George Whitefield

A Select Collection of Letters of the Late Reverend George Whitefield

Vol. II

George Whitefield

A Select Collection of Letters of the Late Reverend George Whitefield
Vol. II

ISBN/EAN: 9783337019266

Printed in Europe, USA, Canada, Australia, Japan

Cover: Foto ©ninafisch / pixelio.de

More available books at **www.hansebooks.com**

OF
LETTERS
OF THE LATE REVEREND
GEORGE WHITEFIELD, M.A.
Of Pembroke-College, Oxford,
And Chaplain to the Rt. Hon. the Countefs of Huntingdon;

WRITTEN TO

His moſt intimate Friends, and Perſons of Diſtinction, in England, Scotland, Ireland, and America,

From the Year 1734, to 1770.

Including the whole Period of his Miniſtry.

WITH

AN ACCOUNT
OF THE
Orphan-Houſe in Georgia,

To the Time of his DEATH.

IN THREE VOLUMES.

VOL. II.

===

LONDON:
Printed for Edward and Charles Dilly, in the Poultry;
and Meſſrs. Kincaid and Creech, at Edinburgh.
MDCCLXXII.

LETTER CCCCXCVIII.

To the Reverend Mr. H———.

London, Dec. 23, 1742.

My dear brother H———,

I Thank you for your kind and very agreeable letter. It was refreshing to my soul, and stirred me to give thanks on your behalf. I am surprized that you are not turned off, since you now so clearly preach the everlasting gospel. But our Saviour has the hearts of all men in his hands, and he turneth them when and wheresoever he pleaseth. O my dear brother, I hope nothing will deter you from preaching the glad tidings of salvation to a world lying in the wicked one. I would not but be a poor despised minister of JESUS CHRIST for ten thousand worlds. This I am persuaded is the language of my dear friend's heart:

I.

For this let men revile my name,
No cross I shun, I fear no shame:
All hail reproach, and welcome pain;
Only thy terrors, LORD, *restrain.*

II.

The love of CHRIST *doth him constrain*
To seek the wand'ring souls of men;
With cries, entreaties, tears to save,
And snatch them from the gaping grave.

LETTERS.

Go on, thou man of GOD; and may the LORD cause thy bow to abide in strength! Glad should I be to come and shoot some gospel arrows in *Devonshire*; but the cloud seems now to point toward *America*. My dear family calls loudly for me. Our LORD has wonderfully of late interposed on their behalf. GOD willing, I intend shortly to send you an account of the Orphan-house, and my last volume of sermons, with some other things. Blessed be GOD for making any of my poor writings of use to your dear soul. Surely I had need proclaim free grace on the house-top; if I did not, the stones would cry out against me. O my dear brother, what a mystery of love is the mystery of godliness? Whilst I am writing the fire kindles. This fire has also of late kindled in many hearts. Our large society goes on well. We have many that walk in the comforts of the Holy Ghost. I hear of glorious things from various parts. I hope ere long we shall hear of persons going from post to post, and crying, "Babylon is fallen, Babylon is fallen." I trust you, my dear Sir, will be made a happy instrument in the Mediator's kingdom, of pulling down satan's strongholds. Pray write me word, how the war is going on between *Michael* and the dragon. For the present, adieu. My tender love to all the lovers of JESUS CHRIST. Accept the same from, my dear brother,

Yours most affectionately in CHRIST,

G. W.

LETTER. CCCCXCIX.

To Mr. R———, in Edinburgh.

Dear Mr. R———,   London, Dec. 24, 1742.

IT has given me some concern that I could not answer your kind and acceptable letter before. As our Saviour will give me freedom, I shall send you a few lines now. I think I may say to you, as *Luther* said to *Melanchton*, *Nimis es nullus*. You are kept in bondage by a false humility. It is good to see ourselves poor, and exceeding vile; but if that sight and feeling prevent our looking up to, and exerting ourselves for our dear Saviour, it becomes criminal, and robs the soul of much comfort. I can speak this by dear-bought experience. How often have I been kept from speaking and acting for GOD, by a sight of my own unworthiness; but now I see that the

more

more unworthy I am, the more fit to work for JESUS, because he will get much glory in working by such mean instruments; and the more he has forgiven me, the more I ought to love and serve him. Fired with a sense of his unspeakable loving-kindness, I dare to go out and tell poor sinners that a lamb was slain for them; and that he will have mercy on sinners as such, of whom indeed I am chief. I wish my dear friend was in this respect not almost, but altogether such as I am. Well would it be with him, and happy would he then be. Upon the receipt of yours, I prayed the LORD to open your mouth. The language of my heart for you, myself, and all the Redeemer's witnesses, is this;

> *Ah!* LORD, *enlarge their scanty thought,*
> *To see the wonders thou hast wrought;*
> *Unloose the stammering tongue, to tell*
> *Thy love immense, unsearchable.*

I bless our LORD for giving you such freedom with himself, though you cannot speak so freely to others. Prayers wrought by his own spirit, he will hear and answer. It is most god-like to be frequent in intercession. It is the constant employment of the Son of GOD in heaven. I rejoice to hear the work of GOD goes on among you in *Scotland*. Blessed be GOD, it prospers in our hands here, in *Wales*, and in various places. That it may prosper more and more, and be daily carried on in your precious soul, is the hearty prayer of, dear Mr. R——,

Yours most affectionately in CHRIST JESUS,

G. W.

LETTER D.

To Miss S——, in Edinburgh.

Dear Miss S——, *London, Dec.* 24, 1742.

CONTINUAL avocations about my master's business, has prevented my answering your kind letter. It gladdened my heart, because it brought me the glad tidings of your being accepted in the beloved; and knowing that you are so, what does the LORD require of you now, but to walk humbly with him? Beg him to shew you more and more of your evil heart, that you may ever remain a poor sinner at the feet of the once crucified, but now exalted Lamb of God. There you will be happy. There you will find shelter from all your enemies. My prayer therefore for you, dear Miss, is this:

> *Continue still thy love, dear Lamb,*
> *Safe hide her in thy wounds;*
> *There may she dwell in all that love*
> *The ransom'd soul surrounds.*

The comforts you have already experienced, as well as your trials, are but earnests of what you will hereafter meet with in the spiritual life. But fear nothing, neither be over thoughtful for the morrow; you have an all-gracious and almighty Saviour to guide and protect you. He will not leave you, until he hath lodged you safe in glory. There the wicked shall cease from troubling, and your weary soul will enjoy an eternal rest. Perhaps I may not see you again, till I meet you in the world of spirits. That grace and peace may be multiplied upon your dear soul, is the hearty prayer of, dear Miss S——,

Your most affectionate friend
and servant in Jesus Christ,
G. W.

LETTER DI.

To Mr. T——.

Dear Sir, *January* 9, 1743.

I Remember, when in *Scotland* last year, how heartily your good people joined in praise and thanksgiving, for the deliverance God had wrought out for the inhabitants of *Georgia*; and I hope I shall never forget how liberally they contributed to the necessities of the orphans, though they knew not but at that time both orphans and Orphan-house were in the enemies hand. As this was an uncommon event, I send you herewith part of the proclamation for a day of thanksgiving to almighty God, for putting an end to this *Spanish Invasion*. It runs thus:

Almighty

ALMIGHTY GOD has in all ages shewn his power and mercy, in the marvellous and gracious deliverance of his church, and in the protection of righteous and religious kings and states, professing his holy and eternal truth, from the open invasion, wicked conspiracies, and malicious practices of all the enemies thereof. He hath by the manifestation of his providence delivered us from the hands of the *Spaniards*: they, with forty sail of small gallies and other craft, came into *Cumberland* Sound; but such a terror came upon them that they fled. With another fleet of thirty-six ships and vessels they came into *Jekyl* Sound, and after a sharp fight became masters thereof; we having only four vessels to oppose their force. We engaged them for the space of four hours, and not one of us was killed, though many of the enemy perished, and five were killed by one shot only. They landed four thousand five hundred men, according to the account of the prisoners, and even of *Englishmen*, who escaped from them. The first party marched up through the woods to this town, and was within sight thereof, when GOD delivered them into our hands, though we were but few in number. They fought and were soon dispers'd and fled. Another party which supported them, also fought; but were soon put to flight. We may truly say, the hand of the LORD fought for us; for in two attacks more than five hundred fled before fifty. At first they seemed to fight with courage; and the grenadiers particularly charged with great resolution; but their shot did not take place, insomuch that none of ours were killed; but they were broken and pursued with great slaughter, and by the report of the prisoners since taken, upwards of two hundred men never returned to their camp. They also came up with their half galleys towards the town, and returned without so much as firing one shot, leaving behind them some cannon, and many things they had taken. Twenty-eight sail attacked *Fort-William*, in which were only fifty men. After three hours fight, they went away and left the province, and were pursued as far as Saint *John's*. So that by this whole expedition, no more than two of ours were taken and two killed. We may therefore truly say, the LORD hath done great things for us, who has delivered us out of the hands of the enemy.

Having taken the premises into consideration, I do hereby order, that *Sunday* the twenty-fifth instant be observed as a day of public thanksgiving to almighty GOD for his great deliverance, in having put an end to the *Spanish* Invasion : and that all persons do solemnize the same in a christian and religious manner, and abstain from drunkenness, and any other wicked and dissolute testimonies of joy.

Given under my hand and seal, this twenty-fourth day of *July*, at *Frederica* in *Georgia*, *Anno Domini* one thousand seven hundred and forty-two.

Signed by,

James Oglethorp.

By his excellency's command,

Francis Moore.

Business prevents my enlarging further at this time, and indeed I chuse rather to leave you to make your own remarks on the inclosed. I only observe in general that as a tincture of piety runs through the whole, and all the glory given to him to whom all glory is due, it will be as acceptable to you as it was to,

Yours,

G. W.

LETTER DII.

To Mr. H——, at Gloucester.

London, Feb. 4, 1743.

My very dear Mr. H——,

I Bless GOD on your behalf. I thank him for visiting your dear soul, and making you useful to others.—Assuredly the LORD has called you to your present work.—Abide in it. Go on and prosper. The LORD will be with you. If we have an association in *Wiltshire* soon, will you chuse to be with us? I expect shortly now to move hence; but my way is quite blocked up from going abroad. I will send you word, when I shall be at *Bristol*. I will salute you and your friend with, "Come in, ye blessed of the LORD." I have just published a fresh account of the Orphan-house, and prefixed the plan. I shall be glad to hear from you often. Be as particular in respect to the society as you can. The LORD is still with us. Blessed be his holy name! My tender love to all. That the glorious *Emmanuel* may be with your soul more and more, is the hearty prayer of, my dear Mr. *H*——,

Yours most affectionately,
G. W.

LETTER DIII.

To Mr. S——.

My dear Sir, *Gloucester, March* 24, 1743.

AN effectual door is opened in these parts. On *Saturday* night I preached here. The LORD was with me. On *Sunday* morning I preached again in a barn. It was a good time to me and the people. Dear Mr. *P*—— was here, and tears of love and joy were running down his aged cheeks almost all the while. He was, like good old *Simeon*, ready to cry out, "LORD, now lettest thy servant depart in peace." At noon I preached at Mr. *F*——*r*'s on the hill, to a glorious auditory indeed. Here JESUS CHRIST displayed his power, and caused much of his glory to pass before us. At four I preached again in a field near *Stroud*, where was a great congregation consisting of many, many thousands. The LORD helped and blessed me much here also. Afterwards I went to the new house at *Hampton*, and the glory of the LORD filled it. It is exceeding commodious for our purpose. I preached in the court-yard on *Monday* noon, to a large auditory. *Monday* evening the LORD gave me a good time at *Pitchcomb*. Both brother *C*—— and brother *A*——'s society met at *Hampton*, and the LORD met with us. Brother *C*—— is certainly called of GOD. All call him a second *Bunyan*. I believe he must give himself wholly to the work. Such a hardy worker with his hands, and hearty preacher at the same time, I have scarce known. On *Tuesday* a man was hung in chains at *Hampton Common*.—A more miserable spectacle I have not seen. I preached in the morning to a great auditory about a mile off the place of execution. I intended doing the same after the criminal was turned off; but the weather was very violent.—Thousands and thousands came and staid to hear; but, through misinformation, kept on the top of the hill, while

while I preached in the bottom. After this I came to *Glou̇cester*, and preached in the evening in a barn : a night much to be remembered! This morning I preached again, and dined with Mr. *E——d I——s* and some more at Mr. *E——*'s. I am just going to my evening lecture, and to-morrow I shall leave *Gloucester* for a few days. The association is put off for a week, so I shall have more time in *Gloucestershire*. Never did I see people more hungry and simple. Many come telling me what the LORD did for their souls when I was here last. To him be all the glory! Brother *A——* is now with me. He must be in the country 'till the house is more settled. I am sure GOD called me here.

Yours, &c.
G. W.

LETTER DIV.

To Mr. S——.

My dear Sir,   *Gloucester, March* 29, 1743.

I Now sit down to fulfil my promise made to you last night. —I think in a former letter I gave you an account of what the LORD had done for and by me since I left *London*, though indeed I cannot tell you the hundredth part. On *Tuesday* evening I preached at *Gloucester* with as convincing, soul-edifying power, as ever I felt in my life. The barn, though made more commodious, was and is generally quite crouded. On *Friday* morning I preached again ; and afterwards went to *Hampton*; the snow falling and freezing on us all the way. In the evening I preached at *Chalford*, upon " walking with GOD :" he was with me and the auditory. On *Saturday* I preached at *Ruscom* in the morning, and at *King-stanley* in the afternoon. In the evening, I visited brother *C——*'s gracious society ; and afterwards rode to *Hampton*, which made about twenty miles. The congregations on account of the weather were not so great, but our Saviour most richly fed us. The word distilled like the dew ; and at *Stanley* I think I was in the very suburbs of heaven. O free grace ! On *Sunday* morning I preached at *Dursley*, about seven miles from *Hampton*, where our dear brother *A——* had been taken down the *Sunday* before ; but no one was permitted to touch or molest us. The congregation consisted of some thousands, and the word came with a moſt glorioufly convincing power. I came away rejoicing, and in the afternoon preached to about ten thouſand on *Hampton* common, at what the people now call *Whitefield's Tump*, becauſe I preached there firſt. I cannot tell you what a ſolemn occaſion that was. I perceive a great alteration in the people ſince I was in theſe parts laſt. They did indeed hang on me to hear the word. It ran and was glorified. In the evening, we had a moſt precious meeting with the two united ſocieties in the new houſe at *Hampton*. Surely many thereabouts will walk with GOD. Laſt night and this morning I preached again with great power; preaching in *Gloucefterſhire* is now like preaching at the tabernacle at *London*. This evening I am to preach again; and after that to hold our firſt love-feaſt.—What our LORD does for us hereafter, you ſhall hear in my next. And now, my dear Sir, help me to be thankful, and bleſs the LORD for all his mercies conferred on

Your unworthy friend, and his worthleſs ſervant,

G. W.

LETTER DV.

To the Same.

Dear Sir, *Gloucefter, April* 2, 1743.

MY ſoul is kept exceeding chearful; and greater and more continued freedom in preaching, I never experienced, than ſince I have been in *Gloucefter* and *Gloucefterſhire*. On *Tueſday* evening we had a bleſſed love-feaſt. On *Wedneſday* morning I preached here with great ſweetneſs; and at noon at *Painſwick*.—In the evening I preached at Mr. F——'s, in the place where the LORD met us remarkably one night about a twelvemonth ago. He met us again moſt delightfully, not in terror, but in love: by which I gueſſed how the goſpel had gained ground in a twelvemonth's time. After this I viſited dear brother C——'s ſociety, and then rode to *Hampton*, with brothers *A*—— and *G*——, praiſing and bleſſing GOD. On *Wedneſday* noon I preached at *Quarhouſe*, from the tump where old Mr. *Cole* uſed to ſtand. It was an alarming time. My ſoul enjoyed exceeding great liberty. In the evening I preached in the new houſe at *Hampton* to

many

many hundreds, and afterwards met the society. Yesterday morning I came hither. At noon and at night I preached in the barn; it was quite crouded. It would have rejoiced you to have been with us. This morning I am to preach again, and shall take my leave at night. My dear Sir, help me to extol free grace, and expect to hear of greater things than these from,

Ever yours, &c.

G. W.

LETTER DVI.

To brother S——.

Waterford (South Wales,) April 7, 1743.

My Dear Brother,

ON *Monday* I received your letter of *April* 2; but till now, have had no opportunity of answering it. I preached and took my leave of the *Gloucester* people with mutual and great concern, on *Sunday* evening last. It was past one in the morning, before I could lay my weary body down.—At five I rose again, sick for want of rest; but I was enabled to get on horseback and ride to Mr. F——'s, where I preached to a large congregation, who came there at seven in the morning, hoping to feel the power of a risen LORD. They were not disappointed of their hope. At ten I read prayers, and preached from these words,—"I am the resurrection and the life," and afterwards was helped to administer the sacrament in *Stonehouse* church. Then I rode to *Stroud*, where I was enabled to preach to about twelve thousand, with uncommon freedom and power, in Mrs. G——'s field. Much of the divine presence was there.—About six in the evening I preached to about the like number on *Hampton Common*; but scarce ever with a more pleasing convincing power. The order and solemnity wherewith the people broke up, was very instructive. After this I went to *Hampton*, and held a general love-feast with the united societies. My soul was kept close to JESUS; my bodily strength renewed; and I went to-bed about midnight, very chearful and very happy. The next morning I went and preached near *Dursley*, to some thousands, with great convictions accompanying the word. About seven I

reached

reached *Bristol*, and preached with wonderful power to a full congregation at *Smith's Hall*; and afterwards spent the evening very agreeably with Mr. C—— of *Bath*, and some other dear friends. On *Tuesday* morning I preached again to a full congregation, and then set out for this place, where we came about eight in the evening, and had sweet and profitable conversation with Mr. B—— and some others of the brethren. We sung an hymn, prayed, and parted in great harmony. On *Wednesday* about noon I opened the association with a close and solemn discourse upon walking with GOD. Indeed much of GOD was with us. The brethren and the people felt much of the divine presence. Afterwards we betook ourselves to business: several matters of great importance were dispatched. We broke up about seven, and met again about ten, and continued settling the affairs of the societies till about two in the morning. On *Thursday* we sat again till about four in the afternoon; then, after taking a little refreshment, and talking warmly of the things of GOD, I preached with great freedom upon the believer's rest, and then we went on with our business, and finished our association about midnight: all acknowledged that GOD had been with us, and blessed him for the same. Perhaps in a month I may come to *London*; but it seems to be the will of the LORD I should stay in *Wales* about a fortnight, and take a tour into *Pembrokeshire*. Great doors are open there. Our Saviour keeps me very happy indeed; and is, I believe, preparing greater blessings, for

Yours, &c.

G. W.

LETTER DVII.

To the Same.

Lantrissant, (in Wales) April 10, 1743.

Dear Sir,

OUR blessed master still countenances my feeble labours. Yesterday I preached at *Cardiff* to a large congregation. The greatest scoffers sat quiet, and the children of GOD felt the divine presence. In the evening I went to *Ful-mon*. Mrs. J—— received us kindly. GOD was pleased to speak for me in the society where I preached: This morning I preached again. It was a most remarkable time. I have been just now preaching with great power here. Dear brother H—— is preaching in *Welch*. The people are very simple. I wrote to you from *Waterford*. I must write a letter or two more, and then away out of town. My kind and tender love to all. The LORD be with you.

I am yours, &c.

G. W.

LETTER DVIII.

To the Same.

My dear Friend,   *Swanzey, April* 12, 1743.

I Hope all is well with you. Great things are doing in *Wales*.—An effectual door is opened for preaching the everlasting gospel. Yesterday I preached at *Neath*, (seven miles from this place) from a balcony, to about three thousand souls in the street. The LORD was with me of a truth. This morning I preached here to about four thousand with great power. About one I preached at *Harbrook*, four miles off; and am now returned to preach here again.—Our Saviour has prepared the way before him. O free grace! Dear brother H—— has discoursed in *Welch* yesterday and to day.

Ever yours,

G. W.

Postscript. Past seven in the evening. I have just now done preaching. Swanzey is taken! I never preached with a more convincing power. Many of the rich and great were present. The congregation larger than in the morning. Free grace for ever!

LETTER DIX.
To the Same.

My dear Friend,   *Larn, April* 15, 1743.

I Wrote to you from several places; and all my letters have, or will I trust come to hand. I can yet send you more glad tidings. But words cannot express what the LORD has done for your unworthy friend, and his own dear people's souls. On *Monday* I preached at a place in the way, and afterwards at *Neath*, a sea port town, to about three thousand people: all was quiet, and the power of JESUS was much there. Then I went to *Swanzey* seven miles from *Neath*. —On *Tuesday* I preached, and the LORD was with me. In the evening I went to *Llanelthy*, eight miles from *Swanzey*. There I preached twice on *Wednesday* with great power to a large congregation; and in the evening near *Aberquilley*, five miles from thence. On *Thursday* I preached at *Carmarthen*, one of the greatest and most polite places in *Wales*; in the morning from the top of the cross: in the evening from a table near it. It was the great sessions. The justices desired I would stay till they rose, and they would come. Accordingly they did, and many thousands more; and several people of quality. JESUS was much with me, and I hope much good work was done. Several sent for me to their houses. Dear brother *H———* exhorts in every place. I have just been preaching, and it would rejoice your heart to see what is doing. I want room and time to tell you all. In about ten days I hope to be near *Bristol*. In the mean while, I am, dear friend,

Ever yours,

G. W.

LETTER DX.
To the Same.

My dear Friend,   *Haverfordwest, April* 17, 1743.

SINCE I left *Larn*, from whence I wrote to you, the LORD has dealt most bountifully with me. I went that evening to *Narbatt*, where I preached to some thousands with great power. On *Saturday* I preached at *Newton*, and afterwards

wards at *Jefferson* to several thousand souls, very like the *Kingswood* colliers. This morning I preached at *Llasfruran*, and had as it were a *Moor-fields* congregation; and this afternoon I preached to about the same number near this town. I also read prayers. Where I have been, the people call loudly again. A most effectual door is opened in *South Wales*. I hope to be with you in a few weeks. I am glad of such news from *Georgia*. Blessed be GOD, he will take care of me and mine. Hearty love attends you and all, from

Yours, &c.
G. W.

LETTER DXI.

To the Same.

Carmarthen, April 20, 1743.

My dear Friend,

SINCE I wrote from *Haverfordwest*, I preached yesterday at eight in the morning to about eight thousand people in this place, and in the afternoon to several thousands at *Narbatt*, both times with great power. This morning I preached at *Larn*, and coming over in the ferry had the unexpected compliment paid me, of one ship firing several guns, and of some others hoisting their flags. This afternoon I preached at a little town called *Kidwilly*, to a large congregation; and came this evening here. One of the ministers preached much against me last *Sunday*, and mentioned me by name; but, like my other opposers (and like the viper biting the file) he only hurt himself. I am as it were in a new, but very unthought of pleasant world. O how many thousands within these few days have heard the word! I thought to see you next week; but as I am here, perhaps it may be best to go round now, and so be at *London* at Pentecost. In about a fortnight, therefore, you may expect to see me.

Ever yours,
G. W.

LETTER DXII.

To the Same.

Bhuadder, *April* 23, 1743.

My dear Friend,

I Wrote to you from *Haverford* and *Carmarthen*. I preached there twice on *Thursday* to about ten thousand people, and dear Mr. R—— preached after me. Yesterday we had another blessed association; and have now settled all the counties in *Wales*. Our LORD was wonderfully with us. You cannot tell how delighted the brethren went away. Indeed they seemed filled as with new wine. Last night we came hither to a little inn. A sweet retreat from the rain. I must away to preach this morning. Help me, my dear man, to be thankful. I kindly salute you and yours, and am,

Ever yours,

G. W.

LETTER DXIII.

To the Same.

Guenfithen, *near the Hay in Radnorshire*, *April* 25, 1743.

My dear Sir,

I Wrote to you on *Saturday* morning; afterwards I preached at *Llangathan* in the church, to a great congregation; I then went about ten miles, and preached at *Landovery* in the evening, and on *Sunday* morning. GOD was with us each time. On *Sunday* evening I preached to a large and polite auditory at *Brecon*, fifteen miles from *Landovery*.—This morning I preached at *Trevecka*, and just now at this place, with as great freedom, power and melting, almost as we have seen: It is now past seven at night, and I have seven or eight *Welsh* miles to go. I am glad you are so happy in JESUS. My body is weak, but I am at the Redeemer's feet, and he reigns king in my heart, and causes me to rejoice and triumph over all. Help me to praise him. Brother H—— salutes you all. The LORD be with you.

Ever, ever yours,

G. W.

LETTER DXIV.

To the Same.

Gloucester, April 29, 1743.

My dear Sir,

I Am at present strengthening myself in the LORD my GOD. These words have much refreshed me, "And the LORD was with *David*, whithersoever he went." After I wrote my last from a gentlewoman's near the *Hay*, I went towards *Builth*, and got into my lodgings about one, and into my bed about two o'clock in the morning. The next day I preached at *Builth*, with much of the Redeemer's presence. Then I rode to the *Gore*, the last place I preached at in *Wales*; and indeed our Saviour kept the good wine 'till last: he made our cup to overflow.—Between eight and nine at night we set out for *Leominster*, and reached there between two and three in the morning. At eleven, and three, I preached. It was quite fallow ground. The LORD broke it up, and gave me a blessed entrance into *Herefordshire*. All glory be to his great Name! The same night I lay at *Hereford*. Even there some of our LORD's disciples were to be found, as also at *Rofs*, where we baited yesterday. In both places I might have preached, would time have permitted; but I was hastening to *Gloucester*, where the good Shepherd of *Israel* brought us in peace and safety about eight in the evening; after having in about three weeks travelled about four hundred *English* miles, spent three days in attending two associations, preached about forty times, visited about thirteen towns, and passed through seven counties. Here then will I set up my *Ebenezer*, thank the adorable JESUS for these and all other his mercies, and from the bottom of my heart give him all the glory. I know my dearest friend will join with me, and say a hearty Amen. "Even so, LORD JESUS. Amen and Amen!"——Last night and this morning I preached here. Since my departure the barn hath been turned into a commodious chapel. I shall preach there again, GOD willing, this evening, and to-morrow morning; in the country on *Sunday* next, and for all as I know, shall come to *London* on *Monday* evening. One of the simple *Apperly* souls died in peace a few days ago. "Praise ye the LORD, for his mercy endureth for ever."

Yours, &c. &c.

G. W.

LETTER DXV.

To the Rev. Mr. I——.

My dear Brother, London, *May* 6, 1743.

YOUR very kind letter I had not the pleasure of receiving 'till yesterday. It was very acceptable, and knits my heart closer to you than ever. I love your honest soul, and long for that time, when the disciples of CHRIST of different sects shall be joined in far closer fellowship one with another. Our divisions have grieved my heart. I heartily approve of the meeting of the chief labourers together. The free grace of the ever-blessed JESUS melts me down. He has been exceeding kind to me of late, and shewn me that, vile as I am, he will not lay me aside. I am just returned from a circuit of about 400 miles. I have been as far as *Haverfordwest*, and was enabled to preach with great power. Thousands and tens of thousands flocked to hear the word, and the souls of GOD's children were much refreshed. I have been also at two associations in *Wales*. The work begins now to shew itself. Many are taking root downward, and bearing fruit upward. Ere long I trust they will fill the land. I am glad the LORD hath opened fresh doors for you, my dear brother. The rams horns are sounding about *Jericho*; surely the towering walls will at length fall down. But we must have patience. He that believeth, doth not make haste. The rams horns must go round seven times. Our divisions in *England* have the worst aspect, while they are now united in *Wales:* but even this shall work for good, and cause the Redeemer's glory to shine more conspicuous. This is my comfort; "The government is upon his shoulders," and he is a "wonderful counsellor."

> *And whatso'er thou wilt,*
> *Thou dost, thou King of Kings!*
> *What thy unerring wisdom plans*
> *Thy power to being brings.*

But where am I running? Pardon me. I am writing to my dear Mr. *I——*. I rejoice in the expectation of seeing you in town. I hope to be in town at that time, and to enjoy some of our former happy seasons. In the mean while, I salute you from my inmost soul, and desire, as often as opportunity offers, a close correspondence may be kept up between you, and, my dear brother,

Your most affectionate unworthy
brother and servant,

G. W.

LETTER DXVI.

To D. T——, in Yorkshire.

London, May 6, 1743.

My dear Brother,

A Day or two ago, I had the pleasure of receiving a letter from you, which I find was written some time since, but came not to hand, as I was out of town. Accept my thanks, though late, and let the blessed JESUS be praised, again and again, for causing his children to love and esteem unworthy, hell-deserving me. O, my dear brother, "Love is of GOD, and he that dwelleth in love, dwelleth in GOD, and GOD in him." Glad am I that our Saviour is getting himself the victory in your parts, and that fresh doors are opened for our dear brother *I——* to preach the everlasting gospel. I have been just writing to him; and now improve a few moments to send you a line also. Blessed be our glorious *Emmanuel,* I can tell you of new and glorious conquests made of late. I am but just returned from a circuit of 400 miles in *Gloucestershire* and *South Wales. Dagon* hath every where fallen before the ark, and the fields are white ready unto harvest. The congregations were very large, and I was never enabled to preach with greater power. I purpose staying here about a month, and once more to attack the prince of darkness in *Moor-fields,* when the holidays come. Many precious souls have been captivated with CHRIST's love in that wicked place. *Jerusalem* sinners bring most glory to the Redeemer. Where I shall go next, I cannot yet tell. If my Master should point out the way, a visit to *Yorkshire* would be very

agreeable.

agreeable. Perhaps *Exeter* and *Cornwall* may be the next places. That is dry ground. I love to range in such places. O my dear brother, continue to pray for me, and help me to praise the blessed Lamb of GOD. Indeed I pray for you, and the redeemed sinners, amongst whom you are. That the great Shepherd and Bishop of souls may fill you with all peace and joy in believing, is the hearty prayer of, my dear brother,

Yours most affectionately in CHRIST.
G. W.

LETTER DXVII.

To Mr. H———.

London, May 21, 1743.

My very dear faithful Friend and Brother,

AFTER watching, and praying, and striving some days for direction and assistance, I now sit down to write you a letter; though I know not well what to say or do. The concern I have felt for you, and my dear family, has had an effect on my body, and increased that weakness, which the season of the year, my constant labours, and continual care upon various accounts, have brought upon me. In the midst of all, my soul I trust grows, and is kept happy in the blessed JESUS. His strength is daily made perfect in my weakness, and I am made more than conqueror through his love. I am somewhat concerned, that scarce any of my letters have reached your hands. I was glad, however, to find that you had received one dated in *May* last. Since that, I hope you have received more. I rejoice that our loving Saviour has not permitted you to want. You are his family, and he would not detain me from you, had not he determined to provide for you in my absence. I fear I have been sinfully impatient to come over. I think, I could be sold a slave to serve at the gallies, rather than you and my dear Orphan-family should want. Sometimes my wicked heart has said, " if I know I should have staid so long, I would not have come over to *England* at all." But GOD's thoughts are not as our thoughts. It is best to be kept at his feet, waiting to know what he would have us to do. By and by we shall know all;

'till then, let us wait patiently; against hope may we believe in hope, and being strong in faith give glory to GOD. After I have fought the LORD's battles in *Moor-fields* these holidays, I think to take a tour into *Cornwall* and *Wales*, and perhaps, to *Ireland*. I have sometimes thought I am detained on purpose to go there. I wonder not at your silence. You may well expect me; but I must not mention it, lest my impatient heart should again say, " LORD, why wilt thou not let me go?" My first fellow-traveller, scarce a day passes without my speaking of, and often praying for you. Old love has revived long since in my soul. I am persuaded, our LORD will reward you even in this life, for your fidelity to unworthy me. " Be strong in the LORD and in the power of his might." While I am writing the fire kindles, and I almost forget my bodily weakness. The LORD be with you. I hear the *Spaniards* intend a second invasion; but those words still follow and comfort me, " The enemies which you have seen, you shall see no more for ever." You are the LORD's family; he will take care of you; fear them not. I have many things to impart, when I see you face to face. 'Till then the LORD JESUS be with your spirit, and grant that you and yours may increase with all the increase of GOD. In bonds of an eternal friendship, with greater affection than words can well express, I subscribe myself,

Ever, ever yours,

G. W.

LETTER DXVIII.

To *Mr. B——*.

London, *May* 21, 1743.

My very dear Brother B——,

LITTLE did I think, when I parted from you at *Bethesda*, that I should be writing to you at this time in *London*. But GOD's ways are in the great waters, and his footsteps are not known. I have essayed to come to you more than once, or twice; but I believe I can say, " the spirit suffered me not." In thought I am with you daily; when I shall come in person, our Saviour only knows: perhaps, at an hour which neither you nor I think of. You will see what I have wrote

(though

(though in much weakness) to my dear Mr. *H——.* The present weakness of my body will not suffer me to enlarge much to you; though, was I to follow the inclination of my soul, I should fill up many sheets. My dear brother, I love you unfeignedly in the bowels of JESUS CHRIST, and heartily thank you for all your works of faith, and the care you have taken of my dear family. Surely our LORD sent you to *Bethesda,* and however cloudy the prospect may have been for some time, I am persuaded a glorious sunshine will succeed, and you shall yet see the salvation of our GOD. When our LORD has any thing great to do, he is generally a great while bringing it about, and many unaccountable dark providences generally intervene. Thus it was with *Abraham, Jacob, Joseph, Moses,* and all the eminent men of GOD in the days of old. Thus our LORD is pleased to deal with me, and my affairs. Many precious promises have been given me in respect to myself, my dear family, and the church of JESUS CHRIST, which I am sure will be fulfilled in due time. I long to be with you, to open our hearts freely, and to tell one another what our good GOD has done for our souls. Great things has he done for me indeed, and greater things is he yet doing, and about to do. The work of GOD is likely to spread far and near, and such are daily added to the church as shall be saved. I am employed every moment for the best of Masters, and only lament that I can do no more. For some days, my body has been much indisposed, but not so as to prevent my preaching. As my day is, so is my strength; and as afflictions abound, consolations much more abound. I know that this will lead you to give thanks on my behalf. I am glad when I hear it goes well with you and yours. I am now like St. *Paul,* who could have no rest, 'till he sent a brother to the church, that he might enquire of their affairs, and know how they did. The person that brings this, loves JESUS in sincerity, and I trust will be a blessing to the house. I would have him employed among the children, or as you and the brethren shall think fit. Our Saviour, I hope, will direct you in every thing. As strength shall permit, I intend writing to Mr. *J——.* Blessed be GOD for raising up such dear friends. He never can or will forsake those that put their trust in him. I hope it is well with you and yours. I doubt not but your souls

prosper.

prosper. Mr. A―― writes to his mother, and tells her how you are instant in season and out of season. Go on, my dear brother, thou man of GOD! and may the LORD make you a spiritual father to thousands. That the LORD of all lords may exceedingly bless you, is the earnest prayer of

Yours most affectionately in JESUS,

G. W.

LETTER DXIX.

To Mr. H――.

London, May 31, 1743.

My dear Mr. H――, Friend and Brother,

ALL last week, do what I would, I could not find freedom to write a line, though I expected our dear brother E――, the bearer of this, to sail every hour. But now I know why he was detained, and I restrained. This morning, to my unspeakable satisfaction, I saw a letter from our dear brother G――, dated *April* 13th, wherein he acquainted me of the welfare of the dear family, and of another out-pouring of the spirit among you. O! my soul does magnify the LORD, and my spirit rejoices in GOD my Saviour. After this, I expect to hear of another shock: but I know you are the LORD's, and he will take care of your souls. As Mr. E―― is going on board, I have not time to say half I would. I fear I am sinfully impatient to see you. The time will come by and by. Hasten it, O LORD, if it be thy blessed will! Our Saviour does greater things for me every day. Last *Sunday* morning, I collected 23*l*. for the orphans in *Moor-fields*. It would amaze you to see the great congregations, and wonderful presence of the LORD. Grace! grace! I have paid all that is due in *England*, and have sent you 25*l*. by the bearer. GOD willing, I shall remit you more soon. Pray give my humble respects to dear Mr. J――, and tell him, our Saviour will enable me to pay him all soon with a thousand thanks. I sent you 100*l*. by my brother's ship, and a packet of letters. I hope they came safe to hand. But I must have done. Salute my dear family, and believe me to be, though now in great haste, dear man,

Ever yours,

G. W.

LETTER

LETTER DXX.

To Mr. G——, of Carlisle.

London, June 9, 1743.

My dear Brother,

I Have been prevented by many things from writing to you. I now redeem a few minutes to send you a line. I believe your way is clear to *London*. The brethren, I am persuaded, will be willing to give you the right-hand of fellowship, since you are determined not to meddle with controversy, or to make *adult baptism* a bone of contention; but simply to preach JESUS CHRIST and him crucified. This I think is the only way to propagate the gospel of the grace of GOD. Our Saviour blesses me in it much, and owns and strengthens me more and more. I have been very weak in body, but every day my strength hath been renewed, and I have been enabled to mount on wings like an eagle. God willing, I shall leave *London* on *Monday* next. If I should be out of town, you will be kindly received. Glory be to GOD, the gospel spreads. I feel myself the chief of sinners. As such, be pleased always to remember to pray for, my dear brother,

Yours most affectionately in JESUS CHRIST,

G. W.

LETTER DXXI.

To Mr. S——.

Burford, June 15, 1743.

My dear Sir,

I Cannot go any farther without writing you a line. Our Saviour hath dealt most graciously with your unworthy friend. On *Monday* I experienced some sweet teachings from above, and was so happy, that I thought our LORD was preparing me for some fresh trials. The prospect pleased me much, knowing how all things had already worked together for my good. Yesterday my body was very weary, but my soul happy, and I preached at *Fairford*; this morning at *Glanfield*, and just now here. It is dry ground; but the LORD has promised to pour water upon such. He has richly watered my soul. Where

I lay,

I lay, was indeed a Bethel, a gate of heaven. I hope GOD has been with you. My tender love to dear brother *A——s.* My fellow-travellers salute you. My love to the Tabernacle people. Their prayers are heard. Grace! grace!

Yours affectionately,

G. W.

LETTER DXXII.

To the same.

Gloucester, June 18, 1743.

My dear Friend,

I Wrote to you from *Burford* on *Wednesday* last. My soul was then so exceeding happy, that I want words to express it. Afterwards, we went to *Bengeworth*, where we came about midnight, and were most heartily received by Mr. *S——* and Mr. *O——*. I was enabled to preach there with such power, that all must confess, GOD was with us of a truth. We dined very comfortably, and then set out for *Gloucester*, shouting, Grace! grace! When I arrived, our Saviour was exceeding gracious; and I had so much of heaven in my soul, that I wanted to lie down any where to praise my GOD. I preached here early the next morning, then rode to *Cheltenham*, and returned hither in the afternoon, and preached in the evening. This morning I preached again, and received your second welcome letter. I thank you for it. I could write much of the love and abiding happiness I have in CHRIST: but I have many letters lying unanswered before me. Adieu at present. The LORD be with you and yours. Salute all the brethren. Forget not to pray for, my dear friend,

Ever, ever yours,

G. W.

LETTER DXXIII.

To the same.

Gloucester, June 21, 1743.

ON *Saturday* I answered your two last letters. Our Saviour sent me to *Gloucester* for wise ends. Much substantial good has been done to several of the society. My mouth
and

and heart were greatly opened in preaching. *Saturday* evening was a time much to be remembered. *Sunday*, was a great day of the Son of Man. I preached at *Gloucester* in the morning, and near *Stroud* in the evening. The word was clothed with much power, both for sinners and saints. I think the congregation at *Hampton* was rather greater than ever. At night we had a precious meeting in *Hampton-house* garden; the house itself being too small to hold the people without almost stifling them. The simplicity, sweetness, and brokenheartedness of the poor souls would have melted your heart. Indeed, much grace was upon them, and many, I believe, to their unspeakable consolation, heard the voice of the LORD GOD in the trees of the garden in the cool of the day. On *Monday* morning I preached again, and came away rejoicing. Whilst I was at *Hampton*, *J. C*—— told me, how he and the people had been abused. My coming at this time, I believe, has much strengthened the persecuted. Indeed there is a glorious work in *Gloucestershire*. Brother *C*—— is truly a great soul! one of the weak things that GOD has chosen to confound the strong. In my journey from *Hampton* hither, our dear Master was graciously with us. We have blessed news from *Scotland*. Brave news also from *Pembrokeshire*. Surely the kingdom of the LORD and his CHRIST is coming on apace. I know you say, "Come, LORD JESUS, come quickly."

Ever, ever yours,
G. W.

P. S. I must acquaint you, by way of postscript, of the following anecdote of the old Mr. *Cole*, a most venerable dissenting minister; whom I was always taught to ridicule, and (with shame I write it) used, when a boy, to run into his meeting-house, and cry, *Old Cole! old Cole! old Cole!* Being asked once by one of his congregation, what business I would be of? I said, "a minister, but I would take care never to tell stories in the pulpit, like the old *Cole*." About twelve years afterwards, the old man heard me preach in one of the churches at *Gloucester*; and on my telling some story to illustrate the subject I was upon, having been informed what I had before said, made this remark to one of his elders, "I find that young *Whitefield* can now tell stories, as well as old *Cole*." Being affected much with my preaching, he was as it were become young again, and used to say, when coming to and returning from *Barn,* " These are days of the Son of Man indeed!" nay, he was so animated, and so humbled, that he used to subscribe himself *my Curate,* and went about preaching after me in the country, from place to place. But one evening, whilst preaching, he was struck with death, and then asked for a chair to lean on 'till he concluded his sermon, when he was carried up stairs and died. O blessed GOD! if it be thy holy will, may my exit be like his!

LETTER DXXIV.

To the same.

Gloucester, June 27, 1743.

FULL of divine consolations, and at the same time, I trust, deeply sensible of my own vileness, I have just arose from the throne of grace, where I have been laying yours, my own, and the affairs of the whole church, before our common Father and our GOD. He was pleased to give me sweet access, and to assure me, that if he gave me his presence, he would freely give me all things; but I must wait his time and season, because that will be better for me. I have therefore just now put my soul, as a blank, into the hands of JESUS CHRIST my Redeemer, and desired him to write upon it what he pleases. I know it will be his own image. Methinks I hear you say, Amen. I know you do from your heart; for I believe you love me in the bowels of JESUS CHRIST, as I do you, GOD knoweth. Our Saviour, by his wise providence has prevented our receiving each others letters so soon as we expected. I preached *Tuesday* last in the evening at *Bristol,* and on *Wednesday* twice; and once at *Kingswood.*—On *Thursday* in the morning I preached there also, and afterwards went to *Bath,* where I was most cordially received by Mr. C——, and one Dr. H——, a christian physician, and Lady C——. Here our Saviour gave me fresh hints, that if I would stand still and wait his time and way, he would make even my enemies to be at peace with me. I returned in the evening to *Bristol,* and preached. I think it was this day the news came of his Majesty's fighting, and coming off conqueror. I had observed for

some

some time past, when praying for him, whether I would or not, out came this petition, " LORD, cover thou his head in the day of battle." Tho' even while I was praying, I wondered why I prayed so, not knowing that he was gone to *Germany* to fight. This gave me fresh confidence towards GOD. I spent almost the whole day on *Friday* in retirement, and prayer. My house was made a Bethel to me indeed, the very gate of heaven. *Saturday* I preached again, and found in the day-time our Saviour had blessed my endeavours to some souls. About three in the afternoon we set out for *Wiltshire*. On *Sunday* I preached at *Brinkworth*, on these words: " Thy Maker is thy husband." It was a day of espousals I believe to many. GOD was with us of a truth. After sermon, I rode to *Longley*, in company with many dear children of GOD, who attended me both on horseback and on foot. We sung, and looked like persons that had been at a spiritual wedding. The LORD helped me in preaching there also. All was quiet. In the evening I preached at *Tetherton*, and a blessed time it was. We rode like as the children of *Israel* passing through the enemies country. Afterwards we set out for *Hampton*, and reached there about midnight. After having travelled about thirty miles, I yet preached thrice. This morning I arose like a giant refreshed with wine, and came hither about eleven. I found my mother recovered from her illness, and my own soul filled and blessed in CHRIST. O grace! how sweet is it? I am glad you are thirsting after an abiding in GOD, after greater degrees of knowledge, both of yourself, and of JESUS CHRIST, whom to know is life eternal. In order to this, you must expect many trials, and well it is to be under the discipline of so tender a Master. I know you will pray to the LORD to make and keep me humble. I recommend you to his care, and wish you all the blessings of the everlasting covenant, from

Yours,
G. W.

LETTER DXXV.

To the Same.

Bristol, July 2, 1743.

I Wrote to you on *Saturday*, and on *Monday* from *Gloucester*. I suppose you have wrote to *Trevecka*. Words cannot express how good our blessed Saviour has been to me, since I wrote last. I preached there on *Monday* night, and *Tuesday* morning. The GOD of love filled my soul, and enabled me to speak of his love with great power. Many felt it also. On *Tuesday* after morning sermon I went to *Abergavenny*; JESUS was with me on the road; and we reached there about ten at night. On *Wednesday* I went to *Trevecka*, where I met with a whole troop of JESU's witnesses. I had some hours by myself, and shed many tears of love before the LORD. At five in the evening, I preached to a larger congregation than ever I had seen at *Trevecka*. JESUS was with us of a truth, and I felt the power of that blood upon my own soul, which I was recommending to others. After I had done, brother H——l D—— and R—— preached and prayed. The holy spirit came down, especially when the latter preached, in a plentiful manner.—About eight we opened the association with great solemnity. Our Saviour was much with me, teaching and helping me to fill my place in a particular manner. The brethren felt the same. About midnight we adjourned; but several of the brethren sat up all night, and ushered in the morning with prayer and praise. About eight we met again, and were greatly delighted at the different and simple accounts the superintendents brought in of their respective societies. Some of their accounts were very particular, as to the state of the people's souls; and several had gone off most triumphantly to glory. We continued doing business 'till two in the afternoon, and broke up with much solemnity and holy joy. Our Saviour kept the new-wine 'till last, and gave us a sweet parting blessing. We had great union with one another. Indeed, JESUS has done great things for *Wales*. The work is much upon the advance. I was surprized to find so much order. Brother H—— D—— has been blessed to the conversion of a young clergyman, Rector of St. B——, *London*. About five in

the

the evening I returned to *Abergavenny*, and preached there on *Friday* morning, and afterwards set out for *Bristol*, where we arrived about eight in the evening. My house, friends, &c. were made a great blessing to the soul of,

Ever yours,

G. W.

LETTER DXXVI.
To Mrs. D―――.

Dear Madam,   *Bristol, July* 9, 1743.

HAVING no time to answer your request concerning the *Hampton* mob, I herewith send you a letter, which I have just now received from my dear fellow-labourer, who is the principal object of their fury. This young confessor, some few years ago came out of curiosity to hear me, when first I preached upon *Hampton Common*, in *Gloucestershire*. Being converted himself, he found himself impelled to strengthen his brethren. GOD has owned him much in *Hampton*, and the adjacent country, in calling by him many poor sinners to the knowledge of the LORD JESUS CHRIST. How satan rages upon the account, you'll see in the inclosed, to which you are referred by, dear Madam,

Yours, &c.

G. W.

A Letter from Mr. A―――, to the Rev. Mr. W―――.

Hampton, July 8, 1743.

Honoured and very dear Sir,

BLessed be the dear JESUS, he hath brought me safe hither. He was also with me on the road, and I am persuaded, that whatsoever sufferings I am to pass through here, all shall work together for good; for JESUS is and will be with me. The mob has breathed out many threatenings against me; but JESUS is greater than all, and I am persuaded he'll let them find him so. I rode all down the town without the least molestation, only many cried, (but silently as it were) "O, he is come home!" which was a surprizing thing to them; for a gentleman had affirmed, that he saw me in prison. I have been walking up the town, without any disturbance; but the mob, they say, continue more and more exasperated. We expect them soon. They generally apprize one another, by ringing a bell. The whole mob consist of about an hundred: but Jesus keeps me without the least fear, and at the same time gives me quietly to wait on him for direction, how to act. A few of the dear disciples are by me. We have been praying together, and the Lord is with us. I believe death in its ugliest shapes would not be terrible to some here, at least I think so of myself; and when I look to the faithfulness of my Saviour, I can loudly say, "As my day is, so my strength shall be." Many of the people of the town have been with me, to tell me the respect they have for me, and how much they are concerned for the abuse that has been given us. I believe all will be well by and by. At the same time, I believe your coming might be much blessed to that end. I must conclude; but I think to give you a farther account on *Monday*, if our Saviour pleases. In the mean time, I heartily beg an interest in your prayers, and the whole society with you. Tell them, O tell them, to get ready for suffering, by cleaving close to the Lamb, rooted and grounded in him: withal please to give my kind love and service to them for Jesu's sake, and be pleased to accept the same your dear self, and many thanks for all the tokens of unfeigned love conferred on

    Your unworthy brother and servant,

            T. A.

LETTER DXXVII.

To Mrs. D——.

My dear Madam,   *Bristol, July* 14, 1743.

NOT doubting but you wait with impatience for dear Mr. A——'s promised second letter, after having just read it once over, I herein inclose it; having only time to beg the continuance of your prayers, and to desire you to send this with the former, as soon as possible, to

      Yours, &c,

         G. W.

Honoured Sir, *July* 11, 1743.

I Promised in my last to write to you again, and to let you know more particularly of our persecutions, which are as follow. On *Saturday* after I wrote to you, I met the society, and after we had sung an hymn, came brother *I——*, with my dear wife from *Bristol*. They came into the society and sat down, while I exhorted them to stedfastness and patience under the cross. They seemed much strengthened, and ready for any suffering; for GOD was with us. After that, I desired brother *I——* to pray, which he did. After that I prayed in faith, and was enabled to plead CHRIST's promises to his church; though we are but a little branch. I had not prayed long, but many of us were persuaded, he would never leave or forsake us. In every prayer we asked direction how to act. I was persuaded, the only way to still the mob, was, not to resist or fly from them, but to give myself up wholly to them, and let them do all that the LORD should permit: for the more we had drawn back, the more our adversaries rejoiced, and vowed they would and should put an end to preaching in *Hampton*. The mob, which consisted of near an hundred, were now about the house, making a terrible noise, and swearing prodigiously. I went down to them and opened the door, and asking them what they wanted. I told them, if they wanted my life, I was willing to deliver it up for JESUS's sake; but withal I desired to know, why they either disturbed me or sought my life? For I did not know I had given them any just cause for either. Some of them said, I had, by bringing in false doctrine, and impoverishing the poor. I told them, that they could prove neither, and that it was really false. They seemed something at a stand; when about five of them begun to be more exasperated, and took me, in order to throw me into a lime pit. I told them, they need not force me, for I was willing to suffer, though unjustly, for JESUS's sake. But while they were pushing me along, some neighbours took me in their arms and carried me into one of their houses; so I was delivered out of their hands. On sabbath-day morning about twenty of the society met again. We spent the morning in prayer. In the evening I preached, and had uncommon strength and courage given me.

me from the Lord, so that death in its ugliest shapes did not at all terrify me. About five in the afternoon we met in my house. I first exhorted them to keep their minds close to the Lord, and if the mob came, not at all to resist, but to make way for them to come to me, and let them do what the Lord would permit. I then prayed and sung that hymn, "*Our lives, our blood, &c.*" When we had so done, in came the mob, demanding me to come down. I asked, by what authority they did so? They swore they would have me. Then said I, so you shall. So they took me to the lime-pit, and threw me in. But O what a power of God fell on my soul! I thought, with *Stephen*, the heavens opened to my sight, and the Lord Jesus was ready, if I had died, to receive me. I believe my undaunted courage shook some. I told them, I should meet them at the judgment, and then their faces would gather paleness. They let me out, and I came home and kneeled down with the people that were there, and prayed to, and praised God. After that, I exhorted from the three first verses of the third chapter of the first epistle of *John*. And when I was just concluding, in came the mob again, and took me to a brook to throw me in there. One, who was a persecutor but a few days before, endeavoured to hinder them; but they took me away, and led me all up the town. I had a sweet walk, and talked and reasoned with the persecutors all the way. My heart was full of love. Before I had gone far, all but one agreed to let me go back again, but he insisted upon my going. I told them, the law was open against them, nevertheless I was willing to suffer any thing for Christ. Then they told me, if I would forbear preaching but for a month, they would let me go; I told them, I would make no such promise. So forward I went. One of them threw me in, and I went to the bottom, but I came up again, with my hands clasped together. I did not desire to come out, till they fetched me. Accordingly, in jumped one or two of them and took me out; but then one maliciously and cowardly pushed me in again, and much bruised and cut one of my legs against a stone. Some of the others were going to throw him in for so doing. I came home talking to them. Many seemed to repent of what they had done, and promised to molest me no more. I believe,

God

GOD has smote some of their consciences. One who was the chief, and would not agree that I should go back, I hear by several, he says he will in no wise touch me again. Many advise us to prosecute them; but if they are quiet, I am content, and can say from my heart, " Father, forgive them." I should be glad if you would be here next *Sunday*. In the mean time pray for me, who am,

Your unworthy brother and servant,

T. A.

LETTER DXXVIII.

To Mr. B———.

Dear Friend, *Bristol, July* 19, 1743.

I Have been so employed for some time past in preaching and travelling, that I could not possibly correspond with you or others as usual; but you see where I am; I came here to preach at the fair; because people from all parts flock hither at that season. Yesterday I preached four times, and twice statedly every day. O that sinners may be made willing to come and buy of CHRIST's wine, and of CHRIST's milk, without money and without price! Last night was such a time as I never saw in *Bristol* society before. To morrow, GOD willing, I set out for *Hampton*, to see what can be done for the poor persecuted sheep of CHRIST there. I hear I am threatened, but JESUS will stand by me. In what manner, expect to hear again soon, from

Yours, &c.

G. W.

LETTER DXXIX.

To the Same.

My dear Friend,

Hampton, July 25, 1743.

ON *Thursday* I came here, and expected to be attacked; because I had heard, that the mob which had been so outragious towards you and others for so long time, had now threatened, that if ever I came there again, they would have a piece of my black gown to make aprons with. No sooner had

had I entered the town, but I saw and heard the signals, such as blowing of horns, and ringing of bells for gathering the mob. My soul was kept quite easy. I preached in a large grass plat from these words, "And seeing the grace of GOD, he exhorted them with full purpose of heart to cleave unto the LORD;" and as it happened, I finished my sermon and pronounced the blessing, just as the ring-leader of the mob broke in upon us, which I soon perceived disappointed and grieved them very much. One of them, as I was coming down from the table, called me *coward*; but I told him, they should hear from me another way. I then went into the house, and preached upon the stair case to a large number of serious souls; but these real troublers of *Israel* soon came in to mock and mob us. But feeling what I never felt before, as you know I have very little natural courage, strength and power being given us from above, I leaped down stairs, and all ran away before me. However they continued making a noise about the house till midnight, abusing the poor people as they went home, and as we hear they broke one young lady's arm in two places. Brother A—— they threw a second time into the pool, in which operation he received a deep wound in his leg. *John* C——'s life, that second *Bunyan*, was much threatened.—Young W—— H—— they wheeled in a barrow to the pool's side, lamed his brother, and grievously hurt several others. Hearing that two or three clergymen were in the town, one of whom was a justice of the peace, I went to them; but alas! I seemed unto them as one that mocked, and instead of redressing, they laid the cause of all the grievances at my door; but, by the help of my GOD, I shall still persist in preaching myself, and in encouraging those (as I know no law of GOD or man against it) who I believe are truly moved by the Holy Ghost. As I came out from the clergymen, two of the unhappy mobbers were particularly insolent, and huzza'd us out of town. "Let us rejoice and be exceeding glad," for now I humbly hope, I begin to be a disciple of JESUS CHRIST; since to suffer for, as well as to believe and preach his precious truths, and own his despis'd people, is now given to,

Yours, &c.

G. W.

LETTER

LETTER DXXX.

To Mr. J—— S——.

My dear Friend,   *Bristol, July* 27, 1743.

ON *Friday* night I reached *Gloucester*, where I received your kind and animating letter. On *Saturday* I came hither. Yesterday was an high day: I preached four times in the fields, and the congregations were as large as at the beginning: blessed seasons indeed! Here are people from all quarters. I am just going out to preach again, and therefore can only add, that perhaps I may set out for *Exeter* on *Wednesday*, from whence you may expect to hear again, from

Yours, &c.

G. W.

LETTER DXXXI.

To the Same.

Dear Sir,   *Exeter, July* 31, 1743.

WE came hither in safety last night. Upon the road my soul was sweetly humbled before GOD, who hath given me near access to his throne. Good Mr. *K——*, our host, and his yoke-fellow, seem to be *Israelites* indeed. In all probability an effectual door will be opened for preaching the everlasting gospel. I am to begin this evening. Brethren, pray for us. I sleep but little; inward comforts support and strengthen both soul and body. Join me in crying, Grace! grace! In great haste and greater affection, I subscribe myself,

Yours affectionately,

G. W.

LETTER DXXXII.

To the Same.

My dear Man,   *Exon, Aug.* 2, 1743.

I Wrote unto you on *Saturday*, and preached the same evening to a great body of people. Several of the clergy attended, with whom this city abounds. Some went off, others staid 'till I had done. All was quiet, and our LORD soon made way for himself into the people's hearts. Yesterday evening

evening I preached on *Southean-hay* to upwards of ten thousand; 'twas just like a *Moor-fields* congregation. GOD was with us of a truth. The people were very desirous of my longer continuance here; but so many things concurred to call me to *London*, that after close application to the throne of grace, and consultation with my friends, I am determined, GOD willing, to leave *Exeter* to-morrow morning, and to preach with Mr. *D*—— in my way to town. I find I am in my element, when evangelizing. Our Saviour fills my heart with his presence, and has in a particular manner prepared the people's hearts in the *West* for receiving the gospel-message. He keeps me happy and chearful amidst all my various trials, for which I pray you to join in thanksgiving with

Your affectionate friend, &c.

G. W.

LETTER DXXXIII.

To Mr. H——, *at Gloucester.*

London, Aug. 20, 1743.

My dear Mr. H——,

HOW wonderfully does our all-wise Redeemer order things for the trial of his children! Alas! alas! how apt are they to judge, censure, and be needlesly prejudiced against each other. Being weak in body, and under great concern of mind upon several accounts, I desired dear Mr. *G*—— to acquaint you, that in our last association we agreed not to separate from the established church, but go on in our usual way. Indeed, the motion to separate, was only made by a very few of more contracted principles. By far the greater part most strenuously opposed it, and with good reason; for as we enjoy such great liberty under the mild and gentle government of his present Majesty king *George*, we think we can do him, our country, and the cause of GOD, more service in ranging up and down, preaching repentance towards GOD and faith in our LORD JESUS, to those multitudes who would neither come into church or meeting, but who are led by curiosity to follow us into the fields. However disorderly this may seem to bigots of every denomination, yet it is a way to which GOD has affixed his seal for many years past, and

therefore

therefore we have no reason to turn to the right hand or to the left, but to press forwards and to do our utmost towards enlarging the kingdom of our LORD JESUS; not doubting, but when we come to stand at his bar, we shall be received with as equal an *Euge-bone* as those, who thro' prejudice, or want of better information, censure us as going beyond our line. That this may be our happy case, you will join in praying with

Yours, &c.
G. W.

LETTER DXXXIV.

To Mrs D——.

Dear Madam, London, Sept. 2, 1743.

A Thousand thanks for your kind solicitude concerning me and mine. My wife has been in trying circumstances, partly through the unskilfulness of a chaise-driver, I mean myself. Being advised to take her out into the air, I drove her as well as myself, through in advertence, into a ditch. Finding that we were falling, she put her hand cross the chaise, and thereby preserved us both from being thrown out. The ditch might be about 14 feet deep, but blessed be GOD, though all that saw us falling, cried out, they are killed, yet, through infinite mercy, we received no great hurt. The place was very narrow near the bottom, and yet the horse went down, as tho' let down by a pulley. A stander-by ran down and catched hold of its head, to prevent its going forwards. I got upon its back and was drawn out by a long whip; whilst my wife hanging between the chaise and the bank, was pulled up on the other side by two or three kind assistants. Being both in a comfortable frame, I must own, to my shame, that I felt rather regret than thankfulness in escaping what I thought would be a kind of a translation, to our wished-for haven. But O amazing love! we were so strengthened, that the chaise and horse being taken up, and our bruises being washed with vinegar in a neighbouring house, we went on our intended way, and came home rejoicing in GOD our Saviour. Not expecting my wife's delivery for some time, I intend making a short excursion, and then you may expect further news from

Yours, &c.

G. W.

LETTER DXXXV.

To the Same.

Dear Madam, London, Oct. 5, 1743.

MY last left me just entering upon another short excursion. Blessed be GOD, it was pleasant because it was profitable to my own, and I trust to many other souls. The last evening of it, I preached from a balcony to many thousands, who stood in the street as comfortable as at noon-day. Upon retiring to my lodgings, news was brought me, that GOD had given me a son. This hastened me up to *London*, where I now am, and from whence after I have baptized my little one, GOD willing, I purpose to set out again on my Master's public business. You will not fail to pray, that I may be taught how to order the child aright, and thereby add to the many obligations already laid on, dear Madam,

Yours, &c.

G. W.

LETTER DXXXVI.

To Mr. S——

Avon, Wilts, October 15, 1743.

My dear Friend,

I Must not be long from *London* without writing to you. Our Saviour brought me hither last night, and filled me as with new wine. I purpose staying till *Monday*; if you write, direct for me at *Bristol*. I trust our LORD hath much people here. This leaves me in spirit sitting at his feet. Praying this may find you there, I am

Yours, &c.

G. W.

LETTER DXXXVII.

To the Same.

Cullompton, Oct. 25, 1743.

I Wrote to you on the 15th inftant, at *Avon*. In the morning I walked to *Tetherton*, and preached there with much of the divine prefence, and to the abundant fatisfaction and comfort of GOD's people. After fermon, I baptized four boys, each about three months old, as near as I can remember. The ordinance was fo folemn and awful that Mrs. G—— (who you know is a quaker) had a mind immediately to partake of it. When I go to *Wiltfhire*, I believe I fhall baptize her and her children, with fome adult perfons that have tafted of redeeming love. About one o'clock I preached at *Clack* in the ftreet. All was quiet. I then rode to *Brinkworth*, and was enabled to preach there with ftill greater freedom, and afterwards adminiftred the Holy Sacrament to about two hundred and fifty communicants. Our LORD made himfelf known to many in breaking of bread. Some ftrangers, that came from *Bath*, went home filled with our Redeemer's prefence. I have preached at *Chippenham*. I hope I managed all things right about the affair of the *Hampton* rioters. It feems, they have compelled us to appeal unto *Cæsar*. Evidences fhall be examined in the country, time enough to fend their examinations up to town. We had a wonderful time in *Wiltfhire*. On *Saturday* laft, when I came to *Wellington*, the Reverend Mr. D—— perfuaded me to ftay there, becaufe the country people had come from all quarters feveral times to hear me, and had been difappointed. I confented, and preached in his meeting-houfe in the evening to a large auditory. The Reverend Mr. F——*t*, formerly pupil to doctor D——, came there, and ftaid all night. The bleffed JESUS gave us much freedom in converfation. I hope both will be inftruments under GOD in promoting a good work in thefe parts. *Sunday* morning I preached again in the meeting-houfe, and in the evening to feven thoufand in the fields. On *Monday* about ten in the morning, and in the afternoon about two, I preached at *Cullompton* with much freedom and power; was kindly received, met fome reputable diffenters, and am now fetting out for

Exeter

Exeter with dear Mr. K——, who came here to meet my dear friend.

Yours, &c.

G. W.

LETTER DXXXVIII.

To the Same.

Exeter, October 28, 1743.

I Have strong conviction that our LORD intends doing something in the west. Since my arrival here, letters of invitation have come from many parts. I thank you for your kind sympathy under the many trials, with which I have been surrounded and exercised. I find there is a needs-be for all; for by our being acquainted with the enemy's work in our own hearts, we see how he works on others, and are enabled to speak better to their hearts. "Whether we are afflicted (says the apostle,) or whether we are comforted, it is for your sake." Besides, by temptation we are kept from sinking into formality, and consequently are taught better to handle our spiritual weapons, and discover what is amiss both in heart and life. For this cause, we are commanded to rejoice when we fall into divers temptations. I thank GOD for giving you some experience of these things. We must now all be *Calebs*; all heart, but at the same time, all humility. Feeling we can do nothing of ourselves, yet believing we can do all things through CHRIST strengthening us. Blessed be his Name, the common people begin to feel. I preached between two and three this afternoon on *Southern-hay*, and expounded in the evening at Mr. K——'s. Even some of the polite were much affected last night; and this morning, O what a blessed season had we! I believe I shall think it my duty to stay in these parts for some time. Continue to pray for me, and assure yourself that you are never forgotten by

Yours, &c.

G. W.

LETTER DXXXIX.

To the Same.

Exeter, Nov. 6, 1743.

ALL being hushed and solemn around me, and my soul filled with the peace of GOD that passeth all understanding, I now sit down to give you a further account of my feeble labours. On *Monday* last I went to *Axminster*, and preached to about two thousand without, and afterward exhorted within the house, where I lay. The next day I preached to a greater number of people, and with more freedom. I gave an exhortation at night, and met the society. Our LORD vouchsafed us a gracious blessing. On *Wednesday* I went to *Ottery*, but just as I named my text, the bells rang. Upon this I adjourned to a field, whither the people ran in droves.—As I stepped into the inn, before I went into the field, a clergyman came, who asked me by what authority I preached, said it was a riot, and that the meeting was illegal. I answered him as I thought pertinently, and afterwards went and shewed him my authority, by preaching on these words: "Go ye to all the world, and preach the gospel to every creature." Between six and seven in the evening, I returned to *Exeter*, where some hundreds were waiting to hear me expound. The LORD was with us. The LORD makes this place very comfortable to me. Prejudices fall off daily, and people begin not only rationally to discern, but powerfully to feel the doctrines of the gospel. To-morrow, GOD willing, I go with Mr. K—— to *Biddeford*. From thence expect to hear again from

Yours, &c.

G. W.

Postscript. Ten at night.—It would have pleased you to have been here this evening. I question, whether near a third part of *Exeter* were not attending on the word preached. All was solemn and awful, and the LORD gave me much assistance from his holy spirit. Help me to praise him. Adieu! Good night! The LORD be with you.

LETTER DXL.

To Mrs. D――――.

Dear Madam,   *Biddeford, Nov.* 11, 1743.

I Thank you for your kind caution to spare myself; but evangelizing is certainly my province. Every where effectual doors are opened, and great freedom is given to me both in public preaching and private conversation. Many are blessed by both. The Rev. Mr. *J――― N―――*, rector of *St. Gennis, Cornwall*, is here. GOD willing, I'll go with him on *Saturday.* Here is also another clergyman about eighty years of age, but not above one year old in the school and knowledge of CHRIST. He lately preached three times and rode forty miles the same day. The dissenting minister and his wife were very hearty, and perhaps here is one of the most settled female christian societies in the kingdom. I cannot well describe with what power the word was attended. Yesterday in the afternoon, and in the evening, it was just like as at *Edinburgh.* The old clergyman was much broken. A young *Oxonian*, who came with him, and many others, were most deeply affected. I suppose there were upwards of two thousand in the evening in the Meeting-house. Dear Mr. *H―――y*, one of our first Methodists at *Oxford*, and who was lately a curate here, had laid the blessed foundation. So far therefore from thinking of nestling at *London*, that I am more and more convinced that I should go from place to place, and therefore question if I shall see *London* for some time. If not too angry with me for prosecuting this rambling way of life, be pleased to pray for, dear madam,

Yours, &c.
G. W.

Postscript. Seven at night. To-day hath been as yesterday, and much more abundant. I am here, as in *Scotland* and *New-England.* Praise to free grace! Here is work enough for some months. The weather is very favourable; range, therefore, I must and will.

LETTER DXLI.

To the Same.

Dear Madam, St. *Gennis, Nov.* 25, 1743.

GLAD I am that GOD inclined my heart to come hither. He hath been with us of a truth. How did his stately steps appear in the sanctuary last LORD's-day? Many, many prayers were put up by the worthy Rector, and others, for an out-pouring of GOD's blessed spirit. They were answered. Arrows of conviction fled so thick and so fast, and such an universal weeping prevailed from one end of the congregation to the other, that good Mr. *J——* could not help going from seat to seat to speak, encourage, and comfort the wounded souls. The *Oxonian*'s father was almost struck dumb; and the young *Oxonian*'s crest was so lowered, that I believe he'll never venture to preach an unknown CHRIST, or deal in the false commerce of unfelt truths. I could enlarge, but I must away to *Biddeford*, just to give satan another stroke, and bid my christian friends farewel, and then return the way I came, namely through *Exeter*, *Wellington* and *Bristol*, to the great metropolis: but journeying, and various other matters that lie before me, I expect will prevent your hearing so frequently as usual, from

Yours, &c.

G. W.

LETTER DXLII.

To Mr. J—— S——.

Brinkworth, December 18, 1743.

My dear Friend,

'TIS past eleven at night, but lest I should not have time to-morrow at *Gloucester*, which I intend to take in my way to *Birmingham*, I'll rob myself of a little sleep to write to you now. On *Friday* evening we reached five miles beyond *Reading*. Last night about nine we got to *Clack*. It rained and snowed much for about seven miles, and the way was dangerous; but the blessed JESUS kept us in safety. In the morning I preached and gave the sacrament at *Tetherton*. This evening

evening I preached here. They were good times. I have a cold, but our LORD warms my heart. To-morrow I must away to *Gloucester*. O follow, follow with your prayers.

Yours, &c.

G. W.

LETTER DXLIII.

To the Same.

Birmingham, Dec. 27, 1743.

WANT of time, not of love, prevented my writing to you from *Gloucester*. Neither have I now leisure to be very particular. It is near eleven at night, and nature calls for rest. I have preached five times this day, and, weak as I am, through CHRIST strengthening me, I could preach five times more. I think I was scarce ever so happy before. Surprizing! how the LORD JESUS hath made way for me in these parts. I lose nothing by being quiet and leaving all to him. O was you here, what could I not tell you? The weather is just like Spring. That the day-spring from on high may visit your heart, till you rise to eternal perfect day, earnestly prays

Yours, &c.

G. W.

LETTER DXLIV.

To the Same.

My dear Friend,   *Birmingham*, Dec. 31, 1743.

WHAT do you think? Since my last, I have stole a whole day to dispatch some private business: however, in the evening I expounded to a great room full of people, who would rush into my lodgings, whether I would or not. On *Sunday* morning at eight I preached in the street to about a thousand, with much freedom. I then went to church and received the sacrament, and afterwards preached to several thousands in the street. The hearers seemed much pleased and delighted. It happened by the providence of GOD, that no minister would come to preach at a house at *Wedgbury*, where a weekly lecture used to be kept up: I was therefore earnestly entreated to come. I went, after my afternoon's

preaching

preaching at *Birmingham*, and preached there at six in the evening to many hundreds in the street. It is about six miles from Birmingham. The word came with power, and only one or two made a noise at a distance. Afterwards we had a precious meeting in private. The power of the dear Redeemer was much amongst us. The person with whom I lodged was a widow fearing GOD. Her husband was an eminent saint, and had been refreshed by my writings, particularly my journals, as had many others that I met with. On *Monday* morning about eight I preached to a large company in a field. By eleven I returned to *Birmingham*, and preached to many thousands on a Common near the town. The soldiers were exercising; but the officers hearing that I was coming to preach, dismissed them, and promised that no disturbance should be made. All was quiet, and a blessed time we had. In the afternoon about three I preached again to about the same company, with the same success. Then I rode to *Wedgbury* and preached there, and afterwards exhorted: but I cannot well tell you, what a sweet melting time there was. Many were in tears. About one I went to bed exceeding happy. In the morning I broke up some fallow ground at a place called *Mare-Green*, about two miles from *Wedgbury*. Much mobbing had been there against Mr. *Wesley*'s friends. A few poor souls began to insult me, but JESUS strengthened me much. Several clods were thrown, one of them fell on my head, and another struck my fingers, while I was in prayer. A sweet gospel spirit was given to me. I preached again at *Birmingham* to larger auditories than before, about eleven the same morning and three in the afternoon. In the evening I expounded twice in a large room. Once to the rich, and once to the poor, and went to rest happier than the night before. In the morning I took my leave of the *Birmingham* people, who wept much and were indeed deeply affected, and shewed great concern at my departure. I then went to *Kidderminster*, about twelve miles from *Birmingham*, where I was kindly received by Mr. *W———ms*, with whom I have corresponded for near two years. Many friends were at his house. I was greatly refreshed to find what a sweet savour of good Mr. *Baxter*'s doctrine, works and discipline remained to this day.

The

The sweet remembrance of the just,
Shall flourish when he sleeps in dust.

I preached about three in the afternoon to a large auditory near the church. Some unkind men, though they promised not to do so, rang the bells; but our Saviour enabled me to preach with power. In the evening and next morning I preached in the meeting house. I then went with Mr. *W———* to *Bromsgrove*, about seven miles from *Kidderminster*, and was kindly received by one Mr. *K———y*, a good man, and several others, among whom were two or three Baptist and one Independent ministers. About three in the afternoon I preached in a field. Some rude people kicked a football and sounded a horn at some distance, but the LORD enabled me to preach with boldness. About six I preached in the Baptist Meeting-house, left *Kidderminster* at eight, and reached *Worcester* about ten at night. Mr. *W———ms* and another friend accompanied us. In the morning the good old Mr. *S———y*, who was supposed to be sanctified from the womb, came to us while we baited. In the evening I reached *Gloucester*, very thankful for my week's progress, and rejoicing greatly in CHRIST for giving me such a delightful and happy Christmas. This day I have preached twice here, and have been enabled to dispatch some private affairs. It is now near twelve. My dear friend, I wish you an exceeding happy new-year. This time twelve-month I was writing to you from *Bristol*. O what has the dear LORD JESUS done for me since that, and since I was born! And O what does he intend to do for me before I die, and when time shall be no more? I am lost in wonder! I must away and cry Grace! grace! Praying that you may be filled with all the fulness of GOD, I subscribe, my dearest friend,

Ever, ever yours wh lst

G. W.

LETTER DXLV.

To Mr. H——, at Gloucester.

Mashfield, Jan. 7, 1744, *(past* 7 *at night.)*

My very dear Mr. H——,

IT being wet and dark, we thought it prudent to stay here this night. I cannot employ part of the evening better than in writing to you, and blessed be our GOD, I can send you good news. Our gracious LORD was with me at *Pitchcomb* and *Hampton*. We have had a wonderful sweet association in *Wales*, with much of the Redeemer's presence, especially when I began to speak about the law affair. The brethren were very generous, according to their circumstances, and one gentlewoman sent me five pounds. After mature deliberation, we determined to prosecute the affair to the utmost, and to set apart next *Tuesday* fortnight (the first day of the term) for a day of fasting and prayer, and to make collections for that purpose. The cause is the LORD's, and much depends on our getting the victory. I believe we shall. I have had a favourable answer from Colonel S——, and also from Colonel *Gar*——. Hitherto the LORD prospers us. I am now going to *London* very happy, and in some measure thankful for the many blessings I have received. Help me, my dear friend, to cry Grace! grace! Inclosed you have some letters: be pleased to peruse and deliver them. I bless GOD that affairs have taken such a turn. I have been at *Abergavenny*, and am settled as to my dear wife's coming down. Blessed be GOD, she and the little one are pretty well. I shall be glad to hear from you when I come to *London*. I hope our LORD blesses you, both in body and soul, and shews you the way wherein you should go. That you may be continually guided by his counsel, and after death conducted to his glory, is the hearty prayer of, dear Sir,

Yours most affectionately in CHRIST JESUS,

G. W.

LETTER DXLVI.

To the Same.

London, *Jan.* 18, 1744.

THIS afternoon I received your kind letter, and thank you a thousand times for your great generosity in lending me some furniture, having little of my own. I know who will repay you. Next week, GOD willing, my dear wife and little one will come to *Gloucester*, for I find it beyond my circumstances to maintain them here. I leave *London*, GOD willing, this day sev'nnight. Your affairs and concerns are mine. I shall lay them before our common Lord. My brother will receive a letter about my wife's coming. She and the little one are brave and well. But why talk I of wife and little one? Let all be absorbed in the thoughts of the love, sufferings, free and full salvation of the infinitely great and glorious *Emmanuel*. Blessed, for ever blessed be his holy Name, for such happy beginnings of another year! How would it rejoice you to see the many thousands in this metropolis, like new-born babes, desiring to be fed with the sincere milk of the word, that they may grow thereby. This, if I know any thing of my heart, is all my salvation, and all my desire. In respect to other things, at present I know this is, and I trust always will be the habitual language of my heart: O blessed GOD,

> *Thy gifts, if call'd for, I resign,*
> *Pleas'd to receive, pleas'd to restore;*
> *Gifts are thy work; it shall be mine,*
> *The giver only to adore.*

That both of us may be always kept thus minded, is the earnest prayer of

Yours most affectionately,

G. W.

LETTER DXLVII.

To Mr. D—— T——

My dear Friend, Gloucester, *Feb.* 9, 1744.

WHO knows what a day may bring forth? Last night I was called to sacrifice my *Isaac*; I mean to bury my my only child and fon about four months old. Many things occurred to make me believe he was not only to be continued to me, but to be a preacher of the everlafting gofpel. Pleafed with the thought, and ambitious of having a fon of my own, fo divinely employed, fatan was permitted to give me fome wrong impreffions, whereby, as I now find, I mifapplied feveral texts of fcripture. Upon thefe grounds I made no fcruple of declaring, " that I fhould have a fon, and that his name was to be *John*." I mentioned the very time of his birth, and fondly hoped, that he was to be great in the fight of the LORD. Every thing happened according to the predictions, and my wife having had feveral narrow efcapes while pregnant, efpecially by her falling from a high horfe, and my driving her into a deep ditch in a one-horfe chaife a little before the time of her lying-in, and from which we received little or no hurt, confirmed me in my expectation, that GOD would grant me my heart's defire. I would obferve to you, that the child was even born in a room, which the mafter of the houfe had prepared as a prifon for his wife for coming to hear me. With joy would fhe often look upon the bars and ftaples and chains which were fixed in order to keep her in. About a week after his birth, I publickly baptized him in the Tabernacle, and in the company of thoufands folemnly gave him up to that GOD, who gave him to me. A hymn, too fondly compofed by an aged widow, as fuitable to the occafion, was fung, and all went away big with hopes of the child's being hereafter to be employed in the work of GOD; but how foon are all their fond, and as the event hath proved, their ill-grounded expectations blafted, as well as mine. Houfe-keeping being expenfive in *London*, I thought beft to fend both parent and child to *Abergavenny*, where my wife had a little houfe of my own, the furniture of which, as I thought of foon embarking for *Georgia*, I had partly fold, and partly given away. In their journey thither, they ftopped at *Gloucefter*, at the *Bell-Inn*, which my brother now keeps, and in which I was born. There, my beloved was cut off with a ftroke. Upon my coming here, without knowing what had happened, I enquired concerning the welfare of parent and child; and by the anfwer, found that the flower was cut down. I immediately called all to join in prayer, in which I bleffed the Father of mercies for giving me a fon, a son, continuing it to me so long, and taking it from me so soon. All joined in desiring that I would decline preaching 'till the child was buried; but I remembered a saying of good Mr. *Henry*, "that weeping must not hinder sowing," and therefore preached twice the next day, and also the day following; on the evening of which, just as I was closing my sermon, the bell struck out for the funeral. At first, I must acknowledge, it gave nature a little shake, but looking up I recovered strength, and then concluded with saying, that this text on which I had been preaching, namely, "all things worked together for good to them that love GOD," made me as willing to go out to my son's funeral, as to hear of his birth. Our parting from him was solemn. We kneeled down, prayed, and shed many tears, but I hope tears of resignation: And then, as he died in the house wherein I was born, he was taken and laid in the church where I was baptized, first communicated, and first preached. All this you may easily guess threw me into very solemn and deep reflection, and I hope deep humiliation; but I was comforted from that passage in the book of Kings, where is recorded the death of the *Shunamite*'s child, which the Prophet said, "The LORD had hid from him;" and the woman's answer likewise to the Prophet when he asked, "Is it well with thee? Is it well with thy husband? Is it well with thy child?" And she answered, "*It is well.*" This gave me no small satisfaction. I immediately preached upon the text the day following at *Gloucester*, and then hastened up to *London*, preached upon the same there; and though disappointed of a living preacher by the death of my son; yet I hope what happened before his birth, and since at his death, hath taught me such lessons, as, if duly improved, may render his mistaken parent more cautious, more sober-minded, more experienced in satan's devices, and consequently more useful in his future labours to the church of GOD. Thus, "out of the eater comes forth meat, and out of the strong comes forth sweetness." Not doubting but our future life will be one continued explanation of this blessed riddle, I commend myself and you to the unerring guidance of GOD's word and spirit, and am

Yours, &c.
G. W.

The HYMN mentioned in the foregoing Letter.

I.

POOR helpless babe! dear little child!
JOHN be thy name, thy nature mild;
Great may'st thou be in JESU's sight,
A babe in whom he takes delight.

II.

Be thou made holy from the womb,
By him who sav'd thee from the * tomb:
In JESU's arms still may'st thou rest,
While sucking at thy mother's breast.

III.

Blest be the parents with the son!
Blest be the GOD that gave you one!
We'll magnify the LORD with you!
Share in your joy, we're sure we do.

IV.

O may you both be taught of GOD,
To teach this Child his SAVIOUR's blood:
That thousands in your bliss may share,
In answer to united pray'r.

V.

And may the Lamb, your Master, grant
This grace, that you may never want
A child to stand before his face,
To preach his Love, his Sov'reign Grace!

* Alluding to the remarkable deliverance that his father and mother had some few weeks before his mother was delivered, when she and her husband being riding in a chaise, they were thrown into a deep ditch, and received no harm, as mentioned in Letter 534, p. 39.

LETTER DXLVIII.

To Mr. G. H———.

London, Feb. 24, 1744.

My dear dear Mr. H———,

MUltiplicity of urgent affairs has kept me from answering your kind letter sooner. Blessed be GOD for giving you such a prosperous journey. I am not sorry that some, after their much joy, have been brought down and plunged into much misery. It is no more than might be expected. Stolen sweets prepare for bitter tears. On *Monday* morning I shall know what the rioters intend doing. There has been dreadful work near *Birmingham*, but satan will be overthrown. We had a glorious fast on *Monday*, and collected above sixty pounds for our poor suffering brethren. We have had two solemn funerals. I hope the work prospers in your hands. Our lawyer hath sent me word, that the rioters stand trial.—I think, GOD willing, to be in *Gloucestershire* by *Monday* sev'nnight. The LORD be with you. I salute all, and am, my dear Mr. H———,

Your most affectionate, though unworthy friend and ready servant,

G. W.

Feb. 26.

P. S. Since I wrote the above, I have consulted with friends, and find it best to come through *Gloucester* to *Abergavenny*.—God willing, I hope to preach with you on *Tuesday* between seven and eight at night. Be pleased immediately on the receipt of this to send word to brother *Adams* to meet me without fail at *Gloucester* on *Tuesday*, to confer about our assize affair. I heard yesterday from *Wales*. I bought a second-hand suit of curtains to-day, so you need not send any thing to *Abergavenny*. "Poor, yet making others rich," shall be my motto still.

LETTER DXLIX.

London, March 12, 1744.

My dear Friend,

THIS leaves me just returned from *Gloucester* assizes, where it has pleased the great Judge of quick and dead to give us the victory over the *Hampton* rioters. You remember I informed you, that I thought we should be obliged to appeal unto *Cæsar*. A solemn day of fasting and humiliation was kept on that account; and accordingly last term we lodged an information against them in the *King's-Bench*. Matters of fact being proved by a variety of evidence, and the defendants making no reply, the rule was made absolute, and an information filed against them. To this they pleaded *Not guilty*, and therefore, according to the method of the Crown-office, the cause was referred to the assizes held in *Gloucester* the third instant. Our council opened the cause by informing the court, that rioters were not to be reformers, and that his Majesty had no where put the reins of government into the hands of mobbers, nor made them either judge or jury. One of them in particular, the *Recorder of Oxford*, with great gravity, reminded the gentlemen on the jury of the advice of *Gamaliel*, " Refrain from these men and let them alone, for if this council, or this work be of man, it will come to nought; but if it be of God, ye cannot overthrow it, least haply ye be found even to fight against God." Our witnesses were then called. Mr. *Adams* and four more, three of which were not reputed Methodists, so clearly proved both the riot and the facts, that the judge was of opinion, there needed no other evidence. The council for the defendants then rose up, and displayed a good deal of oratory, and I think said all that could be said to mend a bad matter. One urged, " that we were enthusiasts, and our principles and practices had such a tendency to infect and hurt the people, that it was right, in his opinion, for any private person to stand up and put a stop to us; and whoever did so, was a friend to his country." He strove to influence the jury, by telling them, " That if a verdict was given against the defendants, it would cost them two hundred pounds; that the defendants rioting was not premeditated, but that coming to hear Mr. *A———*, and being offended at his doctrine, a sudden quarrel arose, and thereby the unhappy men were led into the present fray, which he could have wished had not happened; but however, it did not amount to a riot, but only an assault." Their other council informed the jury, " That they would undertake to prove, that the Methodists began the tumult first." He was pleased to mention me by name, and acquainted the court, "That Mr. *Whitefield* had been travelling from common to common, making the people cry, and then picking their pockets, under pretence of collecting money for the colony of *Georgia*; and knowing that *Gloucestershire* was a populous county, he at last came there; that he had now several curates, of which Mr. *Adams* was one, who in his preaching had found fault with the proceedings of the clergy, and had said, that if the people went to hear them, they would be damned." He added, that "there had lately been such mobbing in *Staffordshire*, that a regiment of soldiers was sent down to suppress them; infinuating, that the Methodists were the authors; that we had now another cause of a like nature depending in *Wiltshire*, and that we were not of that mild pacific spirit, as we pretended to be." This, and much more to the same purpose, though foreign to the matter in hand, pleased many of the auditors, who expressed their satisfaction, in hearing the Methodists in general, and me in particular, thus lashed, by frequent laughing. But our LORD not only kept me quite easy, but enabled me to rejoice in being thus honoured for his great Name's sake. To prove what the defendants council had infinuated, they called up a young man, who was a brother to one of the defendants, and one of the mob. He swore point blank, "That Mr. *Adams* said, if people went to church, they would be damned, but if they would come to him, he would carry them to JESUS CHRIST." He swore also, "that the brook into which Mr. *A——* was thrown, was no deeper than half up his legs." He said first, that there were but about ten of them that came to the house of Mr. *A——*; and then he swore, that there were about threescore. He said, there was a bell, and that one of the defendants did ask Mr. *A——* to come off the stairs, but that none of them went up to him: upon which Mr. *A——* willingly obeyed, went with them briskly along the street, and as he would have represented it, put himself into the skin-pit and brook, and so came out again. He said also some other things; but through the whole, his evidence appeared so flagrantly false, that one of the council said, "It was enough to make his hair stand an end." The judge himself wished, "That the man had so much religion as to fear an oath." So he went down in disgrace. Their second evidence was an aged woman, mother of one of the defendants;

fendants; she swore, "That her son did go up stairs to Mr. *A——*, and that Mr. *A——* tore her son's coat;" but she talked so fast, and her evidence was so palpably false, that she was sent away in as much disgrace as the other. Their third and last evidence, was father to one who was in the mob, tho' not one of the defendants. The chief he had to say was, " That when Mr. *A——* was coming from the brook, he met " him and said, Brother, how do you do? Upon which he an-" swer'd, that he had received no damage, but had been in the " brook and came out again." So that all their evidences, however contrary one to another, yet corroborated ours, and proved the riot out of their own mouths. The book was then given to a justice of the peace, who had formerly taken up Mr. *C——* for preaching near *Stroud*, and had lately given many signal proofs that he was no friend to the Methodists. But he intending to speak only about their characters, and the council and judge looking upon that as quite impertinent to the matter in hand, he was not admitted as an evidence. Upon this, his Lordship with great candor and impartiality summed up the evidence, and told the jury, " That " he thought they should bring all the defendants in GUILTY; " for our evidences had sufficiently proved the whole of the " information, and also, that the riot was premeditated."— He said, " That, in his opinion, the chief of the defendants " evidence was incredible; and, that supposing the Methodists " were heterodox, (as perhaps they might be) it belonged to " the ecclesiastical government to call them to an account; " that they were subjects, and rioters were not to be their re-" formers." He also reminded them " of the dreadful conse-" quences of rioting at any time, much more at such a critical " time as this; that rioting was the forerunner of, and might " end in rebellion; that it was felony without benefit of clergy, " to pull down a Meeting-house; and for all as he knew, it was " high treason to pull down even a bawdy-house.—That this " information also came from the *King's-Bench*; that his Ma-" jesty's justices there, thought they had sufficient reason to " grant it; that the matters contained in it had been evidently " proved before them; and consequently they should bring in " all the defendants guilty." Upon this the jury were desired to consider of their verdict, and for a while there seemed to be

some

some little demur among them. His Lordship perceiving the cause of it, immediately informed them, "they had nothing to do with the damages, (that was to be referred to the *King's-Bench*) they were only to consider, whether the defendants were guilty or not." Whereupon in a few minutes they gave a verdict for the prosecutors, and brought in all the defendants *guilty* of the whole information lodged against them. I then retired to my lodgings, kneeled down, and with my friends gave thanks to our all-conquering *Emmanuel*. Afterwards I went to the inn, prayed and returned thanks with the witnesses, exhorted them to behave with meekness and humility to their adversaries; and after they had taken proper refreshment, I sent them home rejoicing. In the evening I preached on these words of the Psalmist, "By this I know that thou favourest me, since thou hast not suffered mine enemy to triumph over me." GOD was pleased to enlarge my heart much. I was very happy with my friends afterwards, and the next morning set out for *London*, where we had a blessed thanksgiving season, and from whence I take the first opportunity of sending you these particulars.

I remain, Sir, your very affectionate friend,

G. W.

LETTER DL.

To Mrs. D――.

Dear Madam, *London, March* 15, 1744.

SHALL I promise and not perform? GOD forbid! This comes in answer to your commands, and to inform you, that through him who has the hearts of all men in his hands, we came off more than conquerors, respecting our *Gloucester* trial. The rioters were brought in guilty, and I suppose will have an execution issued out against them next Term. I hear they are hugely alarmed; but they know not that we intend to let them see what we could do, and then to forgive them. This troublesome affair being now over, I must prepare for my intended voyage. They tell me there is a ship going from *Portsmouth*. GOD willing, I purpose to take my passage in it, and though calls come to me from every quarter, yet I must once more visit my dear family in *America*. Some well-meaning

LETTERS.

ing people threaten me with I know not what, if I embark at this time; but my absence hath been so long and unexpected, that come what will, I am determined to prosecute my intended voyage; and therefore whether we meet any more in the flesh, I trust we shall meet in the world of spirits, where parting, weeping, and breaking of hearts will no more disturb and try the affections of, dear Madam,

Yours in the dear *Emmanuel*,

G. W.

LETTER DLI.

To the Same.

My dear Friend,   *Plymouth*, *June* 26, 1744.

YOU see by this where I am. Doubtless you'll wonder at the quick transition from *Portsmouth* to *Plymouth*. To the former I intended going when I wrote last; but just before I took leave of the dear tabernacle people, a message was sent to me, that the captain in which I was to sail from thence, would not take me for fear of spoiling his sailors. Some interpreted this as a call from providence not to embark at this time; but I enjoined them silence 'till I had taken my leave, and then, hearing of a mast-ship that was going under convoy from *Plymouth*, I hastened thither, and have taken a passage in the *Wilmington*, Capt. *Dalby*, bound to *Piscataway*, in *New-England*. My first reception here was a little unpromising. A report being spread that I was come, a great number of people assembled upon the *Hoe*, (a large green for walks and diversions) and somebody brought out a bear and a drum; but I did not come 'till the following evening, when, under pretence of a hue-and-cry, several broke into the room where I lodged at the inn, and disturbed me very much. I then betook myself to private lodgings, and being gone to rest, after preaching to a large congregation, and visiting the *French* prisoners, the good woman of the house came and told me, that a well-dressed gentleman desired to speak with me. Imagining that it was some Nicodemite, I desired he might be brought up. He came and sat down by my bedside, told me he was a lieutenant of a man of war, congratulated me on the success of my ministry, and expressed himself much concerned for being detained

tained from hearing me. He then asked me, if I knew him. I answered, no. He replied, his name was *Cadogan*. I rejoined, that I had seen one Mr. *Cadogan*, who was formerly an officer at *Georgia*, about a fortnight ago at *Bristol*. Upon this, he immediately rose up, uttering the most abusive language, calling me *dog, rogue, villain*, &c. and beat me most unmercifully with his gold-headed cane. As you know I have not much natural courage, guess how surprized I was; being apprehensive that he intended to shoot or stab me, I underwent all the fears of a sudden violent death. But, as it providentially happened, my hostess and her daughter hearing me cry *murder*, rushed into the room and seized him by the collar; however, he immediately disengaged himself from them, and repeated his blows upon me. The cry of *murder* was repeated also, which putting him into some terror, he made towards the chamber-door, from whence the good woman pushed him down stairs. About the bottom of which, a second cry'd out, "Take courage, I am ready to help you;" accordingly, whilst the other was escaping, he rushed up, and finding one of the women coming down, took her by the heels and threw her upon the stairs, by which her back was almost broken. By this time the neighbourhood was alarmed. Unwilling to add to it, I desired the doors might be shut, and so betook myself to rest, not without reflecting, how indispensibly necessary it was for christians and christian ministers to be always upon their guard, and with what great propriety we are taught to pray in our excellent Litany, "from sudden," that is, "from violent and unprepared death, good LORD deliver us." That this may be our happy lot, is the hearty prayer of, dear Madam,

Yours, &c.

G. W.

LETTER DLII.

To the Same.

Plymouth, July 4, 1744.

SINCE my last, I have had some particular information about the late odd adventure. It seems, that four gentlemen came to the house of one of my particular friends, kindly enquiring after me, and desired to know where I lodged,

that

that they might come and pay their refpects. He directed them. Soon afterwards I received a letter, informing me that the writer was a nephew to Mr. S———, an eminent attorney at *New-York*; that he had the pleafure of fupping with me at his uncle's houfe, and defired my company to fup with him and a few more friends at a tavern. I fent him word, that it was not cuftomary for me to fup out at taverns, but fhould be glad of his company, out of refpect to his uncle, to eat a morfel with him at my lodgings. He came; we fupped; and I obferved that he frequently looked around him, and feemed very abfent; but having no fufpicion, I continued in converfation with him and my other friends, 'till we parted. This, I now find, was to have been the *affaffin*; and being interrogated by his other companions on his return to the tavern about what he had done, he anfwered, that being ufed fo civilly, he had not the heart to touch me. Upon which, as I am informed, the perfon who affaulted me laid a wager of ten guineas that he would do my bufinefs for me. Some fay, that they took his fword from him, which I fuppofe they did, for I only faw and felt the weight of his cane. The next morning, I was to expound at a private houfe, and then to fet out for *Biddeford*. Some urged me to ftay and profecute; but being better employed, I went on my intended journey, was greatly bleffed in preaching the everlafting gofpel, and upon my return was well paid for what I had fuffered: curiofity having led perhaps two thoufand more than ordinary to fee and hear a man, that had like to have been murdered in his bed. Thus all things tend to the furtherance of the gofpel, and work together for good to thofe that love GOD.

Thus fatan thwarts, and men object,
And yet the thing they thwart, effect.

Leaving you to add an *Hallelujah*, I fubfcribe myfelf,
Ever, ever yours,
G. W.

LETTER DLIII.
To Mr. S———.

Plymouth, July 21, 1744.

I Expected a line from you this morning; but I fuppofe you think we are gone. This day came in a privateer, which saw the *Brest* squadron that has pursued two of our men of war, the *Dreadnought* and *Frederick*; so that had we sailed, we should in all probability have been carried into *France*. We are now to go under convoy of the grand fleet; many letters from our friends at *Portsmouth* inform us, that they are to sail on *Sunday*; but the wind hath not been very favourable, so we may yet stay some days longer. I never was so easy in this respect before. In one or two things I find my will reluctant; but JESUS will bring all things in subjection to him. I have been greatly refreshed this evening in preaching his blood. The congregations grow visibly every day. You will see the letter from *Kingsbridge*.—Last night many from the *Dock* came and guarded me home, being apprehensive there was a design against me. Without my knowledge, they insulted a man who intended to hurt me, for which I am sorry. We had a wonderful good time last night. O help me to praise my Saviour! My health is better. I hope you got to *London* well. Whether we sail or not, expect to hear again from dear, dear *J*———,

Ever, ever yours, &c.
G. W.

Open a door, which earth and hell
May strive to shut, but strive in vain;
Let thy word richly with them dwell,
And let their gracious fruit remain!

LETTER DLIV.

To Mr. T———.

My dear Friend,   *Plymouth, July* 26, 1744.

ACCEPT some few hasty lines from one, who, properly speaking, may at present be stiled a prisoner at large. I am still here waiting for the promised convoy, and as I humbly hope, really waiting for the convoy of death to carry me to *Abraham*'s bosom. Could you think it? I have been preaching a confirmation sermon. Do you ask me where? In a *Quaker*'s field. As I saw thousands flocked to the church to have the Bishop's hands imposed upon them, I thought it not improper to let them have a word of exhortation suitable to the occasion. I have also made an elopement to *Kingsbridge*, where I preached to many thousands a few days ago. It was really a most solemn occasion. A calling, inviting, persuasive gift was vouchsafed me. The hearts of the auditory seemed to be bowed as the heart of one man. Many tears were shed; but I was obliged to ride off as soon as my discourse was ended, and to return hither in the night. But blessed be GOD, our night was as it were turned into day. I was accompanied by several old and new converts, and we conversed in some degree, as became persons who ought to be employed every hour and every moment in trimming their lamps to be ready for the midnight cry, "Behold the bridegroom cometh!" As I am at present in this unsettled state, continually engaged in preaching, and in talking privately with many, very many awakened souls, you and my other friends must be content with receiving short, but I hope truly loving letters, from

Yours, &c.

G. W.

LETTER DLV.

To Mr. J—— S——,

Plymouth, July 27, 1744.

MATTERS go on better and better here. I begin to think myself in *London*. We have our regular morning meetings; and our LORD is pleased to grace them with his presence. We are looking out for a place proper for a society, and to expound in. People come daily to me, especially from the *Dock*, under convictions. Some, I believe, have really closed with CHRIST; and here are several aged persons perfectly made young again. We are just now entered upon our singing hours.—The souls come forward greatly in many respects, and friends are more and more hearty. Fresh news from *Kingsbridge* of souls being awakened; but I am kept close prisoner on account of the convoy. Yesterday morning we were called up at the *Dock*, very early, by a false alarm that our convoy was come. Many poor souls much lamented it. We hastened hither, and I expounded upon our LORD's bidding his disciples to watch. This waiting is much blessed to me. I am kept passive; notwithstanding, satan attempts to disturb me, but JESUS refreshes me, and overcomes him. I need not bid you to pray for me. Brother C—— must come into these parts soon.

Yours, &c.
G. W.

LETTER DLVI.

To the Same.

Plymouth, July 29, 1744.

OUR LORD has been giving us blessings in drops, but now he is sending them in showers. This morning we have had a most precious meeting. Perhaps more good hath been done by that one sermon, than by all I have preached before. When GOD will work, who shall hinder? The wind is yet against us. Our LORD detains me here for wise reasons. Some persons, formerly prejudiced against me, have offered to give me a piece of ground surrounded with walls, for a society room. I believe that one will be built soon. Brother C—— must stay in the *West* some time. The LORD JESUS blesses me with health, and a sweet preaching spirit. O grace, grace! I will join with thee in praising it. Adieu, my friend. I am yours, in the bonds of eternal love, whilst

G. W.

LETTER DLVII.

To the Same.

My dear, dear Friend,　　*Plymouth, August 3, 1744.*

IT is past ten, or I would write you a long letter. Our convoy is come, and perhaps we may sail to-morrow. It is delightful to be here. We come from Dock in the evenings, in great companies, singing and praising GOD. Our parting there has been more awful than words can express. I shall have sailed before you can answer this.

I.

Eternal JESUS, *bless thy sword,*
　Be mindful of thy child;
Behold thy servant; be thou, LORD,
　His helmet, sword, and shield.

Close

II.

Close by thy side him ever keep;
Still hold him in thy hand,
Till he and all thy ransom'd sheep,
Shall rest in their own land.

III.

The preachers and the people there,
Shall thee in fulness see;
Shall keep the long sabbatic year,
The feast of jubilee.

If we never meet again in this suffering world, GOD grant that we may ere long see each other in the heavenly paradise, where all tears shall be wiped from our eyes, and death, sin, and sorrow we shall know no more. Farewel.

Ever, ever yours,

G. W.

LETTER DLVIII.

To Mr. E————.

Plymouth, August 4, 1744.

My very dear Brother E————,

I Thank you for your last kind and loving letter, and as a token of my unfeigned love to you, I send you these few lines by way of answer, before I embark. Our convoy is now come, and in all probability we shall sail this day or to-morrow. I need not stir up my dear brother, and other dear souls with you, to pray for me and mine. I am quite easy about the trust, having put all things into the hands of the LORD JESUS, upon whose shoulders the government of all is placed. He will, he does order all things well: I bless him for it, and for what he has, and is doing among the soldiers. I desire you all to bless him for what he is doing in these parts; for preaching at the *Dock* is now like preaching at the *tabernacle*. It would delight your dear soul, my brother, to be a spectator of the people's seriousness. Last night we had a most awful and solemn parting; many wept sorely. After sermon we walked pleasantly over the fields, blessing and praising GOD. Our morning lectures are very delightful. O the thousands

thousands that flock to the preaching of Christ's gospel! If brother C—— is in *London*, pray salute him in my name, and all the dear dear brethren and sisters, wishing you all thousands and millions of blessings, and earnestly intreating an interest in your prayers for me the chief of sinners. I subscribe myself, my dear brother *E*——,

Yours most affectionately in the
most adorable Redeemer,
G. W.

Postscript. I must tell you one thing more. There is a ferry over to *Plymouth*; and the ferrymen, which were like *Levi* the publican at the receipt of custom, are now so much my friends, that they will take nothing of the multitude that come to hear me preach, saying, "God forbid that we should sell the word of God." O! the hearts of all men are in the hand of the Lord!

LETTER DLIX.

To Mr. ————.

On board the *Wilmington*, *Oct*. 20, 1744.

My dear Friend,

YOU know in what a poor state of health I was, when I embarked. The length, and seeming tediousness of the voyage, hath occasioned no small addition to the violent pain in my side; however, blessed be God, in a week or two after we sailed, we began to have a church in our ship. Two serious *New-England* friends finding how I was served at *Portsmouth*, came from thence to *Plymouth* in order to bear me company. We had regular public prayer morning and evening, frequent communion, and days of humiliation and fasting. Being time of war, and sailing out with near 150 ships, we had several convoys. Their taking leave of each other at their several appointed places, was striking: but ours was ordered to convoy us all the way. We were soon, and have been often alarmed. Once with the sight of a *Dutch* fleet, whom we took for an enemy; and again at the sight of Admiral *Balchen*, who rode by us receiving the obeisance of the surrounding ships, as though he was Lord of the whole ocean.

It was full six weeks ere we reached the *Western* Islands, off which it being calm weather, we continued floating for some days; during which interval we were like to suffer much damage. The wind having brisked up a little, and orders being given for tacking about, one of the ships, I know not by what accident, having missed her stays, in turning, came directly upon us; I happened at that time to be singing a hymn upon deck with my little family, and thinking it best to keep there to receive the shock, I had the opportunity of seeing what passed. The ship struck her mainsail into our bowsprit, but our ship being of a large, and theirs of a smaller size, our hull received but little damage, whilst theirs received such a blow, that when disentangled from us, they were immediately apprehensive of sinking. As they again passed by us, when we expected another touch, their cries and groans were awful. O how eagerly did they cry for some signal to be given! It was done. A little after that, we came up with the convoy, and our captain informed them of what had happened. The answer was, " This is your praying, and be damned to ye." With many expressions of the like nature. This, I must own, shocked me more than the striking of the ships. I called my friends together, and broke out into these words in prayer: " GOD of the sea and GOD of the dry land! This is a night of rebuke and blasphemy: shew thyself, O GOD, and take us under thy own immediate protection; be thou our convoy, and make a difference between those that fear thee and those that fear thee not!" The disabled ship was taken into tow. Next morning they were saluted in like manner as the night before, and orders were given us to follow our convoy into *Fial*; but on a sudden a violent euroclydon arose, which not only prevented our going into *Fial*, but battered and drove away our convoy, so that we saw him no more all the voyage. For my own part, I thought it no loss; we sailed very comfortably on, 'till we were again alarmed with the sight of two ships, making up to us with all the sail they could well croud, and which our captain took to be enemies. The preparations for an engagement, to me, who you know am naturally a coward, were formidable. Guns mounting, chains put about the masts, every thing taken out of the great cabin, hammocks put about the sides of the ship, and all, except myself, seemed ready for fire and smoke. My wife, after having dressed herself to prepare for all events, set about making cartridges, whilst the husband wanted to go into the holes of the ship, hearing that was the chaplain's usual place. I went, but not liking my situation, and being desired by one of my *New-England* friends to say something to animate the men, I crept up on deck, and for the first time of my life beat up to arms by a warm exhortation. The men seemed pleased, the apprehended enemy approached, but upon nearer view we found them not only to be friends, but the two masts ships that were going with us under the same convoy. This pleased us all. The captain taking this opportunity to clean the cabin, said, " After all, this is the best fighting:" with which you may be sure I readily concurred, praying, and believing at the same time, that all our various conflicts with spiritual enemies might, and would under the conduct of the all-conquering captain of our salvation, at last terminate in a thorough cleansing, and an eternal purification of the defiled cabin of our hearts. Committing you to his almighty guidance and protection, I subscribe myself,

Yours, &c.

G. W.

LETTER DLX.

To Mr. ———.

York (New-England,) Oct. 30, 1744.

Dear Friend,

DONT judge me for not writing more frequent. It was impracticable. I have been laid on a bed of sickness, and was, in the apprehension of myself and others, at the very mouth of the heavenly harbour; but as that more than once hath been the case, I am putting out to sea again. O who would but follow the Redeemer blindfold? No convoy like him who is the GOD of the sea and the GOD of the dry land. After eleven weeks passage he hath brought us hither, but through my impatience and imprudence I and my friends were like to suffer loss. A little smack coming up to us just as we were near port, and being told that she would be in several hours before the ship, I, with others in complaisance to me,

though

though perfuaded to the contrary, ventured in her. It foon grew dark, our pilots miffed their inlet and we were toffed about all night. My pain was great, having had for fome time a nervous cholic, and I was fo hungry that I could have gnawed the very boards. The fifhermen had nothing but a few potatoes, of which I partook moft eagerly; but withal, thought my fituation to be like the poor difciples, who were rowing and toiling all night, when the wind was contrary. About the fourth watch of the night, deliverance came; the men difcovered the proper inlet; but what paffed before our arrival is fomewhat ftriking to me. One of my friends, on afking what news, was anfwered, that the *New-England* people were turned *new lights*; which with us you know is a term for *heterodoxy*; but however, added the man, not knowing that I was lying down at his elbow, they are all expecting one Mr. *Whitefield*; and my fifter, and a great company of her ftamp, were yefterday all praying for his fafe arrival. This made me to take courage. I continued undifcovered; and in a few hours, in anfwer I truft to *new light prayers*, we arrived fafe at *York*, a few miles off *Pifcataway*, the place to which we were bound.—But you muft excufe enlarging; as I recover ftrength you fhall hear again from

Yours, &c.
G. W.

LETTER DLXI.

To Mr. ———.

Dear Sir, *York, Nov.* 6, 1744.

HOW thankful ought I to be to him, whofe mercy endureth for ever! GOD has commanded a phyfician (once a notorious deift, but through grace converted at my laft vifit in *New-England*) to receive me here. Worthy Colonel *P———*, who lives at the very mouth of the harbour, on feeing our fhip, went with fome other friends in his own boat to invite and conduct me to his princely habitation. But GOD appointed otherwife. In about half an hour after my arrival, I was put to bed, racked with a nervous cholic, and convulfed from the wafte down to my toes. A total convulfion was immediately apprehended,

My wife and friends stood weeping by,
In tears resolv'd to see me die.

Filled with divine consolation, I begged them not to be shocked. My Saviour whispered that all was well, and therefore I desired them not to be surprized if I should be totally convulsed, or be suffered in a delirium to speak things that were wrong. Many, many of GOD's dearest children, through the infirmities which crazy constitutions more especially are liable to, have been called to drink such a bitter cup before me. But an all-compassionate Redeemer disappointed our fears, and exceeded our strongest expectations. Apprehended convulsions were kept off; and though I was so weak as not to be able to bear the sound of a tread of the foot, or the voice of friends who came to see and pray with me, yet my heart was kept in perfect peace. After undergoing, for about four days, fomentations and exercises of different kinds, by having my feet put into warm water, &c. nature was relieved, and what I had taken four days before came away hardly discoloured. After this, whilst carried about by my tender nurse and a servant, still racked with pain, and like an helpless child, I could only say, "Look and learn what a poor creature I am." The scene affects me yet. May it never be forgotten! I must retire, and leave enlarging to another opportunity. In the mean while, assure yourself of my being, though less than the least of all,

Yours, &c.

G. W.

LETTER DLXII.

To Mr. ———.

Portsmouth, (New-England) Nov. 16, 1744.

My dear Friend,

AS I promised, I must employ a little of my new-gained strength in writing to you. Soon after I began to recover, good old Mr. M—— the minister of *York*, who feared the LORD greatly from his youth, came to and accosted me thus: "Sir, you are first welcome to *America*; secondly, to *New-England*; thirdly, to all the faithful ministers in *New-England*;

England; fourthly, to all the good people in *New-England*; fifthly, to all the good people of *York*; and sixthly and lastly, to me, dear Sir, less than the least of all." He then urged me to give them a sermon. Too forward to reingage in my old delightful work, I complied, notwithstanding at the same time word had been sent to *Boston* that I was dying; upon which, my dear *Gaius* and a beloved physician came, either to take care of me, or attend my funeral; but to their great surprize they found me in the pulpit. GOD was with me; but imprudently going over the ferry to *Portsmouth*, I caught cold, immediately relapsed, and was taken, as every one thought, with death, in my dear friend Mr. *Sherburne*'s house. My pains returned; but what gave me most concern was, that notice had been given of my being to preach the next evening. A great number of ministers and people flocked to hear; three physicians attended me, and Colonel *Pepperel* with many others were so kind as to pay me a visit and sympathize with me. GOD dealt so bountifully with me, that I was enabled to tell the Colonel in particular, from heart-experience, that I felt a divine life distinct from my animal life, which made me as it were to laugh at pain; this made me determine to get up and preach, though the General and all had left me, and the person appointed to lecture in my stead was just going out of the house. My dear *York* physician was then about to administer a medicine. I on a sudden cried, " Doctor, my pains are suspended: by the help of GOD I'll go and preach, and then come home and die." With some difficulty I reached the pulpit. All looked quite surprized, as though they saw one rose from the dead. Indeed, I was as pale as death, and told them " they must look upon me as a dying man, that I came to bear my dying testimony to the truths I had formerly preached amongst them, and to the invisible realities of another world." Nature (by my continuing an hour in my discourse) was almost quite exhausted; but O what life! what power spread all around! All seemed to be melted, and were drowned in tears. The cry after me, when I left the pulpit, was like the cry of sincere mourners when attending the funeral of a dear departed friend. Upon my coming home, I was laid on a bed upon the ground near the fire, and I heard them say, " He is gone;" but still you find by this

I am alive, and if spared to be made instrumental in making any poor dead soul alive to GOD, I shall rejoice that the all-wise Redeemer has kept out of heaven a little longer,

Yours, &c.

G. W.

LETTER DLXIII.

To Mr. ———.

My dear Friend, *Boston, Jan.* 18, 1745.

BY this time I suppose you have heard, by your brother's letter, how good old Mr. *Moody*, in his honest way, said, I was welcome to all the faithful ministers in *New-England*. But the good old man judged too much by his own honest feelings. You see I am now at *Boston*, whither I was brought from *Piscataway* in a coach and four. The joy with which I was received by the common people, cannot well be described; but many of the ministers how shy? — And how different from what once they were? When last in *Boston*, governor *Belcher* was in the chair: then, *reges ad exemplum, totus componitur orbis*, he honoured me with great honour, and the clergy paid the nod, and obeyed. In many I then perceived it was quite forced, and I think when at his table I whispered to some and said, if ever I came again, many of those who now seem extremely civil, will turn out my open and avowed enemies. The event has proved, that in this respect I have been no false prophet. You know where it is written, "There arose a king, who knew not *Joseph*." Freed therefore from their former restraint, many have appeared in *puris naturalibus*. Some occasions of offence had undoubtedly been given whilst I was here and preached up and down the country. —Nothing however appeared but a pure, divine power working upon, converting, and transforming people's hearts, of all ranks, without any extraordinary phænomena attending it. Good Mr. *T*—— succeeded me; numbers succeeded him. Lecture upon lecture were set up in various places; one minister called to another, to help drag the gospel net; and by all the accounts that I can have from private information, or good Mr. *Prince*'s weekly history, which I send you with this, one would have imagined the millennium was coming indeed.

But

But you know, in this mixed state of things, wild-fire will necessarily blend itself with the pure fire that comes from GOD's altar. This the enemy long waited for; at last it broke out and spread itself; and it must be confessed, through the instrumentality of many good souls both among clergy and laity, who for a while mistaking fancy for faith, and imagination for revelation, were guilty of great imprudence. What these were, I have not time now to particularize; I can only inform you, that all is laid to me as being the *primum mobile*, though there was not so much as the appearance of any thing of this nature when I left *New-England* last. But, maugre all, my poor labours are yet attended with the usual blessings, and therefore I must entreat you as usual to pray and give thanks in behalf of

Yours, &c.

G. W.

LETTER DLXIV.

To Mr. ———.

My dear Friend, *Boston, Feb.* 6, 1745.

I Remember you once told me, that you heard one of the good old *Puritans*, who went over to *New-England*, wrote back again, that he went from *Old-England* to avoid the Lord Bishops, and came to *New-England* to get under the Lord Brethren. Well is it at present that they are the Lord Brethren; for finding some of their pastors without cause shy of me, they have passed votes of invitation for me to preach in the pulpits, and some time ago prevailed upon me, as they heard I had done in *Scotland*, to set up a lecture at six o'clock in the morning. Not expecting a very great auditory, I opened a lecture in one of the smallest meetings, upon these words, "And they came early in the morning to hear him;" but how was I disappointed? Such great numbers flocked to hear, that I was obliged for the future to make use of two of their very largest places of worship, where I believe seldom less than two or three thousand attentive hearers hung as it were upon me, to hear the word preached. I began with the first of *Genesis*, and have now lectured in order, till I am almost come to the story of *Abraham* sending his servant to fetch a

wife

Many I trust have been made willing to go with the GOD-man, even *Isaac*'s GOD." It is impossible to describe the eagerness and punctuality of these early visitants. To see so many hundreds of both sexes neatly dressed, walking or riding so early along the streets to get food for their souls, has feasted my own heart. The *Pharaohs* who used to say, " Ye are idle, ye are idle," now are struck dumb: for lecture, and family prayer, and breakfast, are now over in many houses before the sun is suffered to come into others windows; and it is now become almost a common proverb, " That between *Tar-water*, and *early rising*, the physicians will have no business." One morning the croud was so great, that I was obliged to go in at the window. The high sheriff, who was once most forward in persecuting good Mr. D———t, being a little convinced under the word, accompanied me, and when he put his head into the window after me, the people were ready to cry out, " Is *Saul* also among the prophets?" Hoping hereafter to send you and other friends a further account of many such real instances of all-conquering grace, I subscribe myself

Yours, &c.

G. W.

LETTER DLXV.

To Mr. A———.

Ipswich, Feb. 7, 1745.

AND how does my very dear brother *A———*? I heard by some friend lately that he was well.—I hope this will find him yet better, and more and more happy in the ever-lovely, ever-loving JESUS.—I suppose you have heard of his great goodness to me and mine.—We have been carried through various trials; and can set up our *Ebenezer*, saying, " Hitherto hath the LORD helped us."—I cannot help thinking but that the LORD JESUS is about to triumph gloriously.—He is pleased to bear me as on eagles wings, and causes both sinners and saints to hear his voice.—I am kept very happy, and see more and more of the mystery of iniquity that lies in my heart. I rejoice in knowing that the blood of JESUS will cleanse me from all.—I long to hear how it is with the dear lambs

lambs in *Gloucestershire.*—I commit you and them to the care of the compassionate bishop and shepherd of souls; and subscribe myself, my dear man,

Yours most affectionately,
G. W.

P. S. My dear wife joins in sending cordial salutations to you, yours, and all.

LETTER DLXVI.

To Mrs. ———.

Dear Madam,   *Boston, Feb.* 17, 1745.

THIS leaves me just retired from my spiritual levee. Our good friend Mr. S—— tells me, while I am here he looks upon his house not as his own, but mine. His parlour is large, and I sit there to receive gospel visitants. Good Mr. P—— told me some time ago, that I should shortly be favoured with the company of a very pensive and uncommon person; a man of good parts, ready wit, and lively imagination, and who had made it his business, in order to furnish matter for preaching over a bottle, to come and hear, and then carry away scraps of my sermons, which it seems were to serve as texts or theses for his tavern harangues. A few nights ago he came for this purpose to Doctor S——'s meeting; upon my coming in, he crouded after amongst the people, and having got sufficient matter to work upon as he thought, attempted to go out; but being pent in on every side, he found his endeavours fruitless. Obliged thus to stay, and looking up to me, waiting for some fresh matter for ridicule, GOD was pleased to prick him to the heart. He came to Mr. P—— full of horror, confessed his crimes, and longed to ask my pardon, but was afraid to see me. Mr. P—— encouraged him to venture. This morning hearing somebody knock at the parlour door, I arose, and upon opening the door, by the paleness, pensiveness, and horror of his countenance, guessed I had met with the person of whom Mr. P—— had apprized me. Immediately he cried with a low but plaintive voice, "Sir, can you forgive me?" I smiled and said, "Yes, Sir, very readily." Indeed, replied he, Sir, you cannot when I tell you all. I then asked him to sit down; and judging

that

that he had sufficiently felt the lashes of the law, I preached to him the gospel. That it may be the power of God through faith unto his eternal salvation, you will join in praying, dear madam, with

Yours, &c.

G. W.

LETTER DLXVII.

To Mrs. ———.

My dear Friend, *Boston, Feb.* 19, 1745.

TEMPORA mutantur; a confederacy, a confederacy! The clergy, amongst whom are a few mistaken, misinformed good old men, are publishing halfpenny testimonials against me. Even the president, professors, and tutors of *Hertford* college, where I was, as you know, some few years ago received with so much uncommon respect, have joined the confederacy. Good Mr. *C———*, that venerable, truly primitive, good old Puritan, as I am informed, had many of these testimonials brought him, in order to judge of their importance. He took them, weighed them in his hand, and having read them before, returned them immediately, saying, " They did not weigh much." However, I thank God, " out of the eater hath come forth meat." They have done me real service. Some unguarded expressions, in the heat of less experienced youth, I certainly did drop. I was much too precipitate in hearkening to, and publishing private informations, and thereby *Peter*-like cut too many ears off: but this is my comfort, when we mean well, though no thanks to our own too forward though well-meant zeal, Jesus, that almighty, all-compassionate physician, will heal and restore the ears again. Some good friends on my side the question are publishing testimonials in my favour. Thus you see what a militant state we are in at present. *Laudatur ab eis, culpatur ab illis.* Amidst all, the word runs and is glorified, and many are so enraged at the treatment I meet with, that they came to me lately, assuring me, that if I'll consent, they will erect in a few weeks time, the outside of the largest place of worship that was ever seen in *America:* but you know ceiled houses were never my aim. I therefore thanked them for, but at the same time begged leave to refuse the accepting of their kind offer. How or when the present storm will subside, for subside I am persuaded it will, is as yet uncertain. I can only, at present, earnestly beg the continuance of your prayers, that whilst tossing in this floating ark I may be purged of some of my corruptions, and be kept in good temper towards those who I believe really think they do GOD's service in opposing, dear Madam,

Yours, &c.

G. W.

LETTER DLXVIII.

Piscataqua, March 6, 1745.

My very dear, dear J.

THIS comes by Captain *Darling*. I hear from *Boston*, a bookseller has got the books you sent over. I have sent a letter to Doctor C——, with my answer to *Harvard* college, which I would have you print, with their testimony, (which is an original :) and my answer to the second part of the observation and remarks upon the charge of the Bishop of L——. May JESUS give them his blessing. I would have them printed so as to be sold cheap : you may collect or print them severally as you will. I cannot yet get time to prepare my sermons, or the other part of my life, for the press. I am writing another *New-England* journal, which I will send when I leave it; when that will be, I know not. I expect Mr. *Habersham* every hour. W—— N—— and J—— are got safe to *Charles-Town*. I heard from friends there last week. *America*, I am afraid, begins to be too dear to me. The LORD smiles upon me and mine, and makes us very happy in himself, and happy in one another. Here is a very large field of action. A very fine and effectual door is opened ; my bodily strength is recovered, and my soul more than ever in love with a crucified JESUS. I could write more to you and other dear friends, but if I do, I shall neglect things of a more public and immediate concern ; neither can my dear wife write, because she is fully employed in copying my letters. However, we do not forget our dear *London* and *English* friends. We pray for them often, and sometimes cannot help wishing some more may come

come over into this delightful wildernefs; it is a fruitful field. JESUS waters it with his bleffings. We expect fifter *W——*. Here are wars and rumours of wars, on this, as well as your fide of the water. But JESUS's difciples may be at peace. O that this may find thy dear heart quite fwallowed up in his amazing love! Be pleafed to remember us moft tenderly to *all*, and lofe no opportunity of fending a line in any *American* fhips. So, my very dear dear man, I reft

Thy very affectionate happy friend,
and fervant in JESUS CHRIST,
G. W.

LETTER DLXIX.

To Mr. C——.

Pifcataqua, March 6, 1745.

My very dear Brother C——,

IT gives me fome concern, that I cannot fend thee a long letter, but at prefent I have fo many things of importance before me, which muft be immediately difpatched, that I defire others to excufe me too. I do not forget any of you as I know of, and, GOD willing, fhall redeem every opportunity of fending to *England*. Our Saviour wonderfully fmiles on us here; feveral years work I think lies before me. The LORD helps me to preach with the demonftration of the fpirit and with power, my ftrength is daily renewed, and my wife and I go on like two happy pilgrims, leaning upon our beloved. O help us to adore and praife free grace. We falute all the conference and truftees, and every particular choir, and the focieties in every place, " Grace, mercy and peace be multiplied upon them, from GOD our father, and from the LORD JESUS CHRIST." To his tender mercy do I commit thee and them, and am, my very dear *C——*,

Yours moft affectionately in CHRIST JESUS,
G. W.

P. S. My dear wife cordially falutes you and all.

LETTER DLXX.

To Mr. J. S. in London.

Piscataqua, March 12, 1745.

I Wrote to you last week, and have sent you by Capt. *Darling* two letters, and a box. This comes by a young gentleman that expects to return to *South-Carolina* by *August* next. By him I send you one of each sort of the pamphlets that I have published here. I would have them sent to *Scotland* as soon as may be. My wife has sent you a few lines in one of my letters. We are more than happy! O grace! grace!— I trust it is so with you. *America* is pleasanter and pleasanter every day. I expect Mr. *Habersham* hourly. The door for preaching opens wider and wider. O my dear friend, I could tell thee what would rejoice thy heart, wast thou here. But I have little time to write. I am now going to prepare my sermons for the press: And am also writing another journal. You shall have them the first opportunity. Our tender love awaits all dear friends. As often as possible, you and others shall hear from, my dear friend, &c.

G. W.

LETTER DLXXI.

On board Capt. Grant, bound from Charles-Town to Philadelphia, May 2, 1745.

My very dear, dear Brother H——,

HOW do you find your heart these trying, sifting, purging times? I hope you are enabled to joy in GOD, and are made more than conqueror through his love. It has given me some concern that I could not write to you oftner: but JESUS knows my heart has been with you; and I have not failed to pray for the preservation of the tossed ark. *Antinominanism*, I find, begins to shew its head and stalk abroad: may the glorious Redeemer cause it to hide its head again, and prevent his children's spirits being imbittered against each other. I am glad to hear the *Welsh* brethren continue steady: and that amongst our *English* friends, *Antinomianism* seems only to be speculative; this is a great evil, but not so great as when it affects the practice, and leads the people of GOD unwarily

into

into licentiousness. The late outward troubles, I hope will do good, and put a stop to the many disputes and various sects which, like so many hydra's, always spring up when the LORD suffers false principles to abound. I expect to hear that JESUS has made thee immoveable like a wall of brass, bold as a lion, but meek as a lamb. Blessed be his name, he continues to be very kind to us: we have been six months in these parts, and are now going northwards for the summer season. The Orphan-house is in a promising way. My temporal affairs begin to be settled; and I am blessed substantially to many souls. JESUS, I trust, has given me a more gospel-heart; and causes many of my professed most imbittered enemies to be at peace with me. I know you will help me to praise him, and beg him to continue to stand by a poor unworthy creature, who simply desires to spend and be spent for the good of precious and immortal souls. You'll remember me to your dear wife, and all our *Welsh* brethren, in the most endearing manner: we frequently talk of, and pray for them; and don't despair of seeing them once more in the flesh. My dear wife loves them exceedingly, and warms her heart often by reflecting on past times. Wishing that grace, mercy, and peace may be multiplied upon you all, I subscribe myself, my very dear brother,

Ever, ever thine in JESUS,

G. W.

LETTER DLXXII.

To Mrs. ———.

Dear Madam, *Boston, July* 29, 1745.

YOU will be surprized to hear that a messenger of the prince of peace, especially such a weak creature as I am, should beat up to arms. No doubt you have judged me, as well you may; but providence seemed to force me to it. You have now heard of the *Cape-Breton* expedition, which was carried on and finished with the greatest secrecy and expedition here, before it could be scarcely known to you at home. Worthy Colonel P——— was fixed upon to command. The day before he accepted of the commission, he purposed to dine with me to ask my advice. I told him, " that I hoped if he " did undertake it, he would beg of the LORD GOD of armies
" to

" to give him a single eye; that the means proposed to take
" *Louisburgh*, in the eye of human reason, were no more ade-
" quate to the end, than the founding of rams horns to blow
" down *Jericho*; that the eyes of all would be upon him; and if
" he should not succeed in the intended enterprize, the widows
" and orphans of the slain soldiers would be like lions robbed
" of their whelps; but if it pleased GOD to give him success,
" envy would not suffer him to take the glory, and therefore
" he should take great care that his views were disinterested,
" and then I doubted not, if providence really called him, he
" would find his strength proportioned to the day, and would
" return more than conqueror." He thanked me, and his Lady
having given her free consent, he commenced general. The
sound now was to arms! to arms! new recruits were eagerly sought after, and my worthy friend Mr. S—— was appointed one of the commissaries. Being at his house, he told
me one evening that he was preparing the flag, and that I must
give him a motto, and that the people must know it too. I
absolutely refused, urging that it would be acting out of character; he replied, that the expedition, he believed, was of
GOD, and that if I did not encourage it, many of the serious
people would not inlist. I still refused; he desired me to consider, and sleep upon it, and to give him my answer in the morning. I retired, I prayed, I slept; and upon his renewing his
request in the morning, I told him, that since he was so urgent,
and as I did not know but divine providence might intend to
give us *Louisburgh*, therefore he might take this motto. *Nil
desperandum Christo duce*. Upon this, great numbers inlisted,
and before their embarkation, their officers desired me to give
them a sermon: I preached from these words: " As many as
were distressed, as many as were discontented, as many as were
in debt, came to *David*, and he became a captain over them."
Officers, soldiers, and others attended. I spiritualized the
subject, and told them how distressed sinners came to JESUS
CHRIST the Son of *David*; and in my application exhorted
the soldiers to behave like the soldiers of *David*, and the officers to act like *David*'s worthies; then, I made no manner of
doubt, but we should receive good news from *Cape-Breton*.
After this, I preached to the general himself, who asked me
if I would not be one of his chaplains: I told him, " I should
" think

"think it an honour, but believed, as I generally preached
"three times a day in various places to large congregations,
"I could do my King my country, and my GOD, more ser-
"vice, by stirring up the people to pray, and thereby strength-
"en his and his soldiers hands." Through divine grace, I
was enabled to persist in this practice for some weeks; but at
last news arrived that the case was desperate. Letter upon letter came from one officer and another to those who planned
this expedition, and did not know the strength of the fortress.
I smiled, and told my friends, that I believed now we should
have *Louisburgh*;—that all having confessed their helplessness,
GOD would now reveal his arm, and make our extremity his
opportunity. I was not disappointed of my hope; for one day
having taken a weeping leave of dear *Boston*, and being about
to preach a few miles out of the town, news was brought that
Louisburgh was taken. Numbers flocked with great joy from
all quarters, and I immediately preached to them a thanksgiving sermon from these words: " By this I know that thou
favourest me, since thou hast not permitted mine enemies to
triumph over me." Here ends, dear Madam, my beating to
arms. It is left to you, to judge as you please of, dear Madam,

Yours, &c.

G. W.

Postscript. I forgot to tell you, to the honour of worthy
Madam P——, that during the time of the expedition, at her
desire, I preached in the General's house, and took the liberty
before sermon, to ask her, how she came to give up the General? She answered, " That it was GOD who enabled her
" to do it for his glory, and her country's good, and that now
" the General was gone, she had the pleasing reflection, that
" thro' divine mercy, home had never been made so disagree-
" able to him by her conduct, as to make him wish to be gone."

LETTER DLXXIII.

To Mrs. L————.

Philadelphia, August 26, 1746.

Honoured Mother,

WHETHER your affections are abated to me or not,
(which one would imagine by your not writing in

two years) yet duty, love, and gratitude oblige me to write to her, to whom, under GOD, I owe my being brought into the world. I am glad to find by a letter from Mr. *Syms*, dated last *March*, that you was well, at least I hoped so, because I heard nothing to the contrary. May the Father of mercies, and GOD of all consolation, grant that your latter end may greatly increase! Whether you ever see me or not any more, you need not be anxious concerning me.—That GOD whom I serve in the gospel of his dear Son, is exceeding good and gracious to me and mine. We have all things pertaining to life and godliness. Many offers are daily made me; but as yet the LORD JESUS keeps me from catching at the golden bait. Favour is given to me in the sight of the rich and great, and the door for my usefulness opens wider and wider. I love to range in the *American* woods, and sometimes think I shall never return to *England* any more. I was never better in health, take all together. My dear wife would send you a few lines, but she is weak by reason of a miscarriage about four days ago. I send you most dutiful respects for her; and praying the LORD of all Lords continually to lift up the light of his blessed countenance upon your dear soul, I subscribe myself, honoured mother,

Your most dutiful, though unworthy son,

G. W.

LETTER DLXXIV.

To the Rev. Mr. Z———.

Bohemia, (Maryland) Oct. 8, 1746.

Rev. and dear Sir,

I Took the freedom some months ago to send you a letter, wherein was inclosed a letter for Professor *Frank*, both which I hope came safe to hand, and were accepted in love. Since that, I have been travelling and ranging the woods, in the service of the best of Masters, who makes his work more pleasant to me every day. I trust that the time for favouring this and the neighbouring southern provinces is come. Every where almost, the door is opened for preaching; great numbers flock to hear, and the power of an ascended Saviour attends the word. It is surprizing, how the LORD causes prejudices to subside, and makes my formerly most bitter enemies to be at peace with me. O Rev. Sir, help me to praise him, whose mercy endureth for ever! I doubt not but he has been wonderfully good to you, and supports you under a feeble tottering tabernacle. The prayers of me and mine are always for you, because we honour and love you in our common head, the blessed JESUS. Be pleased, when you write, to present my most dutiful and affectionate respects to the Professor, and Mr. *Uspurgher*. I have had some sweet times with several of the *Lutheran* ministers at *Philadelphia*. I love them dearly. Mr. *Driselzer* does bravely at *Frederica*. Mr. *Boltzius* and his collegue I hear are well. By and by, I trust, *Georgia* will lift up its drooping head.—All is well at the Orphan-house. I am, Rev. and very dear Sir,

Your most affectionate, though unworthy younger
brother and servant in CHRIST,

G. W.

LETTER DLXXV.

To Mr. H—— H——.

Anapolis, (*Maryland*,) *Nov.* 8, 1746.

My very dear, dear Brother,

JUst now received a wished-for packet from *England*, in which are two or three letters from you. My dear fellow pilgrim will exceedingly rejoice at the receipt of them. She is gone forward with a *Boston* young lady towards *Georgia*.—I hear they traverse the woods bravely.—I wrote to you very lately.—I can only send you a few loving lines now.—I am just setting out.—Lately I have been in seven counties in *Maryland*, and preached with abundant success.—Our LORD gives me health, and his work (O free grace!) prospers in my unworthy hands. I shall consider of the calls sent me to return to my native country.—My tender love to all.—I am, my very dear man,

Ever yours whilst

G. W.

LETTER DLXXVI.

To a friend at the Tabernacle, London.

Anapolis, November 8, 1746.

My very dear Brother,

JUST now I have received your kind letter with some others, but have not time to read them all, being just setting out from this place. I shall consider of your *loud call*, and pray our LORD to direct me.—Poor *English* friends! May JESUS heal their divisions! Courage, my dear brother—Land is in sight.—Ere long we shall sail into the haven of eternal rest.—The harvest is great here. I have lately been in seven counties in *Maryland*, and preached to great congregations of people with great power.—I have now a journey of seven hundred miles before me.—My tender love to all. GOD willing, you shall hear again shortly from,

Ever yours in our triumphant JESUS,

G. W.

LETTER DLXXVII.

To Mr. H―― H――.

Hanover county, (Virginia) Nov. 16, 1746.

My very dear Brother,

ABOUT a week ago I had the pleasure of receiving a long letter from you, which I immediately answered at *Anapolis.*—That you wrote to my dear wife is gone to her, and I suppose will rejoice her exceedingly.—She is well, and enjoys much of GOD.—I was glad to find that the *Tabernacle* was given up to your care.—Whether its breaches are yet repaired, or whether it be entirely fallen down, I know not.—I suppose when I come to *England*, I shall have all to begin again.—It is the LORD, let him do what seemeth him good.—The account of dear brother *H――*'s trial affected me much. I rejoice that he comes bright out of the furnace of affliction. I salute him and all my dear friends most tenderly.—Sometimes affection works strong, and I almost determine to come over.—But the cloud does not seem to move that way as yet.—However, my eyes are to the LORD.—Whenever his providence

dence points out the way, the language of my heart is, "Lo I come."—I wrote to brother *H—— J—* and *A——* lately, and since have received their kind letters.—I have lately been in seven counties in *Maryland*, and ere long think to preach in as many in this province.—There is a sweet stirring among the dry bones.—I have a thousand tender things to say, but time will not permit.—Well, my dear dear man, heaven is at hand;—there we shall have talk enough.—O let us take as many souls with us to that blessed place as we can.—Blessed be GOD, my soul springs with fresh desires to hunt after poor straying sheep, which JESUS has purchased with his dear heart's blood.—O that I may begin now to do something for him, who hath done and suffered so much for me! But I can no more.—I am lost, I am quite overcome when I think of this.—LORD, I believe and worship!—Pray remember me to *all* most tenderly.—Remember me before the LORD as the *chief of sinners*, but, my very dear brother,

Ever, ever yours,

G. W.

LETTER DLXXVIII.

To a Friend in London.

My dear Brother,   *Bethesda, Dec.* 24, 1746.

I Thank you heartily for your very kind letter, which I now snatch a few moments to answer. The account you gave of things, made me mourn that they were in so bad a situation, and at the same time I could not help rejoicing they were no worse: You and all that attended on my preaching, and had opportunities to converse with me privately, cannot be ignorant how many hints I gave of what has happened. It might have been foreseen and spoken of without a spirit of prophecy, and consequently did not so much surprize me when I found it came to pass; but I trust the storm is now blown over, and that the little flock will enjoy a sweet calm. O that your eyes may be looking towards and waiting on the blessed JESUS: from him alone can come your salvation, he will be better to you than a thousand *Whitefields*.—I am afraid you are too desirous of having me with you; and indeed I long to see you and my other dear christian friends, but *America* seems to be

my

my scene of action for some time. The harvest is great in many places, and the labourers are very few. I am resolved in the strength of JESUS to range more and more; hunting for souls is a delightful work, and I am ashamed that I do no more. O my dear man, pray for me; indeed I do for you and yours.—I am glad the LORD has appeared for you; he never fails those that put their trust in him; only remember, " In the world, and yet not *of* it," is the real christian's motto.—That JESUS may continually lift up the light of his blessed countenance upon you, and give you and yours all peace and joy in believing, is the earnest prayer of, my dear man,

Your very affectionate friend,
and servant for JESUS sake,
G. W.

P. S. My tender tender love to all enquiring friends; my dear yoke-fellow joins heartily: we are happy in JESUS, and happy in one another.

LETTER DLXXIX.

My dear Brother,   *Bethesda, Dec.* 24, 1746.

I Must not let your kind letter which I received a few days ago lie long unanswered. And now what shall I say? why that I would have you comfort yourself with this promise, " That all things shall work (nay *do* work) for good to those that love GOD."—Blessed be GOD for that little, that great word ALL.—Could we always act faith upon that, nothing could move us.—It is this promise that makes me now to rejoice in the midst of all the tribulations that has befallen my dear *Tabernacle* friends.—For ere long you shall sing,

———— O happy Rod!
That brought us nearer to our GOD !

Courage, therefore, my brother, courage.—The LORD will yet uphold you with his right hand.—Only live near to JESUS, and let the language of your heart be, " LORD, *let me know myself and thee!*" All trials are sent for these two ends, that we may be better acquainted with the dear LORD JESUS, and with our own wicked hearts.—That you may increase in this knowledge more and more, is the earnest prayer of

Your affectionate friend, and servant in CHRIST,

G. W.

P. S. My dear wife joins in sending hearty salutations to all.—I must refer you to other letters for news.

LETTER DLXXX.

To Mr. A———.

Bethesda, Dec. 29, 1746.

My very dear Brother A———,

SINCE I wrote to you from *Maryland*, I have received two or three kind letters from you, in which I have had a particular account how affairs stand in *England.*—I bless GOD for the gracious assistance he has been pleased to afford you, and pray for a continuance and increase of it to your dear soul ever more and more—O my very dear brother, it is no small favour to be kept steady and humbly bold for the glorious *Emmanuel* in a cloudy dark day.—This honour the LORD JESUS has conferred on you—May his past goodness strengthen your faith, and encourage you to trust in him amidst all future trials!—I say future trials—for we must never expect an entire cessation of arms, till we bow down our heads and give up the ghost—Our trials will be changed in order to discover to us the remainder of corruption in the heart; but they will not, they must not be entirely removed—The captain of our salvation was made perfect through sufferings, and so must we—Be strong therefore, my brother, in the grace which is in CHRIST JESUS—Endure afflictions—make full proof of thy ministry—Truth is great, and will prevail—Fail not writing—Other letters will acquaint you with particulars about me.—Continue in prayer, and it may be, sooner than your expectations, you may see

Your very unworthy, but affectionate brother and servant in JESUS CHRIST,

G. W.

P. S. My dear yoke-fellow joins in sending most cordial salutations to you, yours, and all that love the precious CHRIST.

Charles-

Charles-Town, Jan. 21, 1747.

Since I wrote the above I have had some sweet seasons at *Bethesda:* I intend staying here some days, and will redeem what time I can to write to friends—May grace, mercy and peace be multiplied upon them all: Amen and Amen.—My dear wife and family are well—GOD willing, we move northward in the beginning of *March.*

LETTER DLXXXI.

To Mr. H—— J——,
My very dear Brother, *Charles-Town, Jan.* 23, 1747.

I Owe you much love, and though I have written to you more than once, yet I look upon myself as indebted to you still.—I therefore now sit down to answer the kind letter which you sent my dear yokefellow.—She is now at *Georgia,* and having not as yet seen it, she cannot answer it herself.—Blessed be GOD she is well, and prospers both in soul and body—We talk of you often, and hope yet to live and have our hearts warmed with our *English* and *Welch* friends ere we go hence, and are no more seen. At present the cloud seems to hang over the *American* parts.—The LORD JESUS is pleased to give me great access to multitudes of souls, and I hope has withal given me as strong an inclination as ever, to go out and preach to them the unsearchable riches of his dying love. I lately came from *Bethesda,* and found my family well, happy in JESUS, and happy in one another.—Our LORD bowed the heavens several times and came down among us, in the power of his eternal Spirit.—In the beginning of *March,* I purpose, GOD willing, to set out for the northward again, and shall not lose any opportunity of writing, that offers in my way. I am sorry to hear the leaven of *Antinomianism* is not yet purged out, and that animosities are not yet ceased.—I can say nothing at this distance, but pray that the GOD of peace and love may direct and rule all my dear friends hearts. You will remember me to all in the most tender manner.—Indeed I omit no opportunity of sending.—I pray for you all continually, and begging a continued interest in all your prayers, I subscribe myself, my very dear brother,

Yours most affectionately in CHRIST JESUS,
G. W.

LETTER DLXXXII.

To a generous Benefactor unknown.

Charles-Town, March, 15, 1747.

WHOEVER you are that delight to imitate the divine beneficence in doing good to your fellow-creatures when they know not of it, I think it my duty, in behalf of the poor orphans committed to my care, to send you a letter of thanks for your kind, generous and opportune benefaction.—That GOD who has opened your heart to give so bountifully, will as bountifully reward you.—I trust you have contributed towards the promoting an institution, which has, and I believe will redound much to the Redeemer's glory.—Blessed be GOD, I hope I can say, that *Bethesda* was never in better order than it is now, in all probability taking root downwards, and bearing fruit upwards.—Since my arrival there this winter, I have opened a *Latin* school, and have several children of promising abilities that have begun to learn.—One little orphan, who this time twelvemonth could not read his letters, has made a considerable proficiency in his *Accidence.*—The blessed spirit has been striving with several of the children's infant hearts, and I hope ere long to see some ministers sent forth from that despised place called *Georgia.* It is true, the constitution of that colony is very bad, and it is impossible for the inhabitants to subsist themselves without the use of slaves. But GOD has put it into the hearts of my *South-Carolina* friends, to contribute liberally towards purchasing a plantation and slaves in this province; which I purpose to devote to the support of *Bethesda.*—Blessed be GOD, the purchase is made.—I last week bought, at a very cheap rate, a plantation of six hundred and forty acres of excellent land, with a good house, barn, and out-houses, and sixty acres of ground ready cleared, fenced and fit for rice, corn, and every thing that will be necessary for provisions. One negroe has been given me.—Some more I purpose to purchase this week.—An overseer is put upon the plantation, and I trust a sufficient quantity of provision will be raised this year.—The family at *Bethesda* consists of twenty-six.—When my arrears are discharged, I purpose to increase the number.—I hope that time will soon come; and that he who has begun, will go on to stir up the friends of *Zion* to help me, not only to discharge the arrears, but also to bring the plantation lately purchased to such perfection, that if I should die shortly, *Bethesda* may yet be provided for.—As you have been such a benefactor, I thought proper to give you this particular account, that you may see it is not given in vain.—I could enlarge, but have only room to subscribe myself, generous friend,

Your most obliged servant,

G. W.

LETTER DLXXXIII.

To Mrs. B.

Bohemia, (Maryland) Sunday night, April. 26, 1747.

Very dear Mrs. B.

IF you will promise not to be sorry, that you set out so soon, I will inform you, that through the singular goodness of a loving Redeemer, we reached *Bohemia* last night, after a pleasant journey of about five weeks from *Charles-Town*. To-day, I trust we have enjoyed some taste of that love, which I pray the LORD of all Lords to shed abroad abundantly in your dear heart by the Holy Ghost. You are entered upon a scene that will call for more than ordinary assistance. JESUS, who himself was once in a wilderness, knows how to succour, support and comfort you. " Out of the eater he can bring forth meat; Out of the strong he can and will bring forth sweetness." My poor prayers do and will follow you. I trust you will return loaded with experience; and however your journey may turn out in respect to your body, I am persuaded it will be for the benefit of your soul. To tell you how bountifully the glorious *Emmanuel* hath dealt with us, would fill a volume. He hath indeed done wonders for us,— some of which I hope to relate to you, when I see you face to face. After two days abode here, I purpose, GOD willing, to take a three weeks circuit in hunting after *Maryland* sinners. In *Virginia*, for the present, the door is shut; but I believe it will be open in the fall to more advantage. I have no thoughts of visiting it this spring. The cloud moves another way. However, night and day I shall remember you in your

little

little hut, praying that you may meet with agreeable company to join in saying, " LORD JESUS, all my springs are in thee." that you may be continually enabled to believe on him, and find him to be a well of water springing up to life eternal, is the hearty prayer of, very dear Mrs. B——,

Your very affectionate, sympathizing friend,
and willing servant for JESUS's sake,
G. W.

LETTER DLXXXIV.

To the Rev. Mr. F——.

Bohemia, April 28, 1747.

Rev. and very dear Brother,

WITH this, I send you a packet from your brother, whom I left well and happy at *Bethesda* about six weeks ago. As I came along I saw Mr. *Davis:* He is licensed, as are the four houses in *Virginia*; but there is a proclamation issued out against all itinerants. Nothing can be done to the purpose, but all will be in the utmost confusion, unless some proper person is always resident among the awakened souls. Pray acquaint your brethren of this. How do you all? Has JESUS warmed your hearts this last cold Winter, and kept you from spiritual frost? He has been very gracious to us southward; and as we came along, " the wilderness seemed to blossom like a rose." About five weeks ago, we left *Charles-Town*, and reached *Bohemia* last Saturday evening. We came from *Hanover* county to this place in five days. I am now dispatching my private affairs, and after about three weeks itinerant preaching in these parts, I purpose, GOD willing, to go towards *Philadelphia.* You will remember me in a particular manner to the young students.—They have a continual share in my poor prayers; and the continuance of theirs and yours is earnestly desired by, my very dear Sir,

Yours most affectionately in CHRIST,
G. W.

LETTER DLXXXV.

To the Honourable J. W——, Esq;

New-Town, (Maryland) May 6, 1747.

Honoured Sir,

A Few days paſt I had the pleaſure of yours, dated November 28th. I embrace this firſt opportunity of returning you my hearty thanks for the unmerited kindneſs and affection expreſſed therein. May the Redeemer give me an humble heart, and grant that all favours conferred upon me by inſtruments, may lead me nearer to him, the ſource and fountain of all! But what ſhall I ſay to dear *New-England's* ſorrowful circumſtances? It pities me to hear that ſhe is ſtill lying in the duſt. However, this has generally been the caſe: trying and diſtreſſing times have generally followed awakening and converting times. May JESUS ſecond them with another alarm of his holy ſpirit, and then all will be well. Glad would I be to come and offer myſelf once more to do *New-England* ſervice; but I am afraid that many miniſters and the heads of the people would not bear it. However, was this my only reaſon, it would ſoon be anſwered. — But here are thouſands in theſe Southern parts (as you have obſerved, honoured Sir), that ſcarce ever heard of redeeming grace and love. Is it not my duty as an itinerant, ſince other places have had their calls and awakening ſeaſons, to go where the goſpel has not been named? Thoſe who think I want to make a party, or to diſturb churches, do not know me. I am willing to hunt in the woods after ſinners; and, according to the preſent temper of my mind, could be content that the name of *George Whitefield* ſhould die, if thereby the name of my dear Redeemer could be exalted. Indeed I am amazed that he employs me at all. But what ſhall we ſay? He hateth putting away, therefore I am not conſumed. Grace, ſovereign free grace! ſhall be all my ſong. Laſt Winter's mercies have renewed my obligations to extol free grace. I could enlarge, but ſeveral things forbid. In heaven, dear Sir, we ſhall have no interruptions. That you may be ſupported through all the fatigues of your journey thither, and with all your dear family, at length arrive at the land of eternal reſt, is the earneſt prayer of, honoured Sir,

Yours, &c.

G. W.

Poſtſcript.

Postscript. Fearing I shall not have an opportunity of seeing you, before you embark for *England*, it being uncertain whether your honour will be at *Philadelphia* upon my coming there, I think it my duty, honoured Sir, in this way to wish you, your honoured Lady and little Miss, an extraordinary good voyage. May the GOD of the seas as well as the GOD of the dry land, be your convoy and pilot! May you and all who sail with you, be preserved from the hand of the enemy, and kept in perpetual peace and safety! As GOD shall enable me, my poor prayers shall follow you. They are your due, honoured Sir. The *Pensylvanians* I am sure will soon regret the loss of you, and all the friends of liberty and loyalty must be constrained to wish you well. O that the great Governor of the universe may so bless you with his holy spirit, that you may bring forth much fruit in old age! O that you may hear the great Judge of quick and dead salute you at the last day, with a " Well done, thou good and faithful servant, enter thou into the joy of thy LORD!" This, honoured Sir, is the native language of my heart. As I trust you think me sincere, be pleased to accept it, as the best acknowledgment I can make you and your beloved consort, for all the kindnesses you have been pleased to heap on, honoured Sir,

Your Honour's most obliged humble servant,

G. W.

LETTER DLXXXVI.

To Mrs. P——.

New-Town, (*Maryland*) *May* 6, 1747.

Dear Mrs. P——,

I Must refrain no longer from returning you thanks for two or three kind letters with which you have favoured me. They seemed to speak the language of a heart concerned for *Zion*'s glory. Well! Blessed are they that mourn for those who will not mourn for themselves, verily they shall be comforted. Blessed are they who are enabled to walk with GOD in a declining day ;—they shall shine hereafter with a distinguished lustre. Thus *Enoch* did,—and *Enoch* was remarkably honoured.—" He was not, for GOD took him."—But shall the harps of *Boston* Christians be always hanging on the willows?

lows? No; JESUS will not be always chiding. He that has brought on this pleasant Spring, after so hard a Winter, can thaw men's hearts, and cause the turtle once more to be heard in the land. Hasten that time, O blessed LORD!—I hope you will keep close to your prayer-days. I have received the memorials from dear Mr. P——, and shall disperse them. I should be glad of a line from him. How are his dear daughters, and the other members of your society? I do not forget you, indeed I do not. If affection guided me, you would soon see me; but the people in these Southern parts are like people that have no shepherd. Surely I ought to go out after them. To-day I have had a sweet season. People are very ready to hear, and the word seems to fasten in some souls. Follow me with your prayers. Remember me to your husband, and to all, in the most cordial manner, and believe me to be

Your very affectionate friend, and willing servant

for CHRIST's sake,

G. W.

LETTER DLXXXVII.

To Madam P——.

Dover, (Pensylvania) May 8, 1747.

Honoured Madam,

THE great though unmerited regard you have always been pleased to express for me, emboldens me now and then to drop you a line to inform you, that you are not forgotten by me before that GOD whose mercy endureth for ever. I trust, your latter end, like that of *Job*'s, will greatly increase, and that you will, as it is said of the righteous, "Bring forth much fruit in old age." Your honoured husband (to whom be pleased to present my dutiful respects) I suppose is now with you. The LORD hath honoured you with many honours, and I hope, amidst all outward favours, does not withhold the comforting influences of his blessed spirit from your soul. I have reason to believe, you esteem this above all earthly things whatsoever. O, dear Madam! how mean and contemptible does every creature appear, when the soul gets a near view of a crucified Redeemer! How easy to bear pain, when one meditates on the agony and bloody sweat of an incarnate

GOD!

GOD! Here then, honoured madam, fix your eye. Look unto JESUS continually. He hath been the author, he will be the finisher of your faith. I find him to be a GOD that changeth not, a tender and compassionate High Priest. Thro' his help, I continue to this day preaching amongst poor sinners the unsearchable riches of his dying love. I am as well in health as I can expect to be, and more and more determined to spend and be spent for the good of precious and immortal souls. Through grace, my labours are rendered very acceptable in various places. Be pleased, Madam, to remember me before the throne. I neither forget you nor the General.— I pray that GOD's loving-kindnesses and fatherly corrections may make you truly great, and beg leave to subscribe myself, honoured Madam,

Your affectionate, obliged humble servant,

G. W.

LETTER DLXXXVIII.

To Mr. B——, Senior.

Dover, May 8, 1747.

Very dear Mr. B——,

I Think it is high time for me to send you a line of thanks, for the favours you have been pleased to shew me, while others were loading me with scorn and contempt. A weak body and continued employ in the service of the best of Masters, occasion my not writing so frequently to my dear friends, as love and gratitude would prompt me to do. You will accept this unfeigned apology, and still increase the obligations you have laid upon me, by continuing to remember me before the LORD. I have need, great need of the united prayers of my christian friends.— For JESUS hath of late so remarkably appeared for me, that I ought to lay myself out more and more in going about endeavouring to do good to precious and immortal souls. At present this is my settled resolution. The Redeemer seems to approve of it; for the fields in the Southern parts are white ready unto harvest, and many seem to have the hearing ear. All next *October*, GOD willing, I have devoted to poor *North-Carolina*. It is pleasant hunting in the woods after the lost sheep for whom the Redeemer hath shed his precious tious blood. May the LORD of the harveſt ſpirit up more to go forth in his ſtrength, to compel poor ſinners to come in! I hope that you and my other *Boſton* friends do go in and out, and find good paſture. I hear it is a Winter time with many. May GOD keep the fatal languor from extending to the circle of my intimate friends! For alas, what is a chriſtian without a holy warmth? Will you remember me to all that you know, in the moſt tender manner? I beſeech them by the mercies of GOD, to live *near* to JESU's croſs, and whatever others may do, let them and theirs ſerve the LORD CHRIST. You will remember me in particular to Mr. F——, and his family, Mr. V—— and wife, your dear ſon, and your whole houſhold, as being, dear Sir,

Your moſt affectionate, obliged friend
and brother in CHRIST,
G. W.

LETTER DLXXXIX.

To Mr. H—— S——.

Dover, *May* 9, 1747.

AS you were my kind hoſt and peculiar friend, I take the liberty of writing to you more frequently than to others. I hope you will accept of this as a token of my unfeigned gratitude and love. It brings you the news of my being advanced thus far, of my being in health, and employed in going about and preaching to poor ſinners the unſearchable riches of JESUS CHRIST. I ſhall be more northward, GOD willing, in *June*, and poſſibly may ſtretch as far as ſome part of *New-England*. —But I am not yet determined. Pray for me, dear Mr. S——, that JESUS may direct my ſteps. I would not willingly go to the right hand or to the left, contrary to his bleſſed will, for ten thouſand worlds.—When ſhall I have another line from you? It may be directed to me at *Philadelphia*. My dear yoke-fellow is there now. We travelled very pleaſantly through the woods, and purpoſe returning to *South-Carolina* and *Georgia* in the fall. We lead a moving life, but I truſt we move heaven-ward. O that JESUS may quicken all his dear people's hearts, and cauſe them to mount on wings like an eagle! I hear that times are yet dead in *New-England*.

It is dreadful to have winter all the year round. May your heart, my dear Sir, and the heart of your dear wife, and the hearts of all my dear friends, be kept close to JESUS, and continually flaming with love! I know you will readily say *Amen*. For the present, adieu. I must go to my delightful work, PREACHING. Pray remember me to all. Let me have a line, and tell me whether the LORD stirs up any to lend an helping hand to, very dear Mr. S———,

Yours most affectionately in CHRIST,

G. W.

LETTER DXC.

To the Reverend Mr. M———, junior.

Dover in Pensylvania, May 9, 1747.

Reverend and very dear Sir,

EVER since I have known and heard of you, the LORD JESUS CHRIST hath made you peculiarly dear to my soul. Your troubles and soul distresses have in some measure been my own. I have looked and learned from your case, that we are indeed but clay in the hands of the heavenly potter, and that a sovereign GOD may deal with us as it seemeth good in his sight. "His ways are in the deep waters, and his footsteps are not known." What he does to us now, we know not, but we shall know hereafter. How will you be surprized, dear Sir, in a very short time, to see that JESUS, whom your soul loves, and who has many a time shed abroad his love in your heart; how will you be surprized to see him receive you into glory, and turning your late or present *Egyptian* darkness into celestial and eternal day? May the compassionate high priest till then support your sinking spirits, and enable you to cope with and overcome all those difficulties and temptations, which either the prevalency of an inveterate melancholy, or the malice of evil spirits, may make you the subject of! Satan hath desired to have you, that he may sift you as wheat; but surely JESUS prays for you, though as it were behind the curtain. Excuse this freedom, reverend Sir; redeeming love constrains me to write thus. I hope you will receive it, as it is written, in much love. If you enquire after me, I would inform you that I am travelling about, and preaching from time to time among poor sinners the unsearchable riches of

JESUS

JESUS CHRIST. I truſt, my labours are not in vain in the LORD. The glorious *Emmanuel* has given me a pleaſant Winter, and I hope is about to cauſe theſe ſouthern wilderneſſes to bloſſom like a roſe. You will follow me with your prayers. My moſt humble and affectionate reſpects await your aged father. My love to your nurſe, and all *York* friends. I am

Yours moſt affectionately in JESUS CHRIST,

G. W.

LETTER DXCI.

To Mrs. B———.

Wicoacommoco, (*Maryland*) *May* 16, 1747.

Dear Mrs. B———,

HEARING by Captain *Adams* that the glorious *Emmanuel* holds your ſoul in life, I cannot help letting you know, paſt kindneſſes are not yet forgotten, and that I wiſh you much ſpiritual and temporal proſperity. How does your ſoul proſper in theſe hard, dull and afflicting times? Has tribulation produced patience, patience experience, and experience hope; and do you find thereby the love of GOD ſhed abroad in your heart by the Holy Ghoſt? Happy then, unſpeakably happy are you in being afflicted. With exultation of heart may you ſing,

O happy rod!
That brought me nearer to my GOD.

I think I can ſay, it is good to bear the yoke of affliction in youth. It teaches one to keep ſilence, and weans us from a too great attachment to all ſublunary enjoyments. I have a few ſtrokes of my father's rod from time to time, as well as you. But I find that his rod as well as his ſtaff do comfort. I am a naughty child, and want much correction; but he that wounds, heals alſo, and in glory we ſhall find, that his loving correction hath made us great. O glory! It is yonder in view; JESUS ſtands at the top of the ladder to receive us into it. Look to him, dear Mrs. B———, for ſurely he is your neverdying huſband.—Death itſelf ſhall not, death cannot part him and you. Had I ſtrength equal to my will, I ſhould write much of the Redeemer's everlaſting love; but my body is weak

weak through continued journeyings and preaching. However, CHRIST's strength is in some degree magnified in my weakness, and my preaching is blessed to poor souls. Amazing love! *Maryland* is yielding converts to the blessed JESUS. The gospel seems to be moving southward. Pray for me, that I may be unwearied in well doing, and follow the Lamb whithersoever he shall be pleased to lead me. Pray remember me in the kindest manner to your aged declining pastor, the other minister who lives about five miles from you, to Mr. *J*——, and all my kind nurses, and dear *York* friends. I find death and sickness have made great havock and alterations among them. May JESUS sanctify all events to the furtherance of his grace, in all their hearts, and give us to meet where the wicked cease from troubling, and the weary are at rest! I salute you and all, and once more praying that you and yours may be watered by the blessed JESUS every momoment, I subscribe myself, dear *Mrs. B*——,

Your most affectionate, obliged
servant in JESUS CHRIST,
G. W.

LETTER DXCII.

To the Reverend Mr. J—— R——.

Wicoacommoca, May 16, 1747.

CAN souls united in JESUS's love ever forget one another? It is difficult, though I believe possible; and in dull seasons I fear too common. However, blessed be the Redeemer, I have not yet forgotten my dear Mr. *R*——. As a proof it, I send you these few lines by Captain *Adams*. You see whence they are dated. Methinks I see you rejoice, and ready to say, " And have the *Marylanders* also received the grace of GOD?" I trust some have indeed received his grace in sincerity. The harvest is promising.—The heat tries my wasting tabernacle, but, through CHRIST strengthening me, I intend persisting till I drop. Since I saw you, the glorious *Emmanuel* has multiplied my obligations to spend and be spent in his service a thousand-fold. The language of my heart at present is,

A will-

A willing and a chearful mind,
That life and all things caſt behind,
  Springs forth obedient to thy call;
A heart that no deſire can move,
But ſtill to adore, believe and love,
  Give me, my CHRIST, *my* GOD, *my all.*

O dear Sir, continue to pray for me, that I may not flag in the latter ſtages of my road. I was in hopes of ſeeing you this Summer, but am afraid my engagements to preach in *North-Carolina* next *October* will prevent me. However, you and the other dear neighbouring miniſters are always upon my heart. I pity them in their preſent diſtreſſing circumſtances, and pray that they and you may have grace given to endure hardneſs like good ſoldiers of JESUS CHRIST. Your dear father I hear is diſcharged from all campaigns.—Ere long, the captain of our ſalvation will command us home alſo. The LORD grant that we may die like ſoldiers, fighting againſt the devil, the world, and the fleſh. How are your dear brothers and ſon? Pray give my hearty love to them, and to your dear wife, and whole houſhold. I ſalute you all from my dear fellow pilgrim now at *Philadelphia*; and praying that you may have thouſands to be your joy and crown of rejoicing in the great day, I ſubſcribe myſelf, reverend and very dear Sir,

Your very affectionate friend, brother and
willing ſervant in JESUS CHRIST,
G. W.

LETTER DXCIII.

To the Reverend Mr. B———.

Near New-Town, (*Maryland*) *May* 21, 1747.

AND how does my dear friend and brother Mr. B——— after ſo long a ſilence? What a pity is it, that the Redeemer's children cannot more frequently correſpond with each other? Bleſſed be GOD, there is a time coming, when our fellowſhip with JESUS and one another ſhall never be interrupted. Now is the time for ſtirring; then will be a time for ſitting, in no meaner place than (O amazing love!) at the right

right hand of the everloving, everlovely Lamb of God.—Well then my dear man, let us go on in his strength, and see what we can do for precious and immortal souls. Indeed they are purchased with the blood of God. This consideration excites me to persist in going out into the highways and hedges. —I have been now a three hundred mile circuit in *Mary-land*, and through one or two counties in *Pensilvania*. Every where people have a hearing ear, and I trust some have an obedient heart. I hope the time of singing of birds is come to *New-England*, and that your hands are full of work. I most heartily wish you very much success. I cordially salute your dear yoke-fellow, and all the followers of the Lamb, and beg you would not forget, my dear old friend,

Your affectionate

G. W.

LETTER DXCIV.

To the Reverend Mr. P——.

New-Town, May 21, 1747.

Reverend and very dear Sir,

IT sometimes gives me concern that I cannot hear oftener from you, and your dear son, whom I love so tenderly. But I suppose your hands are full of work for the best of masters. I pray him daily, that you may be crowned with much success. Though I have deserved a thousand and a thousand times over to be cast off, yet such is the divine goodness, that my labours in fresh places are made very acceptable daily. I have now been upon the stretch, preaching constantly for almost three weeks. I hope I can say with sincerity (O that I may say it with humility!) that God hath been with me of a truth. My body is often extremely weak, but the joy of the Lord is my strength, and by the help of my God I intend going on till I drop, or this poor carcase can hold out no more. These southern colonies lie in darkness, and yet, as far as I find, are as willing to receive the gospel as others. If some books could be purchased to dispose among poor people, much good might be done. Pray, Sir, have you any Latin school-books to spare? I shall want some for the Orphan-house. I hope to hear from you at *Philadelphia,*

phia, where I expect to be in a week's time. In the mean while, reverend Sir, I beg you would make my most cordial and humble respects acceptable to all your reverend brethren, that honoured me with their acquaintance, as well as to your dear family and all other friends. I wish you and them millions and millions of blessings, and intreat the continuance of their and your prayers, for, reverend and very dear Sir,

Your most affectionate, though unworthy
younger brother, and servant in CHRIST,
G. W.

LETTER DXCV.

To Mr. H——— H———.

Philadelphia, May 30, 1747.

My dearest Brother,

HAD I strength equal to my will, you should now receive from me a very long letter; but at present I have such a fever upon me, that I can scarce send you a few lines. However I will try. Your dear letters in *August* last came to my hands last Lord's-day.—They variously affected me, and put me on the search, whether I had neglected writing to my very dear man. Upon enquiry, I found that I wrote to you about the same time as I wrote to Mr. *J———*, and brother S———, and four or five times since. Blessed be the GOD and Father of our LORD JESUS CHRIST, I am not suffered to forget old love and old friends. Indeed you are very dear to me,—all of you very dear to me still. I thank you ten thousand times for all expressions of your tender love, and for your steadiness in the truths and cause of CHRIST; and hope sometimes that your prayers will draw me to *England* more speedily than I imagine. But what shall I say, my dear friend? Here are thousands and thousands in *America* who as to spiritual things know not their right hand from their left; and who are ready to hear the gospel from my mouth. Since my coming this time from *Georgia*, I have been within these five weeks a circuit of 400 miles, and every where found the fields white ready unto harvest. Nobody goes out scarcely but myself. As you are in *England* and *Wales*, the power of religion I trust will be kept up; and though my coming should be delayed some time longer, yet when I am sent, it will be with the greater blessing. I am daily finishing my outward affairs, and shall think my call clearer home, when I have provided for the support of the Orphan-house. The generous benefactor's letter pierced my heart, made me to shed tears of love, and to put up many prayers for him. I sent him a letter from *Charles-Town* under cover to Mr. *B——.* If the person be unknown, I see no impropriety in printing my letter in the *Daily Advertiser* or *Evening Post*. I am glad you have printed my letter to the *Litchfield* clergy, and want to know what effect my sermon on the rebellion has had. Our LORD has blessed it much in these parts. I shall be glad when the great Head of the church unites dear brethren again. I trust nothing shall be wanting on my part when I come over. An union before perhaps may not be so well. However, I leave it to you, my dear Sir, and think that the bar being taken away against people's coming to the tabernacle, may be one good step towards it. I wait upon the LORD. As his grace increases in the heart, I am sure his children will grow less positive and more child-like, yet more steady. O my dear man, I could write all night long, but am so giddy by hard riding and preaching constantly in the heat of the day, that I must defer being more particular till another opportunity. I hope my dear wife will supply all my deficiencies. Remember me in the tenderest manner to all. Bid them to pray me to *England*; and in the mean while, they may assure themselves they are not forgotten by, my very dear brother,

Yours, &c.

G. W.

LETTER DXCVI.

Philadelphia, June 1, 1747.

My dear Mr. H——,

I Make no apology for troubling you with the inclosed. I hear you have taken the Tabernacle outward affairs into your hands. I am glad of it, and pray the LORD of all Lords to make you a faithful steward of his manifold gifts. You will remember me most tenderly to dear Mrs. *H——,* and to all

all friends. Perhaps I may see you yet before I die. GOD is delivering me out of my embarrassments by degrees. With the collection made at *Charles-Town*, I have purchased a plantation and some slaves, which I intend to devote to the use of *Bethesda*. When a sufficient fund for the future support of that house is raised, so that it may not lie as a dead weight upon me when absent, I shall think my call clearer to *England*. At present I have full work here; the congregations yesterday were exceeding large, and for this month past I have been preaching to thousands in different places. I am sick and well, as I used to be in *England*; but the Redeemer fills me with comfort, and gives me to rejoice in his salvation day by day. I am determined in his strength to die fighting, and to go on till I drop. He is a JESUS worth dying for. Once more, remember us to all. We remember you, and am, as much as as ever, dear Mr. H——,

Your affectionate friend, brother and
willing servant in CHRIST,
G. W.

LETTER DXCVII.

To Mr. J—— S——.

Very dear Sir, *Philadelphia, June* 4, 1747.

YESTERDAY I received your very kind and judicious letter. In answer to it, must inform you, that in all probability I shall once more see my dear *New-England* friends this summer. I suppose it will be some time in *July*. At present my whole frame of nature seems to be shocked. — I have had several returns of my convulsions, and have almost always a continual burning fever. With great regret I have omitted preaching one night (to oblige my friends,) and purpose to do so once more, that they may not charge me with murdering myself; but I hope yet to die in the pulpit, or soon after I come out of it. Dying is exceeding pleasant to me: for the LORD, though my body is so weak, causes my soul to rejoice exceedingly. Letters from *England* refreshed me; all of them call me home loudly. May JESUS direct my steps! I am poor and needy, but the LORD, I am persuaded will be my helper. Outward affairs when I am weak pull me down; but the LORD can and will raise and keep me up.—I preach here

with

with great acceptance. Congregations are as large as ever. Next *Monday* sevennight I purpose, GOD willing, to set out for *New-York*. I wrote lately from *New-Town*, to Messrs. *Prince*, *W—*, *R—*, &c. but am apt to believe the packet has miscarried. I think to come by way of *Long-Island*, and to return by *Connecticut*. You will not be slack in getting all to pray for me, who am, very dear Sir,

Yours, &c.

G. W.

LETTER DXCVIII.

To Mr. P———.

Very Dear Sir,   *Philadelphia, June* 5, 1747.

THOUGH this frail nature of mine has lately received several very great shocks, yet I cannot, if strength admits, omit writing you a line. Glad was I when I came to town, to hear by Captain *G———* that you was so far recovered, as to be able once more to go to the house of GOD. I heartily wish you, dear Sir, what the noble Colonel *Gardiner* once wished me, "A thriving soul in a healthy body." Or however it may be with the one, I earnestly pray that the other may prosper. Sickness is often made use of as a means, in the hands of an all-gracious Father, to ripen our graces and fit us for heaven. Through grace, I can say it is good for me to be sick, though I am afraid I am too impatient to be gone. Well! He that cometh, will come, and cannot tarry long: till then may I be resigned, and work the works of him that sent me whilst it is day, before the night cometh when no man can work. I could proceed, but indeed, dear Sir, strength faileth me. However, I hope to see you and my other dear *Charles-Town* friends in *November*. O that till then we may every moment grow in grace and in the knowledge of JESUS CHRIST. I would write to many, but weakness forbids. I must refer you to Mr. *S———* for particulars concerning me. My dear yoke-fellow joins in sending cordial respects to yourself and all friends. Neither you nor they are forgotten by, very dear Sir,

Yours, &c.

G. W.

LETTER DXCIX.

To Mr. B——.

Philadelphia, June 6, 1747.

My very dear Friend,

I Love you dearly, and therefore muſt, though in much weakneſs, ſend you a line. It informs you of my being ſick, but withal of the LORD's comforting me, and cauſing me to triumph over the king of terrors. Mr. *B——* I ſuppoſe, ere this reaches you, will let you know that the word has run, and hath been glorified in *Mary-land*. Satan has attempted to ſtop the progreſs of the everlaſting goſpel in *Virginia*; but I believe he has overſhot himſelf. How can it be otherwiſe? ſince eternal Truth hath ſaid, "The ſeed of the woman ſhall bruiſe the ſerpent's head." I hope you find this true, by the daily conqueſt you get over the corruptions of your heart. Remember who hath promiſed to make you more than conqueror through his love. Our kind reſpects attend dear Mrs. *B——*, your ſon, and daughter, and all friends. O that we may meet grown in grace, and the knowledge of our LORD and Saviour JESUS CHRIST. I ſubſcribe myſelf, very dear Mr. *B——*,

Yours moſt affectionately in CHRIST,

G. W.

LETTER DC.

To the Reverend Mr. S——.

Philadelphia, June 23, 1747.

Reverend and dear Sir,

SINCE my laſt, I have been ſeveral times on the verge of eternity. To-day I have got a few more ſpirits. I would improve them in anſwering your kind letter, which I received yeſterday. I am obliged to *Charles-Town* friends: their example will certainly influence many here. Something is upon the anvil. Particulars expect in my next. To-morrow, GOD willing, I ſet out for *New-York*, to ſee if I can gain ſtrength. At preſent I am ſo weak, that I cannot preach. —'Tis hard work to be ſilent; but I muſt be tried every way. Friends are exceeding kind. What is the beſt of all, the

friend

friend of sinners looks in upon, and comforts my heart. I have had loud calls to *England*. Matters go on bravely there, and in *Wales*. My *State Sermon* has gone through two editions. They have also my five last sermons, which have convinced my friends that I am firm to my principles. May JESUS keep me steady till I die! I am glad Mr. P—— went off so well. His children I look upon as my own. The things which he had belong to me. I would have them taken to *Providence:* for that also *Deus providebit*. Your father is well, and always talking of you. Why did you not mention his wife in your letter? She is a discreet woman, and desired to be remembered to you. Every day she expects to lie in. You will excuse my enlarging.—Strength begins to fail me. However, whilst I have strength I would employ it in praying for you and yours. I subscribe myself, reverend and very dear Sir,

Yours most affectionately in CHRIST JESUS,

G. W.

LETTER DCI.

To Mr. R——.

New-York, June 28, 1747.

My dear Brother,

THANKS be to GOD, for revealing his dear Son in you. Thanks be to his great name for calling you to preach his everlasting gospel. I give him all the glory, and adore him for making ill and hell-deserving me, the happy instrument of alarming and awakening your dead soul. Ere long, I hope we shall meet in eternity, to sing endless praises to him who has redeemed us unto GOD by his blood, and has made us kings and priests unto GOD, and enables us to reign over death, hell, and sin, even whilst here on earth. I abhor all those bad principles which you mention, and cannot join so as to labour in the same place, and upon the same plan, with those that hold them. However, let us behave with meekness, my dear brother, and we shall soon find that every plant that our heavenly father hath not planted, shall be plucked up. "He that believeth doth not make haste." JESUS reigneth; let our eyes wait on Him. All things shall work, and even now are working, together for good to all that

love

love him. In due time you will see me, perhaps next year. I am as willing to hunt for souls as ever. I am not weary of my master or his work, though he might long ago have been weary of me. But his name is Love. Proclaim it, my dear Sir, proclaim it till thou diest. By the strength of God I will. My love to all. I can now write no more, being recovered from a great illness. Continue to pray over

Your affectionate friend, brother
and servant in CHRIST,
G. W.

LETTER DCII.

To Dr. B———.

Dear Sir,   *New-York, June* 29, 1747.

SINCE I wrote to Doctor S———, I have preached to a very large auditory, and, blessed be GOD, do not find myself much worse for it this morning. As I am bound to thank you for all favours, so especially would I send my acknowledgments for promoting this northward excursion. I believe it will be a great means of restoring my health, which I value upon no other account, than as it renders me more capable of doing good to mankind. A pleasing prospect of action lies before me. I am willing once more, in the strength of JESUS of *Nazareth*, to enter the field, and hope through his blessing, I shall return to *Philadelphia* laden with fresh experiences of unwearied and redeeming love. Whether I shall leave *New-York* this week is uncertain. But wherever I am, assure yourself, dear Sir, your favours shall not be forgotten. That the great physician of souls may bless you and yours with the choicest of his mercies, is and shall be the hearty prayer of, dear Sir,

Your most obliged humble servant,
G. W.

LETTER DCIII.

To ———.

New-York, June 29, 1747.

My very dear, dear Brother,

IT is with much pleasure I now sit down to answer your kind and welcome letters, dated *April* 11th and 13th. And to keep you no longer in suspence, I would inform you, that they have had such an effect upon me, that, GOD willing, I am determined to embark for *England* or *Scotland* early next Spring.—'Till *Christmas* I am already under indissoluble engagements, and am making a strong effort, in dependance on the great Head of the church, to get free from my outward embarrasments.—I thank my dear *English* friends for what they have done for me in this respect, and must beg you, my dear and faithful brother, still to do what you can further. The LORD JESUS seems *to assure me* that the time of my deliverance is at hand.—I hope before this year is out, to stock my new plantation in *South-Carolina* as a *visible fund* for the Orphan-house, and upon news of something more being done in *England*, (so that my poor heart may no more be oppressed as it has been for many years by outward difficulties,) my answer shall be, Lo! I come once more to see my dear, very dear friends on the other side of the mighty waters. 'Till then, I shall as it were count the hours, and long for them to glide away a-pace. My dear yoke-fellow now at *Philadelphia* is like-minded, being exceedingly desirous to see her dear friends once more. May JESUS grant it, if it be agreeable to his holy will! Indeed, I have lately thought I should never see you any more. For some weeks past, I have been exceedingly indisposed. GOD has been pleased to bring my body to the very brink of the grave by convulsions, gravel, a nervous cholic, and a violent fever. But as pain and afflictions abounded, consolations much more abounded, and my soul longed to take its flight to JESUS. For this week past I have not preached; but since my leaving *Philadelphia*, about three days ago, I seemed to have gathered strength, and hope once more, to-morrow, to proclaim amongst poor sinners the unsearchable riches of JESUS CHRIST. From hence

I purpose to go to *Boston*, and return by land so as to reach *Charles-Town* by *November*.—Glad shall I be to receive an answer to this, about that time there.—For upon that in a great measure will depend my coming to you, or staying longer in these parts. Blessed be the LORD of all Lords, the door is yet open here, and I am exceedingly rejoiced to find it is kept so sweetly open at home. I can easily guess how my dear man has been tried. I find more and more that through much tribulation we must enter into glory, and by sufferings be prepared for farther usefulness here below.—O that patience may have its perfect work in our hearts. O that underneath thee may be the everlasting arms, and that by happy experience thou mayst daily prove the strength of JESUS to be thine. I intend, GOD willing, to write to brother *J*——, &c. I rejoice that brother *E*—— still continues in his place.—It is a token for good. You will return my most humble and dutiful respects to good Lady *H—g—n*, the Marquifs, and Mrs. *E*——*n*. If possible I will write to them. —I sent letters to the Marquifs, Lord *L*——*n*, and Lord *R*——*a*, about *October* last, but suppose they have miscarried. —I leave my affairs to you, and depend on you, under GOD, to transact them all.—The trouble is great, but JESUS will support and reward thee.—Near forty pounds yearly were subscribed in *England* to the *Orphan-house*, but I have not received I think above five.—I have rather more confidence in you, if possible, my very dear Man, than ever. May JESUS reward thee for all thy works of faith, and labours which have proceeded of love!—I wish you joy of your little one, and most heartily salute your dear wife, and all the lovers of the blessed JESUS every where. I wrote to you about a month ago in extreme weakness, and shall neglect no opportunity of sending to you. —I beseech you to continue to pray me over, and assure yourself none of you are forgotten by, my very dear Brother,

Yours most affectionately in CHRIST JESUS,

G. W.

LETTER

LETTER DCIV.

To the Rev. Mr. S———.

New-York, July 4, 1747.

Rev. and very dear Sir,

LAST week I left a letter for you at *Philadelphia.*—Since that, through the divine blessing, I have recovered a little more strength, and find my appetite restored. I have been here about eight days, and to-morrow, GOD willing, intend posting away to *Boston*, and then I shall take a long, if not a final farewel of all my northward friends. I have preached twice with great freedom. People flock rather more than ever, and the LORD vouchsafes us solemn meetings. I hope to be back again in six weeks. I shall go, if JESUS gives strength, like an arrow out of a bow. I have therefore left my dear yoke-fellow at *Philadelphia*, and expect to meet her again at *New-York*. Among these three northward provinces, I trust something considerable will be done towards paying off the orphan-house arrears. When that is effected, I care not how soon I sing my *Nunc dimittis*; but I must wait 'till my blessed change come. You will be pleased to remember me to all, and you may expect, GOD willing, at the appointed time, Reverend and very dear Sir,

Yours, &c.

G. W.

LETTER DCV.

To Mr. A———.

New-York, July 4, 1747.

My very dear Brother A———,

I Have just now been reading over your kind letter, dated *November* 23d, the second or third time.—It affected me much, and with the other letters, have constrained me to set my face towards *England*.—What is due in *America*, for the *Orphan-house*, I hope to discharge this year.—I am of your mind in respect to the work in *England*, and therefore am willing so to settle my affairs, that when I come over, I may stay with you for a long season, if the LORD JESUS is pleased to give me health and strength.—At present I am very weakly, and scarce able to preach above once or twice a week.—But if our Saviour hath further work for me to do, he can make me young and strong as an eagle.—If not, I shall go to him whom my soul loveth, and whom I long to see.—Blessed be his Name that there are yet a few names left in *Sardis*, that have not defiled their garments, but have kept close to his truths and cause in this declining day.——You will remember me to all most tenderly.—I pray for you continually, and whilst I am writing, it being *Friday**, comfort myself with this consideration, that many are praying for me.—You will see my letter to dear brother *H——*, and excuse my being so short, because I am so weak.—Our LORD continues to deal graciously with me, and was I well, I have rather a wider door than ever opened before me.—But our thoughts are not as his thoughts.—For the present, adieu.—I send most cordial love to you, yours, and all, and am, more than ever,

Yours, &c. in the blessed JESUS,

G. W.

LETTER DCVI.

To Mr J—— C——.

My dear John,   *New-York, July,* 5, 1747.

THOUGH I am quite sick and weak in body, yet the love I owe thee for JESU's sake, constrains me to answer your last kind letter, dated *Febuary* 5th. The other mentioned therein, never came to hand. I am sorry to hear there are yet disputings amongst us about brick-walls. I was in hopes, after our contests of that kind about seven years ago, such a scene would never appear again; but I find fresh offences must come, to search out and discover to us fresh corruptions, to try our faith, teach us to cease from man, and to lean more upon him, who by his infinite wisdom and power will cause, "that out of the eater shall come forth meat, and from the strong sweetness." I am glad you find yourself happy in the holy JESUS. I wish thee an increase of such dearbought happiness every day, and pray that thy mouth may not be stopped, as others have been before thee, from publishing the glad tidings of salvation, by a crucified Redeemer. It has

* A stated weekly day of prayer, at the *Tabernacle, London.*

been

been thy meat and drink to preach among poor sinners the unsearchable riches of JESUS CHRIST. May'st thou continue and abide in this plan, and whether I see thee or not, whether thou dost ever think of, or write to me any more, I wish thee much success, and shall always pray that the work of the LORD may prosper in thy hands. Whether you have changed your principles with your situation, I know not. I would only caution thee against taking any thing for *gospel* upon the mere authority of man. Go where thou wilt, though thou shouldest be in the purest society under heaven, thou wilt find that the best of men are but men at the best, and will meet with stumbling blocks enough, to teach thee the necessity of a continual dependence on the LORD JESUS, who alone is infallible, and who will not give that glory to another. Blessed be his Name, for the trials I have met with from the friends of *Zion*. At present, I can rejoice in being deserted by one, and used unkind by another, who at the great day must own me to be their spiritual father. Such trials are very salutary.—They lead me to the Cross, and I trust in the end will conform me to him, who in his bitterest agony had no one to watch with him, no not for one hour. My dear man, you will excuse me, as my heart at present is affected with the thoughts of the divisions that subsist between the servants and churches of JESUS CHRIST. May JESUS heal them, and hasten that blessed time, when we shall all see eye to eye, and there shall be no disputings about houses, doctrine, or discipline in all GOD's holy mountain! GOD willing, I purpose seeing *England* next year, and shall be glad to converse with thee once more, about the things which belong to our Saviour's kingdom—If my present sickness ends in death, we shall converse in a better world, and without the least discord and contention. Remember me to *Brampton*, and to all. I thank them for not forgetting the chief of sinners. Tell them JESUS is yet with me, and causes my rod to bud and blossom. The bush burns, but is not consumed. Adieu.

Thine in the glorious *Emmanuel*,
G. W.

LETTER

LETTER DCVII.

To Mrs. R——.

Dear Madam, New-Port, August 20, 1747.

I Hope that since I left you, Mr. M——'s conversation has been blessed, and that you are steadily and deliberately resolved to know nothing but JESUS CHRIST, and him crucified. Indeed he is the fairest among ten thousand. The more you know him, the more you will love him. O what a happy change will you experience when you enter into the world of new creatures! May JESUS hasten the time, and enable you to come as a poor, lost, undone sinner, to be clothed with his everlasting righteousness! Accept these few hasty lines. They are the language of a heart truly concerned for your eternal welfare. I salute Miss *M*——; may JESUS make her a wise virgin, and give you and dear Mr. *R*—— grace to bring her up in the nurture and admonition of the LORD! I at present add no more. As opportunity offers, you shall hear again from me. Dear Madam,

Your affectionate friend and servant
for CHRIST sake,
G. W.

LETTER DCVIII.

To Mrs L——.

Dear Madam, New-port, August 20, 1747.

DOES not JESUS take his lambs into his arms, and dandle his little ones on his knees? Ought not his ministers then to follow his good example, and strive with him, not to quench the smoaking flax or break the bruised reed. This consideration causes me to write you a few lines. May they find you as in an agony to enter in at the straight gate! Courage, dear Mrs. *L*——, courage. CHRIST, heaven, glory, are worth your acceptance. They are all yours, if you will give him your heart. May JESUS make you willing, and enable you to say henceforward, "GOD forbid that I should glory, save in the Cross of JESUS CHRIST." You will remember me to Mr. L——, and all dear friends. As opportunity offers, they and you shall hear from, dear Madam,

Your most affectionate friend and willing
servant for CHRIST's sake,
G. W.

LETTER DCIX.

To Mr. D——.

Dear Mr. D——,   *New-York, August* 27, 1747.

IS it not just, that I should pay off my old debts? consequently I must write to you. I owe you many letters, and more love. Accept this in part of payment. It brings you news of my safe arrival, through the good hand of my GOD upon me, at *New-York.* We were detained upon the water three or four days. I believe it was for good; for the LORD blessed it to the recovery of my health, so that I eat like a sailor. At present I find my nature recruited considerably, and met my dear yoke-fellow and friends well at this place. O that my heart glowed with thanks to the LORD of all Lords, whose mercy endureth for ever! Help me, my dear Sir, to be thankful. My obligations to my glorious JESUS are increased by my late excursion to *Charles-Town, Portsmouth, Boston,* and other places in *New-England.* If I forget her, let my right-hand forget her cunning. I think of, and pray for you and yours, and all my dear friends daily. O let us so live, that we may meet in heaven. You know the way; "JESUS is the way, the truth and the life." Walk before him, look continually to him, and you shall be enabled to trample upon sin, death, and hell. Excuse the brevity of this. Next time, GOD willing, you shall have a longer letter. My tender love awaits your dear spouse and family. You will remember me to all enquiring friends, and as GOD enables, you shall all be remembered by, dear Mr. D——,

Yours most affectionately in CHRIST JESUS,
G. W.

LETTER DCX.

To Mr. A——.

New-York, Aug. 27, 1747.

TO convince you that I remember your desire when at *Boston,* I send you almost my first letter. It comes full

of

of thanks for all past favours. May the GOD whom I serve, reward you ten thousand fold! He will, he has promised, he also will do it. Will you give me leave to ask one favour more? You may guess what it is. I beseech you to entreat the giver of every good and perfect gift to grant me an humble and a thankful heart; for indeed, mercies are renewed to me every moment. GOD has given me a pleasant journey, and brought me this day to *New-York* in safety. My health is considerably restored, and I know not why my dear friends yet cruelly hinder me. Well, GOD's will be done! O that it may be to the Redeemer's glory, and the good of precious and immortal souls! I am of the same mind as when at *Boston*,—resolved to preach and work for JESUS, 'till I can preach and work no more. I doubt not, but in your sphere, you are like-minded. May the LORD strengthen, stablish, settle you in it, and give you to abound in every good word and work. CHRIST is a good Master: he is worthy of all our time, and of every thing that we possess. Is not one heart too little for him? And yet he requires no more. Amazing love! I am lost when I think of it. I can only say, LORD, I adore and worship! But how does dear Mrs. *A*——? Bid her, not be faithless, but believing. JESUS shall do more for her than she can ask or think. I salute you both most heartily, as does my dear yoke-fellow.—That JESUS may plentifully reward you for all favours, and give you so to live here, that you may sit at his right-hand eternally hereafter, is the hearty prayer of, dear Mr. *A*——,

Yours, &c.
G. W.

LETTER DCXI.

To Mr. W——, *at Portsmouth.*

New-York, Aug. 27, 1747.

Very dear Sir,

IS it right when we have committed a fault, to persist in, and not confess and amend it? By no means. I must therefore write to you, whom (though you have received no letter from me) I dearly love in the bowels of the ever-loving, ever-lovely JESUS. I thank you, dear Sir, for all favours, and exhort you,

you, as the best return I can make, to walk worthy of that God, who has called you to his kingdom and his glory. May you be enabled to live above, and overcome the world! O that Jesus may be at all times, your only All! O that you may look up continually to him for light, life, and every thing! Then will he direct your steps, and cause every change and scene of life to be a means of changing and transforming your dear soul more and more into his own divine likeness. You are shortly to enter into a new and untried state. Dear Sir, call Jesus and his Disciples to your marriage; marry in and for the Lord, or your life will be exceedingly uneasy and miserable. Remember, that new states call for new strength. Let your eyes then be fixed on Jesus. From him every good and perfect gift cometh. He alone can teach you to use the world, and every worldly enjoyment, so as not to abuse it. I commend you to his tender mercy. I pray continually for you, and humbly intreat you to remember unworthy, ungrateful, ill and hell-deserving me. I can now only most heartily thank you for all favours, beg to be remembered to all friends, and subscribe myself, dear Sir,

Yours in Him that liveth for ever,

G. W.

LETTER DCXII.

To the Rev. Mr. G. T——.

New-York, Aug. 29, 1747.

Rev. and very dear Sir,

NOT want of love, but of leisure, has prevented my writing to you for some time past. Blessed be God, I can now send you good news from the Northward. My reception at *Boston*, and elsewhere in *New-England*, was like unto the first. Arrows of conviction fled and stuck fast. Many, I hear, were wounded. Congregations were rather larger than ever, and opposers mouths were stopped. Will you now take another trip? I believe it would be blest to the good of your own and many other souls. I would be more particular, did I not expect to see you next week. I am better in health than when I left *New-York*. God gives me grace to spend it to the utmost in the Redeemer's service. I am determined in his strength, to die fighting, though it be upon my stumps. I trust you pray for me. I remember you and your flock. I salute all tenderly, and am, Rev. and very dear Sir,

> Your most affectionate younger brother
> and servant in JESUS CHRIST,
>
> G. W.

LETTER DCXIII.

To Mr. Henry S——, Junior.

New-York, Aug. 29, 1747.

My dear Mr. S——,

LAST *Thursday* noon the keeper of *Israel*, who neither slumbereth or sleepeth, brought me hither in safety. We were detained three days on the water. It was over-ruled for good. I recovered my appetite, and am now much better than when I left *New-England.* Next *Tuesday,* GOD willing, I shall set forward, and hope to be at *Charles-Town* the beginning of *November.* Will you write to me? GOD willing, you shall hear from me every opportunity. I have good news from *Providence,* my plantation in *South-Carolina,* and from *Bethesda:* both families are well, and several negroes are under conviction. I hope those that were under concern at *Portsmouth,* find their convictions to abide. I pray GOD, they may have no rest, 'till they find rest in JESUS CHRIST! I salute them, and all the Redeemer's true followers. I join with my dear yoke-fellow, in sending you, and dear Mrs. S——, ten thousand thanks for all favours, and am, very dear Sir,

Your most affectionate, obliged friend and brother, &c.

G. W.

LETTER DCXIV.

To Mr. D——.

New-York, Aug. 30, 1747.

MY dear brother *Daniel,* thou man greatly beloved, why weepest thou? Why art thou so cast down? All is forgiven, all is forgotten long ago; be strong, and GOD shall establish thy heart. Look up, and put thy trust in the LORD. He is a merciful Redeemer; otherwise what could worthless, ungrateful, unfruitful, ill, hell-deserving I do? O how great is his love to us-ward! How kindly hath he brought me to

New-York! Pray let your mourning be turned into praise, and give thanks to the LORD of all lords in behalf of your unworthy friend. You are my old friend. I have loved thee, and do love thee with a peculiar love. May the LORD increase thee more and more, even thee and thy children! I send you and yours most cordial salutations. We set out, GOD willing, to-morrow on our southern journey. I have good news from the Orphan-house, and my new Plantation. Some negroes are brought under conviction. Mr. B—— was well the latter end of *July.* I shall take care of his father's letter. My dear yoke-fellow intends writing to you soon. In the mean while accept hearty love from, yours as usual,

G. *W.*

LETTER DCXV.

To Mrs. S——, at New-York.

Philadelphia, Sept. 6, 1747.

SHALL I promise and not perform? GOD forbid. I must then drop a line to my afflicted friend. How is your little one? Is it yet languishing? Is it quite emaciated and panting for breath? Or is it gone into the world of spirits? Whatever be your answer, I am ready to reply, Remember your father *Abraham*; how chearfully did he offer up his dear *Isaac,* his son, whom he loved? How kindly did the LORD take it at his hands? Go thou and do likewise. If JESUS hath restored it to you, nurse it for him; pray to him continually for grace to order it aright, and learn how soon GOD may imbitter the dearest comforts to us. Happy, happy they, who can lean on and trust in JESUS, whilst they are going through this howling wilderness, this world of woe. I trust you are one of these happy ones. O free grace! Sovereign, electing, distinguishing love! You will join with me in saying, "Why me, LORD, why me?" I could enlarge. Whilst I am writing, the fire kindles; but my Master's business calls me away. He is with me here. Remember the Pilgrims. My dear yoke-fellow is gone forward; perhaps I may follow this week. I desire to be remembered in the kindest manner to dear Mr. S—— P——, wife, and all friends. I thank them and you a thousand times for all favours, and am, dear Mrs. S——,

Your affectionate and willing servant for CHRIST's sake,

G. *W.*

LETTER

LETTER DCXVI.

To Captain S——.

Philadelphia, Sept. 9, 1747.

My very dear Mr. S——,

THOUGH I wrote to you lately by my friend Mr. *V*——, yet the receipt of your kind letter makes me to write again. The deadly blow I see is given. Well! Thanks be to GOD, you are so resigned. You doubtless remember, that you took one another only " 'till death you should part." That *shocking clause*, as Mr. *B*—— calls it, is very instructive. Blessed be GOD, that she gave you any comfortable evidences of her being for ever with the LORD. If so, do not wish her here again, but remember how soon your own great change must necessarily come. You are now on the decline of life. You have seen that all below is vanity. O that you may bring forth much fruit in old age! Take heed, watch and be sober, since you know not at what hour the blessed bridegroom may come to call you. I write thus freely to you; because you are pleased to stile me your father. Pray for me then, that I may give to JESUS all the glory, and study to glorify him more and more. Next *Monday*, GOD willing, I intend leaving this place. Be pleased to acquaint our dear friend Mr. *V*—— that I intend writing to him soon. I hope he reached home in safety. I salute him, Mr. *P*————, and all friends most heartily. Accept of the same yourself, in the most cordial manner, from, very dear Sir,

Yours most affectionately in CHRIST JESUS,

G. W.

LETTER DCXVII.

To Mr. IV——.

Very dear Sir,   *Philadelphia, Sept. 9. 1747.*

LAST night I heard of Dr. *Coleman*'s sudden death. I bless GOD for granting him such an easy passage. Soon after the news reached me, I bowed my knee before the GOD and Father of our LORD JESUS in behalf of your bereaved (and I could almost say desolate) church. O may the LORD of all lords direct you in the choice of another, who may rule and feed you diligently with all his power. I shall be glad to hear what the great head of the church does for you. You may direct to me at *Charles-Town*. GOD willing, I set forward on my journey *Monday* next. Our glorious *Emmanuel* has been pleased to open my mouth, and enlarge my heart in preaching the unsearchable riches of his grace.—I hope my dear *Boston* friends are warm and lively. I salute all most heartily. Pray remember the poor pilgrims; and if you write to *Scotland* or *South-Carolina*, let them know how affairs go. My dear yoke-fellow is gone to *Bohemia*, otherwise she would write. I intend writing to dear Mr. S———— by next post. In the mean while, I beg leave to subscribe myself, very dear Sir,

Yours most affectionately in CHRIST,
G. W.

LETTER DCXVIII.

To Mr. and Mrs. F————.

Philadelphia, Sept. 9, 1747.

My very dear, dear Friends,

THOUGH I hope to see you ere this reaches *Charles-Town*, yet I cannot but embrace every opportunity that offers to let you know how we do. I have lately been eleven hundred miles journey northward, and have found the Redeemer's strength magnified in my great weakness. The word ran and was glorified. I am now posting towards, and hope to reach you the beginning of *November* next. I am better in health than usual, and through grace am determined to die fighting the Redeemer's battles. On *Long Island* I saw Mr. B————. He still loves his *Charles-Town* friend. If you are not provided, it is my opinion, that it is best for you, for him, and the church of CHRIST, that he should be at *Charles-Town*. But this is only my opinion. With this, you will receive a packet of letters from him. If it be not done before you receive this, I wish you would be pleased to send my bureau, with my other things that were packed up, to *Providence*. I would not willingly have it to do when I come to *Charles-Town*. I hear you have had a dry season. I trust it has not been so in spirituals,

rituals. O that JESUS may water you every moment! I think you may plead this promife before a prayer-hearing GOD; "He that watereth, fhall be water'd again." Surely the bowels of the faints have been, and are daily refrefhed through your means. Happy ye that are determined to make to yourfelves friends of the mammon of unrighteoufnefs. When natural lives fail, you fhall be received into everlafting habitations. O happy time, when we fhall be, foul and body, for ever with the LORD! I have lived in hopes fome time, that my departure was at hand; but I feem to be gathering ftrength again, and truft fhall be made inftrumental in calling fome more fouls to the precious JESUS. O that I may be humble and thankful! Dear friends, pray for us.—My dear wife is gone to *Bohemia*, otherwife fhe would write. We have written by every fhip. Some of our letters, I believe, have been taken. Our tender love to all. I am,

Ever yours, whilft

G. W.

LETTER DCXIX.

To the Rev. Mr. H———.

Philadelphia, Sept. 9, 1747.

My very dear Mr. H———,

I Thank our gracious GOD for all the good news contained in your kind letter. It gladened my heart, and gave me reafon to hope, that the *Indian* land would be a chriftian land indeed. When I received your letter, I was juft returned from an eleven hundred miles journey northward, in which the rock of ages was pleafed to let much of his glory pafs before his dear people. I was enabled to preach about 30 times in *New-England*, and am now coming forward towards you, and hope to fee you in *November*. My dear yoke-fellow would anfwer Mrs. H———, but fhe is gone to *Bohemia*. Accept thanks and love in her name. I have been frequently at the gates of death within thefe few months, and thought to have reached my defired port; but it feems I muft put out to fea again. My heavenly Father's will be done. I have good news from *England*. I have fome thoughts of feeing it next year. JESUS will direct me. Captain *Grant* is failed

from

from *Jamaica*. Ere long I hope to owe no man any thing but love. Something confiderable hath been done fince I left *Charles-Town*. The LORD will never fail thofe that put their truft in him. I have remembered the book with the hymn tunes. I hope we fhall not differ about an earthly matter. We are brethren; let us dwell in unity, and the GOD of love and peace will dwell amongft us. O that his divine love may be fhed abroad abundantly in our hearts by the Holy Ghoft! How fhall we then bear with, and forbear one another? I hope all around you are well, and watered with fpiritual as well as natural rain. I falute all moft tenderly; and hoping to fee you fhortly, I fubfcribe myfelf, very dear Mr. *H——*,

Yours moft affectionately in CHRIST,

G. W.

LETTER DCXX.

To the Rev. Mr. T——.

Philadelphia, Sept. 10. 1747.

Reverend and very dear Sir,

I Suppofe, ere this comes to hand, you will have heard how near I have been to my wifhed-for harbour, and how I have been obliged to put out to fea again. Bleffed be GOD, fince I muft live, he does not permit me altogether to live in vain. The word ran and was glorified much in *New-England*. The gathering of the people, and the power that attended the word feemed to be near the fame as when the work begun feven years ago. I parted from my friends with great reluctance. Since my coming fouthward, I have feen and dined with Governor *B——*. He ftill retains his former affection, and I hope will be a great bleffing to thefe parts. I have lately heard of the death of Doctor *Coleman*. I pity his poor congregation, fearing it will much dwindle. There are now many deftitute flocks in *New-England*. Mr. *B——*'s death hath taught me a good leffon. May the LORD JESUS keep me from trimming! fomething confiderable hath been done fince I faw you, towards eafing me of my Orphan-houfe embarraffments. The particulars expect in *November:* then I

hope

hope to see you once more. I still intend, GOD willing, to see *Bermudas.* Blessed be GOD, I have good news from *Bethesda* and *Providence.* I am helped here, as I was at *New-York,* in preaching; but find little conviction-work going on. As you observe, " that is GOD's work." I hope you have been carried comfortably through the Summer's heat, and that we shall have a warm Winter when we meet at *Charles-Town.* Your father's child is dead. I have a letter for you from him. I salute you and all for my dear yoke-fellow, who is gone forward to *Bohemia.* I follow on *Monday* next. You will remember me in the kindest manner to all. I have written to many friends, but believe the vessels have been taken in which the letters were sent. I have now just time to beg the continuance of your prayers, and subscribe myself, Rev. and very dear Sir,

Yours as usual,

G. W.

LETTER DCXXI.

To Mr. H—— H——.

Philadelphia, Sept. 11, 1747.

My very dear Brother,

I Wrote to you within these few months from this place, *Boston* and *New-York.* My last letters were to inform you, that, GOD willing, some time next year I purpose to see *England,* if my outward affairs can be settled. Surely the LORD will deliver me from money matters by and by.—He will, he will.—LORD, I believe, help my unbelief! I have good news from *Georgia,* and from my new plantation in *South-Carolina.* Many negroes are brought under conviction. We saw great things in *New-England.* The flocking and power that attended the word, was like unto that seven years ago. Weak as I was, and have been, I was enabled to travel eleven hundred miles and preach daily. I am now once more going to *Georgia* to settle all my affairs, and shall get ready to embark as soon as I receive letters from you. My dear yoke-fellow is gone forwards. She exceedingly longs to see her old friends. But death may intervene. I have been daily waiting for it. Few have expected my life, but at present I seem to be getting

strength.

strength. By the grace of God, it shall all be employed in the dear Redeemer's service. I find no inclination to settle. My heart (O free grace!) is yet springing for God, and I am determined to die fighting. I hope matters go on well with you. Indeed I remember you daily, and pray that you all may be filled with all the fulness of God. I am here travelling through a wilderness; but I trust leaning on my beloved. Jesus is my rock, my stay, my God, and my all. Various are the scenes I pass through; various are the comforts and supports I meet with. Sometimes the Lord feeds me as it were by the ravens, and teaches me daily that man's extremity is his opportunity to help and succour. O, my dear brother, if ever we meet in this world, how much have we to say to one another, concerning the loving-kindnesses of the Lord? But when we meet in heaven.—I am lost at the thought—What!

> Make slaves the partners of thy throne,
> Deck'd with a never-fading crown?

O Jesus! thy love is indeed immense, unsearchable.—Shed it abroad in the dear man's heart to whom I am writing, and the hearts of all with whom he is concerned, and the hearts of all thy dear children. Even so, Lord Jesus. Amen! I can no more. My heart is almost too full to subscribe myself

Ever yours,

G. W.

LETTER DCXXII.

To the Rev. Mr. J. W——.

Philadelphia, Sept. 11, 1747.

Dear and Rev. Sir,

NOT long ago I received your kind letter, dated in *February* last. Your others I believe came to hand, and I hope ere now you have received my answer. My heart is really for an outward, as well as an inward union. Nothing shall be wanting on my part to bring it about; but I cannot see how it can possibly be effected, 'till we all think and speak the same things. I rejoice to hear, that you and your brother are

are more moderate with respect to *sinless perfection*. Time and experience I believe will convince you, that attaining such a state in this life, is not a doctrine of the everlasting gospel. As for *universal redemption*, if we omit on each side the talking for or against reprobation, which we may do fairly, and agree as we already do in giving an universal offer to all poor sinners that will come and taste of the water of life, I think we may manage very well. But it is difficult to determine such matters at a distance. Some time next year, (if the Redeemer spares my life,) I hope to see you face to face. In the mean while, the language of my heart is,

> O let us find the ancient way,
> Our wond'ring foes to move;
> And force the heathen world to say,
> See how these brethren love.

I rejoice to find that the rebellion has been over-ruled for the awakening of many souls. Our LORD generally builds his temple in troublesome times. I cannot, upon the maturest deliberation, charge myself with a design to flatter in my sermon on that occasion. You know my attachment to the present establishment. Out of the fulness of my heart my pen wrote. But it may be I know not myself. LORD, keep me from trimming! At present, my heart seems as free for JESUS as ever. I have been once more in *New-England*. My entrance was as at the first, about seven years ago. Perhaps I may embark from thence for my native country. Our LORD will direct. I am now going to *Georgia* to winter. At *New-York* and here, JESUS has enlarged my heart, and opened my mouth to shew forth his praise. I have news of the awakening of several negroes at my new plantation, lately purchased at *South-Carolina*. I hope ere long to be delivered from my outward embarrassments. I long to owe no man any thing but love. This is a debt, Reverend Sir, I shall never be able to discharge to you, or your brother. JESUS will pay you all. For his sake, I love and honour you very much, and rejoice as much, in your success as in my own. I cannot agree with you in some principles, but that need not hinder love; since I trust we hold the foundation, even "JESUS, the same yesterday, to-day and for ever." Will you salute, in the kindest manner,

all

all the followers of the Lamb within your sphere of action? Grace, mercy and peace be multiplied upon all their dear souls! I thank them for remembering a poor pilgrim, who though faint is still pursuing, and determined, in the strength of JESUS, to spend and be spent more and more for the good of poor sinners. Perhaps before I see you, I may visit *Bermudas* and *Cape-Breton*. You will pray that the LORD may order my steps aright. What have you done with the *Moravian Brethren?* their affairs are in confusion here. I think their foundation is too narrow for their superstructure. I believe in their plan there are many plants that our heavenly Father hath not planted. The LORD bless what is right, and rectify what is wrong in them, in us, and in all. Even so, LORD JESUS, Amen!—O for heaven! where we shall mistake, judge, and grieve one another no more. Lately I thought myself sailing several times into the blessed harbour; but it seems I must put out to sea again. My Redeemer's will be done! Forgive, Reverend Sir, the prolixity of this. Love indites. I salute you for my dear fellow pilgrim, who is gone forwards.—Continue to pray for us, and assure yourself, that you are always remembered by, Reverend and very dear Sir,

Your most affectionate, though unworthy younger brother and willing servant for CHRIST's sake,

G. W.

LETTER DCXXIII.

To the Rev. Mr. C—— W——.

Very dear Sir, *Philadelphia, Sept.* 11, 1747.

BOTH your letters and your prayers I trust have reached me. May mine reach you also, and then it will not be long ere we shall indeed be one fold under one Shepherd. However, if this should not be on earth, it will certainly be effected in heaven. Thither I trust we are hastening apace. Blessed be GOD that you are kept alive, and that your spiritual children are increasing. May they increase more and more! JESUS can maintain them all. He wills that his house should be full. Some have wrote me things to your disadvantage. I do not believe them. Love thinks no evil of a friend. Such are you to me. I love you most dearly. I
could

could write to you much more, but time and business will not permit. You will see my letter to your dear brother. That you may be guided into all truth, turn thousands and ten thousands more unto righteousness, and shine as the stars in the future world, for ever and ever, is the hearty prayer of, very dear Sir,

Yours most affectionately, &c.
G. W.

LETTER DCXXIV.

To the Rev. Mr. M——.

Bohemia, (Maryland) Sept. 17, 1747.

Honoured Sir,

WILL you permit a young soldier of JESUS CHRIST to write to an experienced veteran, before he goes hence, and is no more seen? Sorry am I that my visit to *York* was short, yet glad that our LORD gave me to see you once more ready to sing your *Nunc dimittis* with steadiness and composure, if not with joy unspeakable, even a joy that is full of glory.—Happy, thrice happy, Reverend Sir! You have gone through that wilderness, which if hoary hairs should be my lot, awaits me your younger son and servant. Well! this is my comfort: I have the same Beloved to lean on, as you have had. The way, though narrow, is not long; the gate, though strait, opens into life eternal. O that I might pass through it when young; but, Father, not my will, but thine be done! Honoured Sir, be pleased to pray for me. I remember you and your dear flock, whom I love in the bowels of JESUS CHRIST. May he who kissed away the soul of his beloved *Moses*, appoint a *Joshua* to succeed you, when he bids you come up to the mount and die! I hope my cordial respects will find acceptance with your dear yoke-fellow. I remember what she said to me, and once more beg a continued interest in your prayers. I beg leave to subscribe myself, honoured Sir,

Your most affectionate tho' unworthy younger son
and willing servant in him that liveth for ever,
G. W.

LETTER DCXXV.

To the Rev. Mr. M—— Jun.

Bohemia, Sept. 17, 1747.

I Have been writing to the father,—Love, love unfeigned constrains me to write to the son also. I hope it will influence you to send me, however unworthy, a line or two in return. Reverend and dear Sir, how do you? Are you yet GOD's mouth to the people? Surely if the prayers of faith keep me alive, the prayers of faith must open your mouth, and constrain you in preaching to shew forth your glorious Redeemer's praise. All things are possible with GOD.

> *Blest is faith, that trusts his power;*
> *Blest are saints, that wait his hour;*
> *Haste, great Conqueror, bring it near,*
> *Let the wish'd-for thing appear.*

But you do not like that I should write about yourself? Will you then permit me to tell you, that in spite of all my corruptions, JESUS still continues to bless unworthy me. He gave me a prosperous journey to *New-York*, and there, as well as at *Philadelphia*, he opened my mouth to shew forth his praise. My outward circumstances are made easier, and I trust, in a short time I shall owe no man any thing but love. I am now posting southward, willing to follow the cloud wheresoever it shall point in the spring. O pray, pray that JESUS may be my comforter and my guide. Great are my trials, but greater my consolations. O free, rich, and sovereign grace! Help me, dear Sir, to extol and praise it. You will remember me to all. Your * *fidus achates*, and your dear faithful nurse, I shall never forget. When you go to *Kittery*, pray make my most dutiful respects acceptable to Sir *William* and his consort. Wishing you, what Colonel *Gardiner* once wished me, " A thriving soul in a healthful body," I subscribe myself, Reverend and very dear Sir,

Yours in CHRIST JESUS,

G. W.

* Bosom friend.

LETTER DCXXVI.

To Mr. J—— S——.

Bath-Town, North Carolina, Oct. 6, 1747.

Very dear Sir,

I Wrote you a few lines just as I was leaving *Bohemia.* They informed you of the receipt of my bills, and by them I also desired you to pay the remainder of what you have of mine into the hands of Mr. D—— V—— of *New-York.* Since that, I have posted forward here, and hope to see some souls in this province all in love with JESUS, and made partakers of the power of his Resurrection. I have preached three times, and purpose, GOD willing, to preach many times more. The LORD seems to have given me the affections of the people, and I am determined in his strength to see what can be done amongst them. The box of books sent hither from Mr. *K*—— and *G*—— never came to hand. Be pleased to make some enquiry about it. I preached once in *Virginia*, and would have preached oftner; but the small-pox was spreading, the assembly did not sit, and I wanted to let *North-Carolina* have as much time as I could. I hope to write to you again from *Charles-Town.* There, I shall be glad to hear that the all-wise head of the church hath directed you to a suitable pastor in the room of Dr. *Coleman.* I sometimes think all will go to heaven before me. I am weak and faint, I long to be dissolved and to be with JESUS, but cannot die. My heavenly Father's will be done! I would have you still pray for me, as a dying man; but O pray that I may not go off as a snuff. I would fain die blazing, not with human glory, but the love of JESUS. I wish you, and yours, and all dear friends, as much of this as your hearts can hold. I remember you daily and hourly. I will thank you in heaven for what you have done for me on earth, and till then shall subscribe myself, dear Sir,

Yours in the best bonds,

G. W.

LETTER DCXXVII.

To Mrs. S——.

Bath-Town, North-Carolina, Oct. 6, 1747,

Dear Madam,

BE pleased to accept this, as a token that you are not forgotten by me ;—no, I loved your deceased husband, I honour and pray for his dear and sorrowful relict. I would give you that advice, dear Madam, which I believe he would do, was he to rise from his grave, " Make sure of a CHRIST, and give the LORD no rest, till you can say, my maker is my husband, the LORD of Hosts is his name." What have you now to do, Madam, but to make sure of a CHRIST? You are desolate, why should you not put your trust in the LORD? Widows, godly ministers widows, are GOD's peculiar care. O that you may have reason to say, " It is good for me that I have been afflicted." Now is your time to learn GOD's law. Come to JESUS, Madam, close with him, and give him your whole heart. I need not tell you, that he will make you happy. He has made me so, even me the chief of sinners. As such be pleased to pray for, dear Madam,

Your real, affectionate friend and servant,

G. W.

LETTER DCXXVIII.

To Mrs. A————.

Bath-Town, North-Carolina, Oct. 6, 1747.

Dear Madam,

BE where I will, the LORD JESUS puts you upon my heart. I often think you happy, because you are so circumstanced that you must necessarily drink of the waters of life at the fountain head. It drinks sweetest from thence. Communion with GOD's children is sweet ; but communion with GOD himself is infinitely sweeter. The woman of *Samaria* found it so. When the disciples came and interrupted her fellowship with their master, she left her water pot and went her way. Blessed be GOD, that happy time is coming when we shall enjoy both him and his without interruption. Till then,

then, dear Madam, be content to have little or much of the company of CHRIST's people, as your heavenly father shall judge most convenient. Heaven is before you, time is flying on eagles wings. Eternity, an happy eternity awaits you when time shall be no more. O that it would approach faster to me! But why so hasty, O my soul! In heaven thou canst not deny thyself for JESUS CHRIST! Dear Madam, pray for me, that my will may be swallowed up in the will of GOD. That it may be so with you, is the hearty prayer of, dear Madam,

   Your most affectionate friend and servant,

            G. W.

LETTER DCXXIX.

To Mr. P————.

Bath-Town, North-Carolina, Oct. 6, 1747.

Dear Mr. P——,

OUR affectionate parting is not yet out of my remembrance. Since that, I hope you have been diligent, and ere now have got an evidence that we shall not be parted hereafter. O for assurance! It is indeed the anchor of the soul. It keeps it steady in the midst of storms. Dear Sir, press after it, as you value your present as well as eternal welfare. Tell the LORD JESUS, you cannot do without it. I once thought dear Mr. P—— would be one of the first-rate christians in *New-England*. What hath hindered you? Whatever it be, whether a right hand or a right eye, may the LORD JESUS take it away! Will you say *Amen* heartily? You will excuse this freedom. I always write so to those I love. Pray remember me to your mother, wife, and all friends. Tell them I am here, hunting after sinners in *North-Carolina* woods. It is pleasant work, though my body is weak and crazy. After a short fermentation in the grave, it will be fashioned like unto CHRIST's glorious body. The thought of this rejoices my soul, and makes me long to leap my seventy years. O pray for me, that I may have patience to tarry the LORD's leisure. I commit you to his care. I charge you in his great name, not to let me miss you in heaven, and with much love subscribe myself, dear Mr. P——,

Your very affectionate friend, and willing

servant for CHRIST's *sake,*

G. W.

LETTER DCXXX.

To Mr. S——.

My dear Mr. S——,   *Oct.* 6, 1747.

LET who will be omitted when I am writing to *New-England*, I think, I am under many obligations not to forget you. Blessed be GOD for making you a christian merchant, and teaching you the holy art of trafficking for the LORD. You trade upon a safe bottom. Your all is insured, and you shall receive your own with good usury at the great day. Go on, my dear man, spend and be spent for CHRIST's people; it is a glorious employ. I would not but be thus engaged for millions of worlds. It is true, I am decaying daily; but resolved in the strength of JESUS to die fighting. At present I am engaged in *North-Carolina*, and hope ere long to send you good news from this ungospelized wilderness. In about a month I expect to see *Charles-Town*. The LORD direct me where to go in the Spring. Several ways present. I am willing to see more of the north before I return to my native country. But alas! why write I thus? How many important hours will intervene? O that every minute may be employed for GOD, even a GOD in CHRIST. Indeed he is a good master. He wounds, but he heals also. He brings down, but raises up again. He humbles, but it is only in order to exalt his dear children. This you and I shall find, as we have found already, times without number, perfectly true, by happy experience. But I cannot enlarge. You will deliver the enclosed. I hope my last to the dear Messrs. M——'s came safe. I will write to more as business, opportunity, and health permit. In the mean while, accept our joint most cordial love to all dear, very dear friends. Accept the same to you and yours. I am, dear Sir,

Yours eternally in the everlasting I AM,

G. W.

LETTER DCXXXI.

To Mr. R———.

Bath-Town, North-Carolina, Oct. 7, 1747.

Very dear Sir,

BY this time (such is your love to unworthy me,) I suppose you are willing to know where I am, and what I am doing. Blessed be GOD, I am still employed in my old delightful work, " calling poor sinners to repentance."—I trust a day of power will shortly come to *North-Carolina*. I have preached three times already, and am now going a small circuit round about. I expect to reach *Charles-Town* in a month's time. But give me leave in my turn to enquire, how it is with you and yours? Are your resolutions more and more invigorated, and hath JESUS at length taken possession of your whole heart? I must not let you alone, till you can fairly and truly say, " 'Tis done, 'tis done." O what a revenue of glory might a person in your station bring to CHRIST, and what a radiant crown of grace might you secure to your own soul, was you but once in earnest to lay up treasure in heaven, where neither moth nor rust doth corrupt, nor thieves break through and steal! Rise, rise, dear Sir, awake and sleep no more. JESUS waits to give you light. May he so fill you with his light and love, that you may rejoice in his great salvation all the day long! Pray let me hear from you in the Winter. I am more concerned for you than ever. Your late favours have increased my obligations to be so. I shall be glad to hear that the LORD hath given you a son. I remember dear Madam *R———*, and hope to drop her a few lines. May the glorious *Emmanuel* make little Miss a wise virgin. My love awaits Mrs. *H———*, and your whole houshold. You will remember me in the kindest manner to Mrs. *G———*, *L———*, &c. and the whole circle of my female friends. Praying that grace, mercy and peace may be multiplied upon all, I subscribe myself, dear Sir,

Yours most affectionately in CHRIST JESUS,

G. W.

LETTER DCXXXII.

To the Reverend Mr. L——.
Bath-Town, North-Carolina, Oct. 11, 1747.

Reverend and very dear Sir,

IT has given me much concern, that I could not comply with your kind invitation to *Plymouth*; but providence plainly pointed my course another way. GOD only knows what a cross it was to me, to leave dear *New-England* so soon. I hope death will not be so bitter to me, as was parting from my friends. Glad shall I be to be prayed thither again, before I see my native land. But future things belong to GOD. I would be just where he would have me, though it be in the uttermost parts of the earth. At present I am hunting after poor lost sinners in these ungospelized wilds. People are willing to hear, and blessed be the LORD of all lords, I am willing to preach. My body is yet weak. A little riding fatigues me; but he that has been, is, and I trust will be my strength, my support, and my guide even unto death. Dear Sir, continue to pray for me. I wish you much of the divine presence, and hope the LORD will yet make you a spiritual father to thousands. Be pleased to remember me in the kindest manner to dear Mr. *F———*, and the whole circle of those reverend brethren, who dare confess CHRIST's work, and CHRIST's truths. I salute your whole large fire side, and am, reverend and dear Sir,

Yours, &c.

G. W.

LETTER DCXXXIII.

To Mr. P——.
Bath-Town, Oct. 11, 1747.

Very dear Mr. P———,

I Am ashamed to think that your short though exceeding sweet and kind letter, lies as yet unanswered. Want of health and of time, (assure yourself) not want of love, has been the cause of it. The searcher of hearts alone knows, what a cordial reverential respect I bear your honoured father and mother, yourself, and dear sister. I must not write much on this

this head, left my eyes should gush out with water. Sorry am I, very sorry, dear Sir, that the church is not to have the benefit of your labours. But what shall we say? GOD is a sovereign GOD. He must do what he will with his own. This comforts me, that I trust you have learned to be in the world, and yet not of it. Well then, since it must be so, go, dear Sir, and trade for GOD. Let merchants see by your example, that JESUS CHRIST can make many saints in a store. O may you daily taste, and feel the efficacy of his all-atoning, heart-cleansing, world-conquering, precious blood! I trust this is dearer and weightier to me than ever. I am now proclaiming it in these uncultivated ungospelized desarts. People hear with great attention, and I trust ere long news will be heard in heaven, that some *North-Carolina* sinners are born of GOD. I stayed but a small time in *Virginia* and *Maryland*, that I might give this province the more time. I hope to be in *Charles-Town* in about a month, and soon after my arrival, expect to determine what course to take in the Spring. Several ways present themselves. May JESUS direct me which to take! Weak as I am, I am willing to spend and be spent for that ever-lovely, ever-loving JESUS, who has done so much for, and borne so long with me. I am afraid some of you have prayed me back into the world again. Well, it cannot be long ere I get my dismission. O for a triumphant exit. LORD JESUS keep me from going off like a snuff! But it is time to bid you good night. I have been on a forty mile excursion, and this tabernacle of mine is weak. You will remember me to all your dear family, and all friends. I will name none, that if possible I may offend none. However, this I must say, *New-England* friends are dearer to me than ever, and glad shall I be, if another sight of them before I die, be permitted to, very dear Sir,

Yours most affectionately in CHRIST JESUS,

G. W.

LETTER DCXXXIV.

To Mr. D——.

Everards-Ferry, Oct. 16, 1747.

Dear Mr. D——,

THE love I owe you for JESUS CHRIST's sake, induces me to send you a few lines. I hope they will find you yet more and more convinced of self-righteousness, and the absolute necessity of being cloathed with the all-sufficient, compleat and everlasting righteousness of JESUS CHRIST. This, and this only is the ground of our acceptance with a holy, just, and sin-avenging GOD. Here the sinner may find a sure asylum, an everlasting, never-failing refuge. Happy they! who begin to see, feel, and taste this, in a realizing spiritual manner. It is the budding of grace, the beginning of the kingdom of GOD in the soul. May I hope that dear Mr. D—— is one of these happy men. I trust so. You seemed beginning to awake out of nature's dream when I left you. O that nothing may prevail on you to lie down to sleep again! It is dangerous to trifle with the spirit of GOD. When he puts into our hearts good desires, he expects that we shall be workers together with him. Strive therefore, or, as the word imports, *agonize* with GOD, yourself, and the world, in order that you may enter into the strait gate of a thorough sound conversion. You know who has told you "that the kingdom of GOD suffereth violence, and the violent only take it by force." And surely heaven is worth striving for; especially since we are sure of a conquest; and JESUS CHRIST, the captain of our salvation, stands ready to assist, support, and strengthen at every rencounter. Learn therefore to endure hardness, like a good soldier of JESUS CHRIST: adopt *Joshua*'s resolution, stand the laugh, quit yourself like a man, put your hand to the plough, and do not look back; fight the good fight of faith, lay hold on eternal life. I could write more, but I want time and paper. Blessed be GOD, I am as well as a pilgrim in my way can expect to be. I am happy in CHRIST, and that is all in all. I wish you and yours this happiness. I pray you may be partakers of it.

This is the best return I can make for all kindnesses shewn to, dear Sir,

Your affectionate, obliged friend and servant,

G. W.

LETTER DCXXXV.

To Mrs. D———.

Everards-Ferry, Oct. 16, 1747.

Dear Mrs. D———,

AS it is uncertain whether I shall ever see you again in this vale of tears, I cannot help expressing my gratitude for kindnesses received, by sending you a few lines. — And what shall I say? Why, that I trust you at length see, that what the world calls an innocent, harmless, decent, sober life, will not be sufficient to carry us to heaven. Such a life I suppose you have led, and assure yourself, you will find it an hard work to give up such a life in point of dependence, and to come as a poor, ill and hell deserving wretch, to be washed in the blood and cloathed with the righteousness of JESUS CHRIST. Nature will struggle, and a reasoning infidelity will stand at the door of your heart, lest JESUS CHRIST's spirit should enter in and make you happy. But all things are possible with GOD. Apply to him therefore, dear Madam, and beg him to let you see that your heart is desperately wicked, and deceitful above all things. Strengthen your husband's hands; be as a goad in his side, if you see him inclined (though I trust you will not) to forget what he hath lately felt and been convinced of. And O that you may be an happy instrument of converting your two daughters! It is sweet when all of one house are agreed to worship the LORD JESUS in spirit and in truth. That you and yours may be all such worshippers, is the earnest prayer of, dear Madam,

Your real friend, and willing servant for CHRIST's sake,

G. W.

LETTER DCXXXVI.

To Mr. T———— A————.

Wilmington, Cape-Fear, Oct. 18, 1747.

My very dear brother A————,

I Have lately written to you and many other dear *English* friends. I am now in my way to *Georgia*, and hope to see my native country some time next year. My sphere of action still increases, and though I hoped this last Summer to have taken my flight to the blessed JESUS, yet it seems I am to live longer. O that it may be for the Redeemer's glory, and the good of many precious and immortal souls! I know you will say *Amen!* I could write much, but am fatigued, having preached several times, and rode on horse-back through the woods an hundred and sixty miles. JESUS makes the barren wilderness to smile. I want to know how affairs go on among you. I expect letters from some of you at *Charles-Town,* and I hope to see you, I repeat it again, some time next year. But future things belong to GOD. My schemes are so frequently disconcerted, that I would willingly put a blank into his hands, to be filled up just as he pleases. But this stubborn will would fain avoid swallowing some wholesome bitter-sweets, which the all-gracious physician reaches out unto me. Nevertheless, through grace, the prevailing language of my heart is, "Not my will, but thine be done." The being so long absent from my friends, sometimes a little affects me; but I have been used to, so many partings, and heart-breakings from various quarters, that I wonder any thing affects, so as to surprize me. But the mystery of the cross is unsearchable. We shall never fully learn it till we die. We must be beginners in this school every day, hour, and moment. But where am I going? I write as though I was conversing with you. Perhaps such a time may come. In heaven I am sure such a time will have existence. The language of my heart is, LORD JESUS, let thy kingdom come! You will remember me to all. I must now say no more. Whilst I am writing, affection works and almost makes me to say, O that I had wings like a dove, for then would I fly away, and see my *English* and *Scotch* friends! I salute all most heartily, as does my dear fellow pilgrim.—That

grace,

grace, mercy and peace may be multiplied upon all your dear souls, is the hearty prayer of, my dear Man,

Yours most affectionately in CHRIST JESUS,

G. W.

LETTER DCXXXVII.

To Mr. B———.

Charles-Town, (South-Carolina,) Oct. 25, 1747.

Very dear Mr. B———,

I Hear a ship sails to-morrow for *Philadelphia*. I cannot help letting you know, that we arrived here last night in health and safety. The barren wilderness was made to smile all the way. I trust good was done in *North-Carolina*. The poor people were very willing to hear. I expected, on my arrival at this place, to have received letters and sundry things from you, or dear Mr. B———. If they are taken, may the LORD JESUS give me a thankful heart! I would write you a long letter, and I would also write to many friends, but you know travellers are weary, and I must away to-morrow to *Georgia*. All is well there, and at my new plantation. You will send the inclosed.———Mr. *Dutton* I believe is lost in his return to *England*. The ship foundered. I have preached this morning, and am to preach again. I snatch a few moments between sermons to write this. Our tender joint love to you all.

Yours, &c.

G. W.

LETTER DCXXXVIII.

To Mr. F———.

Bermudas, May 27, 1748.

My dear Mr. F———,

INCLOSED you have a letter which you may print in your weekly paper. It brings good news from this little pleasant spot. If you could print it on half a sheet of paper, to distribute among the *Bermudas* captains, it might perhaps be serviceable. The inhabitants here have received me so well, that I think publishing their kindness is a debt justly due to them. I am now waiting for a fair wind, and then we shall

sa.l

sail for *England*. The Governor's lady goes with me. His Excellency is very civil to me, and I believe many souls have been benefited by this visit to *Bermudas*. I desire to give the LORD JESUS all the glory. You will remember me to Mrs. F——, and all my dear *Philadelphia* friends. I do not forget them, and hope they will always remember, dear Sir,

Their and your most affectionate,
obliged friend and servant,
G. W.

LETTER DCXXXIX.

To Mrs. F———.

On board the Betsy, June 2, 1748.

TILL last night, I did not know that the last letter I wrote to you never came to hand. Mr. B—— tells me, that as he did not go according to his design he destroyed it. Accept therefore, dear Madam, a few more parting lines. They bring you good news indeed. The LORD JESUS has blessed my being at *Bermudas* very much. A good work I trust is begun in many hearts. I am now on board, and the wind is fair. We expect to sail this day. According to my present view, I intend to return to beloved *America* next year; which is one of the reasons, why I leave my dear yoke-fellow behind. O that I knew how it was with her! But I see that GOD will make those he loves, to live by faith and not by sense. Glorious privileges, though difficult to flesh and blood! As you are so dear a friend, I know you will do your utmost to comfort her. I have so ordered matters, that she need not be under any concern about providing for the families. GOD has caused the people in *Bermudas* to devise liberal things. Yet a little while, and I trust I shall, on the Orphan-house account, owe no man any thing but love." But I find I must fight every inch of my ground. Well! JESUS is on my side. I can do all things through him strengthening me. An entrance is now made into the *Islands*. The LORD, that has begun, can and will carry on his own work. You will all help me with your prayers. I must be content with dealing in general salutations, having not time to write more particulars. Pray remember me in the kindest manner to all your relations and all our dear friends. That grace,

mercy,

mercy, and peace may be multiplied upon all, is the earnest prayer of, dear Mrs. T——,

Your most affectionate friend, brother, and servant, in CHRIST JESUS,

G. W.

LETTER DCXL.

To the Rev. Mr. S——.

On board the Betsy, June 24, 1748.

Rev. and very dear Sir,

THOUGH we are about two hundred leagues from land, yet lest hurry of business should prevent me when we get a shore, I think proper to write you a few lines whilst I am on board.—Long before this reaches you, I suppose you will have heard of what the LORD of all Lords was pleased to do for me and his people at, and also when we sailed from, *Bermudas.* We sailed from thence just twenty-one days this morning, and have lived, as to the conveniencies of eating and drinking, like people that came from the continent, rather than one of the islands; so bountiful were our friends, whom we left behind us. Hitherto we have met with no storms or contrary winds, only it begins to head us now. But GOD, in his own time, I trust will carry us to our desired port. The first day we came out we were chased, and yesterday a large French vessel shot thrice, at and bore down upon us. We gave up all for gone. I was dressing myself in order to receive our expected visitors. In the mean while, our Captain cries, " the danger is over." The Frenchman turned about and left us. He was quite near, and we almost defenceless. Now we are so near the channel, we expect such alarms daily. If any thing happens extraordinary, I shall be particular. As for other things, I cannot say much. The Captain is exceeding civil, and I have my passage free; but all I have been able to do in the great cabbin in respect to religious duties, is to read the church prayers once every evening, and twice on the LORD's day. I have not preached yet; this may spare my lungs, but it grieves my heart. I long to be ashore, if it was for no other reason. Besides, I can do but little in respect to my writing. You may guess how it is, when we have four

gentle-

gentlewomen in the cabin. However, they have been, and are very civil, and I believe my being on board has been somewhat serviceable. My health I think is improved, and I have finished my abridgment of Mr. *Law*'s serious call, which I have endeavoured to gospelize. Yesterday I likewise made an end of revising all my journals. Blessed be GOD, for letting me have leisure to do it. I purpose to have a new edition before I see *America*. Alas! alas! In how many things have I judged and acted wrong.—I have been too rash and hasty in giving characters, both of places and persons. Being fond of scripture language, I have often used a style too apostolical, and at the same time I have been too bitter in my zeal. Wild-fire has been mixed with it, and I find that I frequently wrote and spoke in my own spirit, when I thought I was writing and speaking by the assistance of the spirit of GOD. I have likewise too much made inward impressions my rule of acting, and too soon and too explicitly published what had been better kept in longer, or told after my death. By these things I have given some wrong touches to GOD's ark, and hurt the blessed cause I would defend, and also stirred up needless opposition. This has humbled me much since I have been on board, and made me think of a saying of Mr. *Henry*'s, " *Joseph* had more *honesty* than he had *policy*, or he never would have told his dreams." At the same time, I cannot but bless, and praise, and magnify that good and gracious GOD, who filled me with so much of his holy fire, and carried me, a poor weak youth, through such a torrent both of popularity and contempt, and set so many seals to my unworthy ministrations. I bless him for ripening my judgment a little more, for giving me to see and confess, and I hope in some degree to correct and amend, some of my mistakes. I thank GOD for giving me grace to embark in such a blessed cause, and pray him to give me strength to hold on and increase in zeal and love to the end. Thus, dear Sir, have I unburdened my heart to you. I look upon you to be my *fidus achates*, and therefore deal thus freely. If I have time and freedom before we land, I think to write a short account of what has happened for these seven years last past; and when I get on shore, GOD willing, I purpose to revise and correct the first part of my life. I know you will pray that I may be directed and owned in every thing. I think often of, and pray for you, and as I intend writing to you again when I send this, I shall content myself at present with subscribing myself, Reverend and very dear Sir,

Your most affectionate obliged though
unworthy brother and servant,
G. W.

LETTER DCXLI.

To Mrs. L——.

Deal, July 5, 1748.

Very dear and Honoured Mother,

ARE you yet in the land of the living, or rather among the dead? shall I have the pleasure of receiving one more letter from you, and asking your blessing once more? Next post, I hope that the two former of these will be answered in the affirmative, and in a week or two I trust God will grant me the last. About a month ago I left the island of *Bermudas*, where my poor labours have been greatly blessed, and your unworthy son has been honoured with many honours. I am now come once more to see my friends in my native country, and settle some affairs, and then return to *America* again. My dear yoke-fellow I have left behind, to take care of two families. I have been several times just upon the brink of eternity since I saw you, but am now a little recruited. O that my health and strength may be wholly employed for that JESUS, who has done such great things for me! His blood and cross, my ever honoured mother, I trust are exceeding precious to your soul. O that I may see you laden with holiness, and bringing forth much fruit in your old age! I could say more, but have several other letters to write. As I know not how your outward affairs are situated, or where you live for a certainty, I can only send cordial and general salutations to all friends and relations. I hope you will be pleased to let me know whether you stand in need of any thing, and not cease to pray for, honoured mother,

Your ever dutiful though unworthy son,
G. W.

LETTER DCXLII.

To Mr. G—— H——.

Deal, July 5, 1748.

AND how does my dear old friend Mr. H——? Surely he will send me a line now! For through the goodness of an infinitely gracious and condescending Saviour, I am once more arrived at my native country. My last excursion was to *Bermudas*. We left those islands a month ago, and GOD was pleased to set his seal to my unworthy ministry in a very glorious manner. I know you will be thankful in my behalf, and let me know next post how the brethren are in and about *Gloucestershire*. I rejoice to find that you still go on steadily and are not ashamed of the gospel of CHRIST. Why should you? Have you not found it by happy experience to be the power of GOD unto salvation? Go on then, my dear Sir, and prove the strength of JESUS to be yours. I long to see you, that we may talk of redeeming love, and feel our hearts warm with an holy fire from GOD's altar. Are the dear old men, the Reverend Messrs. S—— and P——, yet alive? Pray send them my most dutiful and affectionate respects, and let them know, that an entrance I trust is now made into one of the islands for the glorious gospel of the Son of GOD. O that I was able to fly from pole to pole upon this blessed errand. But alas! my wings are clipped. My bodily health is much impaired, and I hoped ere now to have taken my last flight to heaven. But it seems that happy hour is not yet come. Well, welcome life, welcome death, so that JESUS, my dear JESUS, may be glorified in both! Pray that we may shortly meet in the fulness of the blessing of the gospel of peace. I subscribe myself, my very dear *Gaius*,

Yours most affectionately in CHRIST,

G. W.

LETTER DCXLIII.

To the Rev. Mr. J—— or C—— H——.

Deal, July 5, 1748.

WILL you not be glad to hear that the GOD of the sea and the GOD of the dry land hath brought me to my native country once more? I came last from the *Bermudas*, where the friend of sinners has been pleased to own my poor labours abundantly. I hope, I come in the spirit of love, desiring to study and pursue those things which make for peace. This is the language of my heart,

> O let us find the ancient way,
> Our wond'ring foes to move;
> And force the heathen world to say,
> See how these Christians love.

I purpose, GOD willing, to be in *London* in a few days. In the mean while, I salute you and all the followers of the blessed Lamb of GOD most heartily.—Be pleased to pray for, and give thanks in behalf of, Reverend and dear brother,

Yours most affectionately in CHRIST,

G. W.

LETTER DCXLIV.

To Mr. F———.

My very dear Friend, London, *July* 7, 1748.

I Have but just time to inform you, that after a pleasant passage of a month, a good and gracious GOD brought me hither in safety, where I have been received by thousands with a joy that almost overcame both them and me. I have preached once, and am this evening to preach again. One large church is open. I cannot now descend to particulars.—I can only send you a thousand thanks for all favours, beg my kindest salutations may be presented to all friends, and entreat the continuance of your most fervent prayers in behalf of, my dear host and hostess,

Yours as usual,

G. W.

LETTER DCXLV.

To Mr. H———.

My very dear Friend, London, *July,* 7, 1748.

THOUGH I suppose you will see my dear wife's letter, yet I must send you a few lines. They bring you news of my safe arrival, and wonderfully kind acceptance in my native country. The blessings bestowed on me, have already, through the thanksgivings of thousands, redounded to the glory of God. Words cannot express the joy that has possessed the hearts of the people. I hear that the minds even of enemies are much softened. I came at a critical juncture. I hear Mr. —— has stood up for me at C——, and that one who preached before the trustees hath spoke honourably of *Bethesda*. If God is pleased to send us a general peace, I hope *Georgia* will lift up its drooping head. You may depend on hearing from me as often as possible. You will remember me to all friends. I can only beg you to give thanks, and pray for, my very dear Sir,

Yours as usual,
G. W.

LETTER DCXLVI.

To the Rev. Mr. H——.

Rev. and dear Brother, London, *July* 8, 1748.

GLAD am I, yea very glad to hear that you are yet alive and have grace given you to adhere to Jesus Christ and his eternal truths. I am very much pleased to find that you appear in print, and that such encouragement is given you to print again. I hope the glorious *Emmanuel* smiles upon your ministerial labours, and gives you many living witnesses, that the truths which you preach are according to Godliness. Go on, my dear old friend, and prove the strength of Jesus to be thine. Through his infinite and unmerited goodness I am once more safe in my native country. *Bermudas* was the last place where I have been preaching. I left many souls under concern. Many precious souls (O free grace!) have received me here in great love, and I have been enabled twice to preach, to a multitude of poor sinners, the unsearchable riches of Jesus Christ. My bodily health is much impared; but through divine assistance, I will go on working for Jesus of *Nazareth*, 'till I can work no more. I could say much of his love, but have a deal of business before me. Accept this as a token of unfeigned love and respect from, my very dear Sir,

Your affectionate though unworthy brother
and servant for Christ's sake,
G. W.

LETTER

LETTER DCXLVII.

To Mr. C——.

Dear Mr. C——, London, *July* 8, 1748.

I Am come over with a sincere desire to pursue the things which make for peace. Consequently I must hear and see for myself, before I determine upon any thing. I have heard nothing of Mrs. D——'s writing concerning you. All I can say is, that by what you have published and I have perused, you have unhappily fallen into some principles, which are contrary to the revealed will of GOD.—But I speak not this to begin a dispute. I shall be glad to see and converse with you. As for your preaching in *Moor-fields*, they are no doubt as free for you as another. I intend preaching there, GOD willing, on *Sunday* evening. That you may have a clear head and a clean heart, is the hearty prayer of, dear Sir,

Your affectionate friend and servant,

G. W.

LETTER DCXLVIII.

To Mr. K——.

My dear Brother, London, *July* 12, 1748.

AT my first arrival, you judged right that I am pretty much taken up; however, I must snatch a few minutes to answer your kind, very kind letter. Blessed be GOD, that the mercies bestowed on hell-deserving me, have, through the thanksgivings of many, redounded to the glory of the blessed JESUS. O that the same prayers that have drawn me hither, may draw down showers of blessings upon GOD's church. Now I am come, do you and my other friends continue to pray and hold up your hands, and in the strength of JESUS CHRIST I will go on fighting. The fields seem to be as white as ever. I trust the shout of a king is among us. O for humility, love and zeal! O for that mind, which was in CHRIST JESUS! I trust that the members of your society are copying after our great Exemplar. As soon as possible I purpose to come down and see you. I thank you for what you have done in respect to the Orphan-house. I could wish the cash was remitted to *London* immediately, because I want to pay it away. Surely the time will come, when I shall owe no man any thing but love. Then, and 'till the day of my death, *Poor, yet making many rich*, shall be my motto. You will remember me in the kindest manner to all the followers of the Lamb; and that you may be filled with all his fulness, is the prayer of

Yours, &c.

G. W.

LETTER DCXLIX.

To Mr. C——.

London, July 12, 1748.

My very dear Friend and Brother,

THOUGH I am pretty much engaged, yet I cannot let your kind letter lie by me two posts unanswered. Blessed be GOD that you yet retain your simple heart, and are determined to know nothing but JESUS CHRIST and him crucified. With this mind, may you climb up higher and higher in the church of *England*, in order that you may move in a superiour orb, and your light shine with greater and more diffusive ardor round the church of GOD! O my dear Mr. C——, what has the Redeemer done for us! What is he still doing! It would gladden your heart to see what a turn affairs take in *London*. I have preached twice in *St. Bartholomew's* church, and helped to administer the sacrament once. I believe on *Sunday* we had a thousand communicants. *Moorfields* are as white as ever unto harvest, and multitudes flock to hear the word. The old spirit of love and power seems to be revived amongst us. What am I, what am I, that JESUS CHRIST should still delight to honour me? O for a single eye and a simple heart unto the end! By what I can judge, satan will allure some with his golden bait. "In all times of our wealth, good LORD deliver us." Blessed be GOD, I am not much in danger of having too much of this world's goods at present. My outward affairs are yet behind hand. I long to owe no man any thing but love. As for your cautions, they shall be observed punctually. Never mind me, let my name die every where, let even my friends forget me, if by that means the cause of the blessed JESUS may be promoted. In

about

about a fortnight I hope to see you at my brother's. I hear he is better. O that he may come out for CHRIST! I think I have now answered your request, and sent you a long letter. I hope to hear from you again before I see you. My hearty respects await Mr. G————. I trust he determines to know nothing but JESUS CHRIST, and him crucified. Commending you to his mercy, and myself to the continuance of your prayers, I subscribe myself, very dear Sir,

Yours eternally in the blessed JESUS,
G. W.

LETTER DCL.

To the Honourable ——— R———, Esq; of Bermuda.

Honoured Sir, London, *July* 12, 1748.

GRATITUDE constrains me to embrace the first opportunity of informing you of our safe arrival at our wished-for port. We struck ground, I think, the 27th day after we set sail, and landed at *Deal* the 30th. We were chased the first afternoon, and prepared for going to prison twice or thrice. But our fears were groundless; there was a cessation of arms with *France*, though we knew it not, and some ships that we thought were pursuing us proved to be *English* men of war. We had plenty of provisions, and met with no storms or bad weather worth the speaking of. Other particulars, I suppose, Captain *E*———, who was very civil, will inform you. The evening after we landed at *Deal*, I was at Mr. *D*——— and *E*———'s, before I came to my own lodgings. They were very glad to hear from *Bermudas*. Since then, words cannot well express how joyful my friends were to see me once more in the land of the living. I find the news-papers had buried me ever since *April* last; but it seems I am not to die, but live: O that it may be to declare the works of the LORD! My obligations to do so, are much increased by the mercies conferred on me at *Bermudas*, and during my voyage. Surely the stones would cry out against me, did I not set forth the riches of redeeming love. Blessed be GOD, I have had several opportunities of doing so, since my arrival. Last Lord's-day I believe we had a thousand communicants. In a few weeks, GOD willing, I purpose to see *Scotland*, and then shall do myself the pleasure of writing to, or waiting on your brother. In the mean time, I shall, as opportunity offers, write to some more of my *Bermudas* friends, whom I desire never to forget at the throne of grace. You and yours, honoured Sir, will be pleased to accept my most cordial salutations. That you and your house may serve the LORD here, and live with him eternally in the kingdom of heaven hereafter, is the hearty prayer of, honoured Sir,

Your most obliged humble servant,

G. W.

LETTER DCLI.

To Mr. H———.

London, July 16, 1748.

My very dear Mr. H———,

I Thank you for your speedy and kind answer to my last poor letter, and heartily pray GOD, if it be agreeable to his will, yet to prolong your life, and make your pen the pen of a ready writer. I shall take it as a great favour, if you will order me a set of your works. I shall peruse them with the greatest pleasure, and send a set of them also abroad. Blessed be GOD, for causing you to write so to suit the taste of the polite world! O that they may be won over to admire Him, who is indeed altogether lovely! But what shall I say to your kind intended present? It is like my dear old friend. Mr. ——— was so kind as to come and see me yesterday. I shewed him your letter. He expects to see me at his house. GOD willing, *possible* I will pay him a visit. O that he may recover his *love*! For ever adored be free grace: many souls seem to *be awakened*. Multitudes flock to hear. My health sometimes *improves*, and our LORD makes it exceeding pleasant to *me to preach* to poor sinners his unsearchable riches. O when shall we get within the veil! Thanks be to GOD, it cannot be long. We are both sickly. LORD give us patience to wait till our bodily change come! To the Redeemer's tender mercy do I most affectionately commit you; and entreat, while life and breath lasts, you will not cease praying for one, who, though less than the least of all, yet for JESUS CHRIST's sake subscribes himself, my very dear friend,

Ever yours,

G. W.

LETTER DCLII.

To Mr. K―――.

Very dear Sir, London, *July,* 19, 1748.

I Thank you for your kind answer to my last, as well as for all other favours. Before I heard from you, I had been informed from several quarters, that Satan hath been sifting all our poor societies. This is no more than I expected. But let us take courage, dear Sir; JESUS CHRIST prays for us. His truths are great and shall prevail. At *London,* affairs seem to be taking a good turn. The LORD JESUS comes among us as in the days of old. I trust by and by we shall see good days at *Exon* again. When I shall go there is uncertain. Next week, GOD willing, I must be at *Bristol,* and after that I must go to the *Welch* association. Glad shall I be to hear whatever you have to offer. May the LORD JESUS give us a right judgment in all things! When the time of my seeing *Exon* is fixed, I will endeavour to send you previous notice. In the mean-while, let you and yours accept most hearty love and cordial salutations from one, who, though less than the least of all saints, begs leave to subscribe himself, very dear Mr. K――,

Yours most affectionately in CHRIST JESUS,

G. W.

LETTER DCLIII.

To the Reverend Mr. C――.

London, *July* 20, 1748.

My very dear Friend and Brother,

NEITHER length of time, nor change of place, I trust, will ever estrange us from each other.—Though through the goodness of GOD I am now in *England,* yet I cannot help daily thinking upon you and my other dear friends in *America.* I have been prayed over hither: do you strive to pray me over again to *South-Carolina.* Much business now lies upon my hands. It is too much for one man, to be received as I have been by thousands. The thoughts of it lay me low, but I cannot get low enough. I would willingly sink into nothing

thing before the blessed JESUS, my All in All. Next week I hope to see *Bristol*, where I shall not fail to enquire about your minister, and send you word accordingly. I hope you do not forget *Bethesda* or *Providence*. O my dear yoke-fellow, how is she carried through the Summer's sultry heat? May the LORD be her helper! You will not fail to give my most cordial respects to Mrs. B——, Dr. B——, his wife, and all friends. Fail not, O fail not to pray heartily for,

Yours most affectionately in CHRIST JESUS,
G. W.

LETTER DCLIV.

To the Reverend Mr. D——.

London, July 23, 1748.

My very Dear Mr. D——.

GLAD was I, yea very glad to receive one more letter from such a valuable and dearly beloved friend and brother. I have often enquired after you since my arrival, and only multiplicity of business prevented your hearing from me. Glory be to the blessed JESUS, for supporting and carrying you through so many difficulties that necessarily attend the pastoral office. I find more and more, my dear Sir, that experience is only to be learned in the school of tribulation; and as we undergo the sufferings mentioned in the scriptures, so far and no farther do we understand the scriptures themselves. O that patience may have its perfect work, and we may be enabled to the end of our days to sanctify the LORD GOD in our hearts! As for poor *Scotland*, what shall I say? Our LORD's words must be fulfilled, "The first shall be last, and the last first." Awakening times are always like the Spring. Many blossoms appear, and perhaps but little solid fruit is produced after all. O that the Lord of the harvest, if I am to see *Scotland* again, may send me to call some backsliders to return. Glory be to GOD, affairs are taking a happy turn here. Old love, and old power, seem to be reviving among us. I preach to multitudes daily. Many are already brought under new awakenings. On *Monday* next I set out, GOD willing, for *Gloucester*, and intend returning in about three weeks.—How glad shall I then be to see Mr. D——. My dear

dear yoke-fellow would rejoice to do so too; but I left her abroad in the tent.—Perhaps she may come over soon. Pray remember her, and, my dear Sir,

Yours, &c.

G. W.

LETTER DCLV.

To Dr. R———.

Honoured Sir, London, *July* 22, 1748.

LOVE and gratitude constrain me to send you a few lines. They come to inform you, that a sense of the almost innumerable favours you was pleased to confer on me, when under your tuition, is yet deeply engraven upon the tables of my heart. That GOD, whom I endeavour to serve in the gospel of his dear Son, will richly reward you in that day. By his assistance, I still continue to preach the everlasting gospel in various places; and, I trust, not without some abiding good effect. Indeed, last year I was in hopes I should have been translated to those blissful regions, where the wicked cease from troubling, and where the weary be at rest. But it seems, I am not yet to die, but live. O that it may be to declare the works of the LORD! I think his glory is the main principle of my acting. I want to bring souls, not to a party, much less to lead them from the established church, but to a sense of their undone condition by nature, and to true faith in JESUS CHRIST, which will be evidenced by a holy life, and an universal, chearful obedience to all the commands of GOD. In this, honoured Sir, however you may judge of the means and method of my proceeding, I am persuaded you wish me success. Your's, both in respect to this life and another, I have much at heart. That the great shepherd and bishop of souls may assist you in the oversight of all under your care, and in the future state receive you with an *Euge bone,* in the presence of applauding angels, and spirits of just men made perfect, is the earnest prayer of, honoured Sir,

Your most unworthy, though dutiful pupil, and very humble servant,

G. W.

LETTER DCLVI.

To Governer Thomas.

Honoured Sir, London, *July* 22, 1748.

THOUGH I am uncertain about your being in town, yet I cannot leave it, without leaving a few lines of acknowledgment, for those many favours you and your worthy lady were pleased to confer upon me and mine abroad. Glad were we, yea exceeding glad to hear of your safe arrival in *England*, and gracious reception at court. May you so live in this world, as to be received with expressions of joy and approbation by the King of kings in the world to come! I hope, honour'd Sir, that the change of climate has been conducive to your health, and the health also of dear little Miss, and her honoured Mamma. I beg my most dutiful respects may find acceptance, honoured Sir, both with them and you. At my return to *London*, which I suppose will be in about three weeks, I purpose doing myself the honour of waiting upon you in person. In the mean while, I beg leave, with the warmest affection, to subscribe myself, honoured Sir,

Your most obliged, obedient humble servant,

G. W.

LETTER DCLVII.

To the Reverend Mr. S———.

London, *July* 24, 1748.

Reverend and very dear Sir,

SINCE my arrival in *England*, (now three weeks) I have sent several packets to *America*. This brings you the welcome tidings of the LORD's continuing to bless my poor administrations, and causing his word to run and be glorified. Particulars I cannot descend to now. My hands are quite full of business. I am assisted also in temporals, and hope, ere I see *America* again, to be delivered from my outward Orphanhouse embarrassments. I have almost fixed on persons to come over to *Bethesda*. With them I intend sending you some things, which I believe you will be glad to see. *Antinomianism* has made havock here, but I trust the worst is over. Our

scattered

scattered troops begin to unite again; and indeed the shout of a king is amongst us. I trust that the glorious *Emmanuel* waves his banner also over you, and causes you to rejoice in his great salvation. That you, and all my dear friends and benefactors may sit under his shadow with unspeakable delight, is the hearty prayer of, reverend and very dear Sir,

Your most affectionate, obliged friend,
brother, and servant in our common Lord,
G. W.

LETTER DCLVIII.

To the Reverend Mr. S———.

Waterford, August 3, 1748.

Reverend and very dear Sir,

I Have written to you more than once since my arrival; notwithstanding that, I must write to you again. The bearer is a man of good report, a *Dissenter*, and brings I believe a testimonial with him. He has met with disappointments in the world, and goes out to be overseer to some gentleman's plantation.—I believe he would be glad to be introduced to some of our religious friends. I write this from *Wales*, where I am come to attend on a quarterly association. Yesterday I left *Bristol*, where great multitudes came to hear, and the arm of the LORD was revealed. Next week, GOD willing, I purpose to return to *London*, and after a short stay there, to go into the *West* and other parts of *England*. I believe that *Ireland* and *Scotland* must be left till next Spring. I am as well in health as I have been for a long while; and GOD is pleased to give me the affections of his people, in a manner I dared not expect. But is there any thing too hard for the LORD? You will continue to pray for me. I expect a loving, chiding letter from you. I have several things to send you, and at present can only beg you and all friends to accept of my hearty love and thanks, and subscribe myself, very dear Sir,

Your most affectionate, obliged friend,
and servant in CHRIST,
G. W.

LETTER DCLIX.

To Mr. Wm. G——.

Waterford, August 3, 1748.

My dear little Man,

I Do not forget the promise I made you when in town. As a proof of it, I snatch a few moments to send you a line. How will it find you? May I answer for you? Upon the stretch for GOD, and giving diligence to make your calling and election sure. O that there may be always in you such a mind! You know how many once did run well; but the devil and the world working upon their wicked hearts, have hindered them. Alas! how is their gold become dim, and their fine gold changed! Let him that thinketh he stands take heed lest he fall. Be jealous of yourself, and hang continually on the LORD JESUS. You are now growing up, and are about to launch into a wicked world. You know how strangely satan will tempt you to love it. Nothing can keep you, but the mighty power of GOD. Ask, and you shall have it exerted in your behalf. I could enlarge, but have not time. Perhaps next week I may be in *London*. The LORD JESUS has blessed my being in the country. The fields are white, ready unto harvest. My love to your sister. May she be a *Ruth*. For the present I must bid you farewel, after having subscribed myself,

Yours, &c.

G. W.

LETTER DCLX.

To the Reverend Mr. M——.

Mitchel-Dean, August 6, 1748.

THOUGH I am now upon the road in my way to *Gloucester*, yet I cannot help dropping you a few lines. Excess of business, not want of respect, has prevented my writing to you before. You, and yours, and all my dear *Scotch* friends, have been, still are, and by the grace of GOD always will be much upon my heart. I long to hear that their souls prosper. Perhaps next Spring I may pay them another
visit

visit. The remainder of this year must be spent in visiting *England* and *Wales*. Blessed be GOD, there is a prospect of a revival where I have been already, at *London*, *Bristol*, and *Wales*, from whence I am just now come. Our LORD hath been pleased to lift up the light of his countenance upon his poor people. I beg, reverend Sir, the continuance of your prayers, that I may be stedfast, unmoveable, always abounding in the work of the LORD. At present, through grace, I am willing to spend and be spent for the good of precious and immortal souls. My native air seems to improve my health, and I trust ere long I shall be lively and strong as an eagle. I suppose you have heard that the word of the LORD has been glorified in *Bermudas*. In a short time, I hope the adjacent islands will know what it is to feel the sun of righteousness arising with healing under his wings.

> *Blest is faith that trusts his power,*
> *Blest are saints that wait his hour;*
> *Haste, great conqueror, bring it near;*
> *Let the glorious close appear.*

Reverend Sir, I could write more; but must away. I beg my most cordial respects may be accepted by your whole fire-side and all friends. I intend writing to dear Mr. *M———* soon. In the mean while, I must haste to subscribe myself, reverend and very dear Sir,

Your most affectionate, obliged younger brother, and willing servant for CHRIST's sake,

G. W.

LETTER DCLXI.

To Lady H———.

London, August 10, 1748.

Honoured Madam,

THIS morning, just after I had begun to put pen to paper, a friend told me, that since I had been in the country, a letter had been sent me by a lady out of *Scotland*. I opened it, and with a pleasing surprize found it was from your Ladyship, to whom I was then writing. Blessed be GOD, that your soul, honoured Madam, is yet held in life! I hope it does and will prosper; and

and however others may grow lukewarm and lose their first love, yet you will say, "A for me and my household, we will serve the LORD." By four years fresh experience, I find that this indeed, in every respect, is the whole of man. O how good has the blessed Redeemer been both to my soul and body! Out of how many and great deaths has he delivered me! And yet, honoured Madam, vile as I am, he is pleased still to honour me. Multitudes flock to hear the word, and our LORD is pleased to administer feed to the sower. Early in the Spring, GOD willing, do I purpose to visit dear *Scotland* once more. That the LORD of all Lords may abundantly bless your Ladyship, and all your connections in this and a better world, is the earnest prayer of, honoured Madam,

Your Ladyship's most obliged,
obedient humble servant,

G. W.

LETTER DCLXII.

To the Reverend Mr. J———.

London, August 11, 1748.

My very dear Mr. J———,

YOUR kind letter, which I received but yesterday, having been taking a little tour in the country, both grieved and pleased me. Glad was I to find, that my dear old friend had not forgotten me, and yet sorry as it were, that I had not wrote to him first. I was just going to put pen to paper, when yours was brought to my hands. I read it with joy, and now embrace the first opportunity of answering it with the greatest pleasure. These words concerning our LORD have always been weighty on my heart, "Having loved his own, he loved them unto the end." They therefore that are most like him, will be most steady in their friendship, and not very readily given to change. O my dear Sir, what has the Redeemer done for us since we used to take such sweet counsel together at *Oxford*! Blessed be his name for giving you a heart still to preach among poor sinners the unsearchable riches of CHRIST. May you go on and prosper, and, maugre all opposition, see Dagon fall every where before the ark. As for me, I am a poor worthless pilgrim, and thought long ere now to be be with him, who has loved and given himself for me.—But it seems I am not yet to die, but live. O that it may be to declare the work of the LORD! I think this is the thirteenth province I have been in within this twelvemonth, in each of which our LORD has been pleased to set his seal to my unworthy ministry. I came from *Bermudas* last, where I left many souls seeking after JESUS of *Nazareth*. In *London, Bristol, Gloucester*, and *Wales*, the glorious *Emmanuel*, since my arrival, has appeared to his people. In about a fortnight I purpose leaving town again in order to go a circuit of about five hundred miles. I need not desire you to pray for me; I need not tell you how glad I shall be whenever opportunity offers, to see you face to face. In the mean while, let us correspond by letter. May JESUS bless it to us both! I return cordial respects to Lady *M*——. I pray the LORD to bless her and her little nursery. For the present adieu. I am, my very dear Mr. *J*-——,

Ever yours,

G. W.

LETTER DCLXIII.

To Mr. S——.

Dear Sir, London, *August* 16, 1748.

GLAD shall I be to have the pleasure of your dining with me on *Thursday* between twelve and one. If you please, you may leave your chaise and horses at the other end of the town, and ride to my lodgings in an hackney coach. Or if you choose to come in your chaise, we have inns near at hand. I shall devote *Thursday* afternoon to you; and if you please to stay the evening and hear me preach, and then sup and take a bed at our house afterwards, I shall be much obliged to you. You need only enquire for the tabernacle new house near *Moorfields*. I hope matters will be so ordered, that you will be *solus cum solo*. I pity persons in your circumstances, and humbly hope that you will be one of *Nicodemus's* children every way. You know, though he came by night at first, yet afterwards he was as bold as a lion. Go on, dear Sir: " To him that hath, shall be given." CHRIST will not quench the smoaking flax, nor break the bruised reed. That his love may be shed abroad in your heart, that you may be enabled

bled to confess him before men, and be confessed by him before his Father and the holy angels in heaven, is the earnest prayer of, dear Sir,

> Your most affectionate friend, and
> willing servant for JESUS CHRIST,
> G. W.

LETTER DCLXIV.

To Lord ———.

My Lord, London, *August* 19, 1748.

THOUGH I expect to be in *Scotland* in about three weeks, yet I cannot defer writing to your Lordship any longer. I hope this will find your worthy lady trampling upon the lust of the eye, the lust of the flesh, and the pride of life, and steadily pursuing the one thing needful. I doubt not but you both have found, that the Redeemer's service has been perfect freedom, and that in keeping of his commandments there is even a present great reward. Blessed be GOD, I can say so by happy and repeated experience. The blessed JESUS is pleased still to own and bless my poor labours, and gives me encouragement to go on fighting his battles. My outward man decays; but I trust I shall die in the field of battle. I want to learn what it is to be a good soldier of JESUS CHRIST. I could enlarge, but multiplicity of business obliges me to be brief. I hope my most dutiful respects will find acceptance with good Lady ———, Lady ———, and all your Lordship's fire side.—That you all may be filled with the fulness of GOD, is the hearty prayer of, my Lord,

> Your Lordship's most obliged, obedient servant,
> G. W.

LETTER DCLXV.

To Mr. B———.

London, *August* 20, 1748.

My very dear Brother,

I Thank you for your kind letter. It was put into my hands just as I was leaving *Bristol*, and ever since, I have been so busy, that till now I could not redeem a few moments to answer

answer it. I am glad that you, and the dear brethren you mentioned, are so well and happy. They are my old hearty friends as well as you. I salute them tenderly, and long for that time when we shall all surround the throne, and throw our crowns before the Lamb who sitteth thereon for ever. There we shall be all unisons: there we shall have clear heads, and perfectly clean and purified hearts. Till then we must agree, to disagree in many things, except to love and serve him, who loved us and gave himself for us, who has redeemed us unto GOD by his blood, hath made us kings and priests unto GOD, and enables us to reign over sin, death, and hell, even whilst we are here on earth. O glorious mystery! Well may the angels desire to look into it. I could enlarge, but other affairs of our LORD's kingdom call me away. For the present, adieu. I return your cordial salutations in the heartiest manner. If our LORD should call me to *Wiltshire*, I would come and see you. At present I am bound to *Scotland*. I trust we can say, JESUS is with us here. That he may be evermore with you and all his sincere followers, is the earnest prayer of, my very dear brother,

Yours most affectionately in him that was dead, but is alive again, and liveth for evermore,

G. W.

LETTER DCLXVI.

To Lady H———.

Honoured Madam, *August* 21, 1748.

I Received your Ladyship's letter late last night, and write this to inform your Ladyship that I am quite willing to comply with your invitation. As I am to preach, GOD willing, at *St. Bartholomew*'s on *Wednesday* evening, I will wait upon your Ladyship the next morning, and spend the whole day at *Chelsea*. Blessed be GOD, that the rich and great begin to have an hearing ear. I think it is a good sign that our LORD intends to give to some at least, an obedient heart. Surely your Ladyship and Madam E——— are only the first fruits. May you increase and multiply! I believe you will. How wonderfully does our Redeemer deal with souls. If they will hear the gospel only under a cieled roof, ministers shall be sent to them there. If only in a church, or a field, they shall have it there.

there. A word in the leſſon, when I was laſt at your Ladyſhip's, ſtruck me. " *Paul* preached privately to thoſe that were of reputation." This muſt be the way I preſume of dealing with the nobility, who yet know not the LORD. O that I may be enabled, when called to preach to any of them, ſo to preach as to win their ſouls to the bleſſed JESUS! I know your Ladyſhip will pray that it may be ſo. As for my poor prayers, ſuch as they are, your Ladyſhip hath them every day. That the bleſſed JESUS may make your Ladyſhip happily inſtrumental in bringing many of the noble and mighty to the ſaving knowledge of his eternal Self, and water your own ſoul every moment, is the continual requeſt of, honoured Madam,

Your Ladyſhip's moſt obliged, obedient humble ſervant,

G. W.

LETTER DCLXVII.

To Judge B———.

Honoured Sir, *London, Auguſt* 22, 1748.

I Think it is now high time for me to ſend you a line of thanks, for the favours you was pleaſed to confer on me when at the *Bermudas.* They are not, and I truſt never will be forgotten by me, whilſt I am on this ſide eternity. The ſame good hand that was with me abroad, hath ſafely brought, and ſince my arrival bleſſed me much at home. I am daily employed in that delightful work of preaching to poor ſinners the unſearchable riches of JESUS CHRIST! Once a week I read prayers and preach in one of the largeſt of the *London* churches. Multitudes flock there and in the fields, and I truſt much good is done to many. I have been lately a three hundred mile circuit, and purpoſe, GOD willing, to ſet out for *Scotland* in about eight days. At my return, I hope to hear by ſome ſhip or another that all is well at *Bermudas.* I beg my moſt dutiful reſpects may find acceptance with his Excellency. I endeavoured to be as obliging as I could to his lady and little maſter, whom I ſuppoſe the Governor will have heard from before this comes to hand. I have taken the freedom to ſend him a volume of my ſermons. I intend writing to Colonel *H———* another opportunity. I have ſent

to

to Colonel G—— and some others already. Multiplicity of business prevents my writing to more at present. Be pleased however to present my most cordial respects to him and his family, to your whole fire side, and all enquiring friends. I hope you will accept the same yourself, from, honoured Sir,

Your most obliged humble servant,

G. W.

LETTER DCLXVIII.

To Captain J—— D——.

Very dear Sir, London, *August* 22, 1748.

I Have already written to you and other friends since my arrival at *London*. With this, I send a box of books to be disposed of among my dear *Bermudas* acquaintance. To some I have affixed their names, and lest I should have forgotten any (as undoubtedly I have, being so much hurried) I have sent half a dozen of my volumes of twenty three sermons, to be disposed of with the small tracts, as you shall think proper. I begin now to expect the *Diana*, or some other ship, to bring me an account of the welfare of you and my other beloved friends. A sense of your manifold kindnesses lies yet upon my heart, and I always endeavour to remember them before Him, who has promised that a cup of cold water given in the name of a disciple, shall in no wise lose its reward. Had I time equal to my will, I would write many letters, but a variety of business prevents. Be pleased therefore to beg my friends to accept general thanks and cordial salutations. In a few days I purpose setting out for *Scotland*, and hope to return to *America* next year. But future things belong to GOD. A wide scene opens here, and I would willingly be disposed of as seemeth best to my heavenly Father. To his tender and never-failing mercy, do I earnestly commend you and dear Mrs. D——, your little ones, all your relations, and the whole circle of my friends. That you may be blessed with all the blessings of the everlasting covenant, is the hearty desire and continual prayer of, very dear Sir,

Your most affectionate, obliged
friend and humble servant,

G. W.

To Mr. ———.

Very dear Sir, London, *August* 12, 1748.

IF any thing I have said or written has been made any way serviceable to your better part, I thank the LORD of all Lords, whose mercy endureth for ever. I trust the language of my heart towards JESUS CHRIST, is this:

If thou excuse, then work thy will,
By so unfit an instrument;
It will at once thy goodness shew,
And prove thy power omnipotent.

I thank you, dear Sir, for your concern about my health. If it should please GOD to bring me back from *Scotland* to winter in town, I have thoughts of submitting to some regimen or another. At present I think it impracticable. On *Tuesday*, GOD willing, I purpose to set out, and to go by the way of *York*. I suppose it will be about a two months circuit. My journals, and last five sermons, I shall send to Mr. D———, with the journal that I have corrected. Alas, dear Sir, so many things want altering, that what you propose for *Andrew* to do, would be for him a too laborious task. I heartily wish that you and doctor D——— and Mr. H——— would be pleased to revise them. I intend publishing a new edition soon. Mr. H——— is of a different opinion from Dr. D——— concerning the seventh of the *Romans*. *Adhuc sub judice lis est.* I always do as you desire in respect to Mr. W———'s sermons. My prayer for him, for myself, and friends, is this; "LORD, give us clear heads and clean hearts." I would recommend bishop Beveridge's sermons more, but they are too voluminous for the common people, and I have not read them all. I expect you will do this yourself, dear Sir, by and by, from the pulpit, and what is more, recommend his and your master to the choice of poor sinners. You have now by your excellent letter publickly confessed him. The eyes of all will be now upon you, to see whether the truths you have delivered to others, are transcribed into your own heart and copied in your life. Now indeed may you cry,

O for

O for a strong, a lasting faith!
To credit what the Almighty saith!

Now the language of your soul should be, "how holy ought I to be in all manner of conversation and godliness." Now, dear Sir, let me entreat you to keep from trimming, or so much as attempting to reconcile two irreconcilable differences, GOD and the world, CHRIST and *Belial*. You know me too well to suppose I want you to turn cynic. No, live a social life. But then, dear Sir, beg of the LORD JESUS to free you from the love of the world; thence, thence arises that fear of man which now so shackles and disturbs your soul. Dare, dear Sir, to be singularly good. If CHRIST be your Saviour, make him a present of your pretty character. Honour him, and he will honour you. He indulges you much, and gently leads you on. Let the same love constrain you, dear Sir, to press forwards, and never rest till you can give up children, name, life, and all into his hands who gave his precious blood for you. I could enlarge, but am called away. I make no apology for this; you say you are my friend.—Accept this, dear Sir, as a token of my believing you sincere in that profession, from

Yours most affectionately in CHRIST JESUS,
G. W.

LETTER DCLXX.

To Lady H——.

Honoured Madam, *London, August* 22, 1748.

EVER since the reading your Ladyship's condescending letter, my soul (as indeed through grace it was in a degree before) has been overpowered with his presence, who is All in All. When your Ladyship stiled me "your friend," I was amazed at your condescension. But when I thought that JESUS was my friend, it quite overcame me, and made me to lie prostrate before him, crying, Why me, why me? I just now rose from the ground, after praying the LORD of all Lords to water your soul, honoured madam, every moment. As there seems to be a door opening for the nobility to hear the gospel, I will defer my journey till *Thursday*, and, GOD willing, preach at your Ladyship's on *Tuesday*. In the mean while

while I will wait upon or send to the Count the *Danish* embassador's brother, who favours me with his company on *Monday* to dine. On *Monday* morning from nine to near eleven I will be at your Ladyship's, and wait to know your order concerning *Tuesday*. O that GOD may be with and make me humble! I am ashamed to think your Ladyship will admit me under your roof, much more am I amazed that the LORD JESUS will make use of such a creature as I am. Under a sense of this, I write to your Ladyship now. It is late, and my poor body calls to rest. But as I am to preach four times to-morrow, I thought it my duty to send these few lines to your Ladyship to night. Quite astonished at your Ladyship's condescension, and the unmerited superabounding grace and goodness of Him who has loved me and given himself for me, I subscribe myself, honoured madam,

Your Ladyship's most obliged, obedient,

humble and willing servant,

G. W.

LETTER DCLXXI.

To Lady H——.

Honoured Madam,   *London, Sept.* 1, 1748.

ALTHOUGH it is time for me to be setting out, yet I dare not leave town without dropping a few lines, gratefully to acknowledge the many favours I have received from your Ladyship, especially the honour you have done me in making me one of your Ladyship's chaplains. A sense of it humbles me, and makes me to pray more intensely for more grace, to walk more worthy of that GOD, who has called me to his kingdom and glory. As your Ladyship hath been pleased to confer on me the honour before mentioned, I shall think it my duty to send you weekly accounts of what the LORD JESUS is pleased to do for and by me. Glory be to his great Name, the prospect is promising. My Lord *Bath* received me yesterday morning very cordially, and would give me five guineas for the orphans, though I refused taking any thing for the books. I send your Ladyship (by the hands of faithful and honest *Betty W——*) a little box of my sermons, and the last account of GOD's dealing with me, and of the money expended

expended for the Orphan-houfe, with my oath before the magiftrates of *Savannah*. The little book in marble paper is for Madam *P——:* I have folded down where I would have her begin to read. What a lovely chriftian will fhe make, when grace hath once refined her heart? I hope GOD intends to honour your Ladyfhip in making you inftrumental of doing good to the nobility. His providence, his peculiar providence hath placed your Ladyfhip at *Chelfea*. I am perfuaded your Ladyfhip will not quit that poft, till he that hath placed you there, plainly gives you a difmiffion. I have good news to-day from *Briftol*. Mr. *C——* intends to be fettered no longer with the fear of man. O that there may be always in him fuch a mind! Mr. *L——*, he informs me too, is coming from under the cloud. He begs his dutiful refpects may be prefented to your Ladyfhip, and is much obliged to your Ladyfhip for being fo much concerned for him. I hope he will fix by and by: But whither am I running? Pardon me, honoured madam, I fear I am too bold and too long. Upon the road, I propofe writing your Ladyfhip my thoughts of what fcheme feems to be moft practicable, in order to carry on the work of GOD, both here and in *America*. I dare add no more but my hearty prayers for the temporal and eternal welfare of your Ladyfhip, and whole houfhold, and fubfcribe myfelf, honoured madam,

Your Ladyfhip's moft obliged humble fervant,

G. W.

LETTER DCLXXII.

To the Rev. Mr. J—— W——.

Rev. and dear Sir,　　　　　　London, Sept. 1, 1748.

MY not meeting you at *London* has been a difappointment to me. But our LORD orders all things well. His time is and will be beft. I fuppofe you will hear of my preaching to fome of the nobility, and I truft the hour is coming when fome of the *Mighty* and *Noble* fhall be called. What have you thought about an union? I am afraid an external one is impracticable. I find by your fermons, that we differ in principles more than I thought, and I believe we are upon two different plans. My attachment to *America* will not permit

mit me to abide very long in *England*; consequently, I should but weave a *Penelope*'s webb, if I formed societies; and if I should form them, I have not proper assistants to take care of them. I intend therefore to go about preaching the gospel to every creature. You, I suppose, are for settling societies every where; but more of this when we meet. I can now only say a few general things. I hope you don't forget to pray for me. You are always remembered by, Reverend and dear Sir,

Yours most affectionately in CHRIST JESUS,

G. W.

LETTER DCLXXIII.

To Mr. J—— W——.

My very dear Brother, London, Sept. 1, 1748.

YOUR kind letter I received with great satisfaction. I chearfully sit down to answer it before I set out for *Scotland*. I have been a mile or two upon the road, but turned back because my chaise was not registered. My hands have been full of work, and I have been among great company. A privy counsellor of the king of *Denmark*, and others, with one of the Prince of *Wales*'s favourites, dined and drank tea with me on *Monday*. On *Tuesday* I preached twice at Lady *Huntingdon*'s to several of the nobility. In the morning the Earl of *Chesterfield* was present. In the evening Lord B——. All behaved quite well, and were in some degree affected. Lord C—— thanked me, and said, " Sir, I will not tell you what I shall tell others, how I approve of you," or words to this purpose. He conversed with me freely afterwards. Lord B—— was much moved, and desired I would come and see him the next morning. I did; and his Lordship behaved with great candour and frankness. All accepted of my sermons, and seemed surprized but pleased. Thus, my dear brother, the world turns round. " In all time of my wealth, good LORD deliver me!" Glad am I, for his own sake, that dear Mr. C—— begins to resolve to play the man. Alas! a triming conduct is uncomfortable to one's self, displeasing to CHRIST, and ridiculous in the sight of the world. CHRIST is worth all, or he is worth nothing. May the LORD enable me to be simple, and honest, and open in all my dealings, and to trust him with the consequences. I have ever yet found, that honesty is the best policy in the end. O that dear Mr. *L*—— may at length show himself a man too! My dear, very dear brother, may you lose no more time, but join in confessing a crucified Saviour. Glad am I to find that Mr. *C*——'s conversation is blest to you. I wish you had always a christian *fidus achates* at your side. Pardon me, dear brother, this freedom. My love is so great to you, and I have put up so many prayers for you, that I cannot rest till you improve those excellent parts GOD has given you, for the glory of his church and the good of his people. I am glad you will send something to our mother. I need not tell you, that the wisest of men has bid us " not to despise one's mother, when she is old." I thank you for the pictures; I have made free with some of them already. I shall not be sorry, if you do not go to *Gloucester*. Alas, so much money spent at music-meetings will make but a poor article at the day of judgment. But where does my affection carry me? My dear brother, good night. GOD willing, you shall hear from me soon again; if you do not answer me immediately, I will impute it to any thing rather than want of love; that, I am sure, is strong towards me, however unworthy of it. GOD has blessed me much in *London*. Congregations are very large. On *Sunday* I was enabled to preach four times: but this body—Well! thanks be to GOD, it is soon to be put off. Once more good night. My love to all friends. I am

Yours most affectionately,
G. W.

LETTER DCLXXIV.

To Mr. S——.

Oulney, (*Northamptonshire*) *Sept.* 4, 1748.

Very dear Sir,

IT was a pleasing surprize to me last week, to receive a letter dated in *July* from my dear, very dear friend Mr. *S*—— of *New-England*. I left town yesterday, but having an immediate opportunity of sending by way of *Philadelphia*, I now sit down to write your answer. Poor *New-England!* I pity and pray for thee from my inmost soul. May GOD arise, and scatter

scatter thy enemies! may those that hate thee be made to flee before thee! I am afraid the scene will be yet darker. But you know it is always darkest before day-break. It has been so in *England*. Matters, as to religion, were come to almost an extremity. The enemy had indeed broken in upon us like a flood. The spirit of the LORD is now lifting up a standard. The prospect of the success of the gospel, I think, was never more promising. In the church, tabernacle, and fields, congregations have been great, and perhaps as great power as ever hath accompanied the word. A door is also opening for the mighty and noble. I have preached four times to several of the nobility at good Lady *H*——'s. All behaved exceeding well, and I suppose in the winter opportunities of preaching to them will be frequent. May the LORD prepare me for whatever he has prepared for me! As for returning to *America*, if I live, I believe there's no doubt of it. I intend keeping myself free from societies, and therefore I hope to see you again next year. But future things belong to GOD. I thank you and dear Mr. *R*—— for your kind invitation. May the LORD direct to what is best! I hope you will continue to write. Pray read, seal and send the inclosed. You will communicate so much of this letter as may be proper. O dear Sir, pray for me, that the glorious *Emmanuel* may give me humility, and lead me on from conquering to conquer. You must remember me to dear Mrs. *S*—— and all in the kindest manner, and entreat them to continue their prayers in behalf of, very dear Sir,

Yours as usual,
G. W.

LETTER DCLXXV.

To Mr. R——.

Very dear Sir,   *Oulney, Sept.* 4, 1748.

THOUGH I am on my journey to *Scotland*, yet I must stop a little by the way to answer your kind letter dated in *July* last. It brought strange things to my ears, and it made me smile. You know, dear Sir, what has often passed between you and me, upon that point, loving honour. Some persons being forced as it were to accept of government places, are like

like other persons saying *nolo episcopare*, when, it may be, they have been making interest for a bishoprick many years. You know how to make the application. However, God may over-rule this for good, and if you could get the government of ———— (though in asking for it, you know not what you ask) it might be of service to *New-England* many ways. But, dear Sir, what can I do in it? I have no interest at court, and supposing I had, you have directed me to no means, neither hath any person been with me concerning it. Be pleased therefore to inform me of particulars. Let Mr. S—— instruct me what steps are to be taken, and if I can be of any service, you may command me. I thank you, dear Sir, for your kind invitation, and if you are to be exalted, I pray the Lord of all Lords to fit and qualify you for, and support you under it. You will not forget to give my most cordial salutations to all my dear *New-England* friends. I pray for them, you, and yours, and am, very dear Sir, with repeated thanks for all favours,

Yours most affectionately in Christ Jesus,

G. W.

LETTER DCLXXVI.

To the Rev. Mr. L——.

Rev. and dear Sir,   *Doncaster, Sept.* 7, 1748.

OUR last short interview at *Stone-house* pleased me. I hope it foreboded something good. I told you the truth when I said, "I had not forgotten you." No, neither have I been suffered to think hardly of you for your shyness to unworthy me; only I have thought you were loosing time, and for fear of displeasing a few mortal men, had acted a part displeasing to the invisible, immortal, and only wise God. Good Sir *John Philips* used to call you *sincere*. I believe that is your right name. I cannot help thinking but you will prove it to be so ere long. That love which Jesus shed abroad in your heart years ago, must constrain you to confess him before man. The light which the Lord hath imparted to you, cannot, I am persuaded, be much longer hid under a bushel. The shackles with which you have been fettered, must be shaken off, or I am much mistaken in the dear man to whom I am writing.—Pardon me, my dear old friend. My heart at present overflows with love towards you. Though weary and on a journey, I cannot help writing to you. Fear not temporal support. Though I went without scrip or shoe, I have lacked nothing; or if I had nothing, in JESUS I have possessed all things. I do not envy those who choose to sleep in a whole skin. Let me have scars, so that they are scars of honour, scars for JESUS CHRIST. I know who will approve of them, when he comes to judgment. O that day! that awful day! GOD enable us so to act, that we may receive an *Euge bone!* Out of the fulness of my heart I write thus. I am now on my way to *Scotland*. The LORD JESUS hath blessed me in *London*. As soon as possible I intend calling upon you. If you have a mind to renew our old delightful christian correspondence, I am quite willing. I wish you and yours the best of blessings, and am, very dear Sir,

Yours most affectionately in JESUS CHRIST,

G. W.

LETTER DCLXXVII.

To Mr. S———.

Morpeth, (Northumberland,) Sept. 10, 1748.

Dear Mr. S———,

TILL now I have not had time to answer your kind letter, and now I am too weary to send you a long one. I thank you for your good wishes and prayers. May they enter into the ears of the LORD of Sabaoth! Hitherto, GOD has been pleased to bless me since my arrival. Let the LORD's people continue to hold up their hands, and by his divine assistance I will go on fighting till I drop. I am now on my way to *Scotland*. I know you wish me good luck in the name of the LORD. When providence opens a door, I shall be glad to embrace.—In the mean while, pray remember me to all in the kindest manner. As for your call to preach, I can say nothing, being a stranger to you. Only I would observe to you what the apostle says, "Not a novice, &c."—You know what follows. If you chuse proper seasons, and keep within the bounds of humility and christian prudence, I pray the LORD to be with and bless you. I can now add no more, but subscribe myself

Your affectionate friend and servant,

G. W.

LETTER

LETTER DCLXXVIII.

To Mr. T―――.

Edinburgh, Sept. 15, 1748.

Dear Mr. T―――,

ERE this can reach *London,* you will find that I have forgot not my promise. No, I love thee too well to do so. Thanks be to GOD, that you begin to awake out of your dream. It has been a dream, though a golden pleasing one. If all was right, such darkness would never come and abide upon your soul. Come, play the man, and, if called to it, leave a worm for GOD. You are not the first that have been called to part with what was as dear as their own souls, or that have seen their beloved object in the possession of another. Better see that, than enjoy the object with guilt upon the mind. How did *Jacob* smart, all his life-time afterwards, for getting the blessing by a lie? The way of duty is the way of safety. I write this on supposition that your father will be against your proceeding. You will let me know what he says: In the mean while, as our LORD enables, I will pray for you. May the LORD JESUS give us a right judgment in all things! But enough of this. You see the bishop's charge has turned out as I supposed. Who could imagine otherwise? LORD, humble thy people for giving such wrong touches to the ark! LORD, keep me from doing so any more! O for zeal according to knowledge! O for grace and wisdom to act aright! Yesterday GOD brought me safe here, and I have been received very kindly. This afternoon I am to preach. The effects of it you may know hereafter. For the present, adieu. I recommend you to Him who is able to keep you from falling, and to raise you when fallen; and subscribe myself,

Yours most affectionately in CHRIST JESUS,

G. W.

LETTER DCLXXIX.

To the Reverend Mr. B——.

Edinburgh, Sept. 16, 1748.

Reverend and dear Sir,

ON *Thursday* noon, through the providence of a good and gracious GOD, I came hither, where I have met with an hearty welcome. Last night I preached to a *Moorfields* congregation for numbers, and the LORD, I believe, was pleased to give it his blessing. I have had the pleasure of hearing, that a serjeant of a regiment, awakened when I was here last, held on, and held out, and died rejoicing; and likewise of several others, who are gone before us to inherit the promises. May the LORD awaken fresh souls to supply their places. I trust he will. I was also much delighted last night, to hear there were so many christian soldiers among the king's forces that came from *Flanders*. A young christian lady, under whose roof they were, told me, that some or other of them were continually praying to, and wrestling with GOD. If any of them return to *England*, I doubt not but Col. G——y will find them out. I intend writing to him soon, and hope to send our good lady some glad tidings next week. In the mean while, pray present my most dutiful respects to her Ladyship. I hope all is well in *London*. The bishop's death, I suppose, will prevent any further stir about *Bartholomew*. I shall be glad to hear how you go on. Pray, dear Sir, how are your circumstances? You will not be offended if I inform you, that more than one have informed me of your being in debt to several. I thought it my duty to apprize you of it, because I know what a burden it is to be in debt; not indeed for myself, but for others. I make no apology for this; you know it must proceed from love. I wish you the very best of blessings, and am, reverend and dear Sir,

Yours most affectionately in CHRIST JESUS,

G. W.

LETTER

LETTER DCLXXX.

To Mr. S—— W——.

Edinburgh, Sept. 19, 1748.

My very dear Mr. W——,

SHALL I promise, and not perform? GOD forbid! Glad am I, yea very glad to open a fresh correspondence with a dear old friend, with whom I have often taken such sweet counsel. O my dear man, how patient, how long-suffering has the blessed JESUS been towards us! Ought not his love to constrain us to obedience? Ought we not to confess him, who endured such contradiction of sinners against himself for us? For my part, when I think that the glorious *Emmanuel* endured the pain, and despised the shame of dying upon a cursed tree for me, I cannot help saying,

> *For this let men revile my name,*
> *No cross I'd shun, I'd fear no shame;*
> *All hail reproach, and welcome pain,*
> *Only thy terrors,* LORD, *restrain.*

Glory be to GOD, I have hitherto found that the cross of JESUS has been lined with love. This has made it easy; this even now makes it exceeding light. I fear prosperity more than affliction; and though there is but little danger perhaps of my being exalted in this world, yet the language of my soul is, " In all time of my wealth, good LORD deliver me." May the LORD keep you, my dear friend, by his mighty power through faith! He has entrusted you with many talents; may you occupy them till he come! I hope he will bless your conversation to those who are yet but weak in the faith, and who cannot, through love of the world, or fear of man, as yet bear much contempt. My service to Messrs. *B*—— and *M*——, when you see them. " prayer for you all is, that you may be good soldiers of JES CHRIST. I am fighting for him here. Vast multitudes come to hear; but what good is done, cannot yet be determined. Many of my dear friends are gone to glory. I purpose being in town about the time appointed. I know you will pray for me. Whether absent or present, assure yourself you are never forgotten by, my very dear friend,

Yours most affectionately in CHRIST JESUS,

G. W.

LETTER DCLXXXI.

To the Countess of H———.

Honoured Madam,   *Edinburgh, Sept.* 20, 1748.

I Suppose, ere this can reach you, your Ladyship will have heard of my being arrived at *Edinburgh*, and of another particular or two mentioned in Mr. B———'s letter. This brings your Lapyship an account of very great multitudes flocking to hear the word; but with what success it is attended, I cannot yet tell. Upon my first coming, I was somewhat discouraged at hearing of the death of many of my valuable and leading friends, and of others losing their first love. Besides, the weather was boisterous, some ministers shy, and GOD was pleased to visit me with a great hoarseness. But the prospect is now more pleasant; and I trust, ere I leave *Scotland*, your Ladyship will have some good news from a far country. Inclosed your Ladyship has an extract of a letter sent from *London* to a pious gentlewoman here: I wish part of the contents may not prove, like the bishop of E———'s charge,—mere imaginary. May GOD hasten the time, when more of the mighty and noble shall be called, and made to stoop to the Redeemer's sceptre! It is now growing late. That your Ladyship and family may be filled with all the fulness of GOD, is the earnest prayer of, honoured Madam,

Your Ladyship's most obedient, willing servant
for CHRIST's sake,

G. W.

LETTER DCLXXXII.

To Mr. H———.

Edinburgh, Sept. 21, 1748.

AND could my very dear Mr. *H———* think, that when he was out of sight he was out of mind? No, my dear friend, I believe it will never be so with you and me. By this

this time, I hope Mr. D——'s letter from *Bermudas*, or the letters sent you from thence by way of *Philadelphia*, will inform you, that I wrote several parting letters to you and many other friends, and sent you bills of exchange to the amount of *eighty pounds* sterling; but, with my letter, books, and several other things, I find they are taken. Of this Mr. D—— writes me lately. As there is now peace, and a commerce opened with *Spain*, I hope the new settlers will be disturbed no more. Courage, my dear man, courage. Surely we shall yet live to see the salvation of GOD in *Georgia*. I am glad Mr. *Fairweather* hath been at *Bethesda*. Whatever has happened, do your best for me in respect to my family. Next year you may see me again. But more of this hereafter. The LORD is exceeding good to me. Great things are doing in *England*; and the LORD is blessing me more and more in *Scotland*. This morning, I hear a gentlewoman has left me an hundred pounds. If so, fifty shall be paid for you on the Orphan-house account, to Mr. *N*————, and as much more as I can spare, as soon as possible.—I have paid Mr. *J*—— thirty pounds sterling. But what does my wife tell me in her letter received this day, about your losing some favourite creature? Is it your wife, or your little daughter? Well, my dear friend, you and I must be made perfect through sufferings; you and I must learn to walk by faith. May the Father of Mercies comfort your heart, and abundantly supply the want of every creature, by communications from his own eternal Self. O pray write to me. Let me bear part of your sorrows, and thereby shew myself your friend. If my wife is embarked ere this arrives, I beg you would open all parcels that are sent to your care, and act as usual for my family. My tender love to all. You will not cease praying, dear Mr. *H*————, for

       Ever yours, &c.

          G. W.

LETTER DCLXXXIII.

To Mr. S―――.

Edinburgh, Sept. 23, 1748.

My dear Brother S―――,

HOW good is GOD! Well may you say, that he never fails those that put their trust in him. How does he make my extremity his opportunity to help and relieve me. If the news about the legacy be true, I hope it will increase my faith, and make me more willing to be upon the stretch for Him, who was stretched upon the accursed tree for me. I thank you for sending my letters. My wife proposes to embark for *England* in *October*. The climate will not agree with her. The physicians advise her to come over, and she entreats all friends to pray for her safe passage to *England*. Affairs here have now a comfortable aspect. I think more people than ever come to hear, and their hearts begin to be warm. Continue to write. My love to all. The not sending the late published account of the Orphan-house, has been of disservice to me. When will the children of light be as wise in their generation as the children of the world? I can now no more, but am, my dear Sir,

Ever yours,

G. W.

LETTER DCLXXXIV.

To Colonel G―――ly.

Very dear Sir, *Edinburgh, Sept.* 23, 1748.

EVER since I have been in *Edinburgh*, I have been attempting to write to you, but could not effect it till now. Though I am absent from, yet I am present with you. I hope this will find you fighting the good fight of faith, and in every respect behaving like a good soldier of JESUS CHRIST. The news of your conversion hath reached the ears of many of the great ones in *Scotland*. May the LORD JESUS keep you stedfast, unmoveable, always abounding in his work. The way you know. A constant looking up to the author and finisher of our faith, and watching unto prayer with all
perse-

perseverance, will keep the soul steady amidst all the temptations of a malicious devil, and ensnaring world. O for grace and zeal to endure unto the end! *Finis coronat opus.* I could say much, but company waits for me. Vast multitudes come to hear, and I trust much good is done. Good Lady H——— has an extract of a letter from a soldier, which will please you. Here are two devout soldiers in *Edinburgh*. May the LORD JESUS add more to his church of such converts as may be saved! You will not forget to pray for me. That you may increase with all the increase of GOD, is the earnest prayer of, very dear Sir,

Your most affectionate friend, &c.

G. W.

LETTER DCLXXXV.

To Mr. H———.

Glasgow, Sept. 28, 1748.

My very dear Mr. H———,

YOU are every day upon my heart. I must not, I cannot refrain writing to you any longer. How do you? Old love revives in my heart towards you, because, I trust, love to the blessed JESUS begins to revive in your heart. May the glorious *Emmanuel* fan the divine spark, till it break out into a holy blaze! Do not lose one moment more, my dear Sir: let this be the language of your soul continually,

> *Be gone, vain world, my heart resign,*
> *For I will be no longer thine:*
> *A nobler a diviner guest*
> *Now takes possession of my breast.*

It pleases me to think, how loud you and I shall sing of infinite, free, and unchangeable love in heaven; for because GOD changeth not, therefore you and I have not been consumed. O pleasant, transporting thought! What a saviour is JESUS of *Nazareth!* How precious was his blood! How profusely, as it were, was it shed for sinners! That you and yours may every moment feel its pardoning, renovating, cleansing, and purifying power, is the earnest prayer of, my very dear friend,

Yours most affectionately in our common LORD,

G. W.

LETTER DCLXXXVI.

To Mr. S―――.

My very Dear Sir, Glasgow, Sept. 28, 1748.

I Have been in pain because your kind letter has lain by me so long unanswered —Nothing but a variety of other necessary business has been the cause. My hands are full, and I trust the pleasure of the LORD will prosper in them. Very great multitudes have flocked to hear; and in *Glasgow* the prospect of doing good is rather more promising than in *Edinburgh*. In a fortnight I purpose, GOD willing, to leave *Scotland*, and to preach at *Oundle* in my way to *London*. Glad shall I be to see two such friends as you and Mr. *H――*, though incog. I will endeavour to send you timely notice. I would have neither of you expose yourselves to needless contempt upon my account. I think I can say, that I am willing to be forgotten even by my friends, if JESUS CHRIST may thereby be exalted. But then, I would not have my friends act an inconsistent part towards that friend of all, that friend of sinners, the glorious *Emmanuel*. You know, my dear Sir, what an inspired apostle hath asserted : " A double-minded man is unstable in all his ways." Whilst you are afraid of men, you will expose yourself to a thousand inconveniences. Your polite company, (unless you converse with them more as their physician, than as their companion) will prevail on you to such compliances, as will make you smart when you retire into your closet, and reflect on the part you have acted. Before I shook off the world, often have I come out of company, shorn of all my strength, like poor *Sampson* when he had lost his locks ! But this is a tender point. Go on, dear Sir, and prove the strength of JESUS to be yours. Continue instant in prayer, and you shall see and feel infinitely greater things than you have seen or felt yet. I am of your opinion, that there is seed sown in *England*, which will in time grow up into a great tree. GOD's giving some of the mighty and noble a hearing ear, forebodes future good. I do not despair, if I live, of seeing you a proclaimer of the unsearchable riches of JESUS CHRIST. GOD be praised, that Mr. *H――* is so bold an advocate for his blessed LORD. I send him my most affectionate

affectionate respects, and entreat him to remember me in his prayers. I wrote to Mr. H—— lately. I herewith send you an extract of a letter I wrote on ship-board to my dear invaluable friend Mr. S——, of *South-Carolina*. If it was judged proper, I would put it in the preface of a new edition of my Journals. I would not have any of my mistakes remain uncensured, uncorrected. I thank you for your hint about my way of preaching. I shall take care to observe it. And now, dear Sir, for the present, adieu. I am afraid I have tired you. I shall be fond of seeing you at *London*. Rejoicing in the prospect of seeing you in the kingdom of heaven, I subscribe myself, very dear Sir,

Yours most affectionately in CHRIST JESUS,

G. W.

LETTER. [DCLXXXVI.]

To Mr. K——.

Dear Sir, *Glasgow, Sept.* 28, 1748.

WHEN I was the other day at *Edinburgh*, your aged father communicated a letter to me, which gave an account of your being translated from the kingdom of darkness into the kingdom of GOD's dear Son. As the news rejoiced the hearts of angels in heaven, no wonder that it gives satisfaction to those who desire to follow the blessed JESUS here on earth. Hoping that I am one of those, and being willing to promote his glorious gospel in every part of the world, I write you this letter at a venture, to wish you joy of your happy change, and to exhort you with full purpose of heart to cleave unto the LORD. The more you know of Wisdom's ways, the more you will find them to be ways of pleasantness. The more you know of the blessed JESUS, the more you will find that his yoke is easy, and his burden exceeding light. Go on then, dear Sir: be strong in the grace that is in CHRIST JESUS, and learn to endure hardness like a good soldier. Who knows what the LORD may do by you in the dark parts where you are? Much good has been done among the soldiers in *Flanders*. What GOD has done for your soul, I trust is only an earnest of what he intends to do for others in St. *Helena*. I salute your companion very heartily.

I wish

I wish you both much prosperity in the LORD. You shall have the prayers of as many as I can engage for you. Remember our LORD's promise. Where there are only two or three gathered together in his name, there is he in the midst of them. Though you have not public ordinances, yet if the GOD of ordinances be with you, there will be no room for complaint. If I can any way be instrumental of promoting the blessed work begun among you, you may readily command, dear Sir,

Your most affectionate friend and
willing servant for CHRIST's sake,
G. W.

LETTER DCLXXXVII.

To Mrs. E——.

Dear Madam,   Glasgow, Sept. 28, 1748.

ALTHOUGH I fear it may be taking too much freedom, yet as I humbly hope that the love of GOD is shed abroad in your heart, I trust you will not be offended at my sending you these few lines. They are lines of joy; for who can help rejoicing that hears what the blessed JESUS hath done for your soul? O Madam, how much are you indebted to that grace which hath made such difference between you and others. To see any one converted is a miracle. But to see a rich person, one of the mighty, one of the noble converted, is yet a greater. May the LORD JESUS add more of your rank to his church, such as shall be saved! Never fear, Madam; all things are possible to the glorious *Emmanuel*. Let him but speak the word, and great shall be the numbers of new creatures. I hope this will find you in good health, and upon the full stretch for him who was stretched and bled upon the cross for you. Great multitudes in *Scotland* flock to hear. Some of my spiritual children, I hear, are gone to heaven, and others come to me, telling what GOD did for their souls when I was here last. I desire to cast my crown before the Lamb; I desire always to be crying out, "Why me, LORD, why me? In about a fortnight I purpose setting out for *London*. I lead a moving life. In heaven I shall have rest enough. Blessed be GOD for giving us to enter into a little of that rest even here! That you may daily increase in faith, and consequently enjoy more and more of this rest, is the hearty prayer of, dear Madam,

Your most obliged humble servant,

G. W.

LETTER DCLXXXVIII.

To some devout Soldiers.

My dear Brethren, Glasgow, Sept. 29, 1748.

IT gave me no small satisfaction, when I was lately at *Edinburgh*, to hear that several of you were enabled to behave like good soldiers of JESUS CHRIST. I rejoice greatly that you are made partakers of his grace, and I earnestly intreat the LORD of all Lords that you may grow and increase in it day by day. This is the christian's duty. He must forget the things that are behind; he must press forward towards the things which are before; he must not stop, till he arrives at the mark of the prize of his high calling. I trust, my dear brethren, you are all thus minded; and that whatever befals you, you will, through divine assistance, hold on and hold out to the end. If I can be any way serviceable to you, be not backward to send to me. I hear of others of your profession, that have lately enlisted under the banner of the ever-blessed Redeemer. Happy they! happy you! You have a good captain, a good cause, good armour, and an exceeding great reward. That you may at all times quit yourselves like men, and be strong; that you may fight the good fight of faith, and at length lay hold on life, eternal is the hearty prayer of, my dear Brethren,

Your affectionate friend, and willing
servant for CHRIST's sake,

G. W.

LETTER DCLXXXIX.

To the Countess of H―――.

Honoured Madam, Sept. 29, 1748.

AM I not too troublesome in writing to your Ladyship so frequently? I fear I am; and yet I am afraid to break your Ladyship's command, " Write weekly." Blessed be GOD, I can yet send your Ladyship word that the glorious *Emmanuel* is with me, and countenances my poor administrations. I have met with some unexpected rubs, but not one more than was absolutely necessary to humble my proud heart. "O my blessed Redeemer, when shall I learn of thee to be meek and lowly! Thou alone, O Lamb of GOD, canst teach me. Sanctify all thy dispensations to this end, and give me always to lie at thy feet." There, honoured Madam, I am safe: There I believe this letter will find your Ladyship.—May you every moment hear the Redeemer's voice, and be built up continually in your most holy faith. In about a fortnight I purpose leaving *Scotland*. Several things concur to make me believe that it was right for me to come here. Particulars your Ladyship may expect at my return to town. In the mean while, I recommend your Ladyship, and your dear offspring, with your whole houshold, to the care of the Father of mercies and the GOD of all consolation, and am, honoured Madam,

Your Ladyship's most obliged humble servant,

G. W.

LETTER DCXC.

To Dr. H———.

My dear Doctor, *Glasgow, Oct.* 1, 1748.

YESTERDAY with great satisfaction I received your kind letter. Being in *Scotland*, I cannot as yet have the pleasure of seeing Captain T———; but, GOD willing, I shall enquire him out at my return to *London*. The GOD of the seas and the GOD of the dry land has brought me safe to my native country; since which I have written to you and many others, and left two boxes of books for my dear *Bermudas* friends, to be sent the first opportunity. Although GOD is pleased to smile upon my poor administrations, and very great multitudes flock to hear both in *England* and *Scotland*, yet I have thoughts of seeing *Bermudas* again next year. But I dare not determine. Future things belong to GOD. Glory be to his great name for sending me to *Bermudas* at all! Glory be to his great name, that you, my dear Sir, are striving to enter at the streight gate of a sound conversion. I hope you will never cease striving, till you know that your Redeemer liveth.—Neither the greatness nor number of your sins can keep you from this unspeakable privilege, if you believe on the LORD JESUS. He is the way, the truth and the life. Come to the Father in and through him, and you, even you shall be made more than conqueror. Ere this can reach you, I hope you will have received redemption through his blood, even the forgiveness of your sins. When you experience this, O how will you rejoice with joy unspeakable, even with joy that is full of glory! You will then have an heaven upon earth. Sin shall not have dominion over you. It shall not reign in your mortal body. My dear Mr. H———, whilst I am musing on, and writing about this blessed change, this present salvation, the fire kindles. I love you with a peculiar love. I travail in birth till JESUS CHRIST be formed in your dear heart. O do not backslide. Study to improve the light and grace already received. " To him that hath shall be given," and he shall have abundance. But I forget myself. Busy as I am, I must, you see, write a long letter. Pray return my hearty love to your dear wife, Mrs. H———'s mother in law, &c. &c. May grace, mercy and peace be multiplied upon you all! I hope you will omit no opportunity of writing to, my very dear Friend,

Yours most affectionately in CHRIST JESUS,

G. W.

LETTER DCXCI.

To Mr. A————.

Dear Mr. A———,   *Glasgow, Oct.* 1, 1748.

I Am not disappointed of my hope. I thought the LORD JESUS had begun a good work in your soul before I left the *Bermudas*. Your welcome letter confirmed me in this opinion. I received it with joy. Though I wrote to you not long ago, yet I must answer yours immediately. And what shall I say? May I not welcome you into the world of new creatures? May I not hope that there has been joy in heaven over you, even you, my dear Man, repenting and turning unto GOD, even a GOD in CHRIST? Surely I may. And what then does the LORD now require of you, now he hath shewn

shewn you that good thing, the pardon of your sins, through a once crucified but now exalted Redeemer? Will you not, out of a principle of gratitude, do justly, love mercy, and walk humbly with your GOD? Methinks I hear you say, "I will, I will through the LORD JESUS CHRIST strengthening me."—And he will strengthen you.—He has promised, that as our day is so shall our strength be.—Despised you must be, and your name shall be cast out as evil; but the glorious Redeemer will enable you to go without the camp, and cause you to rejoice when loaded with his sacred reproach. "Increase and multiply," must now be your motto. Strive as much as in you lies, by your life and conversation, to win others to the blessed GOD. The eyes of men and angels will now be upon you. May the LORD enable you to walk circumspectly to those that are without. I hope your wife and all your relations will join in going to heaven with you. I return them my most hearty love, and pray that they may be filled with all the fulness of GOD. You will join in praying me over to the *Bermudas* again. I suppose Dr. H—— will shew you his letter. Remember me in the kindest manner to all, and accept this as a token of love unfeigned, from, dear Mr. *A*——,

Yours most affectionately in CHRIST JESUS,

G. W.

LETTER DCXCII.

To Mr. D——.

My very dear Friend,   *Glasgow, Oct.* 1, 1748.

WHO is like unto GOD, who makes his creatures extremity, the opportunity to help them? Your kind letter hath confirmed the news of the death of Mrs. *B*——, and of her leaving me a legacy of a hundred pounds. Well! though she is gone, yet I shall meet her at the great day, when the LORD JESUS shall remember this and all her other works of faith, and labours which have proceeded from love. I am glad she has left such an executor; I doubt not of your taking care of my interest. Your love is founded upon the rock of ages, and so is mine; for indeed I love you and yours in the bowels of the dear Redeemer. I

know

know you will be glad to hear of my prosperity in this work. Indeed GOD makes way for his own gospel. Many come to me, telling me what the LORD did by me the last time I was in *Scotland*, and also the time before. Congregations are very large. I am pressed to stay three or four days more than I intended. Some that were prejudiced, have had their prejudices removed, and I believe will be greater friends than ever. O that I was humble and thankful! I have good news from *Bermudas*. I return you and yours love and thanks. I desire to be remembered to dear Mrs. —— and every inquiring friend. As I need them so much, I hope none will cease putting up earnest prayers in behalf of, very dear Sir,

Yours most affectionately in CHRIST JESUS,

G. W.

LETTER DCXCIII.

To Mr. S——.

My dear Sir,   *Glasgow, Oct.* 3, 1748.

I Thank you for your kind letter. I am so ill with a hoarseness and cold, and in straining to reach large congregations, that I must send you but a short answer. The depending upon CHRIST's immediate teachings, without making use of books and proper means of instruction, you may assure yourself is a *terrible temptation*. It is the very quintessence of enthusiasm, and will lay you open to a thousand delusions. " Give thyself to reading," says *Paul* to *Timothy*. If thou cannot think of being a *Latin*, strive to be an *English* scholar. At my return I will endeavour to assist you. At present I am quite ill; but I am afraid I shall not be able to leave *Scotland* in less than a fortnight. You must remember me to all. The LORD JESUS has appeared for me. Particulars expect to hear another time.

Yours most affectionately in CHRIST JESUS,

G. W.

LETTER DCXCIV.

To Mr. ——.

Very dear Sir,   *Glasgow, Oct.* 5, 1748.

I Received yours this morning; though I am engaged this evening, yet I think it my duty to send you an immediate answer. You might well inform, and almost assure, *my Lord of Exeter*, that I knew nothing of the printing of his Lordship's pretended charge, or of the pamphlets occasioned by it. When the former was sent to me in manuscript from *London* to *Bristol*, as his Lordship's production, I immediately said, it could not be his. When I found it printed, I spoke to the officious printer who did it out of his own head, and blamed him very much. When I saw the pamphlet, I was still more offended; repeatedly in several companies I urged the injustice as well as imprudence thereof, and said it would produce what it did, I mean a declaration from his Lordship, that he was no Methodist. I am sorry his Lordship had such an occasion given him to declare his aversion to what is called Methodism; and though I think his Lordship in his declaration hath been somewhat severe concerning some of the Methodist leaders; yet I cannot blame his Lordship for saying, "that he thought some of them were worse than ignorant and misguided," supposing that his Lordship had sufficient proof, that they either caused to be printed, or wrote again when printed, a charge which his Lordship had never owned nor published. If you think proper, dear Sir, you may let his Lordship see the contents of this. I will only add, that I wish a way could be found out, whereby his Lordship and other of the Right Reverend the Bishops, might converse with some of us. Many mistakes might thereby be rectified, and perhaps his Lordship's sentiments in some degree altered. If this cannot be effected (I speak only for myself,) I am content to wait till we all appear before the great shepherd and bishop of souls. In the mean while, I heartily pray, that their Lordships may be blessed with all spiritual blessings, and wishing you the like mercies, I subscribe myself, very dear Sir,

    Your affectionate, obliged humble servant,

           G. W.

LETTER DCXCV.

To Mr. H——.

My dear Mr. H——, *Cambuslang, Oct. 9, 1748.*

HAVE you not suspected, that I have forgotten you? but indeed I have not. As a testimony of it, though late, accept a line of love, even love unfeigned. I hope you are well, and that affairs go on at the Tabernacle as well as can be expected. I trust the shout of a king is amongst you. Blessed be GOD, he has caused his gospel to triumph in *Scotland*. I have been humbled and exalted; humbled first, in order to be exalted afterwards. Thus it is.—The LORD wounds and then heals. At present I am in the place where the great awakening was about six years ago. The fruits of it yet remain. To morrow, GOD willing, I take my leave at *Glasgow*. I believe we shall have a sorrowful parting. As I expect to stop in *Yorkshire*, I suppose I cannot reach *London* till the latter end of this month, if so soon. O for a warm winter! You must remember me to all. I cannot now descend to particulars. I can only pray, that you and yours may be filled with all the fulness of GOD, and subscribe myself,

Yours most affectionately in the glorious JESUS,

G. W.

LETTER DCXCVI.

To Mr. B——.

My dear Sir, *Edinburgh, Oct. 12, 1748.*

LAST night, after wondering at your being silent so long, I received your wished-for letter. The reading it brought tears from my eyes. I felt for you, and for your father, and for all parties concerned. How lovingly does the LORD deal with you? Is not the way of duty the way of safety? Should you not both agree to let matters lie as they are, and not go one step further till you know your father's mind? You have given him your word; you must not go back. My affair came to as near a crisis, and yet I was called to sacrifice my *Rachael*. It may not be so with you. But prepare for the worst.

worst. Assure yourself, that your present passion, at least as to the excess of it, is sinful. If all is right, why such uneasiness for such a small space of time? Why such a long eclipse in the soul? Alas! B——'s has been almost total. I hope you are now coming out of it. Thanks be to that JESUS, who has promised "that we shall not be tempted above what we are able to bear," but will with the temptation make a way to escape. You see, my dear man, my love by my sympathy and plainness. Pray remember me to your aged father in the kindest manner. Dear old man! he is worthy of your greatest regard. His account of the legacy is true.—Yes, my dear friend, the LORD JESUS does reign indeed, and therefore I shall be delivered out of all my troubles. You will give thanks in my behalf. He has appeared for me here. Congregations have been very large, and several things have concurred to prove that providence did indeed call me to *Scotland*. I would not but have come for the world. Last night I came hither from *Glasgow*, and thought to leave this place as next *Tuesday*, but perhaps it may be the *Tuesday* following. I fear I cannot write to any more this post. But whether I write or not, whether absent or present, you must always remember me, as

Your assured friend, and willing
servant for CHRIST's sake,
G. W.

LETTER DCXCVII.

To Mr. W——.

Edinburgh, Oct. 12, 1748.

Reverend and dear Sir,

THOUGH I have not written to you, yet not one day hath passed since my being this time in *Scotland*, without my thinking of you. The love and respect I owe you, as an aged minister of JESUS CHRIST, will not suffer me to be silent any longer. How do you, reverend Sir? I doubt not but you find that promise true, "The righteous shall bring forth much fruit in old age." This leaves me, though faint, yet pursuing, and resolved, in the blessed JESUS, to spend and be spent in the blessed cause wherein I have embarked. Indeed,

deed, when I confider my blunders, miftakes, and imprudencies, I wonder the glorious *Emmanuel* does not lay me afide; but his grace is like himfelf, *infinite* and *eternal*. I hope he has given me a fight of, and humbled me for fome of my miftakes; and I truft as I grow in years, if I am to live longer, I fhall grow in knowledge and every chriftian virtue. Reverend and dear Sir, be pleafed to pray for me. I do not forget you, though perhaps you may judge otherwife. O for heaven! There chriftian minifters fhall fee eye to eye.—But I muft not weary you. In a few days I fuppofe you will hear what has happened in the *Weft*. Dear Mr. M—— perhaps may acquaint you with particulars. With this, I fend you a few of my laft accounts of the Orphan-houfe. You may difpofe of them as you think proper. When you fee Mr. B—— or R——, or any of the minifters that were friendly to me, be pleafed to remember me to them in the moft refpectful manner. I hope Mrs. W—— and your whole houfhold enjoy much of Him whofe prefence is better than life. I earneftly entreat the LORD to fill you with all his fulnefs, and beg leave to fubfcribe myfelf, reverend and dear Sir,

Your moft affectionate, though unworthy younger
brother and fervant in JESUS CHRIST,

G. W.

LETTER DCXCVIII.

To the Reverend Mr. E——.

Edinburgh, Oct. 12, 1748.

Reverend and dear Sir,

BY the providence of a good and gracious GOD, I came hither laft night, after having preached at *Falkirk* in the morning. Mr. A—— behaved very kindly. Mr. N—— has Mr. M——'s letter. I am to fee him at five this evening. On *Tuefday* next, GOD willing, I intend preaching for Mr. G——, and to leave *Scotland* the *Tuefday* following. In the mean while you may write what you pleafe. But whither am I going? Let GOD direct. Let my name be forgotten, let me be trodden under the feet of all men, if JESUS may thereby be glorified. I wifh you or Mr. M—— would write a line to Mr. W——; I would not have any good, though miftaken man,

man, uneasy upon my account. Well! In heaven all will be over. When I meet you there, I will thank you for all the pains you have taken with, reverend and dear Sir,

Yours most affectionately in CHRIST JESUS,

G. W.

LETTER DCXCIX.

To the Countess of H———n.

Honoured Madam,   *Edinburgh, Oct.* 15, 1748.

THOUGH it is late and nature calls for rest, yet I cannot with satisfaction close my eyes unless I write once more to your Ladyship: and what shall I say? I am the chief of sinners, and the LORD JESUS magnifies his grace in being long suffering and infinitely bountiful unto me. At *Glasgow* he has magnified his strength in my weakness, and out of the eater hath brought forth meat. Next week I purpose, GOD willing, to send your Ladyship the substance of a long debate about poor unworthy me, in the synod of *Glasgow*. Since that, I find the presbytery of *Perth* (I mean the new-fashioned part of it) has made an act against employing me. Ill-nature shews itself here, but I feel the benefit of it. Congregations are large, and I am enabled to preach with greater power, and feel unspeakable great comfort in my own soul. My hoarseness is quite gone off, my bodily health much repaired, and if my enemies shew themselves, I am persuaded the blessed JESUS will bless me to his people more and more.— Some give out, that I am employed by the government to preach against the *Pretender*; and the *Seceders* are very angry with me for not preaching up the *Scotch Covenant*. Blessed be GOD, I preached up the covenant of grace, and I trust many souls are taught to profit. The inclosed, dear Madam, will shew your Ladyship a little how I have been dealt with. Particulars your Ladyship shall have when the LORD is pleased to bring me to *London*. Next *Tuesday* sevennight I am to leave *Scotland*. Lady *Mary H*—— Lord *L*—— and Lady *F*—— beg their compliments may be presented to your Ladyship. Many in *Scotland* pray most earnestly for you, and Mr. *R*—— intends writing your Ladyship a letter. I pray for you, honoured Madam, continually. I am quite happy in Him who died upon the cross to save me. I believe he will deliver me out of all; and if I die for him, so that I am not suffered to deny him, it will exceedingly please, honoured Madam,

Your Ladyship's most obliged humble servant,

G. W.

LETTER DCC.

To the Same.

Honoured Madam,   *Topcliff, Nov. 1, 1748.*

THUS far has a gracious and good GOD brought me in my way to *London*, which I hope to reach some time next week. Your Ladyship may expect to see me the next day I come to town. Thanks be to the LORD of all Lords for directing my way to *Scotland*. I have reason to believe some have been awakened, and many, many quickened and comforted. My old friends are more solidly so than ever, and a foundation I trust has been laid for doing much good, if ever the LORD should call me thither again. Two synods and one presbytery brought me upon the carpet; but all has worked for good. The more I was blackened, the more the Redeemer comforted me. I desire to cry, Grace! grace!

> *The love of* CHRIST *doth me constrain,*
> *To seek the wandering souls of men;*
> *With cries, entreaties, tears, to save,*
> *And snatch them from the gaping grave.*
>
> *For this let men revile my name,*
> *No cross I'd shun, I'd fear no shame;*
> *All hail reproach, and welcome pain,*
> *Only thy terrors,* LORD, *restrain.*

At present I add no more, but my most dutiful respects to your Ladyship, and with hearty prayers for your temporal and eternal welfare, I beg leave to subscribe myself,

Your Ladyship's most obliged humble servant,

G. W.

LETTER DCCI.

To Mr. R——.

My dear Friend, *Topcliff, Nov.* 1, 1748.

HERE, with thankfulness of heart, will I set up my *Ebenezer*; for hitherto assuredly hath the LORD helped me. We reached *Fetton* on Saturday night. There being no public worship on the Lord's-day, I came on to *Morpeth* to worship there; got to *Ferry-hill* on *Monday* evening, and to-night am writing at *Topcliff*. Though I do not preach, yet I hope I am preparing for it. Reading, prayer, and meditation are three necessary ingredients. Riding, and getting proper rest, have recruited me; but I am apt to believe I have strained myself inwardly. I feel sensible pain in my breath.—But no matter; it is for a good master, who bore inexpressible pain for me.

> O LORD, *enlarge my scanty thought,*
> *To see the wonders thou hast wrought;*
> *Unloose my stammering tongue to tell,*
> *Thy love immense, unsearchable.*

I could write much, but my body calls for rest. My very dear Sir, good night. May the Lord of all lords reward you, and my other dear honoured friends, a thousand-fold. I intend writing to more very soon. In the mean while, pray present my sincerest respect and thanks to all. Inclosed you have Mr. *M*——'s letter and my answer. Be pleased to shew what Mr. *M*—— and Mr. —— writes, and let them tell you how the affair between them was. I know you will act as a peace-maker. That the GOD of peace and love may dwell and rule in your dear heart, is the earnest prayer of, my very dear friend,

Yours, &c.
G. W.

LETTER DCCII.

To the Honourable Lady D——.

Wantfworth (Northamptonshire), Nov. 5, 1748.

Honoured Madam,

THOUGH I am now eighty miles from *London*, yet gratitude, and the unfeigned respect I bear to you and yours, will not suffer me to go any further, without sending your Ladyship my repeated acknowledgments for your very many and repeated favours. Your kindnesses, when last at *Edinburgh*, were indeed surprizing. They have often humbled me, and as often led me to the throne of grace in behalf of your Ladyship and honoured family. May the promise made to those who are not ashamed of CHRIST, his gospel, and ministers, descend upon you all! O that you may have grace given you to shine as lights in the world, and to dare to be singularly good, since it is too apparent that we live in a wicked and adulterous generation. Honoured Madam, let us look up: as our day is, so shall our strength be. All things are possible to those that believe. May the LORD JESUS evermore give your Ladyship and children a large share of precious, purifying, operative faith! This is the earnest desire of my soul. Upon this I could enlarge, but travelling wearies me. Thanks be to GOD, I have that place in view, where the weary are at rest. In a post or two I purpose writing to my Lord *B———*, his honoured lady, &c. I never forget any of them. They have my constant prayers and most cordial respects. Be pleased to accept the same, honoured Madam, from

Your Ladyship's most obliged humble servant,

G. W.

LETTER DCCIII.

To Lady ———.

Honoured Madam,   *London, Nov.* 10, 1748.

I Wrote a line to dear Mr. *R———*, when about the middle of my journey. I must write a line to you, now the LORD of all lords hath brought me to the end of it. I trust I can say,

say, JESUS was with me on the way. My health was sensibly improved; but, by sitting up late to preach, I am grown a little sick again. Good Lady H—— is come to town, and I am to preach at her Ladyship's house twice a week to the Great and Noble. O that some of them may effectually be called, and taste of the riches of redeeming love! I need not inform your Ladyship, that this, and this alone, can give true rest and peace to any soul. You have felt the beginnings of it. May you experience an increase of it more and more. I desire my most tender and affectionate respects may find acceptance with dear Mr. R——, and with all who are pleased to honour me with their acquaintance. That grace, mercy, and peace may be multiplied upon you, is the continual prayer of, honoured madam,

Your Ladyship's most obliged humble servant,

G. W.

LETTER DCCIV.

To Lord R——.

My Lord, London, Nov. 10, 1748.

I Believe I am not mistaken, in thinking that your Lordship will not be offended with me for sending you a short letter. It is the effect of that unfeigned love I bear to your honoured father, yourself, and that dear and honourable family with which your Lordship is now so closely allied. And what shall I say? Can I wish your Lordship any thing greater, than that you may be a good soldier of JESUS CHRIST. It is a blessed thing to be engaged in fighting his battles; and not only to be almost, but altogether a christian. It is this half-way religion that undoes the professing world. The heart can never be at unity with itself, till it is wholly centered in GOD. This can only be done by faith in JESUS CHRIST; and when once a soul begins to taste of this faith, then that soul's heaven begins on earth. I trust I can say this by happy experience. I wish your Lordship a very large share of it; and with hearty acknowledgments for all favours, beg leave to subscribe myself, my Lord,

Your Lordship's most obedient,

obliged humble servant,

G. W.

LETTER DCCV.

To Lady Mary H——.

Honoured Madam, London, *Nov.* 10, 1748.

THOUGH absent from, yet I am not unmindful of you. The regard your Ladyship has been pleased to shew to a poor unworthy worm, calls for and claims my sincerest and most repeated acknowledgments. This letter brings them, and shall be followed, honoured Madam, as the Lord enables, with fervent prayers for your temporal and eternal welfare. O that you may be enabled to make a stand this winter for the Lord Jesus, and not in the least countenance any of those diversions that have already brought religion so low in poor *Scotland!* I need not inform your Ladyship, what a blessed thing it is to be singularly good, and to be consistent in our whole walk and conversation. To be uniform, and all of a piece, is the very life of a christian. It is this, and not a compliance with the polite world in any of their fooleries, that will gain proselytes to Jesus Christ. I could enlarge on this head, but I am persuaded it is needless for your Ladyship. The glorious Jesus hath let you see too much of his love, for you ever to be taken up with any thing short of his own eternal life! That he may knit your heart yet closer to himself, he is pleased to visit you with crosses. They are the christian's portion, honoured madam: They are the believer's birthright. " In the world you shall have tribulation;" but what follows? " Be not afraid, I have overcome the world." Look, therefore, to Him, honoured madam, who, as he hath been the author, will also be the finisher of your faith. That you may increase with all the increase of God, is the earnest prayer of, honoured madam,

Your Ladyship's most obliged humble servant,

G. W.

LETTER DCCVI.

To the Rev. Mr. M———.

London, Nov. 10, 1748.

Reverend and dear Sir,

OUR bountiful and good GOD brought me here in safety the beginning of this week. I have already waited upon, and preached at good Lady H———'s. About thirty have defired to come, and I fuppofe they will bring thirty more. I have heard of two or three more dear chriftians among the *Great Ones.* I know you will pray the LORD of all lords to increafe the number. Her Ladyfhip hath a great regard for all thofe in *Scotland,* who ftand up for vital religion. She intends to fend you down the picture of poor *Aaron* the late negroe preacher. I find the public papers give ftrange lying accounts of my reception in *Scotland.* At prefent, bleffed be the glorious JESUS, I am content to be blackened. I fend you my repeated thanks for all favours; and, with hearty love to dear Mr. G———, your family, and all friends, I fubfcribe myfelf, reverend and very dear Sir,

Your moft affectionate, obliged, though unworthy
younger brother and fervant in CHRIST JESUS,

G. W.

LETTER DCCVII.

To the Reverend Mr. S———.

London, Nov. 12. 1748.

Reverend and very dear Sir,

BY my not hearing from you with my wife's letter, I fufpect you are not yet reconciled to my leaving *America,* though but for a feafon. Every thing concurs to prove that I have done the will of GOD. As I am ftreightened in time, I will refer you to the inclofed, which I defire you will read, feal, and fend. Here are loud calls; but I think to come over to you again next year. Pray write to me. I will endeavour to anfwer you. I wrote to you lately from *Scotland.* Not a day paffes, but I think of you and my other *Charles-Town* friends. I intend to write to you very foon. In the

mean

mean time, be pleafed to remember me to all in the moſt tender manner. Ere this can reach you, I expect to fee my wife in *England*. I purpofe to perfuade her to fettle here. I want to make the Orphan-houfe a feminary of learning. If fome fuch thing be not done, I cannot fee how the *Southern* parts will be provided with minifters. All are afraid to come over. May the LORD JESUS direct me. I believe he will. Pray remember me to Mr. Z——, Mr. O——, &c. if with you. I have not time at prefent, or otherwife they fhould have a line from, reverend and very dear Sir,

Yours moſt affectionately in CHRIST JESUS,

G. W.

LETTER DCCVIII.

To the Countefs of H————.

Honoured Madam,   *London, Nov.* 14, 1748.

THE inclofed brings good news from a far country. The perfon's mother belongs to the Tabernacle fociety: I lay at his houfe when in *Virginia*; but he and others went to cards, I thought on purpofe to affront me. We retired to prayers for him. I hope they were heard. Your Ladyfhip will be pleafed to let me have the letter again; as likewife that I fent to your Ladyfhip from *Scotland*, from one Capt. K. of St. *Helena*. Your Ladyfhip fhall have copies of them all. I am getting the *New-England Chriſtian Hiſtory*, and *Bifhop Hall's Works* in folio, bound for your Ladyfhip. I find there has been a great ſtir in the fynod of *Edinburgh* about unworthy me. Mr. W——, Mr. J——, Mr. R—— W——, have protefted againft their proceedings, and appeared quite hearty. Your Ladyfhip wrote to Mr. R——. A word or two of encouragement now from your Ladyfhip, would ftrengthen the hands of thefe minifters of CHRIST. I hear the affair is to come before the affembly next *May*. News alfo was brought me laft night, that the negroes are allowed by the truftees for *Georgia*. If fo, that province, under GOD, will flourifh. Bleffed be GOD, I am more hearty than I have been for a long feafon. I hope to be enabled to preach here on *Sunday* evening, and to come and preach at your Ladyfhip's afterwards. Laft night the gofpel was indeed preached with

the

the Holy Ghost sent down from heaven. I was shewing the dignity of a christian, and in what sense christians were kings. The King of kings was amongst us. When I hear or receive any thing that is new and good, I naturally inform your Ladyship of it, because I believe it will give your Ladyship satisfaction. I hope your new house is agreeable to your Ladyship. That the Redeemer's glory may fill it, and that it may prove a gate of heaven to many of the rich and great, is the earnest prayer of, honoured madam,

Your Ladyship's, &c.

G. W.

LETTER DCCIX.

To the Honourable Lady T———.

Honoured Madam, London, *Nov.* 19, 1748.

WHEN I was lately in *Scotland*, Col. G———*ly* wrote me word, that your Ladyship was pleased to desire my poor prayers. Before his writing, they had been put up to the throne of grace in behalf of your Ladyship very frequently; and I would then have written to your Ladyship, had I not feared it would have been making too free. Yesterday good Lady H———*n* informed me that your Ladyship was ill. Had I judged it proper, I would have waited upon your Ladyship this morning. But I was cautious of intruding. However, the regard I bear to your Ladyship, constrains me to inform your Ladyship, that my heart's desire and prayer to GOD is, that this sickness may not be unto death, but to his glory, and the present and eternal good of your better part, your precious and immortal soul. This, no doubt, is the end of afflictions: GOD's name and nature is Love. He cannot, therefore, chastise us for any other purpose, than that we may be made partakers of his holiness.—Every cross and disappointment, every degree of pain, brings this important call with it, " My son, my daughter, give me thy heart." O that your Ladyship's soul may echo back, " My heart, LORD JESUS, will I give." O that from a feeling, spiritual, abiding
sense

sense of the vanity and emptiness of all created good, you may, in a holy resentment, cry out,

> *Be gone, vain world, my heart resign,*
> *For I must be no longer thine:*
> *A nobler, a diviner guest,*
> *Now claims possession of my breast!*

Then, and not till then, will your Ladyship's mind be at unity with itself. Then, and not till then, will your Ladyship, upon truly rational principles, with chearfulness wait for the approach of death, and the coming of the LORD from heaven. It is faith in JESUS, a true and living faith in the Son of GOD, that can alone bring present, real peace, and lay a solid foundation for future and eternal comfort. I cannot wish your Ladyship any thing greater, any thing more noble, than a large share of this precious faith: and a large, yea a very large share, is the glorious Redeemer ready to give to all that sincerely ask for, and seek after it. He waits to be gracious. He giveth liberally; he upbraideth not. When, like *Noah*'s dove, we have been wandering about in a fruitless search after happiness, and have found no rest for the sole of our feet, he is ready to reach out his merciful hand, and receive us into his ark. This hand, honoured madam, is he reaching out to you. May you be constrained to give your heart entirely to him, and thereby enter into that rest which remains for the happy, though despised people of GOD. But whither am I going? I forget that your Ladyship is indisposed, and I almost a stranger to you. I will only make this apology: "The love of JESUS constrains me." Hoping, therefore, your Ladyship will excuse the freedom I have here taken, I beg leave to subscribe myself, honoured madam,

Your Ladyship's most obliged humble servant,

G. W.

LETTER DCCX.

To the Reverend Mr. P——.

London, Nov. 19, 1748.

Reverend and dear Sir,

IT is a concern to me, that I cannot write to more of my *New-England* friends than I do; for indeed a multiplicity of business renders a more frequent correspondence impracticable. However, I would willingly send you, dear Sir, a few lines. They are lines of love, and bring you news of my being better in health than I have been for many years last past. Several things have concurred to prove it was the divine will I should return this time to my native country. Matters were in great confusion by reason of Mr. *C——*'s going over to the *Moravians*; but blessed be GOD, we are now easy at the Tabernacle, and the word falls with weight and power. In *Scotland* the LORD JESUS was pleased to appear for me; I found no diminution in respect to the number of hearers; and, I believe, (thanks be to free grace) my preaching was more acceptable than ever to GOD's people, and to those ministers who were pleased formerly to own and encourage me. Some of the opposite party begun a like stir with that which was made in *New-England* by Dr. *C——*, &c. but I believe it will only make the people more eager to hear, and in the end be productive of great good. Our LORD orders all things well. I never enjoyed more settled peace and joy than now. I trust he has given me to see many things that were wrong, and withal a disposition to confess and amend them. At present, this is the language of my heart:

Correct me when I go astray,
And lead me in the perfect way.

I suppose you will be acquainted with particulars by some of my dear friends from *Scotland*. In all probability I shall go to *Scotland* again in the Spring; and, in the latter end of the year, I propose embarking for *America*. But future things belong to GOD. Thanks be to his great name, I am willing to go any where, so that I may but glorify the dear Redeemer. Ere this reaches you, doubtless you will have heard of his giving me favour in the sight of Lady *H——n*, a Lady as good as she is great. Two or three among the great, I trust have been made the happy subjects of redeeming love. I have heard lately also of the conversion of two or three clergymen; there is likewise a great awakening in *Ireland*, and in *Wales* the work goes on. Upon the whole, I believe the gospel is getting ground, and next spring, when it is proper to range about and preach in the fields, I hope to see yet greater things. I repeat my old request, reverend and dear brother, " Pray for us." I continually pray for you, and the people committed to your charge. I wish you and yours an increase of blessings, and beg leave to subscribe myself, Reverend and very dear Sir,

Yours, &c.
G. W.

LETTER DCCXI.

To the Rev. Mr. L——.

My very dear Brother, London, *Nov.* 19, 1748.

WORDS cannot well express what I felt when your welcome letter came to hand. It drew me to my knees; it made me shed tears of joy, and with two or three of my dear friends I was enabled to wrestle for you at the throne of grace. Blessed, for ever blessed be the GOD and Father of our LORD JESUS CHRIST, for opening your eyes, and giving you such an experimental and soul-ravishing knowledge of the doctrine of grace. No wonder that people take notice of you. I hope the fame thereof, as it hath reached heaven, will also be spread abroad upon the earth, and thro' the thanksgivings of thousands redound to the glory of GOD. I think it a happiness, that you are surrounded with many souls that have indeed tasted that the LORD is gracious, and consequently will be fed with the sincere milk of the word, now communicated to them, under GOD, by you. Now, my dear friend will you begin to live, now will you begin to preach indeed. Go on in the name of JESUS, and as *Paul* did, so shall you, " increase with all the increase of GOD." Glad shall I be to give you all the assistance that lies in my power. *Henry on the Scriptures* will now suit your taste, and *Jenks upon the Righteousness of* CHRIST might do you immediate service. *Flavel's Sermons* would be food for you, and *Boston upon the Covenant*, and his *fourfold State*, I believe would delight you. *Bishop Hall's Contemplations* are excellent, *Bishop Hopkins* and *Beveridge* will do for you, and indeed almost all the writers a century ago. The doctrines you now preach are no new doctrines; you are now got into the good old way. May the LORD keep and succeed you in it, ever more and more. I believe he will. I could say more, but I expect another letter from you before I come down. Lady *H*—— is rejoiced to hear of you. I read part of your letter to her last night before I preached. Some of the great ones hear the gospel gladly. That you may be made a very great blessing to thousands and ten thousands, is the hearty prayer of, my dear Mr. *L*——,

Ever yours,

G. W.

LETTER DCCXII.

To the Rev. Mr. P——.

London, Nov. 21, 1748.

Reverend and very dear Sir,

I Was glad to hear, by a letter sent by Mr. *R*——, that you had been in *New-England*. I hoped you would have come further, even to Old *England* and *Scotland*. I have been endeavouring in *Scotland* to do all the service I could to the *Indian* school and the *New-Jersey* college whilst I was there; but I believe nothing will be done to purpose unless you or some other popular minister come over, and make an application in person. In all probability, a collection might then be recommended by the general assembly, which sits next *May*, and large contributions be raised among private persons that wish well to *Zion*. If one of the Indians was brought over with the minister, and a proposal made to educate some of the late awakened *Indians* in the *New-Jersey* college, it would certainly be of service. Mr. *M*—— and several other faithful ministers are hearty in the affair; but I believe will do nothing, unless you or some other such like minister come over.

Probably

Probably I shall be in *Scotland* next spring again. GOD has been pleased to countenance me there; and some of the clergy, in order to stop my progress, have followed Dr. C——y's example. But if GOD be for us, who can be against us? Thanks be to his holy name, I am kept quite chearful in soul, and healthy in my body. Blessed be GOD, the word falls with weight, and I hear of several brought under fresh convictions. A clergyman or two have been lately converted, and there is a great awakening in *Ireland*. I shall be glad to hear that *New-York* is full of new creatures. I beg that my most cordial respects and love may find acceptance with all my dear friends, and am, reverend and dear Sir,

Ever yours,

G. W.

LETTER DCCXIII.

To Mr. E———.

Dear Mr. E———, *Gloucester, Dec.* 5, 1748.

WHY no letter from you all this while? I have written to you several times. Lately I sent a case full of divers things for *Bethesda*. When I return to *London*, I purpose to send more. I hear that my wife hath lessened the family; but how it stands now, I cannot expect to know for a certainty till I see her. I expect her daily, though I am apt to believe she will not embark till she sees *Betty W———*. I hope ere now you have welcomed her to *Bethesda* in the name of the LORD. I expect to be over with you again by this time twelvemonth. In the mean while, I trust we shall make some better advances towards heaven than we have hitherto done, and be more conformed to the blessed and glorious JESUS. Thanks be to his great name, he continues to deal bountifully with me. I am pretty well in health, and hope to hear that you are so. I send you all my blessing, and am

Yours, &c.

G. W.

LETTER DCCXIV.

To the Honourable Trustees of Georgia.

Honoured Gentlemen,   *Gloucester, Dec.* 6, 1748.

NOT want of respect, but a suspicion that my letters would not be acceptable, has been the occasion of my not writing to you these four years last past. I am sensible, that in some of my former letters, through hurry of business, want of more experience, and in all probability too great an opinion of my own sufficiency, I expressed myself in too strong, and sometimes unbecoming terms. For this I desire to be humbled before GOD and man, knowing that, *Peter*-like, by a misguided zeal, I have cut off as it were those ears which otherwise might have been open to what I had to offer. However I can assure you, honoured gentlemen, to the best of my knowledge, I have acted a disinterested part, and notwithstanding my manifold mistakes and imprudence, I have simply aimed at GOD's glory and the good of mankind. This principle drew me first to *Georgia*; this, and this alone, induced me to begin and carry on the scheme of the *Orphan-house*; and this, honoured gentlemen, excites me to trouble you with the present lines. I need not inform you, honoured gentlemen, how the colony of *Georgia* has been declining for these many years last past, and at what great disadvantages I have maintained a large family in that wilderness, through the providence of a good and gracious GOD. Upwards of five thousand pounds have been expended in that undertaking, and yet very little proficiency made in the cultivation of my tract of land, and that entirely owing to the necessity I lay under of making use of white hands. Had a negroe been allowed, I should now have had a sufficiency to support a great many orphans, without expending above half the sum which hath been laid out. An unwillingness to let so good a design drop, and having a rational conviction that it must necessarily, if some other method was not fixed upon to prevent it. These two considerations, honoured gentlemen, prevailed on me about two years ago, through the bounty of my good friends, to purchase a plantation in *South-Carolina*, where negroes are allowed. Blessed be GOD, this plantation hath succeeded; and though at present I have only eight working hands, yet in all probability there will be more raised in one year, and with a quarter the expence, than has been produced at *Bethesda* for several years last past. This confirms me in the opinion I have entertained for a long time, that *Georgia* never can or will be a flourishing province without negroes are allowed. But notwithstanding my private judgment, I am determined that not one of mine shall ever be allowed to work at the Orphan-house, till I can do it in a legal manner, and by the approbation of the honourable trustees. My chief end in writing this, is to inform you, honourable gentlemen, of the matter of fact, and to let you know, that I am as willing as ever to do all I can for *Georgia* and the Orphan-house, if either a limited use of negroes is approved of, or some more indented servants sent over. If not, I cannot promise to keep any large family, or cultivate the plantation in any considerable manner. My strength must necessarily be taken to the other side. I would also further recommend it to your consideration, honourable gentlemen, whether or not as the Orphan-house was and is intended for a charitable purpose, it ought not to be exempted from all quit-rents and public taxes, as I believe is customary universally for such institutions to be? And as most of the land on which the Orphan-house is built, is good for little, I would humbly enquire, whether I may not have a grant for five hundred more acres that are not taken up, somewhere near the Orphan-house? My intention is, if you, honourable gentlemen, are pleased to put the colony upon another footing, (I mean in respect to the permission of a limited use of negroes) to make the Orphan-house not only a receptacle for fatherless children, but also a place of literature and academical studies. Such a place is much wanted in the southern parts of *America*; and if conducted in a proper manner, must necessarily be of great service to any colony. I can easily procure proper persons to embark in such a cause, and I do not know but several families would go over, supposing I could give them a probable prospect of a support upon their honest industry. I could say more, but I fear I have been already too prolix. I humbly recommend what has been urged to your consideration, and beg leave to subscribe myself, honourable gentlemen,

Your most obedient humble servant,
G. W.

LETTER DCCXV.

To the Countess of H——.

Honoured Madam, *Bristol, Dec. 10, 1748.*

THOUGH I am afraid of taking too much freedom, yet the duty I owe to your Ladyship constrains me to send you a few lines from hence. I came hither last night, after having preached five times in *Gloucester*, and once in *Gloucestershire*. The glorious *Emmanuel* pleased to shine upon my administrations, and many told me they received a blessing. The bishop behaved respectfully when I was at sacrament at the cathedral, and my old tutor, Dr. R——, one of the prebendaries, was very cordial when I waited upon him. I told him that my judgment (as I trust) was a little more ripened than it was some years ago, and that as fast as I found out my faults I would be glad to acknowledge them. He said, as I grew moderate, the offence the Governors of the Church had taken against me, would lessen and wear off. Blessed be God, I am pretty easy about that: so that I can but act an honest part, and be kept from trimming, I will, through the divine assistance, leave all consequences to him who orders all things well. Thanks be to his great name, a wonderous change is wrought on Mr. L——. He came to see and hear me at *Gloucester*: his worldly shackles are dropping off apace, and his feet begin to be set in a large room. The news of his conversion hath reached Mr. W———, who wrote him a long letter; but to send dissuasives to a man that hath seen and felt so much, is like throwing chaff against a brass wall. He begged me to send his duty to your Ladyship when I wrote, as does my brother, at whose house I am. I trust he is coming forwards, and that he will at length fairly shake hands with the world, and act as one alive to God. I think your Ladyship meets with great encouragement. My continual prayer to the blessed Redeemer in your Ladyship's behalf is, " that your bow may abide in strength, and the arms of your hands be strengthened by the hands of the mighty God of *Jacob*." He is the rock of ages. He is the LORD our righteousness. In him is our strength found. Thanks be to the GOD and Father of our LORD JESUS CHRIST,

Christ, for shewing your Ladyship the way to fetch continual strength and supplies from him! I could enlarge, but am streightened in paper. If Mr. C—— hath courage enough, I expect to see him, and then I shall have it in my power to send your Ladyship word how matters stand at *Bath*. In the mean while, I beg leave with all dutiful respects to subscribe myself, honoured madam,

Your Ladyship's most obliged humble servant,

G. W.

LETTER DCCXVI.

To Mr. B——.

My dear Tommy, *Bristol, Dec.* 12, 1748.

THE love I bear to you, will not suffer me to omit answering your letter the very first opportunity. I find you are in danger of being led into temptation. If only your preparations for business keep you from attending on the word preached, how will it be when you are totally immersed in it? O my dear man, let that promise of our LORD's be written on the tables of your heart, " seek you first the kingdom of GOD and his righteousness, and all those things shall be added unto you." If you act inconsistent with this, assure yourself your endeavours will be blasted, and GOD out of love will curse your temporal blessings. But enough of this. I hope a word to the wise is sufficient.—Since I wrote thus far, I have received a letter from good Lady H——n, desiring I would come up to town. I therefore propose to be with you, GOD willing, by *Saturday* night, and to preach at the Tabernacle next *Sunday*. Be pleased to apprize all friends of it. If you are at the tabernacle-house on *Saturday* evening, it would be very agreeable to,

Yours, &c. in great haste,

G. W.

LETTER DCCXVII.

To Mr. H—— H——.

London, Dec. 18, 1748.

I Can assure you, my not being able to write to you during my last excursion, has given me much concern. I love to be punctual. Journeying, preaching, and a train of bufineſs for the beſt of maſters, has prevented my being ſo now. I have been at *Gloueceſter*, in other parts of *Glouceſterſhire*, and at *Briſtol*, where I truſt the ſound of my Redeemer's feet was heard behind me. My brother I hope is coming on. I like him better than I have for ſome years. He greatly regards you, and intends anſwering your kind letters. I propoſed his meeting you here. What do you think of it? He likes it well. I wrote for him to come up next week. I expect to know by *Wedneſday* or *Thurſday*. If you could be here on a LORD's day, or a *Thurſday*, you might ſee our aſſembly at the other end of the town. I truſt, abiding good will be done among ſome at leaſt of the rich and great. I thank you a thouſand times for your advice in reſpect to my health.—For near theſe two months paſt, my uſual reachings have left me. I find that keeping from too much fatigue, under GOD, muſt be my cure. I will endeavour to keep within bounds every way. I have ſhewed the doctor's letter to Lady *H*——, but ſhe is of opinion, the journals as now corrected ought to be reprinted. In the multitude of councils there is ſafety; the language of my heart is,

> LORD, *teach me when I go aſtray,*
> *And lead me in thy perfect way.*

O that my zeal may increaſe with prudence. I have had too little of both. I am now thirty-four years of age, and alas! how little have I done and ſuffered for Him, who has done and ſuffered ſo much for me! Thanks be to his great name, for countenancing my poor adminiſtrations ſo much! I know not how it is, but perhaps it may be to diſplay the riches of free grace, that notwithſtanding the firſt zeal of moſt, I might add, all men of GOD, is generally mixed with much wildfire, yet their firſt times have been generally bleſt moſt, eſpecially for awakening and converting ſouls. Bleſſed be our good GOD that Mr. *H*—— is coming out. May the LORD JESUS make him a ſpiritual father to thouſands! I ſmiled when you ſaid, he would avoid the name of *Methodiſt*, if he could. Alas, my dear man, he might as ſoon think to waſh a blackmoor white. The *Methodiſts* are now as it were a ſkreen for others. Formerly, if a perſon was ſerious, or preached CHRIST, he was termed a *Puritan*, now he is a Methodiſt:

But

But do you go on as you are able to bear it. Oppofition fhall follow you; without it, be as prudent as you will, your fincerity towards GOD and love for fouls cannot be evidenced. Self, love of praife, and love of the world, muft come down. Our LORD always does this, by way of fufferings inward or outward, or rather by both. One Mr. L—— of *Gloucefterfhire*, whom Mr. H—— knows, though he has begun to preach CHRIST but lately, yet is already warned to leave his cure. Our LORD will provide for him. He is a new creature indeed. I do not blame you for your conduct towards Mrs. D——. She is a good woman, and I believe thirfts for the Redeemer's glory. I wifh fhe would not write fo much. And what fhall I fay more? I hope you have had enough from me now. My very dear Sir, when am I to hear that you are a preacher of CHRIST crucified? I long for the time, and earneftly pray that you may be freed from worldly hopes and worldly fears: for till then, I cannot believe a man, let his other accomplifhments be ever fo great, will be much owned and bleffed by the great head of the church. I fhould be glad to know what my LORD of *Exeter* faid. I thank the LORD of all Lords for giving you fo much encouragement. Let this excite you to prefs forwards, and never fear what man or devils fay of, or can do unto you. Dear, very dear Sir, my heart is enlarged towards you. I thank you, for remembering an unworthy worm before him who is the great high-prieft and bleffed apoftle of our profeffion. As he enables, I fhall return the favour, being, for his great name's fake, very dear Sir,

Yours moft affectionately,

G. W.

LETTER DCCXVIII.

To the Rev. Mr. H——.

London, December 18, 1748.

Reverend and dear Sir,

THOUGH I am not perfonally acquainted with you, yet I owe you much love. Thanks be to our great high Prieft for giving you fuch light and heat, and enabling you to preach among poor finners the unfearchable riches of redeeming love. Earth and hell will be up in arms againft you; your own mother's children will foon be angry with you,

you, and many of the members of that church of which you are a minister, whenever you preach her doctrine with power and purity, will think it doing GOD's service to caſt you out. Thus it has been, thus it will be in all ages, ſo long as thoſe two ſeeds of the woman and the ſerpent remain ſtruggling in this lower world. Welcome, welcome dear Sir, into the field of battle! Now the common people will hear you gladly. Now the ſelf-righteous will ſpeak all manner of evil againſt you. I am told the corporation have rejected you for preaching CHRIST crucified. I wiſh you joy. May you, like bleſſed *Paul*, increaſe the more in ſtrength, and be made a ſpiritual father to thouſands! Excuſe this freedom from one who loves you in the bowels of JESUS CHRIST. I thank you for your intended interview. Could no way be contrived for a private viſit? however that be, aſſure yourſelf your intereſt will be much upon my heart, and if you will remember a poor unworthy worm before his throne, whoſe compaſſions fail not, you will much oblige, reverend and dear Sir,

Your moſt affectionate brother
and ſervant in JESUS CHRIST,
G. W.

LETTER DCCXIX.

To Doctor D——.

London, Dec. 21, 1748.

Reverend and very dear Sir,

GLAD was I, yea very glad to receive your letter dated *November* 7th, though it did not reach me till laſt night. I thank you for it a thouſand times. It has led me to the throne of grace, where I have been crying, "LORD, counſel my counſellors, and ſhew them what thou wouldſt have me to do."—Alas, alas! how can I be too ſevere againſt myſelf, who, *Peter* like, have cut off ſo many ears, and by imprudencies mixed with my zeal, have diſhonoured the cauſe of JESUS? I can only look up to him, who healed the high-prieſt's ſervant's ear, and ſay, "LORD, heal all the wounds my miſguided zeal has given." Aſſure yourſelf, dear Sir, every thing I print ſhall be reviſed. I always have ſubmitted my poor performances to my friends corrections. Time and
experience

experience I find ripen men's judgments, and make them more
solid, rational, and confiftent, both in their conduct and writings. O that this may be my cafe! O that the bleffed JESUS
may enable me to hold on, and hold out, and keep me from
flagging in the latter ftages of my road. I thank you, dear Sir,
for your folemn charge in refpect to my health. Bleffed be
GOD, it is much repaired fince my return from *Scotland*, and
I truft by obferving the rules you prefcribe (if I muft live) I
fhall be enabled to declare the works of the LORD. But what
fhall I fay concerning your prefent trial? fhall I wifh you
joy? Surely I may with great propriety, fince an infpired
writer hath faid, " count it all joy when you fall into divers
temptations." But at the fame time, reverend Sir, I moft earneftly fympathize with you, having had the fame trial from
the fame quarter long ago. The *Moravians* firft divided my
family, then my parifh at *Georgia*, and after that the focieties
which, under GOD, I was an inftrument of gathering. I fuppofe not lefs than four hundred, through their practices, have
left the tabernacle. But I have been forfaken otherways. I
have not had above an hundred to hear me, where I had
twenty thoufand, and hundreds now affemble within a quarter of a mile of me, who never come to fee or fpeak to me;
though they muft own at the great day that I was their fpiritual father. All this I find but little enough to teach me to
ceafe from man, and to wean me from that too great fondnefs
which fpiritual fathers are apt to have for their fpiritual children. Thus bleffed *Paul* was ferved, thus muft all expect to
be treated who are of *Paul*'s fpirit, and are honoured with any
confiderable degree of *Paul*'s fuccefs. But I have generally
obferved, that when one door of ufefulnefs is fhut, another
opens. Our LORD bleffes you, dear Sir, in your writings; nay
your people's treating you as they are now permitted to do,
perhaps is one of the greateft bleffings you ever received from
heaven. May patience have its perfect work, and may you
be enabled to fanctify the LORD GOD in your heart! I know
of no other way of dealing with the *M———s*, than to go on
preaching the truth as it is in JESUS, and reft upon that promife, " Every plant which my heavenly father hath not
planted fhall be plucked up." Seven years will make a great

alteration.

alteration. I believe their grand design is to extend their oeconomy as far as possible. This I believe is now kept up by dint of money, and I am apt to think that the very thing by which they think to establish, will destroy their scheme. *John Lapidee* went on in the same manner in *Maryland*. His plan was raised as high, and fell as remarkably. GOD is a gracious Father, and will not always let his children proceed in a wrong way. Doubtless there are many of his dear little ones in the *M———n* flock; but many of their principles and practices are exceeding wrong, for which I doubt not our LORD will rebuke them in his own time. But I fear that I weary you. However, dear Sir, I must thank you for your sermon. It contains the very life of preaching, I mean sweet invitations to close with CHRIST. I do not wonder you are dubbed a Methodist on account of it. As it was designed for the poor, I wish it was cheaper. I think practical books cannot be too reasonable. The poor must have them cheap, and the rich will like them the better for it. And now methinks I hear you say, " But how is it at the other end of the town ?" Blessed be GOD, the prospect is promising. Last *Sunday* evening I preached to a most brilliant assembly indeed. They expressed great approbation, and some I think begin to feel. Good Lady H——n is indeed a mother in *Israel*. She is all in a flame for JESUS. You may guess by a word or two in this, that she hath shewn me your last letter. I suppose she will write to you soon. But whither am I running? I quite forget myself. Love makes my pen to move too fast, and too long. Excuse it, dear Sir, and for JESUS's sake never cease praying for, Reverend and very dear Sir,

Your most affectionate though unworthy
younger brother, and willing servant
in our common LORD,
C. W.

LETTER DCCXX.

Dear Mr. T———.

London, Dec. 21, 1748.

HAVE you not thought it unkind, that I answered not your letter before now. You will be pacified when I tell

tell you, that not want of love but leisure hath been the cause of so long a silence. I will now redeem a few moments to pay this debt, and acknowledge a much greater debt of love that I owe, and intend indeed to be always owing to you and yours. CHRIST alone can pay you. He will. Whatever is done to his ministers, he looks upon as done to himself. What a blessed master do we serve! Thanks be to his great name, he continues to deal lovingly with me. I have been blessed in my late excursion into the country, and likewise since I came to town. The prospect of doing good at least to some of the rich, is very encouraging. I know you will pray, that the foolishness of preaching may be a means of bringing some of them to believe on him who justifies the ungodly. You find, that not gifts but grace, sovereign, all powerful grace alone, can reach the heart. But how is dear Mr. B——? Is he yet fled to the world of spirits? Since the LORD has been pleased to hinder his preaching, I think it was cruel to desire he should stay any longer out of heaven. Doctor *Watts* is now gone. Blessed be GOD we shall ere long follow

Where sin and pain and sorrow cease,
And all is love and joy and peace.

I am now thirty four years of age. Little did I think of living so long. And yet when I consider how I have lived, shame and confusion cover my face. O my dear Mr. T——, as you are preparing for the ministry, lose not one moment of time, but labour to be always on the stretch for Him, who was stretched on the accursed cross for you. Study books and men, but above all, study your own heart and the knowledge of JESUS CHRIST, and him crucified. Get your heart free from worldly hopes and worldly fears, and you will avoid thousands of those snares, into which young ministers for want of this too often fall. O let the language of your heart be, "GOD forbid that I should glory, save in the cross of CHRIST, by whom the world is crucified unto me and I unto the world." You will excuse this freedom. It proceeds from the love I bear you. Be pleased to present my cordial respects to your honoured father, your brother, and all enquiring friends, and

accept

accept of the same yourself in the most tender manner, from, my dear Sir,

Yours most affectionately in CHRIST JESUS,
G. W.

LETTER DCCXXI.

To Mr. B——.

My dear Brother, London, *Dec.* 26, 1748.

AS soon as I received your kind letter, I was willing, but till now could not get leisure, to answer it. Accept my thanks, though late, and let the glorious *Emmanuel* have eternal thanks ascribed unto him, if he has been pleased to work upon your soul by any of my poor writings. Since that, I doubt not but you have experienced much of his love, and know more of GOD, even a GOD in CHRIST, and also of your own heart. In these two things consists all our happiness in time and for eternity. Blessed be his name for calling you to witness the efficacy of his death, and the unsearchable riches of his grace to poor sinners. My dear brother, it is an angelic employ. Go on in the name and strength of JESUS. He will not send you a warfare on your own charges. As your day is so shall your strength be. Only wait upon him, and eternal truth has declared, that you shall mount on wings like an eagle, you shall walk and not be weary, nay run and not be faint. Should providence bring me your way in the Spring, I shall rejoice to see and converse with you, and shall tell all that come in my way, of the present as well as future great salvation that is to be had in JESUS CHRIST. In the mean while, I entreat you to pray for me, and as enabled you shall be remembered by, my dear Brother,

Your affectionate brother and servant
for CHRIST's sake,
G. W.

LETTER DCCXXII.

To Lord B——.

My Lord,   *London, Dec.* 30. 1748.

I Had the honour of your Lordship's letter. Gratitude constrains me to send my heartiest acknowledgments. Though absent from, yet I am often present with you. That benign, that sweet disposition of which your Lordship is possessed, must make you appear amiable to all who know you. Add but the christian to it, and then, O then, how happy will your Lordship be! Thanks be to GOD, that your Lordship begins to feel there is no being happy without real christianity. O that this conviction may be abiding, and that your Lordship may have no rest, till you find it in Him who is the Alpha and Omega, the author and finisher of our faith. He longs to make you happy, he is ready to receive you with open arms. He cries, " My son, give me thy heart." To engage you to love him more, he has let you have a worthy lady, who I am persuaded will be glad to go hand in hand to heaven. O that you may both walk in all the ordinances and commandments of the LORD blameless. No greater thing can be desired for you at the throne of grace by, my Lord,

Your Lordship's most obedient, obliged humble servant,

G. W.

LETTER DCCXXIII.

To Lady B——.

Honoured Madam,   *London, Dec.* 30, 1748.

HAVE you not wondered at my not answering your Ladyship's kind letter before now? But I am persuaded you are well assured, that a variety of avocations, and multiplicity of business for the best of masters, not want of respect, hath been the cause. My Lady, your family are always upon my heart. My constant desire and prayer to GOD is, that you all may be filled with all the fulness of GOD. As my Lord mentions nothing to the contrary, I hope your indisposition is removed, and that the language of your heart is, " what shall I render unto the LORD?" I know that the love of JESUS

which

which you have felt, must necessarily constrain your Ladyship to live to Him, who lived and died upon the accursed tree for you. O how is the power of the Redeemer's resurrection displayed in Lady H———n. She is a mother in *Israel* indeed. It would please you to see the assemblies at her Ladyship's house. They are brilliant ones indeed. The prospect of catching some of the rich in the gospel net is very promising. I know you will wish prosperity in the name of the LORD. But how does good Lady D———, dear Mrs. C———, and Mrs. I———? All, I hope, putting off the old man, and putting on the new with greater earnestness than ever. O that I may begin to be in earnest! I am now thirty-four years of age. Is it not time for me to begin to spend, and be spent, for him who has loved me and given himself for me? I beg your Ladyship's prayers, and the prayers of all your dear and honoured relations. I send them all my humble and hearty respects, and beg you will accept the same from, my Lady,

Your Ladyship's most obliged humble servant,

G. W.

LETTER DCCXXIV.

To Mr. H——— H———.

My dear Brother,   *Chelsea, Jan.* 12, 1749.

I Can now send you but a few lines. Thanks be to GOD, that weeping doth not hinder sowing. I think it is cruel to wish our little ones back into this cold world again. Go on, JESUS will be better to you and yours than seven daughters. I hope Mrs. H——— joins with you in saying, "it is well." But a word or two in answer to the other part of your letter. Cannot you be at *Gloucester* the 24th of this month? That would be abundantly more convenient for me than the 27th. I would appoint our *English* meeting at that time, and, GOD willing, would go with you to *Builth*, and after that to the west. I am now here waiting for LORD B———ke, and some others, who are coming to hear the glorious gospel. Lord L——— is in town. Our good Lady is going on, and every day increasing her reward in heaven. I have much to say when we meet. When will you leave off being a spiritual rake? For the present, adieu! Pray fail not being at *Gloucester.*

cester. In the mean while, let us ply the throne of grace in behalf of each other, and do you pray that an humble, child-like, obedient heart, may be given to, my very dear fellow-soldier,

Yours, &c.
G. W.

LETTER DCCXXV.

To the Reverend Mr. H——.

Chelsea, Jan. 13, 1749.

Reverend and very dear Sir,

YOUR kind and loving answer to my last poor scrawl, humbled me much before Him who alone worketh all things in and by us. But if he will work, who shall hinder? I trust the language of my heart to the ever-blessed JESUS is this,

> *If thou excuse then work thy will,*
> *By so unfit an instrument;*
> *It will at once thy goodness shew,*
> *And prove thy power omnipotent.*

You will not be offended if I tell you, that good Lady H——n saw your letter. She was much pleased with it, and has a great regard for you. She goes on from strength to strength. The prospect of doing good to the rich that attend her Ladyship's house, is very encouraging. I preach twice a week, and yesterday Lord B———ke was one of my auditors. His Lordship was pleased to express very great satisfaction. Who knows what GOD may do? He can never work by a meaner instrument. O dear Sir, pray for me. I want humility, I want thankfulness, I want a heart continually flaming with the love of GOD. Blessed be his name for the share imparted to you. May you go on and increase with all the increase of GOD! I thank you for your kind invitation to your house and pulpit. I would not bring you or any of my friends into difficulties, for owning poor, unworthy, ill and hell deserving me. But if providence should give me a clear call, I should be glad to come your way. I rejoice in the prospect of having some ministers in our church pulpits that dare own

a crucified

a crucified Redeemer. I hope the time will come that many of the priests also shall be obedient to the word, and that of the honourable women there will be not a few. I know you will say *Amen*. For the present, my dear Sir, adieu. Remember me to the doctor, and Mr. *H———*, when you write to or see them, and assure yourself of a constant remembrance in the poor but sincere petitions of, very dear Sir,

Yours most affectionately in the best bonds,

G. W.

LETTER DCCXXVI.

To Dr. S———.

Very dear Sir, London, *Jan.* 17, 1749.

I Received your last kind letter, soon after I had been informing dear Mr. *H———* that I did not chuse to bring my friends into trouble; but that if providence should give me a clear call, I might accept of his invitation. This perhaps may never happen. But if it should, wherefore should dear Mr. *S———* be so much alarmed? What if his people are prejudiced against me? Might not a sermon, under GOD, lessen their prejudices, and perhaps awaken some souls to a sense of the divine life? Such things have been done, such a thing, through the divine blessing, may be repeated again. The way of duty is the way of safety. Our LORD requires of us to confess him in his gospel members and ministers. To be afraid of professing the one, or publicly to own, associate with, and strengthen the hands and hearts of the other, especially when they are set for the defence of the gospel, is, in my opinion, very offensive in the sight of our common LORD, and can only proceed from a want of more love to him and his dear people. I am quite of your mind, my dear friend, that our LORD recommends to us the wisdom of the serpent, but then it is always to be blended with the innocence of the dove. How this is done, in effect, by disowning the open and avowed proclaimers of his eternal truths, I cannot I must confess at present see into. You say, " we are most of us too warm already:" but I hope you do not think, that being ashamed of any of your LORD's ministers is an instance of it? Thanks be to GOD that Mr. *H———* seems, as you express it, " to

court

court the enmity of mankind;" it is an error of the right fide. Better fo than to be afraid of it. The LORD never threatned to fpew any church 'out of his mouth for being too hot; but for being neither hot nor cold he has. It is too true, my dear Sir, " we have but few faithful minifters." But is keeping at a diftance from one another the way to ftrengthen their intereft? By no means. I rather think thofe that hold the fame principles at leaft, and are embarked in the fame caufe, fhould jointly and publicly appear for GOD.—And to tell you my whole mind, I do not believe GOD will blefs either you or your friends to any confiderable degree, till you are more delivered from the fear of man. Alas, how was you bowed down with it, when I faw you laft! And your letter befpeaks you a flave to it yet. O my brother, deal faithfully with yourfelf, and you will find a love of the world, and fear of not providing for your children, have gotten too much hold of your heart. Do not miftake me. I would not have you throw yourfelf into flames. I would only have you act a confiftent part, and not for fear of a little contempt be afhamed of owning the minifters of CHRIST. After all, think not, my dear Sir, that I am pleading my own caufe. You are not in danger of feeing me at N——n. I only take this occafion of faying a word or two to your heart. You will not be offended, as it proceeds from love. You may fhew this to dear Mr. H——. I falute him, the dear doctor, and dear Mr. H——, moft cordially. I hope the feed is fown among the rich to fome purpofe. Laft *Thurfday* Lord B——*ke* was one of my hearers. Brethren pray for us; you are never forgotten by, very dear Sir,

Yours, &c.
G. W.

LETTER DCCXXVII.

To Mr. S——.

London, Jan. 18, 1749.

My very dear Mr. S——,

I Have received from you two very kind letters, the laft of which made me to fmile indeed. Alas, my dear man, what airy caftles are you building? Were your fanguine expectations

pectations to take place, might I not justly say to my friends, "*Quid vultis, ut peream?*" But blessed be GOD, there is yet no danger. The gospel is not got so near the court as you imagine. However, some of the mighty and noble come twice a week to hear at good Lady H———n's, and the prospect of doing good amongst them is very encouraging. One or two I trust are effectually touched. Pray on, and who knows what a great fire a little spark may kindle? I wish the LORD may answer your request, and give you a religious governor. I cannot see how I can serve dear Mr. B———. I should be very shy of asking any favours, supposing I had interest, lest I should be thought to preach for myself and not for CHRIST JESUS my LORD. I would fain convince all, that I seek not theirs but them. I am sorry you have met with so many losses of late; but all our losses will be found to be gain in the end. Blessed are they that love GOD! All things are even now working together for their good. About *August* I purpose, GOD willing, to embark for *Carolina*; though my friends say not, I believe they will be mistaken. Ere this reaches you, I hope GOD will have raised you up Pastors after his own heart. Pray remember me in the most endearing manner to all that I was acquainted with, and tell them I live in hopes of seeing them once more in the flesh. I heartily salute all, and am, very dear Mr. S———,

Yours most affectionately in CHRIST JESUS,

G. W.

LETTER DCCXXVIII.

To Lady H———n.

Honoured Madam, *Bristol, Jan.* 28, 1740.

I Think it is now high time for me to trouble your Ladyship with a few lines. They come to thank your Ladyship ten thousand times for all favours, and to inform you that our glorious Redeemer orders all things well. On *Wednesday*, through winds, rain and frost, I reached *Gloucester*, and preached there the same evening. The next day we held our association, and, thanks be to GOD, affairs turned out better than expectation. I came hither this evening, where I f my brother in the very temper I could wish, "seemingly quite fixed to leave the world for GOD." He tells me of a Colonel, who heard me once in the Summer, that now wants to know if his sins are forgiven. My brother's visit to town has been greatly blessed to him. Surely your Ladyship will never know, till the day of judgment, the great ends GOD had in view in calling your Ladyship to *London*. I rejoice in the prospect of seeing your Ladyship happy amidst a crowd of your spiritual children, who will come to you from time to time to be built up in their most holy faith. You will suffer many pangs for them; but all shall work for your Ladyship's present and eternal good. I suffer much in my bodily health for preaching to the nobility; but, thanks be to GOD, that some seem to have an hearing ear, and an understanding heart. My warmest prayers are continually ascending to the throne of grace for your Ladyship, and for all those who have heard the word; especially those honourable women that used to join with your Ladyship in receiving the sacred symbols of the Redeemer's blessed body and blood. My cry to our LORD in their behalf is this,

> *Take their poor hearts, and let them be*
> *For ever clos'd to all but thee.*

I forgot to tell your Ladyship, that the *Welch* justices have ordered the twenty pounds, exacted of the Methodists by Sir *W———*, to be returned. I can add no more, but my most grateful acknowledgements for all kindnesses, and subscribe myself, honoured Madam,

Your Ladyship's most dutiful and willing servant
for CHRIST's sake,

G. W.

LETTER DCCXXIX.

To Lady H———n.

Honoured Madam, *Bristol, Feb.* 1, 1749.

YESTERDAY I had the favour of your Ladyship's letter; and am glad to find that Lady G———'s journey will not be altogether in vain. Our LORD will note, in his book, your Ladyship's endeavour to serve her, and reward you openly before men and angels, for this and all other your works of faith, and labours of love. I am glad your Ladyship approves of Mr. *W*——'s conduct, and that he hath preached at your Ladyship's. The language of my heart is, "LORD, send by whom thou wilt send, only convert some of the mighty and noble, for thy mercy's sake! Then I care not if I am heard of no more." I am much obliged to those honourable ladies who are pleased to send me their good wishes. In return, they have my earnest prayers that they may be filled with all the fulness of GOD. For my own part, I long to take the field. I trust we shall see a glorious Spring, and hear of many souls crying out, "What shall we do to be saved?" Blessed be GOD, we have solid seasons here. I trust I can with truth say, "The gospel has been preached with the Holy Ghost sent down from heaven." Next *Monday*, GOD willing, I shall travel further *Westward*. In the mean while, I purpose to preach here, and at *Kingswood*, and to take a step to *Bath*. Mr. C—— was here yesterday, and brought me a benefaction from Miss S——, of fifteen guineas, most or all of which I purpose paying to Mr. ———, towards discharging what is due to him for the Orphan-house. Thus doth the LORD help me, who long ago deserved to be banished from his presence for ever, and to be employed in his work no more. I am glad your Ladyship approves of Mr. G——: He is, I think, a worthy man. By taking this method, your Ladyship will have an opportunity of conversing with the best of all parties, without being a bigot, and too strenuously attached to any. Surely in this your Ladyship is directed from above. The blessed JESUS cares for his people of all denominations. He is gathering his elect out of all. Happy they, who, with a disinterested view, take in the whole church militant, and, in spite of narrow-hearted bigots, breathe an undissembled catholic spirit towards all. That your Ladyship may increase and grow in this spirit, and consequently increase in true divine happiness every day, is and shall be the constant prayer of, Madam,

   Your Ladyship's most obliged, obedient
    humble servant,

          G. W.

LETTER DCCXXX.

To the Countess of D——.

Honoured Madam, *Bristol, Feb.* 1, 1749.

WILL your Ladyship pardon me, if I inform you, that love and gratitude constrain me to send your Ladyship a few lines? As I am daily praying for the temporal and eternal welfare of your Ladyship, and your honourable sister, so I cannot help informing you, that I trust you have both such a view of the present great salvation, purchased for the very chief of sinners by the blood of CHRIST, that you will neither of you be at rest, till made real partakers thereof. Has not your Ladyship already had a taste of this inward happiness? Assuredly you have. Should not this encourage your Ladyship to expect, seek after, and pray for unspeakably more? Undoubtedly it ought. The fulness which is in JESUS is inexhaustible. Out of that fulness your Ladyship may be always receiving grace for grace. Thanks be to GOD for teaching you the way! Let not your honoured sister think herself too unworthy of such a mercy. Jesus is worthy; she hath nothing to do but to bring all her unworthiness to the LORD our righteousness, and accept of compleat salvation as a free gift. Hearing, when last in town, that your Ladyship would not be offended if I wrote, encouraged me to take the liberty of troubling your Ladyship with this. As the glorious *Emmanuel* enables, it shall be followed with my most fervent prayers, which have been, are, and, through JESUS CHRIST strengthening, shall always be put up in behalf of yourself, and your honourable sister, by, honoured Madam,

Your Ladyship's most obliged, obedient
humble servant,

G. W.

LETTER DCCXXXI.

To Mr. ————.

My dear Sir, *Bristol, Feb.* 4, 1749.

THE contents of your letter surprized me; and yet it is time for me to learn to be surprized at nothing. But what shall we say? It must needs be that these trials should come, to wean us from every creature, and teach us to live by faith in the Son of GOD. Had you succeeded, you certainly would have met with some thorn in the flesh, to keep you from being elated too much. Persons of such sanguine dispositions as you and I are, always need one from some quarter or another. By your letter, this trial has done you good already. Be thankful for it, therefore, my dear Sir, and say from your inmost soul, " the cup, which my heavenly Father hath given me, shall I not drink it?"—We are but poor choosers for ourselves. GOD sees not as we see. It is a comfort when we can say, we have eyed GOD in any affair; but if that affair be plainly disconcerted by his providence, we may be certain it is for good. I found it so in a like circumstance, when my affections were much more engaged than yours necessarily must have been. I wish you joy of being called to leave a worm for GOD, and in your submission to his divine appointment. " Surely, (says the prophet that was sent to anoint one of *Jesse*'s sons) " the LORD's anointed is before me." He guessed several times; but always guessed wrong, till little *David* was sent for, who was thought nothing of. And if a prophet was mistaken, when thus sent in a peculiar manner, and no doubt particularly engaged in prayer for direction, is it any wonder, that we should find ourselves mistaken in many things, even when we have been most earnest with GOD for guidance and direction? GOD often guides us by disappointments; and I doubt not but you will find some better thing is prepared for you. What the LORD hath done to you, though you know not now, yet you shall know hereafter.

I.
Leave to his sovereign sway
  To choose and to command;
So shalt thou wond'ring own his way,
  How wise, how strong his hand.

II.
Far, far above thy thoughts,
  His counsel shall appear,
When fully he the work hath wrought,
  Which caus'd thy needless fear.

You

You see, dear Sir, my concern for you by the length of this letter. As you are, I trust, my own son in the faith, so I cannot avoid naturally caring for you. My letter shall be followed with my prayers. Be resigned. I am better in health than when I left town; and am much blessed in preaching. You know how to give thanks in behalf of

Your sympathizing friend,
G. W.

LETTER DCCXXXII.

To Lady H———n.

Honoured Madam,   *Exon, Feb.* 9. 1749.

YOUR Ladyship's laying your commands upon me to write often, makes me uneasy unless I can redeem time to send to your Ladyship at least once a week. Blessed be GOD, I can inform your Ladyship, that there was a great stirring among the dry bones at *Bristol* and *Kingswood*. Last Lord's-day was a great day of the Son of Man. The power of the LORD attended the word, as in days of old, and several persons, that had never heard me before, were brought under great awakenings. A counsellor came once, and was so affected, that when he got home he invited others to come and hear, which so alarmed his lady, (ready to die of a consumption) that she is afraid her husband will go mad. Last night I came hither, and had the pleasure of seeing some spiritual children that were begotten unto GOD when I was here last. This evening I am to begin to spread the gospel-net; and shall continue in *Exeter* till *Monday*. Affairs have been so confused, that it requires some time to settle them. I find a death must come upon all we do, that the life of it may appear to be wholly of GOD. I hope your Ladyship finds that the Redeemer's work flourishes in your hands. I long to hear, whether my letters were kindly received, and whether the seed sown by me or any other springs up. Whoever plants, or whoever waters, I know it is the LORD must give the increase. Mr. C—— is vastly attached to your Ladyship's interest, and, I believe, prays continually for your success. Many do so, whom your Ladyship knows not. Your Ladyship's letter to Mr. R—— I find is blessed much. It is the good man's lot, that whatsoever he doth shall prosper. May this be fulfilled in your Ladyship more and more every day! I could enlarge, but must away to my delightful work. People are waiting. This late journey has been blessed to the recovery of my health. I have not had any of my usual disorders since I left town. I am sometimes faint. But, "Faint, and yet pursuing," must be the christian's motto. I hope my most dutiful respects will find acceptance with those honourable persons whose faces are set *Zion-wards*, and that your Ladyship will accept the same from, honoured Madam,

Your Ladyship's most obliged, obedient,
and willing servant for CHRIST's sake,
G. W.

LETTER DCCXXXIII.

To Lady H———n.

Honoured Madam,   *Plymouth, Feb.* 16, 1749.

THE last time I wrote to your Ladyship, I was at *Exeter*, where I begun on *Sunday* evening to preach in the open air.—Abundance of souls attended, and I trust real good was done. In the morning, grace flowed richly round the congregation; and many knew experimentally that CHRIST was risen, by his giving them to experience the power of his resurrection in their hearts. On *Monday* I went to *Bovey-Tracey*, about 12 miles from *Exeter*, where I found several poor simple souls. Here also the fountain of life was open, and I believe some drank at, and others felt the want of it. The next morning I preached at a place called *Mary-Church*, where are supposed to be near a score of awakened souls, who have undergone much outward trouble for adhering to the cross of CHRIST. Most of their bitterest opposers were present. All was calm; and the power of the LORD accompanied the word. After sermon I rode twenty miles to *Kingsbridge*, where, to my great surprize, I found about a thousand souls waiting till eight in the evening to hear the word. The tender nature said, "Spare thyself," I thought faith and love said, "Venture upon the LORD's strength, and speak to them." I did, from these words of our dear LORD's: "I must work the works of him that sent me, while it is

day:

day: the night cometh when no man can work." I preached in the street. The moon-shone. All was quiet; and I hope some begun to think of working out their salvation with fear and trembling. The next morning I preached there again; four ministers attended. Our LORD was pleased to make it a very fine season. After sermon I had the pleasure of hearing, that by two or three discourses preached at this place about 5 years ago, many souls were awakened. One young man, then called, is since a preacher; he was in a tree partly to ridicule me. I spoke to him to imitate *Zaccheus*, and come down and receive the LORD JESUS. The word was backed with power—He heard, came down, believed, and now adorns the gospel. From *Kingsbridge* to *Plymouth*, is near twenty post miles. Hither I came last night. About ten miles from the town, I met several of my spiritual children, who came on horseback to see me. When I came into the town, many hundreds were waiting to hear the word, and received me with great joy. Though it was past seven at night, and I had preached at *Kingsbridge* in the morning, I thought it my duty to comply with the people's importunity, and accordingly I called upon them, (in a place stiled the tabernacle, built since I have been absent) to behold the Lamb of GOD. I find a strange alteration in the people since I came first here, now above four years ago. Many were then awakened, and truly converted to the blessed JESUS. I write in a house belonging to a married couple, who call me their spiritual father. *Plymouth* seems to be quite a new place to me. I have also just now parted from a truly converted neighbouring clergyman, who has invited me to preach in his church. Ere long I hope to send your Ladyship some more good news. In the mean while, I wish your Ladyship the best of blessings; and entreat your Ladyship to pray, that a chearful, humble, simple, and guileless heart may be given to, honoured Madam,

   Your Ladyship's most dutiful, though unworthy
    servant for CHRIST's sake,

           G. W.

LETTER DCXXXIV.

To the Reverend Mr. C——.

Reverend and dear Sir,   *Plymouth, Feb.* 20, 1749.

I Had the pleasure of receiving your letters dated *December* 29th and 31st. I thank you a thousand times for this, and all your other favours. I did not think Mr. *H——*'s friendship would hold long. It will be time enough for me to speak to and of him, when I see *Bermudas* again, which I propose doing, GOD willing, as soon as possible. In the mean while, I would only observe, that if I am a *Roman Catholic*, the Pope must have given me me a very large dispensation. Surely Mr. *H——* has acted like one, to pretend so much friendship, and express it in the strongest terms, and yet have nothing of it in his heart all the while. But thus it must be. Dear Sir, we must be tried every way. *Hic murus aheneus esto*, &c. As for any secrets that I told him, he is very welcome to reveal them. You know me too well to judge I have many secrets. May the secret of the LORD be with me! and then I care not if there was a window in my heart for all mankind to see the uprightness of my intentions. I long to have *Bethesda* a foundation for the LORD JESUS. If I can procure a proper solid person of good literature, who will be content to stay two or three years, something may be done. I am now in the *West*, and have begun to take the field. Great multitudes flock to hear; and our LORD is pleased apparently to countenance my poor unworthy ministrations. I have the pleasure of seeing the seed, which was sown just before I embarked last for *America*, spring up, producing an hundred-fold. May JESUS have all the glory! Perhaps (O amazing love!) he has not done with me yet. I am better in bodily health than usual, but expect to be sick again when I return to *London.* Thither I must go in about a fortnight, to preach again to some of the Rich and Great, as well as the Poor. I find it is a trial, to be thus divided between the work on this and the other side of the water. I am convinced I have done right in coming over now; and I keep myself quite disengaged, that I may be free to leave *England* the latter end of the Summer, if our LORD is pleased to make my way clear.

clear. I hope, as you say nothing to the conrrary, that all friends are well. I beg to be remembered to them all in the kindeſt manner, and depend much on their not forgetting to pray for, reverend and dear Sir,

Yours, &c.

G. W.

LETTER DCCXXXV.

To Lady H———.

Honoured Madam, *Plymouth, Feb.* 21, 1749.

I Believe it will much rejoice your Ladyſhip's heart to hear what is doing in the *Weſt*. I could not have thought that the ſeed ſown four years ago, would have met with ſuch a great increaſe. But what cannot GOD do? I have now proclaimed here ſeven times the riches of redeeming love, to very large, attentive, and affected auditories. Generally about two thouſand attend every night; and the *Sunday* evening, in the field, I believe there were above five thouſand hearers. On *Wedneſday*, GOD willing, I move hence. My ſhort ſtay affects the people. But our LORD orders all things well. I hope to be in town at my appointed time, at leaſt within a few days of it. If Mr. *B———* is not returned, I ſhall be grieved to think how your Ladyſhip will want the ordinance; but, thanks be to GOD, the fountain is open, and your Ladyſhip knows the way to it. Laſt Lord's-day I adminiſtered the ſacrament to ſome few ſouls that had no paſtor; and I could have wiſhed your Ladyſhip preſent to have ſeen an affecting ſight,—two parents, both believers, preſenting two daughters and a ſon, in the moſt ſolemn manner, for the firſt time to be communicants. I received them with all joy; and our LORD graced the feaſt with much of his divine preſence. Indeed, my good Lady, affairs bear a very promiſing aſpect. I hear that much good has been done at *Briſtol*. Every where freſh doors are opening, and people flock from all quarters. Prejudices, I find, do ſubſide, and, through grace, ſtrong impreſſions are made on many ſouls. I have not been ſo well, for ſo long a ſeaſon together, for many years, as I have been ſince I left town. A proof, I think, that the LORD calls me into the fields. I hear how your Ladyſhip has been, by the

B———p.

B——p. Alas! how does the enmity of the heart sometimes make persons to forget good manners! Your Ladyship has been taught of GOD to forgive and pity. Well, if the great shepherd and bishop of souls has work to be done, he will raise up instruments, and find ways to send them out.

I.

Thoughts are vain against the LORD,
All subserve his powerful word;
Wheels encircling wheels must run,
Each in course to bring it on.

II.

Blest is faith, that trusts his power,
Blest are saints that wait his hour;
Haste, great conqueror, bring it near,
Let the glorious close appear.

I know that your Ladyship will say heartily, *Amen.* I doubt not but your Ladyship enjoys much of his presence, which is better than life. I hope your honourable and right honourable visitants share richly with you. I beg leave to send them, and your Ladyship, my most dutiful respects, and subscribe myself, honoured Madam,

Your Ladyship's most dutiful, though
unworthy servant,

G. W.

LETTER DCCXXXVI.

To Lady G——.

Honoured Madam, *Plymouth, Feb.* 22, 1749.

YOUR Ladyship's letter I received yesterday; I trust under some sense of the honour your Ladyship has done me, through the King of kings making me instrumental in quickening or building up your Ladyship's precious and immortal soul. Like a pure chrystal, I would transmit all the glory he is pleased to pour upon me, and never claim as my own, what is his sole propriety. Thanks be to his great and glorious name, for putting it into your Ladyship's heart to say sincerely, "LORD, increase my faith." When I had read your Ladyship's letter, I could not help observing what a connection

nection there was between the present frame of your Ladyship's heart, and your present circumstances in respect to your servant. For how is it, honoured Madam, that our faith is to be increased, but by our being exercised with trials? By these the christian grows; and faith, like the burning bush amidst the furnace of affliction, flourishes unconsumed. Blessed be GOD, that your Ladyship hath taken hold of a great and precious promise. Our LORD has promised, "that he will not suffer us to be tempted above what we are able to bear." And he is faithful that hath promised. We have nothing to do, but to plead his promise in prayer. Be pleased, therefore, honoured Madam, to solace yourself, under your present distress, with these lines:

I.
With joy we meditate the grace
Of our High-priest above;
His heart is made of tenderness,
His bowels melt with love.

II.
Touch'd with a sympathy within,
He knows our feeble frame;
He knows what sore temptations mean,
For he has felt the same.

III.
He, in the days of feeble flesh,
Pour'd out his cries and tears;
And in his measure feels afresh,
What every member bears.

IV.
Then let our humble faith address
His mercy and his power;
We shall obtain delivering grace,
In the distressing hour.

This is, and shall be, honoured Madam, my daily prayer on your behalf. Fear not; our LORD will take care that all shall work for good. Those who are sincere, will soon get over such stumbling blocks; and those that are not, will stumble at any thing, nay every thing. I bless GOD, that
some

some have got their faces set *Zion-wards*. Of the honourable women, ere long, I trust, there will be not a few who will dare to be singularly good, and confess the blessed JESUS before men. O with what a holy contempt may the poor despised believer look down on those, who are yet immersed in the pleasures of sense, and amidst all the refinements of their unassisted, unenlightened reason, continue slaves to their own lusts and passions. Happy, thrice happy they! who begin to feel and experience what it is to be redeemed from this present evil world. Well may they count all things but dung and dross for the excellency of the knowledge of CHRIST JESUS their Lord. Well may they look upon the few righteous, as the only truly excellent ones of the earth; and choose rather to suffer affliction with the people of GOD, than enjoy the pleasures of sin for a season. You, honoured Madam, I trust, are one of this happy number. May all your children add to it, and follow your Ladyship, as they see you follow CHRIST. I hope that some have been inclined to list under his banner, since I left town. Indeed the glorious Redeemer has dealt bountifully with his people, and with unworthy me. The good Lady H———n, I suppose, hath informed your Ladyship of some pleasing particulars. I hope to acquaint you of more at my return to town. In the mean while, I beg leave to subscribe myself, honoured Madam,

Your Ladyship's most obliged, &c.
G. W.

LETTER DCCXXXVII.

To the Countess of D———.

Honoured Madam,   *Plymouth, Feb.* 22, 1749.

YESTERDAY I had the favour of your Ladyship's letter, which I would have answered immediately, but was engaged both in company, and in preaching the everlasting gospel. Your Ladyship's answering my poor scrawl, was an honour I did not expect; but, since your Ladyship is pleased thus to condescend, I am encouraged to make a reply. And give me leave to assure your Ladyship, that your own case, and that of your honoured sisters, have been, and are always upon my heart. I pray for both in public and private,

though

though none knows whom I mean. Blessed be the God and Father of our Lord Jesus Christ, who, I trust, hath imparted a saving knowledge of his eternal Son to your Ladyship's heart. Your letter bespeaks the language of a soul which hath tasted that the Lord is gracious, and hath been initiated into the divine life. Welcome, thrice welcome, honoured Madam, into the world of new creatures! O what a scene of happiness lies before you! Your frames, my Lady, like the moon, will wax and wane; but the Lord Jesus, on whose righteousness you solely depend, will, notwithstanding, remain your faithful friend in heaven. Your Ladyship seems to have the right point in view, to get a constant abiding witness and indwelling of the blessed Spirit of God in your heart. This the Redeemer has purchased for you. Of this he has given your Ladyship a taste; this, I am persuaded, he will yet impart so plentifully to your heart, that out of it shall flow rivers of living waters. This Jesus spake of the Spirit, which they that believe on him should receive. As you have, therefore, honoured Madam, received the Lord Jesus, so walk in him even by faith. Lean on your beloved, and you shall go on comfortably through this howling wilderness, till you arrive at those blissful regions,

> *Where pain, and sin, and sorrow cease,*
> *And all is calm, and joy, and peace.*

And O that your honoured sister may go hand in hand with your Ladyship! Wherefore doth she doubt? Wherefore doth she fear? Why does not her Ladyship say,

> *To the blest fountain of thy blood,*
> *Incarnate* God, *I fly;*
> *Here let me wash my spotted soul,*
> *From sins of crimson dye.*

Honoured Madam, is it not a fountain opened? Opened for all that will come, and wash at, and drink of it? Entreat her Ladyship, therefore, honoured Madam, not to be faithless, but believing. Beg her to come, or rather be pleased to inform her Ladyship, that her Saviour entreats and commands her to come just as she is, and to accept of salvation as a free-gift. O that with Queen *Esther* she may say, "If I perish, I perish." Then shall she see the King of kings holding out a golden sceptre, and not an iron rod. But I forget myself again. Honoured Madam, be pleased to pardon me, and accept what I have written as the overflowings of a heart that hath been wrestling with GOD, for the salvation of your Ladyship, your honoured sister, and of all related to you. This is the best proof I can give of my being, honoured Madam,

Your Ladyship's most obliged, obedient,
and willing servant for CHRIST's sake,

G. W.

LETTER DCCXXXVIII.

To the Countess of H———n.

Honoured Madam,   *Exeter, Feb.* 24, 1749.

AFTER I wrote to your Ladyship last post, from *Plymouth*, I received the letters you was pleased to communicate to Mr. C———. They came quite unexpected. I think it is enough, that my letters are received, not without being answered; but the LORD JESUS will humble me by mercies. O that they may have that blessed effect upon my soul! Inclosed, your Ladyship hath my answers. I have sent them open, that your Ladyship may (if not too long) peruse them. Whilst I was writing, the fire kindled, and I did not well know how to leave off. I rejoice that your Ladyship hath such a promising prospect of doing good among the rich and great. Mr. C———, in his last, writes thus: "Mr. G——— went with me to wait on her Ladyship; where he owns he spent two hours with more pleasure, than he ever remembered to have done in any company before: and, I must freely own, he spoke my own sentiments." I believe that your Ladyship will daily reap the fruit of a catholic spirit, and a free conversation with the truly gracious of all denominations. It is a conduct truly god-like. Dear Mr. T——— has much of it. I parted from him on *Thursday* afternoon. He was once almost blinded by weeping under the word. He was rejoiced to see the flocking at *Plymouth*. Indeed it was very encouraging. Our LORD seemed to keep the best wine until the last. At *Tavistock*, ten miles from *Plymouth*, I preached last *Thursday*, but was rudely treated. For, whilst I was praying, some of the baser sort brought a bull and dogs, and disturbed us much. But I hope that good was done. Blessed be GOD, we know some has been done. I conversed with three or four, that have been awakened by the reading of some of my printed sermons. Surely the Apostle spoke like himself, when he said, "GOD has chosen the weak things of this world, to confound the strong; and things that are not, to bring to nought the things that are." I am now come thus far in my return to *London*. I purpose, GOD willing, being there in about ten days. On *Monday* next I shall set out for *Bristol*; where, as I am informed, the infinitely condescending Redeemer has been pleased greatly to bless my last visit. When I think of *London*, I feel a kind of fear and trembling, lest my bodily sickness should return again, and I should not speak to the Mighty and Noble, so as to win them to the ever-blessed JESUS. But I desire to throw myself blindfold into his hands, believing, (LORD, help my unbelief!) that as my day is, so shall my strength be. At present, honoured Madam, this is the language of my heart, to Him, whose I am, and whom I desire to serve:

> *A life that all things casts behind,*
> *Springs forth obedient to thy call;*
> *A heart, that no desire can move,*
> *But still t'adore, believe, and love,*
> *Give me, my* LORD, *my life, my all!*

I hope this will find your Ladyship quite happy under the shadow of redeeming love. I wish your Ladyship an increase of that happiness every moment, as being, honoured Madam,

Your Ladyship's most dutiful, though most
unworthy humble servant,

G. W.

LETTER

LETTER DCCXXXIX.

To Mr. C———.

My dear Mr. C———,   *Exeter, Feb.* 25, 1749.

YOUR last, with the inclosed, you may be sure gave me satisfaction, at the same time as they, I trust, humbled me before him, who will send by whom he will send. This post carries answers to the honourable women. I suppose that you will be pleased to find I am thus far in my return to *London.* O my friend, my friend, I come with fear and trembling. To speak to the rich and great, so as to win them to the blessed JESUS, is indeed a task. But wherefore do we fear? We can do all things through CHRIST strengthening us. But why does Mr. C——— think it strange, that no-body can be found to help me in the country? Is it not more strange, that you should lie supine as it were, burying your talents in a napkin, complaining that you have nothing to do, and yet souls every where are perishing about you for lack of knowledge? Why do you not preach or print? At least, why do you not help me, or somebody or another, in a more public way? You are in the decline of life, and if you do not soon reassume the place, you are now, through grace, qualified for, you may lose the opportunity of doing so for ever. I write this in great seriousness. May the LORD give you no rest, till you lift up your voice like a trumpet! Up, and be doing, and the LORD will be with you. I can now no more, but inform you, that, GOD willing, I am to be at *Bristol* next *Tuesday,* where letters on *Wednesday* morning may find, very dear Sir,

    Yours most affectionately in CHRIST JESUS,

                              G. W.

LETTER DCCXL.

To Mr. S———.

Very dear Mr. S———,   *Exeter, Feb.* 27, 1749.

I Am ashamed to think that your last kind letter has lain by so long unanswered; but journeying, preaching, and a multiplicity of other business has prevented me. I shall not carry on the debate; only I must thank you for receiving my letter in so friendly a manner, and entreat you, though a host of enemies are behind, and a whole sea of troubles before you, to go forwards. That was the command the great JEHOVAH gave to his servant *Moses*, when under very pressing circumstances, so that he knew not what to do. The LORD's impressing and affecting persons under your exhortation, is a token for good. It is good to be led on step by step into whatever plan providence intends to call us. " He that believeth doth not make haste." Our business is to follow, and improve the light we have, and that is the way to get more. You know who hath said, " to him that hath shall be given, and he shall have more abundance." May this promise be fulfilled in your heart! But why does my friend write so about assurance, or think he is too sinful to expect such a favour? Have you learnt CHRIST no better yet? Who more sinful than *Paul* or the jaylor, *Zaccheus* or *Magdalene?* and who more assured of their salvation? My dear Mr. S——, do not think so hardly of the glorious Redeemer. Draw near to him with boldness, though the greatest of sinners, and urge that as an argument, why he should give you the greatest and most abiding assurance of his everlasting love. This is the only argument I can use in respect to my own soul. Fear not, dear Sir, though clouds return after the rain; ere long I trust the glorious and ever-blessed spirit will not, as to his comforts, be like a way-faring man, tarrying only for a night, but come and make a continued abode in your heart. The language of my soul for you is, " Come LORD JESUS, come quickly!" May I expect an answer to this in *London*. Thither I am now going from the west, where I have been for about a month, and through grace have seen that the seed sown just before my embarking last for *America*, has sprung up and produced fruit unto GOD. To him be all the glory. The impressions made upon some of the great ones do remain. Good Lady H—— sends me good news. Be pleased to remember me as usual to doctor D—— and Mr. H——, and believe me to be, very dear Sir,

Yours most affectionately in our common LORD,

G. W.

LETTER DCCXLI.

To the Rev. Mr. H——.

Bristol, March 1, 1749.

Reverend and dear Sir,

I Am much obliged to you for your last kind letter. It was so agreeable, that I sent it to good Lady H——. Her Ladyship writes me word " that it was a letter after her own heart." She loves a Catholic spirit, and I trust you are not deceived in your thoughts concerning me in this respect. If I know any thing of my desperately wicked and deceitful heart, I truly love all that love the glorious *Emmanuel*, and though I cannot depart from the principles which I believe are clearly revealed in the book of GOD, yet I can chearfully associate with those that differ from me, if I have reason to think they are united to our common head. This induced me to call upon good Mr. *L*——, whose books many years ago were blessed to my soul, when the work that is now spreading, was then only in embryo. I am just come from the west, where I have had the pleasure of seeing the seed sown just before I last embarked for *America*, sprung up and bearing much fruit. All glory be to Him who alone giveth the increase. I have also had two letters from some honourable women, who I trust have received the grace of GOD in truth; and Lady *H——n* writes me word, that " the prospect of doing good at my return to *London* is very encouraging." Thither I am now bound. I go with fear and trembling, knowing how difficult it is to speak to the great, so as to win them to JESUS CHRIST. I sometimes am ready to say, " LORD, I pray thee have me excused, and send by whom thou wilt send." But divine grace is sufficient for me. I can do all things through CHRIST strengthening me. My dear brother, fail not to pray for me, that I may hold on and hold out to the end, and in prosperity and adversity press forward with an even, chearful, meek and lowly mind towards the mark, for the prize of our high calling in CHRIST JESUS. I am glad to hear that doctor *S*—— goes on so well. I guess he will not be suffered long to halt. It is no matter how soon all worldly shackles are knocked off, and persons set at liberty

(supposing

(supposing they have a proper call) to range for GOD. I find there is no hopes of compromising matters. Nobody can be ordained that is a Methodist. Well! the time may come, when many of the priests also shall be obedient to the word. They come last; but then many of them come together. I know you will say, Amen! Let me hear from you shortly again. You shall have as quick returns as can be given you, by, my dear brother,

   Yours most affectionately in our common LORD,
         G. W.

LETTER DCCXLII.

To Lady H―――.

Honoured Madam,   *Gloucester, March 4, 1749.*

HAVING been moving this week from place to place, I could not write to your Ladyship as usual; and even now my body is so fatigued, that I cannot say much. However, I would beg leave to inform your Ladyship that the glorious *Emmanuel* continues to smile upon my poor labours; and that about the middle of the week, by his leave, I purpose waiting upon your Ladyship in *North Audley-street*. I doubt not but I shall find your Ladyship riper for heaven, than when I left *London*. There you will be always thronged with company, and yet free from the least distraction. On earth it is otherwise. However, as we advance in the divine life, we shall be more and more conformed to those ministring spirits, who, though waiting on us below, do always behold the face of our heavenly Father above. This divine lesson, honoured madam, GOD has begun to teach you. May you daily make a proficiency therein, so that your progress may be made known unto all men! I will follow as fast as I can, though alas! with too slow a pace. I must now add no more, but my usual prayers for your Ladyship's temporal and eternal welfare, and hasten to subscribe myself, honoured madam;

   Your Ladyship's most dutiful though
    unworthy humble servant,
        G. W.

LETTER DCCXLIII.

To Mr. B——.

Dear Billy, London, *March* 10, 1749.

I Have juſt now heard, that a ſhip will ſail for *Philadelphia* in a day or two. I cannot therefore miſs the opportunity of acknowledging the receipt of your laſt kind letter. I am ſorry it brought me ſuch bad news concerning the ſtate of religion in your parts. My conſtant prayer for you, and my other *Philadelphia* friends is this, " LORD, revive thy work in the midſt of the years." Notwithſtanding ſo wide a door is opened here, and a proſpect of doing much good lies before me, yet I have ſettled thoughts of embarking for *America* in the fall. But future things belong to GOD. His I am, and I deſire to be entirely at his alwiſe diſpoſal. My wife is not yet arrived; I hear ſhe is yet upon the water. May the LORD JESUS be her convoy! I am juſt returned from an excurſion of about ſix hundred miles in the weſt, where I had the pleaſure of ſeeing, that the ſeed ſown before I embarked laſt for *America*, had been bleſſed abundantly. Glory be to Him, who alone has given the increaſe. The news you have had of my preaching to ſome great ones, is true; I have done it for ſome time twice a week, and thanks be to the bleſſed Redeemer, it has already produced good effects. Lady H—— is a mirror of piety indeed. In time, I truſt of the honourable women there will not be a few, who dare to confeſs the LORD JESUS before men. You muſt remember me to all. I have ſcarce time to write this, ſo can only ſend one general ſalutation. The LORD JESUS be with all your ſpirits, Amen and Amen! The bearer, Mr. *H*——, ſeems to be well recommended as an honeſt man. He is an entire ſtranger to every body in *America*, and I believe has a mind to ſettle in *Philadelphia*. I am deſired to write a line in his behalf. You will do what you can for him, becauſe he is a ſtranger. I could write much more, but am interrupted. Adieu, my dear man, for the preſent. Pray keep near the ever-bleſſed Redeemer, and fail not to pray for and write to

Yours moſt affectionately in our common LORD,

G. W.

LETTER DCCXLIV.

To Mr. S——.

London, March 11, 1749.

My very dear Mr. S——,

I Wish you joy. I trust you may now say, "Now I begin to be a disciple of JESUS CHRIST." You know who has commanded us to rejoice and be exceeding glad when men separate from our company, and speak all manner of evil against us falsely for his name's sake. Thanks be to GOD, you have at length found out, that whosoever attempts to reconcile GOD and the world, is attempting to reconcile two irreconcilable differences. They are as opposite as light and darkness, heaven and hell. You have nothing to do, but to go on doing, and then sing with an holy triumph,

> *For this let men revile my name,*
> *I shun no cross, I fear no shame;*
> *All hail reproach, and welcome pain,*
> *Only thy terrors,* LORD, *restrain.*

You know he is faithful, who hath promised, " that he will never leave nor forsake you." Wait on him therefore, dear Sir, and you shall renew your strength, nay you shall mount on wings like an eagle; you shall walk and not be weary, you shall run and not be faint. Various are the trials inward and outward that you will meet with. It is in the spiritual as in the natural birth. The after-pangs are sometimes sharper than those that precede the new-birth itself. If you are made use of by JESUS CHRIST, no wonder that satan desires to have you, that he may sift you as wheat. But fear not; JESUS prays for you; your faith therefore shall not fail. How was *Paul* humbled and struck down before he was sent forth to preach the everlasting gospel? Prayer, temptation, and meditation, says *Luther*, are necessary ingredients for a minister. If GOD teaches us humility, it must be as *Gideon* taught the men of *Succoth*, by thorns. This I suppose is what dear Mr. *H*—— means; he has been conversant with Mr. *L*——, and writes much therefore in his way. I find he is for making thorough work of it, and digging deep in order to build high. He is certainly right;

right; but why we should not press after and continually plead for assurance, which is every where through the holy scriptures spoken of as the common portion of GOD's children, I cannot yet see. It is a false humility to be content without that which GOD offers and promises to give. Let him give it in his own way and time; but, "LORD give me a full assurance of faith, that I may joy and rejoice in thee evermore!" should be the constant cry of your soul. My dear Sir, I could enlarge, but I must away to our good Lady H——n's. You must not expect to see her till *August*. I preached at her Ladyship's on *Thursday*, and am to do so weekly. I expect to leave town in about a month. Pray let me see you if possible. A new scene will open to you, now you begin to act publickly for CHRIST; but I must bid you farewel. Adieu. May the LORD JESUS be with your spirit! Write often, and you shall be answered, GOD willing, as speedy as possible by, my very dear friend,

Ever yours whilst
G. W.

LETTER DCCXLV.

To the Rev. Mr. G——.

My dear Brother, London, *March* 17, 1749.

WHAT a blessed thing it is, that we can write to, when we cannot see one another! By this means we increase our joys, and lessen our sorrows, and as it were exchange hearts. Thanks be to the LORD JESUS, that the work flourishes with you. I am glad your children grow so fast; they become fathers soon; I wish some may not prove dwarfs at last. A word to the wise is sufficient. I have always found awakening times like spring times. Many blossoms, but not always so much fruit. But go on, my dear man, and in the strength of the LORD you shall do valiantly. I long to be your way, but I suppose it will be two months first. My love awaits Mrs. H—— and all that love the LORD JESUS in sincerity. Pray tell my dear Mr. I—— that I cannot now answer the *Preston* letter, being engaged in answering a virulent pamphlet, entitled, "*The Enthusiasm of the Methodists and Papists compared*," supposed to be done by the

Bishop

Bishop of *E———*. Thus it must be. If we will be temple builders, we must have temple builders lot; I mean, hold a sword in one hand and a trowel in the other. The LORD make us faithful *Nehemiahs*, for we have many *Sanballats* to deal with! but wherefore should we fear? If CHRIST be for us, who can be against us? *Nil desperandum, christo duce*, is the christian's motto. My dear brother, good night. May the LORD JESUS be with your spirit, and make you wise to win souls, even wise as an angel of GOD! Remember me in the kindest manner to honest hearted Mr. *I———*, and tell him, that in a post or two I hope he will hear again from

His and your most affectionate though unworthy
brother and fellow-labourer in CHRIST's vineyard,
G. W.

LETTER DCCXLVI.

To the Rev. Mr. W———.

Reverend and dear Sir, London, *April* 5, 1749.

YOU cannot well tell how much satisfaction your last kind letter gave me. It was like yourself, like a father in CHRIST, to write to strengthen the hands of one, who is not yet half your age, but I trust ready to spend and be spent for the good of precious and immortal souls. I see that you have heard how kind my enemies have been to me. They have told me of my faults, and by their opposition have given me an opportunity of confessing them. I am just now publishing a pamphlet, in answer to one published against the Methodists, upon the title-page of which I intend to have these words, " Out of the eater came forth meat." O how good, how infinitely wise is JESUS CHRIST! How careful to cause all things to work together for good to those who love him. I have reason to speak well of him, as a promise-keeping Saviour. I doubt not, but he will greatly bless and own you in the latter stages of the road, and cause you to go off like a ripe shock of corn. It will rejoice you to hear that conviction work is going on in *England* and *Wales*. I believe the holy spirit is powerfully working on some of the Rich, and the Poor seem rather more eager than ever to hear the gospel. I am much engaged, so that I have scarce time to see or write to any; but in heaven there will be time enough, and but just enough too;

> *For O eternity's too short,*
> *To utter all* CHRIST'*s praise.*

You will be pleased to return my most cordial salutations to your wife, and all that desire the welfare of such a worthless worm. As our common Lord enables, you and they shall be remembered by, Reverend and very dear Sir,

Yours most affectionately,

G. W.

LETTER DCCXLVII.

To the Rev. Mr. H———.

Rev. and dear Sir, London, *April* 5, 1749.

YOUR kind letter would not have lain by me unanswered so long, had I not been necessarily employed in affairs of immediate consequence. At Lady H——'s request, I read part of it to some of the nobility, who approved of it very much. By your leave, I will put a sentence or two of it, without mentioning names, into a pamphlet I am now fitting for the press. I suppose you have seen it advertised. I want to own and publicly confess my public mistakes. O how many, how great have they been! How much obliged am I to my enemies for telling me of them! I wish you could see my pamphlet before it comes out. I just now wrote to Doctor S——— to see if he cannot meet me this day sevennight, or contrive some way for conveyance of my little piece to him. O that it may be blessed to promote GOD's glory, and the good of souls! You will be glad to hear that our LORD has given us a good passover, and that the prospect is still encouraging among the Rich. I intend leaving town in about a week, and to begin ranging after precious souls.—But I shall wait for the doctor's answer. You judge right when you say, " it is your opinion that I do not want to make a sect, or set myself at the head of a party." No, let the name of *Whitefield* die, so that the cause of JESUS CHRIST may live. I have seen enough of popularity to be sick of it, and did not the interest of my blessed Master require my appearing in public, the world should hear but little of me henceforward. But who can defert fuch a caufe? Who, for fear of a little contempt and fuffering, would decline the fervice of fuch a Mafter? O that the Lord JESUS may thruft out many, many labourers into his harveft? Surely the time muft come, when many of the priefts alfo fhall be obedient to the word. I wait for thy falvation, O LORD!—But I muft bid you farewel. Praying that you may grow under the crofs, and be enabled to flourifh unconfumed in fire, I fubfcribe myfelf, Reverend and dear Sir,

Yours moft affectionately in our common LORD,

G. W.

LETTER DCCXLVIII.

To Lady H———n.

Honoured Madam, *Gloucefter, April* 15, 1749.

IT has given me fome concern, to think that I was fo long in town after I took leave of your Ladyfhip, and could neither fee nor write to you. The laft letter I was about to write, I found myfelf too ill to hold a pen long enough in my hand to finifh it. Bleffed be GOD, I find myfelf now much better. Travelling, as ufual, does me fervice, and the joy of the LORD fupplies the want of bodily ftrength. Ere long I hope to fend your Ladyfhip fome good news out of the country. I came hither this morning, and am to preach to night. In a poft or two your Ladyfhip may expect to hear from me again. In the mean while my prayers will be continually putting up, that you may increafe with all the increafe of GOD. I hope the elect countefs is perfectly recovered of her late indifpofition, and that Lady *Fanny,* H——, C——, &c. are determined to go on in that narrow way which leads to everlafting life. Before I left town, I defired Mr. H—— to fend your Ladyfhip a dozen of my pamphlets, to be prefented to the forefaid Ladies, and to whomfoever your Ladyfhip fhall pleafe befides. As many more may be had as your Ladyfhip fends for. May the LORD give it his bleffing, and caufe me to grow wifer and better by all his various difpenfations towards me. I fhall now take my leave; and after wifhing your Ladyfhip, and the other honourable women that are feeking JESUS,

much

much of that rest which remains for the people of God, I shall subscribe myself, honoured Madam,

Your Ladyship's most obliged humble servant,

G. W.

LETTER DCCXLIX.

To the Countess D——.

Honoured Madam,   *Bristol, April* 19, 1749.

THE unfeigned regard I have for your Ladyship, will not suffer me to be long out of *London* without sending a line to enquire after your Ladyship's welfare. I hope this will find you perfectly recovered from, or meekly resigned under, your late bodily indisposition. I believe your Ladyship hath reason to say, " It is good for me, that I have been afflicted ;"—and sanctified afflictions are undoubtedly signs of special love. To come purified out of the furnace, and to find that some of our dross is purged away by the Lord's putting us into the fire, is indeed an evidence that he is praying for us, and that our faith, however tried, shall not finally fail. O Madam, what a blessing is it to be able to say, " I know in whom I have believed !" How does such an assurance sweeten every bitter cup, and make even death itself to appear with an angel's face ! O that all who are destitute of this unspeakable gift, were convinced of their want thereof, and set upon hungering and thirsting after it ! I hope your honoured sister will be one of these. I have her Ladyship much upon my heart, and do earnestly pray that she may be strengthened, established, and settled in the love of God, and determine to know nothing but Jesus Christ and him crucified. I send her Ladyship my most dutiful respects, and beg you would accept of the same, from, honoured Madam,

Your Ladyship's most obliged humble servant,

G. W.

LETTER DCCL.

To Lady H———n.

Honoured Madam,   *Portsmouth, May* 8, 1749.

GLAD, very glad was I to hear, in a letter sent me by Mr. H——, that your Ladyship was better ; and glad am I,

yea

yea very glad, that I can send your Ladyship good news from this part of the country. The night after I came here, I preached to many thousands, a great body of whom was attentive, but some of the baser sort made a little disturbance. A very great opposer sent for me to his house immediately, and could scarce refrain weeping all the time I was with him. On the *Friday* evening I preached at *Gosport*, where the mob has generally been very turbulent, but all was hushed and quiet, and as far as I could find, all approved. Every time the word has seemed to sink deeper and deeper into the people's hearts, and their affections seem to be more and more drawn out. In short, I hope I can inform your Ladyship that *Portsmouth* is taken, and that we shall hear of many who will in earnest seek after the one thing needful. I have a great mind to go to the isle of *Wight*, but am not yet determined. Here is a knot of sincere souls, that seem to love the LORD JESUS in sincerity. Several date their awakenings from their hearing T——— G———, who I hear is to be ordained by the Bishop of W———, but I doubt it. Last night I had sweet conversation with two of the devout soldiers that have been abroad. They are soldiers indeed. Blessed be GOD, that there are so many of his children scattered up and down, who I trust will give him no rest, till he makes *Jerusalem* a praise through the whole earth. I do not forget Lady F———, the Countess, or any of those who seemed inclined to follow JESUS of *Nazareth*. O that they may be steady, and be enabled with full purpose of heart to cleave unto the LORD! I beg that my most humble and dutiful respects may find acceptance with them and your Ladyship, from, honoured madam,

Your Ladyship's most obliged, obedient
humble servant for CHRIST's sake,
G. W.

LETTER DCCLI.

To the Rev. Mr. M———.

Portsmouth, May 11, 1749.

Rev. and very dear Sir,

IT concerns me much, that one whom I so much honour, and so dearly love in the bowels of JESUS, should hear so seldom from me. Twice have I endeavoured to answer your last kind letter, but have been prevented, by want of health, a multiplicity of business, and frequent removes from place to place. About three weeks ago I was sent for up to *London* to see my wife, but she is not yet arrived. However, it has been over-ruled to the bringing me here, where I have been preaching every day for this week past, to very large and attentive auditories, who come to hear with great eagerness. I hear of many that are brought under convictions, prejudices seem to be universally removed, and a people that but a week ago were speaking all manner of evil against me, are now very desirous of my staying longer amongst them to preach the everlasting gospel. What cannot GOD do? After I remove hence, I purpose, GOD willing, to take a tour into *Wales*, where Mr. H—— tells me the work is upon the advance. We have lately renewed our connection, and whether I stay in *England* or go abroad, he and some more have agreed, in the strength of the LORD, to continue preaching at the Tabernacle and elsewhere as formerly. At *London*, matters have advanced successfully. Real good has certainly been done among the Rich, and the Poor receive the gospel with as much gladness as ever. My outward embarrassments are much lessened, and I hope ere long to be able to say, "I owe no man any thing but love." Many doors are open, and I have thoughts, if possible, of seeing *Scotland* this year. But at present I am in a strait, and continually saying, "LORD, what wouldest thou have me to do?" Sometimes I think I must either drop my *English* or *American* work; but our LORD knows best how to dispose of me. I would be as clay in his hands, and ready to go whithersoever he is pleased to call me. I should be glad to hear of a revival at *G*———; but, dear Sir, you have already seen such things as are seldom seen above once in a century. I am afraid that some good men's calculations about the latter-day glory are premature, and that it is not so near at hand as some imagine. This is our comfort, a thousand years in the LORD's sight are but as one day. He that comes, will come, and will not tarry. Take courage, my dear Mr. *M*———; look up, and go on your way rejoicing. You will remember me most kindly to your dear yoke-fellow, *Nathaniel*, little *R*———, and the young student in your house, and all dear friends. Indeed I do not forget though I cannot write to you. God will not forget your works of faith, and the many favours conferred on, my very dear Sir,

Yours most affectionately in CHRIST JESUS,

G. W.

LETTER DCCLII.

To the Countess D——.

Portsmouth, May, 12, 1749.

Honoured Madam,

I Just now rose from my knees, and have been interceding for you at the throne of grace. The same principle that led me to pray for, excites me also to write a few lines to your Ladyship. Ere now your late bodily indisposition, I hope is entirely removed, and you are up and ministring to JESUS CHRIST. I doubt not but your Ladyship will be helped to sing with a dear saint now with GOD,

―――― *O happy rod,*
That brought me nearer to my GOD.

The end of all affliction, outward and inward, is to make us more and more partakers of a divine nature. The father of mercies hath dealt bountifully with your Ladyship; he hath blessed you in the decline of life. O that your latter end may greatly increase! May you be filled with all the fulness of GOD! This, Madam, is the privilege of a real christian, always growing, and making perpetual advances in the divine life. The path of the just shines more and more unto the perfect day. The way, thanks be to GOD, your Ladyship knows. We must always come by faith, and be continually drawing out of the Redeemer's inexhaustible fulness. If we are enabled to lean on him, we shall go comfortably on in a wilderness. That is the best name this world deserves. Cieled houses, gaudy attire, and rich furniture, do not make it appear less so to a mind truly enlightened to see the beauties that are in JESUS of *Nazareth*. These are things, which a watchful, well-informed christian will always look on with a jealous eye, lest they should divert him from looking unto JESUS the author and finisher of his faith. But I need not write

write thus to your Ladyship, the native language of whose heart I trust is, "GOD forbid that I should glory save in the cross of CHRIST, by whom the world is crucified unto me, and I unto the world." The preaching of the cross hath been much blessed here. Multitudes daily attend, and many are much affected. It would please your Ladyship to see the alteration that has been made in a week's time. But what cannot GOD do? All things are possible to him. I hope your Ladyship will not forget a poor pilgrim in your prayers. Neither you nor your honoured sister are forgotten by him. I send most dutiful respects and grateful acknowledgments to her Ladyship and Lady G—— H——, and shall only now add, that I am, honoured Madam,

Your Ladyship's most obliged, obedient humble servant, for CHRIST's sake,

G. W.

LETTER DCCLIII.

To Lady F——— S———.

Portsmouth, May 12, 1749.

Honoured Madam,

AS I am uncertain whether good Lady *H*—— be in town, I make bold to inclose a line to your Ladyship in a letter I have just written to the elect Countess *D*——. Gratitude constrains me to take the freedom, and the conviction I have that your Ladyship's face is set *Zion*-wards, makes me think it will not be altogether unacceptable. With great pleasure I often reflect on that good work, which I trust the ever-blessed GOD has begun in your soul. My heart's desire and continual prayer unto him is, that your Ladyship, having put your hand to the plough, may be kept from looking back! Satan will not be wanting to exert his utmost efforts to divert you from the cross. He knows of what influence your Ladyship's example must necessarily be, and therefore will always be striving to persuade your Ladyship at least to compound matters, and to attempt to reconcile two irreconcilable differences, CHRIST and the world. But your Ladyship is too well grounded to hearken to his delusive insinuations, and too noble to refuse to give your whole heart to Him who has bought it with no less price than that of his own most precious blood. —What a price is now put into your Ladyship's hands! What a glorious opportunity is now afforded you, to shew even before kings, that we are made kings indeed, and priests unto GOD, and that it is our privilege as christians to reign over sin, death, hell, the world, and ourselves, even whilst here on earth. Methinks I see angels gazing to see how your Ladyship acts your part. O that the angel of the everlasting covenant may always accompany you, and by the power of his eternal and all-conquering spirit, enable your Ladyship to fight the good fight of faith, and run with patience the glorious race that is set before you! He is never wanting to those that put their trust in him. Ask and you shall receive, seek and you shall find, be always knocking, and a door of mercy shall be always opened unto you. O the happiness of a life wholly devoted to, and spent in communion and fellowship with the ever-blessed GOD! It is indeed heaven begun on earth. May your Ladyship taste of it more and more every day and every hour! Blessed be GOD, I trust some in these parts, who a few days ago had never heard of, now begin to look after this kingdom of GOD. A more visible alteration I have not seen made in a people for some time. At first some of the baser sort made a noise, but ever since, thousands have attended in the greatest order, numbers have been and are affected, and through their importunity I have been prevailed on to stay longer than I designed. O to be instrumental to bring only one soul to JESUS CHRIST! But whither am I running? Honoured Madam, your goodness will excuse this freedom. I believe your Ladyship will be glad to hear such tidings. It is the best way I can think of to express my gratitude for the many unmerited favours your Ladyship hath been pleased to confer on, honoured Madam,

   Your Ladyship's most obliged
      and ready servant for CHRIST's sake,
          G. W.

LETTER

LETTER DCCLIV.

To the Countess of H———.

Portsmouth, May 13, 1749.

Honoured Madam,

WITH some degree of impatience have I been waiting to hear from your Ladyship, being very solicitous for your Ladyship's welfare. This morning your Ladyship's unexpected letter surprized me. I only expected to have a line from Mrs. C———. Your Ladyship's writing under such weakness, put me in mind of Mr. C———, who, when his friends advised him not to write on account of his illness, made this reply, "What! would you have my master come and find me idle?" Perhaps our LORD is fitting your Ladyship for some new work. *Luther* observed, that " he was never employed in any new thing, but he was beset with some temptations, or visited with a fit of sickness." I only wish I could bear it for your Ladyship; but then your crown would not be so bright, nor the inward purity of your heart so great. The more trials when sanctified, the more conformed we shall be to the ever-loving ever-lovely JESUS. O that the LORD of all Lords may water you every moment, and cause you to flourish like the burning bush unconsumed in fire! I have more good news to send your Ladyship from *Portsmouth.* Ever since my last, the prospect of doing good has increased. Thousands have attended, and even when it rained, when one could reasonably expect but very few, some thousands came to hear the word. I have contracted a cold by preaching in the rain ; but what is that, if any soul can but get good !.

My life, my blood, I here present,
If in thy cause they may be spent ;
Fulfil thy sov'reign counsel, LORD ;
Thy will be done, thy name ador'd.

On next *Monday* evening I intend, GOD willing, to set out for *Salisbury,* and from thence shall write to your Ladyship again. Yesterday I wrote to the Countess and Lady F———, but did not send the letters to your Ladyship, not knowing
but

but you might have set out for *Bristol*. My brother would be highly delighted to have your Ladyship under his roof. That GOD may restore you to perfect health, and make you a blessing to thousands, is and shall be the constant prayer of, honoured Madam,

  Your Ladyship's most obliged, dutiful, sympathizing,
   though unworthy humble servant,

             G. W.

LETTER DCCLV.

To Lady H———n.

Honoured Madam,   *Bristol, May* 22, 1749.

SINCE I wrote last to your Ladyship, several things have concurred to prove that Providence directed my way hither. I have preached three times, and each time our LORD caused the word to leave a blessing behind it. Yesterday, congregations were very large in the fields. This evening I am to preach again, and to-morrow, GOD willing, I set out for *Wales.*—Though my brother is sorry for the occasion, yet he rejoices very much that he is to be honoured with your Ladyship's company. I believe you will find his house very commodious, and I am persuaded your Ladyship's coming will prove a blessing to him. Surely our LORD is only purging you that you may bring forth more fruit. I am always thinking of, and praying for your Ladyship's perfect recovery. I am now reduced to great weakness myself, but the joy of the LORD is my strength, and through his help I shall leap over every wall. Gladly would I help to bear all your Ladyship's burdens, and thereby evidence how much I am, honoured Madam,

  Your Ladyship's dutiful, sympathizing,
   obliged, though most unworthy servant,

             G. W.

LETTER DCCLVI.

To Lady H———.

Abergavenny, May 27, 1749.

Honoured Madam,

THOUGH I suppose your Ladyship will not be at *Bristol* so soon as this reaches it, yet as this is the most leisure time I am likely to have these three weeks, I cannot help writing a few lines to wait for your Ladyship at my brother's house. I think (as I am persuaded he does also) that he is highly honoured in having your Ladyship under his roof, and I earnestly pray the LORD of all Lords to bless the waters, for the recovery of your health. Though I want to die myself, yet methinks I would have others live, especially such as, like your Ladyship, are placed upon a pinnacle, and in a particular manner set up as lights in the world. For two days past I have been at my wife's house for the sake of a little retirement. It has been sweet, yea very sweet, so sweet that I should be glad never to be heard of again. But this must not be. A necessity is laid upon me, and woe is me if I do not preach the gospel of CHRIST. GOD willing, I therefore purpose to-morrow to begin a three weeks circuit, and to see what the LORD will be pleased to do by me. The country is alarmed, and I hear very numerous congregations are expected. Your Ladyship shall hear from time to time. May the ever blessed GOD fill you with all his fulness, and after you have done and suffered what he hath appointed for you here, translate you to partake of an exceeding and eternal weight of glory in his kingdom hereafter. So prays, honoured Madam,

Your Ladyship's most dutiful, obedient,
obliged humble servant, &c.

G. W.

LETTER DCCLVII.

Abergavenny, May 27, 1749.

My very dear Brother,

INCLOSED you have a letter for our good Lady *H———,* whom I suppose you will have the honour of receiving in
a few

a few days under your roof. Both before, and ever since I left *Bristol*, I have been frequently thinking of the unspeakable mercies, that the infinitely great and glorious GOD is pleased to pour down upon us.—Surely the language of both our hearts ought to be, "What shall we render unto the LORD?" For my part, I am lost in wonder, and want a thousand lives to spend in the Redeemer's service. O let not my dear brother be angry, if I intreat him at length to leave off killing, and begin to redeem time. A concern for your eternal welfare so affects me, that it often brings bodily sickness upon me, and drives me to a throne of grace, to wrestle in your behalf. Even now, whilst I am writing, my soul is agonizing in prayer for you, hoping I shall see that day, when you will have poured out on you a spirit of grace and of supplication, and look to him whom we have pierced, and be made to mourn as one mourneth for a first-born. Till this be done, all resolutions, all schemes for amendment, will be only like spiders webs. Nature is a mere Proteus, and till renewed by the spirit of GOD, though it may shift its scene, will be only nature still. Apply then, my dearest Brother, to the fountain of light and life, from whence every good and perfect gift cometh. A worthy woman in all probability is going to throw herself under GOD, into your hands. A considerable addition will be then made to your present talents, and consequently a greater share of care and circumspection necessary to improve all for the glory of Him, who hath been always preventing and following you with his blessings. Should you prove any otherwise than a pious husband, it will be one of the greatest afflictions I ever met with in my life. At present you can only hurt yourself, which is hurt enough; but then (forgive me, my dear Brother,) I am jealous over you with a godly jealousy. My fears shall be turned into prayers, and I will follow this letter with strong crying unto GOD in your behalf. My retirement here these two days hath been very sweet; but to-morrow I begin a three weeks circuit. Next sabbath I am to be at *Carmarthen*, the *Friday* following at *Haverford-west*. For the present, adieu. That you may take CHRIST to be your All in All, and that the remainder of your life may be one continued sacrifice of love to him, who hath shed his precious blood for you, is the hearty prayer of, my dear Brother,

Yours most affectionately,
G. W.

LETTER DCCLVIII.

To Mr. D———.

Abergavenny, May 27, 1749.

My very dear Friend,

YOUR kind letter I received at *Bristol*, but have not had time to answer it till now. You know what a moving life I lead. It is for one, who laid down his life for me. I want my last remove to come. Blessed be GOD for your recovery from your late indisposition. Many of GOD's people will have reason to be thankful on your behalf. I trust I am; and earnestly pray the LORD of all Lords, that as your day is, so your strength may be. I thank you for minding the poor widows, and the other poor tabernacle petitioners. What an honour is put upon you! To be CHRIST's almoner is no mean office. You shall be rewarded ere long before men and angels. Mrs. D—— shall share with you; and as you have been helpers of each others faith, so shall you be partakers of the same glory. May your latter end greatly increase, and may you be enabled to bring forth fruit even to a good old age! I hope good has been done at *Bristol*. We had three good seasons there. To-morrow I set out on a three weeks circuit through *Wales*. I have been here these two days for a little retirement: it has been very sweet. On *Thursday* I saw Mr. E—— I——, the dissenting minister I before spoke of, and found him very meanly apparelled. He is a most worthy man, and from his zeal for GOD some time ago, he sold fifteen pounds worth of his books to finish a small Meeting-house in which he preaches. He has but three pounds per annum from the fund, and about as much from his people. He lives very low, but enjoys much of GOD, and hath as great understanding in the figurative parts of scripture as any one I know of in the world. He is a *Zachary*, and his wife an *Elizabeth*. Four or five guineas might be bestowed on them. What a scene will open at the great day!

How many *rich Priests* will stand confounded, whilst the poor despised *faithful Ministers* of CHRIST shall enter, after all their tribulation, into the joy of their LORD. I tremble for the one, I rejoice in the foresight of the happiness of the other. May my latter end and future state (however I may be disposed of in the mean while) be like theirs! I know you will say, *Amen.* But what am I doing? I am robbing the poor of your time. Away to your work in the strength of GOD, and whilst you are feeding others, may the LORD JESUS feast your soul! My heartiest respects attend Mrs. D——. She always shares in the petitions put up for you by, my very dear Sir,

Yours most affectionately in our common LORD,

G. W.

LETTER DCCLIX.

To Mr. I—— C——.

Dear Jemmy,   *Carmarthen, June* 5, 1749.

AS I have a peculiar love for you and your wife, I need not inform you that your letter, which gave me an account of her great illness, affected me much. I have not failed to remember her at the throne of grace, and I trust this will find her either relieved from her pain, or resigned to his will who orders all things well. Parting is hard to those who, like you two, have walked in love. But we can do all things through JESUS CHRIST strengthening us. She, when dead, will live for ever, and GOD will be to you better than seven wives. Pray salute the dear woman for me in the tenderest manner. O that she may be strong in the LORD, and in the power of his might, and be enabled to say, " the cup which my father hath given me, shall I not drink it ?" I sympathize with poor Mrs. N—— as well as you. GOD comfort and support you all. We must all be tried. I am still in suspense about my wife: but, what is best, (Glory be to GOD !) the gospel runs and is glorified! I have been enabled to preach fourteen times within these eight days, and the word has every where fallen with weight and power. Yesterday was a great day here indeed. This morning I am going toward *Haverford-west*, and am to be at *Abergavenny* to-morrow fortnight.

I know you will continually pray for me. You know under what character, even as the chief of sinners, but

Yours, &c.

G. W.

LETTER DCCLX.

To Lady H——.

Haverford-west, June 8, 1749.

Honoured Madam,

SINCE my coming into *Wales*, and leaving *Carmarthen*, the infinitely great and infinitely condescending Redeemer has been pleased to ride on in the chariot of the everlasting gospel. Congregations grow larger and larger, and all the towns here about are quite open for the word of GOD. Yesterday I preached very near *Pembroke*, to-day and next LORD's day I am to preach here, and to-morrow at *St. David's*. Not a dog stirs a tongue. The mayor and gentlemen at *Pembroke* were very civil, and the justices here are very fond of having me in *Haverford-west*. I wish I had more time in these parts. The fields are indeed white, ready unto harvest, and the young men bred up at *Carmarthen* Academy were much taken. The congregations consist of many thousands, and their behaviour is very affecting. Indeed we have blessed seasons. O free grace! Here is a dear young man, just ripe for orders. He has good parts, and hath made some proficiency in the languages, is solid, and of some influence in this town. He can get testimonials, and if ordained I believe would be eminently useful in the church. I wish a way could be found out for his admission: but I fear it is impracticable. However, I thought it my duty just to hint it to your Ladyship. May the great Shepherd and Bishop of souls find out means for sending him, and many more like-minded, into his vineyard! But how is your Ladyship's health? I begin to be quite uneasy, because I have received no letter from my brother. I despair of hearing now till *Tuesday* sevennight, when I hope to be at *Abergavenny* again. In the mean while, my prayers are always going to the throne of grace in behalf of your Ladyship, and every branch of your noble family. That they

may

may take root downwards, and bear fruit upwards, is the ardent desire of, honoured Madam,

Your Ladyship's most dutiful,
though unworthy servant,
G. W.

LETTER DCCLXI.

To Dr. S——.

Dear Sir,   *Landovery, June* 14, 1749.

A Few days ago, I received a letter from Mr. C——, in which yours to him dated *May* 20th was inclosed. It gave me some concern, and would have given me more had not the same letter informed me that good Lady H——n had written to you herself. Alas, my dear friend, what needless trouble do you give yourself, and into what difficulties does your fear of man, your too great attachment to the world, and an over-weening fondness for your pretty character, every day bring you! Is it not time to drop our correspondence, when, on so slight an information, you could so much as suspect that I had betrayed that confidence you reposed in me, or believe that I read a letter wherein you declared yourself a *Methodist*, when I had never such letter from you. The only passage, as far as I can remember, that was read (and that too at my Lady's request, if I mistake not) was that noble one wherein you said, "Let the world take my character, and tear it to pieces, &c." Are you ashamed, my dear friend, of the resolution? Or think you to put that in practice, and shun being called a *Methodist?* You might as well attempt to reach heaven with your hand; for, blessed be GOD, such an honour has he put upon the Methodists, that whoever renounces the world and takes up CHRIST's cross, and believes and lives the doctrines of Grace, must be stiled a Methodist whether he will or not. Formerly it was "You are a Puritan," now it is, "You are a Methodist." And why does my dear Mr. S——. take such pains to declare, he never will join the Methodists? Who ever asked him? Or what service could you do their cause by joining, unless your heart was more enstranged from the world than at present it is? Would to GOD you was more like-minded with Mr. H——! He seems to have set down, and counted the cost. He seems to have begun at the right end, and to be fully convinced that there is no reconciling CHRIST and the world, GOD and *Mammon*. My dear Mr. S——, suffer me to be free with you. Our LORD I trust has begun a good work in your soul: but indeed you have many lessons yet to learn. The great physician must give many a bitter portion, in order to purge out the opinion you have of your own importance, and the too great desire you have to keep in with the world. Reproach you cannot shun, if you appear but a little for CHRIST; and you will not have more, perhaps not so much, if you shew quite out. Perhaps you may say, I have done this already; do not then be ashamed of it, but go on, grow in grace, press forwards, and then I care not what declaration you make of your not intending to be a *Methodist*. Be a consistent christian, live above the world, call not the fear of man christian prudence, and then underneath you shall be GOD's everlasting arms. Thanks be to his great name, they have upholden me for some weeks last past. I have now been a circuit of several hundred miles. At *Portsmouth* and *Gosport* the word ran and was glorified. In *South Wales* every where the fields have been white ready unto harvest. Not a dog stirs his tongue. Last *Sunday* I believe I preached to near twenty thousand souls. Grace! grace! In about ten days I hope to be at *Bristol*. Soon after I propose to go to *London*, and from thence to *Yorkshire* and *Scotland*.— Follow me with your prayers, and in return you shall be remembered by, very dear Sir,

Your affectionate friend,

G. W.

LETTER DCCLXII.

To the Reverend Mr. H——.

Landovery, June 14, 1749.

Reverend and dear Sir,

YOURS, dated *May* 24th, gave me both pleasure and pain. I was pleased to read the sweet observations made up and down in it, but pained to find that you have been much indisposed. But what says our LORD? "Those that abide in him, he will purge;" but it is only in order that they may bring forth more fruit. Perhaps our LORD is about to employ you in some fresh work. I wish you may be enabled to draw your pen on the topic you mentioned; it may be of great service to the church of CHRIST. Your remark upon

my

my pamphlet is juſt. I wrote ſhort, becauſe I know long compoſitions generally weary the reader. Perhaps hereafter I may write more; but at preſent I find I have enough to do, to travel, and preach, and anſwer my correſpondents. I publiſhed my confeſſion of ſome miſtakes and imprudencies, to ſatisfy my own conſcience, and ſtop the mouths of adverſaries, and ſtrengthen the hands of real diſintereſted hearty friends: but where are ſuch friends to be found? That phantom called *Contempt* keeps them in fetters, and makes them afraid to appear in defence of a cauſe, which, (notwithſtanding the many imprudencies that have attended it) is undoubtedly the cauſe of GOD. If we think to be free from theſe, in this imperfect ſtate of things, and to ſee either a perfect ſaint or a perfect church till we come to heaven, we ſhall find ourſelves much miſtaken. Daily experience, and more mature confideration, may leſſen our blunders and imperfections; but death alone will put a final ſtop to their mixing in all we do. Thanks be to GOD that we have a CHRIST, who amidſt all does love, and can uphold us. If our infirmities lead us to his croſs, and our ſufferings only make us more willing to be conformed to him in his death, we are gainers by all our loſſes, and riſe by all our falls. Bleſſed be the LORD, that you, dear Sir, have had grace given you to ſit down and count the coſt. I wiſh the beloved phyſician was more reconciled to the croſs. I am perſuaded, let him ſay what he pleaſes, that a too great attachment to the world makes him reaſon as he does in many things. Well,—he is in good hands. He muſt either come or be dragged to the croſs. That pretty character of his muſt be crucified and ſlain: and as well as others, he muſt be content (as Mr. *Gurnall* expreſſes it) " to go to heaven in a fool's coat." O my dear Sir, what pains is the LORD JESUS obliged to take with us, before we can be reconciled to ſuffer ſhame for his great name's ſake!

Briſtol, June 24.

Thus far I wrote, but was obliged to ſtop, being called out to preach. Yeſterday GOD brought me here, after having carried me a circuit of about eight hundred miles, and enabled me to preach, I ſuppoſe to upwards of a hundred thouſand ſouls. I have been in eight *Welch* counties, and I think we have not had one dry meeting. The work in *Wales* is much

much upon the advance, and likely to increase daily. Had my dear Mr. *H——* been there to have seen the simplicity of so many dear souls, I am persuaded he would have said, "*Sit anima mea cum Methodistis!*" But every one to his post. During this excursion I have been kept happy inwardly, and well in body till the latter end of last week, when the LORD was pleased to lay his hand upon me, so that I was almost brought to the grave. But he that wounds, heals also. Thanks be to his holy name for ever and ever! On *Monday* or *Tuesday* next, GOD willing, I set out for *London*. Good Lady *H——* is here, and goes on in her usual way, doing good. She is recovered from her indisposition. I hope this will find you recovered also. That the LORD of all Lords may give you a thriving soul in a healthy body, is the hearty prayer of, reverend and dear Sir,

Yours, &c.
G. W.

LETTER DCCLXIII.

To the Reverend Mr. P——.

London, July 10, 1749.

Reverend and dear Sir,

YOUR kind letter came safe to hand, and it was the more welcome, because it gave me a proof of your being recovered from your late threatening indisposition. Blessed be GOD, it found me as well as can be expected in my body, and I trust steady in promoting the welfare of precious and immortal souls. I have lately seen great things in *Wales*, and the seed sown among the Rich, has in some sprung up and brought forth fruit; but what you have heard from *Scotland* is all a mistake. I heartily wish all was true. The time I hope will come, when princes shall adorn the Redeemer's train. Is there no prospect of your coming over? Your Mr. *T——* might do much for *New-Jersey* college; but I have told you my mind in a former letter. May GOD direct for the best! I am looking up, to know what the great Head of the church would have me to do. I have a great mind to return to my beloved *America* this fall, but am not yet determined. My wife arrived about a fortnight ago, and joins in sending
cordial

cordial salutations to all. O that we may all increase with all the increase of GOD! Your sentiments concerning Mr. H——'s book, are very just. It has gone through six editions. The author of it is my old friend; a most heavenly-minded creature, one of the first of the Methodists, who is contented with a small cure, and gives all that he has to the poor. He is very weak, and daily waits for his dissolution. A neighbouring clergyman near him preaches the gospel; and a physician, formerly a noted Deist, has lately espoused the interest of JESUS of *Nazareth*. We correspond with, though we cannot see one another. We shall ere long meet in heaven:

There pain, and sin, and sorrow cease,
And all is calm, and joy, and peace.

I recommend myself most earnestly to your prayers, and am, reverend and dear Sir,

Yours most affectionately,

G. W.

LETTER DCCLXIV.

To Mr. J—— D——.

My dear Friend, London, *July* 12, 1749.

I Am obliged to you for your kind letters; for the trouble you have been at about the money, and for all favours. Was I to follow my own inclinations, I would come and thank you in person; but I fear providence will not permit me to embark for *America* this fall. However, I am looking up, and looking about me, and trust our LORD will point out his way before me. I am not at all uneasy at what one of your clergy may have said of me; I am only sorry upon his own account; having known more than once, that GOD delights to plead the cause of the injured. I trust I can say, that with simplicity and godly sincerity I desire to have my conversation in the world; and I hope it is my daily study to keep a conscience void of offence towards GOD and towards man. Whilst this is the case, we need not fear what men or devils can say, or do unto us. They can only speak all manner of evil against us falsely: and that our LORD hath taught us to expect. They can only kill the body; blessed be GOD, the

soul

foul is out of their reach. I am content to wait till the day of judgment for the clearing up of my character: and after I am dead, I defire no other epitaph than this, "Here lies G. W. what fort of a man he was, the great day will difcover." O my dear Sir, what a bleffed thing is it to have the Redeemer to be our friend. If we can but truly fay, "I know that my Redeemer liveth," how fafely may we put our fouls into his hands, as into the hands of a faithful creator! I hope my dear Mr. D―― will not reft till he can fay fo.―The frequent indifpofitions of body that you are under, are fo many loud calls to prepare for another world —Nothing but the righteoufnefs of CHRIST imputed, and the holinefs of CHRIST imparted to your foul, can make you happy in a dying hour. I could enlarge, but muft away. With this, I have fent you a dozen of my nine fermons, to be difpofed of as you think beft. I would fend more, but have very few left. I would write to Efquire R――――, and fome other gentlemen, but have not the leaft leifure. Be pleafed to remember me to them in the kindeft manner, as they come in your way, and let them know they are not forgotten by me. Will your dear yokefellow, and all your family, accept of my hearty love? I owe you much! May the LORD JESUS reward you a thoufand-fold! He will, he will. Laft night Capt. H―― did me the pleafure to fup with me. I took it extremely kind, and fhould be glad to wait upon *Bermudas* friends every day. My wife hath been arrived about a fortnight, and joins in fending cordial falutations with, my dear Mr. D――,

Yours moft affectionately,

G. W.

LETTER DCCLXV.

To Lady Fanny S――――.

Honoured Madam, *Briftol, Aug.* 1, 1749.

THOUGH I had the pleafure of hearing of your welfare, by your laft to good Lady H―――n, yet I cannot help taking the freedom of fending your Ladyfhip a few lines. They come to inform you, that you never are, and, by divine affiftance, never fhall be forgotten by me at the

throne

throne of grace. To that, I truſt, your Ladyſhip finds free acceſs every day, and every hour, through the blood of the Lamb, who was ſlain to take away the ſins of the world. Your Ladyſhip's preſent ſituation, I hope, will be ſanctified to this end. It is in the ſchool of affliction that we muſt learn the way to, and reap benefit from the croſs.—Happy they who come purified out of the furnace, and, like the burning buſh, flouriſh unconſumed in fire. This, Madam, is the privilege of all believers. Trials, which harden others, purify and ſoften them. The love of GOD turns every thing into what is more valuable than gold. It brings light out of darkneſs, and cauſes others blindneſs to increaſe our ſpiritual ſight. O glorious privilege! happy change! How much are you indebted, honoured Madam, to free grace, for making you in any degree a partaker of it! Alas! alas! but few of your Ladyſhip's ſtation in life chooſe to ſtrive to enter into that ſtrait gate which leadeth unto life eternal. The noiſe of coaches, and the continual attention to what they call innocent diverſions, drowns the ſmall ſtill voice of GOD's bleſſed Spirit ſpeaking in their hearts. Since I have been here, many in high life have attended; whether to any valuable purpoſe, the great day will diſcover. Good Lady *H———n* ſtill continues to abound in the work of the LORD, and is brightening her crown every day and hour. She is quite well, and intends ſtaying ſome days longer for the benefit of the waters. Your Ladyſhip is remembered when we are feaſting at the Redeemer's table. In a few days I ſhall move hence; and it may be, that I ſhall go to *Georgia* this fall. May the LORD direct me, and bleſs all thoſe who are the orphan's friends! That your Ladyſhip may be bleſſed with all the bleſſings of the everlaſting goſpel, is the hearty prayer of, honoured Madam,

Your Ladyſhip's moſt obliged, obedient
humble ſervant,
G. W.

LETTER

LETTER DCCLXVI.

To Mr. L―――.

Dear Mr. L―――,   *Bristol, Aug.* 4, 1749.

PROVIDENCE, for wise reasons, prevented my seeing you both at *Gloucester*, and at the *Hill*. This comforts me, " What is, is best." Since I came here, I have seen your letter about the intended charity-school, and wish you success in the name of the LORD. I communicated it to our elect lady, who immediately contributed five guineas, another two, and Colonel G―― one. These I have sent for you, to Mr. ―――, who, I suppose, will take care to convey them to you. Mrs. E――, I believe, intends to do something. Mr. C―― likewise spoke to the Bishop, who, I think, has promised to contribute: so that you see no time has been lost. Only, my dear friend, take this caution, " sit down, and count the cost, before you begin to build." Do not lay out more than you know you can pay. Go the cheapest way to work; and if you cannot build, rather keep a stock in hand to pay the schoolmaster, and hire a house convenient from year to year, and, if possible, find the children in books. You well know what I have suffered for running too far into debt for others. I am glad you are likely to settle at S――. May the LORD JESUS bless you and yours more and more! He continues to be kind to me, and will at length, I am persuaded, (though I pass through many tribulations) land me safe in glory. There we shall meet, never to part again. In the mean while, that we may both behave like good soldiers of JESUS CHRIST, is the hearty prayer of, my dear friend,

Yours, &c.

G. W.

LETTER DCCLXVII.

To the Bishop of W―――.

My Lord,   *Bristol, Aug.* 7, 1749.

THE occasion of my troubling your Lordship in this manner, is as follows. I have, more than once, been very credibly informed, that your Lordship has been pleased to charge me, at the public Wells, with being guilty of *Perjury*. This comes, therefore, to beg the favour of your Lordship, only to let me know, (in whatever manner your Lordship shall judge most proper) upon what foundation such a charge is built: and I hereby promise, by divine assistance, that a full, fair, and explicit answer shall be given to your Lordship, by, my Lord,

    Your Lordship's dutiful son and servant,

            G. W.

LETTER DCCLXVIII.

To the Bishop of W———.

My Lord,   *Bristol, Aug.* 7, 1749.

I Thank your Lordship for your kind and cordial letter. I shall take care to do your Lordship justice, by shewing it to such persons as I think have been more immediately concerned. This, I imagine, will be as much satisfaction as your Lordship will desire. I suppose the mistake has lain here: your Lordship might have insinuated, that by my present way of acting, I had broken the solemn engagement I had entered into at my ordination: and that might have been interpreted to imply a charge of *Perjury*. The relation in which I stand to the Right Honourable the Countess of *H———*, made me desirous to clear myself from such an imputation; and at the same time to give your Lordship an opportunity of vindicating yourself in the manner you have done. Was I not afraid of intruding too much upon your Lordship's time, and of shewing the least inclination to controversy, I would endeavour, in the fear of GOD, to answer the other part of your Lordship's letter; and, as far as lies in me, give your Lordship a satisfactory account of whatever may seem irregular and exceptionable in my present conduct. This I would be glad to do, not only before your Lordship, but all the Right Reverend the Bishops; for I highly honour them on account of the sacred character they sustain, and would make it my daily endeavour to obey all their godly admonitions. This, I presume, my Lord, is the utmost extent of the promise I made at my ordination. If I err or deviate from this, in any respect, it is through ignorance and want of better information, and not (as far as I know

know my own heart) out of obstinacy or contempt of lawful authority. But I forget myself. I beg your Lordship's pardon for taking up so much of your time; I thank your Lordship for your prayers in my behalf; and beg leave to offer mine in return for your Lordship's present and eternal welfare, who am, my Lord,

Your Lordship's dutiful son, and obliged
humble servant,

G. W.

LETTER DCCLXIX.

To Lady H———.

Honoured Madam,   *Plymouth, Aug.* 15, 1749.

I Hope this will find your Ladyship recovered from the fatigue of your journey, and sitting under the Redeemer's shadow with unspeakable delight at *Abby-Place.* My prayers have constantly followed you, ever since I left your Ladyship at *Bristol*; and the LORD of all lords has dealt bountifully with me in my way *Westward.* At *Wellington,* as I was riding through the town, a good woman stopped me, and entreated me to give the people a sermon. I complied, and preached to a great company; and the next day to a much larger at the same place. I have also preached once at *Exeter,* twice at *Kingsbridge,* and once here at *Plymouth,* where, by the providence of an infinitely condescending GOD, I came yesterday in the afternoon. Several, I find, were awakened when I was here last; and the fields are every where white, ready unto harvest. My late pamphlet has been greatly blest. My Lord of *Exeter* was asked, Whether he had seen it? He answered, "Yes," and said, "I wrote like an honest man, had recanted several things, but he goes on in the same way yet." Being asked, Whether he did not intend publishing his second part? he replied, "You may expect a second." GOD be praised! I wish it may come out before I embark. I find he did not proceed to sentence Mr. *T———*; he only threatened to pull off his gown. Mr. *T———* immediately pulled it off himself, and said, "He could preach the gospel without a gown," and went out. Upon which the Bishop sent after him, and soothed him. In a few days I hope to see Mr. *T———,* and then your

Ladyship shall have further particulars. Blessed be GOD, all things turn out for the furtherance of the gospel. " Out of the eater comes forth meat, and out of the strong comes forth sweetness." In about a fortnight I hope to reach *London*, and in the mean time shall take care to send your Ladyship historical letters. I count it my highest honour and privilege to wait upon your Ladyship; but I fear shall never have it in my power to express my gratitude as I ought, for those unmerited favours your Ladyship hath been pleased to confer on, honoured Madam,

Your Ladyship's most dutiful, obliged, though
unworthy servant for CHRIST's sake,
G. W.

LETTER DCCLXX.

To Mr. S———.

Dear Sir,   *Plymouth, Aug.* 18, 1749.

I Thank you for your kind letter, which I have not had an opportunity of answering until now. I rejoice that so much gospel seed has been sown in *Yorkshire*, and that so much hath sprung up and brought forth fruit. No wonder that the enemy has been busy to sow tares of various kinds amongst it. This always was, and, in all probability, will always be the case, till time shall be no more. Happy they! who are enabled to distinguish truth from error, and who, amongst the different sentiments of CHRIST's disciples, maintain a catholic love for all. Your letter bespeaks you to be thus minded. This is what I would aim at, because it is the glory of a christian, and a temper of mind which sweetly prepares us for the communion of saints in heaven. Be pleased, therefore, to give my love to all that love the LORD JESUS in sincerity. If any of my poor writings have been blessed to any, let CHRIST have the glory, and me your prayers. I want them much. I am the chief of sinners, less than the least of all saints; but, I trust, am willing to spend and be spent for souls. The beginning of next month, I have thoughts of being your way. If it is best, providence will direct my course thither. In the mean while, and at all other seasons, whether I come or not,

I recommend myself to your prayers, as being, though unknown, yet, for Jesus Christ's sake,

Your affectionate friend and servant,
G. W.

LETTER DCCLXXI.

To Captain W———.

My very dear Brother,   Plymouth, *Aug.* 19, 1749.

I Do not love to be long out of *Bristol* without writing to you. I want to know how it is with you after the loss of my noble patroness, and whether dear Mr. H—— goes on. I have been preaching as usual in the *West*, and for some days past have been comforted and refreshed in a peculiar manner. Last night I heard that the Bishop had published a second pamphlet, of half-a-crown price, with a preface to me. Have you seen it, or do you think it worth answering? He told a clergyman some time ago, that he might expect a second part. He said, "My answer was honest; that I had recanted many things, but that I went on in my usual way still." God forbid I should do otherwise. I am informed, that upon threatening to pull Mr. T——'s gown off, he threw it off himself, and said, "He could preach the gospel without a gown," and so withdrew. Upon which the Bishop sent for him in, and soothed him. Particulars I expect to hear on *Tuesday* at *Biddiford*, where I hope to see Mr. T——; and to-morrow se'nnight, God willing, I intend to preach at *Exeter*, in my way to *London*. I hope you find retirement blessed to you. Whether retired, or in public life, that you may be entirely devoted to the most adorable Redeemer, is the hearty prayer of, my very dear brother,

Yours most affectionately,
G. W.

Postscript to Lady H———n.

Honoured Madam,

SINCE I wrote the above, God has given me a glorious season at the dock, where I preached to a great multitude. This morning the King of kings shewed himself in the gallery of his ordinances indeed; and this evening I preached to many thousands in *Plymouth* fields. It was a folemn meeting. Since that, a youth, laden with a fenfe of fin, came crying, "What fhall I do to be faved?" May JESUS give him reft! May the fame JESUS ftill fill your Ladyfhip with all his fulnefs! To-morrow, GOD willing, I fet out for *Biddiford*. I have now a clergyman with me, who is made a rural Dean, and who, I believe, preaches CHRIST in fincerity.

LETTER DCCLXXII.

To Lady H———n.

Biddiford, Aug. 24, 1749.

SINCE I had the honour of writing to your Ladyfhip, I have feen the Bifhop's fecond pamphlet, in which he hath ferved the Methodifts, as the bifhop of *Conftance* ferved *John Hufs*, when they ordered fome painted devils to be put round his head, before they burned him. His preface to me is moft virulent. Every thing I wrote in my anfwer, is turned into the vileft ridicule, and nothing will fatisfy, but giving up the glorious work of the ever-blefled GOD, as entirely cheat and impofture. I cannot fee that it calls for any further anfwer from me. Mr. *Wefley*, I think, had beft attack him now, as he is largely concerned in this fecond part. I hope to be in *London* fome time next week. I think of leaving this place to-morrow, and to preach at *Exeter* next Lord's-day. The glorious *Emmanuel* has given me feveral fpiritual children in this place, who do indeed adorn the gofpel of GOD their Saviour. Here is a little flock, to whom, I believe, it will be our heavenly Father's good pleafure to give an eternal kingdom. I have preached once publicly to a large auditory, and this evening am to preach again. I am afhamed I do no more for Him, who hath done and fuffered fo much for me. O what fhall I render unto the LORD of all lords, whofe mercy endureth for ever! A thought of his infinite patience and long-fuffering ftrikes me dumb. His goodnefs, in bringing me into the acquaintance of your Ladyfhip, quite amazes me; and the many peculiar providences that have attended me this laft year, encourage me to believe that goodnefs and mercy fhall follow me all the days of my life, and that I shall dwell in the house of the LORD for ever. There, shall I see your Ladyship; and will there thank you before men and angels for all you have done for unworthy me, and that blessed cause in which I am embarked. That your Ladyship in the mean while may be watered every moment by the dew of the Redeemer's heavenly blessing, is and shall be the continued prayer of, honoured Madam,

Your Ladyship's most dutiful, obliged, though unworthy servant for CHRIST's sake,

G. W.

LETTER DCCLXXIII.

To the Countess of D————.

Honoured Madam, Biddiford, Aug. 24, 1749.

AS I am always praying for, so I cannot help sometimes writing to your Ladyship. I think I can say, "The love of CHRIST constrains me." Thanks be to GOD that your Ladyship knows what these words mean. I hope you find it every day constraining you more and more to every good word and work. My greatest pain is, to find that I can do no more for Him, who has done and suffered so much for me. Blessed be his name, that the fields are yet every where white, ready unto harvest. Since I have been in the *West*, I have been preaching as usual, and a divine influence hath every where attended the word. This, I think, is the best way to answer those that oppose themselves. If GOD be for us, who can be against us? I suppose your Ladyship hath seen the Bishop's second pamphlet. Surely it is an original. May the LORD JESUS open his eyes, and change his heart! Well might the glorious *Emmanuel* break out into this blessed exclamation, " I thank thee, Father, Lord of heaven and earth, that thou hast hid these things from the wise and prudent, and hast revealed them unto babes. Even so, Father, for so it seemed good in thy sight." Honoured Madam, how much are you indebted to divine grace, that hath singled you out from among the Mighty and Noble, and placed your Ladyship to the number of those happy few to whom it is given to know the mysteries of the kingdom of GOD! I trust your honoured

honoured sister will ere long bear you company, and travel with you in that narrow road which leads to eternal life. When I remember you, I always think of her, and beg my most dutiful respects may find acceptance with her Ladyship. Some time next week I hope to be in town for a few days, and then shall do myself the honour of calling upon your Ladyship. In the mean while I recommend you to the tender mercies of the ever-loving, ever-lovely JESUS, and beg an interest in your Ladyship's prayers, in behalf of, honoured Madam,

Your Ladyship's most obedient, obliged humble servant,

G. W.

LETTER DCCLXXIV.

To Lady Fanny S——.

Honoured Madam, Exeter, *Aug.* 26, 1749.

THOUGH I took the freedom of writing to your Ladyship before I left *Bristol*, and though I hope to be in town by next *Thursday* evening, yet gratitude and respect even compel me to trouble your Ladyship with another letter from this place. Here I came last night, after having preached the everlasting gospel to many thousands in the *West*. Sometimes I have been weak in body; but He, whose I am, and whom I endeavour to serve in the gospel of his dear Son, hath carried me through, and greatly refreshed and comforted my soul. Alas! to what a heaven are they strangers, who deny the influence of the Blessed Spirit, and cry down the felt and abiding joys of the Holy Ghost, as fancy, enthusiasm, and delusion. Ye poor dry Rationalists! I honour your parts in other respects, but pity your ignorance in the things of GOD. By this time, I suppose your Ladyship hath seen the Bishop's second performance. I think it is an original, and so very scurrilous, unchristian, and profane, that I cannot think it will be worth my while to answer him again. I have satisfied my conscience in publishing my last pamphlet; and I now commit our cause to him who judgeth righteously. O honoured Madam, what a happy thing is it to be despised for the sake of JESUS! When *John Hufs* was burnt, the Bishop of *Constance* painted devils upon paper, and put them round his head; how soon were they exchanged for a crown of glory! Yet a little while,

while, and He that cometh will come, and will not tarry. Till then, may your Ladyship be kept by the mighty power of God through faith, and stand impregnable as a wall of brass! May you be kept a stranger to names and parties, and by a holy, humble, uniform imitation of the blessed JESUS, evidence to the world, that you are indeed experimentally acquainted with the power of his resurrection. High is your station, great are your difficulties; but he that dwelleth on high is mightier, and hath engaged to make you more than conqueror through his love. To his tender mercy do I now, and likewise every day, commend your Ladyship; and this, by divine assistance, shall always be the employ of, honoured Madam,

Your Ladyship's most obedient, obliged,
ready servant for CHRIST's sake,
G. W.

LETTER DCCLXXV.

To Lady H———n.

Honoured Madam,   *London, Sept. 4. 1749.*

BY the providence of a good and gracious GOD, I came to town on *Thursday* evening, after having had a pleasant circuit in the *West*. The day after I wrote to your Ladyship, I preached twice at *Exeter*, and in the evening I believe I had near ten thousand hearers. The Bishop and several of his clergy stood very near me, as I am informed. A good season it was. All was quiet, and there was a great solemnity in the congregation; but a drunken man threw at me three great stones. One of them cut my head deeply, and was like to knock me off the table; but, blessed be GOD, I was not discomposed at all. One of the other stones struck a poor man quite down. As I came from *Exeter*, I visited one *John Haynе*, the soldier that, under GOD, begun the great awakening in *Flanders*. He is in *Dorchester* goal for preaching at *Shaftsbury*, where there has been, and is now a great awakening. Every where the work is upon the spread; and since I have been here, we have had some of the most awful, solemn, powerful meetings, as I ever saw at the Tabernacle. Congregations have been very large, and I have had several meetings with the preachers. On *Saturday* I had the honour

of

of being almost all the day long with Lady *F*——, Lady *H*——, Lady *C*——, and the Countess of *D*——. Lady *F*—— and the Countess received the blessed sacrament before the others came: and I think they both grow. If I stay over *Sunday*, (as perhaps I may) I hope to have another day with them. I am sorry to inform your Ladyship, Mr. *D*—— died last *Sunday* about noon. He had been sick about a fortnight, was in doubts for a while, but two or three days before his death he rejoiced in GOD his Saviour. This morning I had the pleasure of a visit from Mr. *P*—— and two *German* ministers, who have been labouring among the *Jews*, and been made instrumental of converting many of them. They seemed to be dear souls. They have preached at the *German* chapel with great power. That your Ladyship may always enjoy a thriving soul in a healthy body, is the continual prayer of, honoured Madam,

Your Ladyship's most dutiful, &c.

G. W.

LETTER DCCLXXVI.

To Mr. B——.

Oundle, in Northamptonshire, Sept. 15, 1749.

My very dear Mr. B——,

THOUGH I have not written to you, yet I know of no one in *America*, for whom I have a more real and abiding esteem. The account of your temporal affairs, which I received from my wife, gave me great concern. I often wish it was in my power to assist you; but as it is not, all I can do is to pray for you, and exhort you to look up to Him, who has engaged, that all things shall work together for good to those who love him in sincerity. This, I am persuaded, may be said of you; and therefore, dear Sir, be of good courage. These light afflictions are but for a moment, and are intended to work out a far more exceeding and eternal weight of glory. Thanks be to GOD, all the hell we are to have, is on this side the grave; there is none for believers beyond it: and even in the midst of our deepest temporal misery, we may enjoy an antepast of heaven. This you know by experience. Thanks be to GOD, for this unspeakable gift in and through CHRIST JESUS our Lord

Lord. Though faint, my dear friend, yet still pursue. Yonder stands the blessed Jesus with a crown in his hand, ready to put on the conqueror's head. Let this animate you, for you shall certainly reap in due time, if you faint not. I could write much, but am surrounded with business from many quarters. Blessed be God, my hands are full of work, though I stand amazed that the Redeemer does not lay me aside. But his grace is free. I commend you and your dear yoke-fellow to his never failing mercy, and begging a continued interest in your prayers, subscribe myself, my very dear friend,

Yours most affectionately in our common Lord,

G. W.

LETTER DCCLXXVII.

To the Rev. Mr. H——.

Binnington, Sept. 17, 1749.

Rev. and very dear Sir,

IF you was uneasy that my last lay by you unanswered, I am sure I have been, it may be, much more so, ever since yours came to hand. Upon reading it, I felt all the springs of sympathy move as it were at once. Glad would I have been of the wings of a dove, to have fled to, and condoled with my suffering friend. Perhaps I have heard from what corner your cross comes. It is a very near one indeed.— A saying of Mr. B—— hath often comforted me; "I would often have nestled, but God always put a thorn in my nest." Is not this suffered, my dear brother, think you, to prick you out, and to compel you as it were to appear for the Lord Jesus Christ? Preaching is my grand *Catholicon* under all domestic, as well as other trials. Methinks the voice of providence now is, "Who is on the Lord's side?"—I fear Dr. S—— has done you hurt, and kept you in shackles too, too long. For Christ's sake, my dear Mr. H——, exhort him, now he hath taken the gown, to play the man, and let the world see that not worldly motives, but God's glory and a love for souls, have sent him into the ministry. Though when I conversed with him he was exceeding weak, yet as I trust there is sincerity at the bottom, I hope he will turn

out

out a flamer at laſt. O when ſhall this once be! who would loſe one moment? Amazing! that the followers of a crucified Redeemer ſhould be afraid of contempt. Surely it muſt be for want of looking more to, and conſidering him who endured ſo much pain, and deſpiſed ſo much ſhame, but is now ſitting at the right hand of the throne of GOD. *O gloriam quantam et qualem!* Riſe, H———, riſe, and ſee thy JESUS reaching out a crown with this motto, *Vincenti dabo*. Excuſe this freedom, I write out of the fulneſs of my heart, not to draw you over to me or a party, but to excite you to appear openly for GOD. I am glad you intend to write. May I know the plan you intend to go upon? Do you think to ſay any thing to the Biſhop of *Exeter?* Have you ſeen his ſecond piece? Would you have me reply? Will you point out to me the faults of my firſt anſwer? A letter may be directed (if you write immediately) to be left for me at the Reverend Mr. J——'s, *Yorkſhire*. Thither I am bound now, and if the ſeaſon of the year ſhould permit, I would ſtretch to *Scotland*. Alas, how ſoon is the year gone round ſince I was there laſt! and how little have I done for JESUS! A thought of it ſometimes breaks my heart. And yet how good is the LORD! In *London* we have had moſt delightful ſeaſons. The glory of the Redeemer filled the tabernacle. If any doubt whether the cauſe we are embarked in be the cauſe of GOD, I ſay, "Come and ſee." Are you free that I ſhould call upon you in my return to town? I think to come by way of *Northampton*. You ſhall hear what is done in *Yorkſhire*. I find GOD has bleſſed my preaching at *Oundle* to ſome ſouls. At *Biddiford, Plymouth, Exeter,* and *Chatham* the word ran and was glorified. But what am I doing? I never wrote to any one ſo freely, I think, that I was not perſonally acquainted with, as to you. Pardon me, if I am too free, and impute it to the love that is borne you by, reverend and dear Sir,

Yours moſt affectionately in our common LORD,

G. W.

LETTER DCCLXXVIII.

To Captain W——.

Newcastle, Sept. 29, 1749.

My very dear Brother,

SINCE I wrote to you last, I have had many proofs that God's providence directed my way into *Yorkshire.* I preached four times at *Abberford*, four times at *Leeds*, and thrice at *Howarth*, where lives one Mr. *G——*. At his church I believe we had above a thousand communicants, and in the church-yard about six thousand hearers. It was a great day of the son of man. At *Leeds* the auditory consisted of above ten thousand. About *Leeds* are Mr. *W——*'s societies. I was invited thither by them and one of their preachers; and Mr. *Charles W——* coming thither published me himself. I therefore complied, and I believe the gospel was welcome. I have preached here once, and am to preach again this evening. On *Monday*, GOD willing, I propose to return to *Yorkshire*, and from thence to *London*. Pray send me word immediately whether the *Port-Merchant* be gone, because I know not but some out of *Wales* may go in her. I forgot to tell you in my last, that I had given over the immediate care of all my societies to Mr. *H——*; so that now I am a preacher at large indeed. I find every thing is turning round strangely. O for simplicity and honesty to the end! I long to know how it is with you. Am I to have my brother at last? Do convictions fasten, and can you at length sing,

> *Be gone, vain world; my heart resign,*
> *For I must be no longer thine?*

For the present, adieu. My love to all. I wish you the very best of blessings, and am, my very dear brother,

Yours most affectionately,

G. W.

LETTER DCCLXXIX.

To Lady H——.

Honoured Madam, *Newcastle, Oct.* 1, 1749.

I Wrote to your Ladyship lately a few lines under great weariness of body. I then promised to send your Ladyship many pleasing particulars. Till now I have not had opportunity; and now what shall I say to your Ladyship? Never did I see more of the hand of GOD in any of my journies than in this. At Mr. G——'s I believe there were above six thousand hearers. The sacramental occasion was most awful. At *Leeds* the congregation consisted of above 10,000. In the morning at five I was obliged to preach out of doors. I was invited to *Leeds* by one of Mr. *W*——'s preachers, and by all his people. The gospel was welcome to them. In my way hither I met Mr. *Charles W*——, who returned back with, and introduced me to the pulpit in *Newcastle.* As I am a debtor to all, and intend to be at the head of no party, I thought it my duty to comply. I have preached now in their room four times, and this morning I preached to many thousands in a large close. This evening I am to do the same again. The power of GOD has attended his own word, and there seems to be a quickening and stirring among the souls. To-morrow, GOD willing, we set out for *Leeds,* and after about a week's stay in those parts I intend returning to *London.* As it is so late in the year, my *Scotch* friends advise me to defer my going thither. Had I known that, I should have embarked for *America* this fall; but I find there were other reasons for my being prevented crossing the waters this winter. I desire to follow the Lamb whithersoever he is pleased to lead me. At *New-haven* there is a great awakening. If any thing offers worthy of notice, your Ladyship shall be sure to hear. In the mean while, I continue to put up my usual prayer, that your Ladyship may be filled with all the fulness of GOD, and to subscribe myself, honoured Madam,

Your Ladyship's most obliged and willing
servant for CHRIST's sake,
G. W.

LETTER DCCLXXX.

To Lady Fanny S——.

Honoured Madam, Newcastle, Oct. 1, 1749.

SOME time last week, my wife sent me the letter your Ladyship was pleased to favour me with about three weeks ago. Though I was sorry it did not reach me before I left town, yet I rejoiced to find that it bespoke your Ladyship's attachment to the ever-loving ever-lovely JESUS, and a desire to partake of the sacred symbols of his most blessed body and blood. I doubt not but your Ladyship, with full purpose of heart, will cleave unto him, and in spite of men and devils go on in that narrow way which leads to life eternal. GOD's grace will be sufficient for you. He hath promised, and he is faithful who hath promised, never to leave nor forsake those that put their trust in him. He is in the burning bush, he is in the fiery furnace. He can and will make us more than conquerors over all. With what courage then may your Ladyship go on through this howling wilderness, whilst leaning on your beloved Saviour? In him alone is all your strength found. Honoured Madam, look to him, consider him, and thereby you will be kept from being weary and faint in your mind. I doubt not but you meet with daily crosses. Persons that stand alone, and in high places, must expect storms. But JESUS is able and willing to uphold you. Thanks be to his great name for giving your Ladyship such a share of prudence and courage. May the glorious *Emmanuel* increase both; and without being attached to any party, may you be preserved unspotted from the world, and be a common friend to all!—Since I saw your Ladyship, I have disengaged myself from the immediate care of the societies, and am now still more at liberty to preach the gospel of the blessed GOD. A series of unforeseen providences brought me down this way. In *Yorkshire* many, many thousands have attended the word, and here at *Newcastle* thousands also hear the gospel gladly. To-morrow I am returning back, and hope to be in town some time this month. I fear it is now too late to embark for *America* this winter; but,

thanks

thanks be to GOD, I hear my family is well, and that the LORD hath given them a plentiful crop. If your Ladyship lives, I believe you will hear of some souls being educated at *Georgia* for GOD. Honoured Madam, my heart's desire and constant prayer is, that you may go on from strength to strength, and be continually growing in the knowledge of yourself and CHRIST JESUS your LORD. I must now add no more, but my repeated thanks for all your Ladyship's favours, and my repeated assurances of being, honoured Madam,

Your Ladyship's most obliged, obedient,
and ready servant for CHRIST's sake,
G. W.

LETTER DCCLXXXI.

To Lady F—— S——.

Honoured Madam, *Estwood in Lancashire, Oct.* 25, 1749.

SINCE I had the honour of writing to your Ladyship from *Newcastle,* fresh wonders of grace and mercy have been shewn us daily. I have now I think preached about thirty times in *Yorkshire,* and above ten times in *Cheshire,* and *Lancashire.* Congregations have been very large, and a solid, convincing, and comforting influence hath every where attended the word. In one or two places I have had a little rough treatment, but elsewhere all has been quiet, and many I hear are brought under concern about the welfare of their better part. At the importunity of many, I am now returning from *Manchester* (where I preached to many thousands) to *Leeds*; from thence I purpose going to *Sheffield,* and next week I hope to see good Lady H——n at *Ashby,* and the week following I hope to be in *London.* Thus do I lead a pilgrim life: GOD give me a pilgrim heart, and enable me to speak of redeeming love to a lost world, till I can speak no more! Surely this is a work that brings with it its own reward. It brings a heaven into the soul, and causes it, amidst all the scoffs and tauntings of a benighted, ill-natured, and ridiculing world, to rejoice with joy unspeakable, even a joy that is full of glory. "To me, (says the blessed apostle) to live is CHRIST." When a person can once say so in reality, then he begins to live indeed. Even death itself is then life, because death to such a one is eternal gain. O how great, how ſtriking, how tranſporting and transforming are the inviſible realities of another world, to a ſoul that is born of God! What meer ſhadows and empty nothings are all ſublunary enjoyments, when compared with theſe! Thanks be to God, who has given you, honoured Madam, a taſte of theſe infinitely important things. My conſtant prayer for your Ladyſhip is, that you may hold on, and hold out, and with full purpoſe of heart cleave unto that Redeemer who hath loved you, and given himſelf for you. Mrs. G—— at *Mancheſter* goes on well, and is not aſhamed to confeſs him, who I truſt has called her out of darkneſs, and made her partaker of his marvellous light. May the glorious *Emmanuel* add daily to the number of his honourable confeſſors, and give the rich to know, that to be rich in faith and good works is the only way to be rich indeed! All is ours, if we can truly ſay, we are Christ's. Honoured Madam, I muſt beg your excuſe for this freedom; but at preſent I have a view of the Redeemer's glory, and therefore know not well how to ſtop when writing of him. Your Ladyſhip will pardon me, and accept theſe poor lines, which ſhall be followed with hearty prayers from, honoured Madam,

Your Ladyſhip's moſt obliged and
ready ſervant for Christ's ſake,
G. W.

LETTER DCCLXXXII.

To the Counteſs D———.

Honoured Madam,   *Halifax, Oct.* 26, 1749.

THOUGH I am jealous of myſelf, leſt I ſhould make too free with perſons in high life, yet when I have good news to ſend concerning the kingdom of Jesus Christ, I am conſtrained as it were to write to your Ladyſhip. Will it not rejoice you very much, honoured Madam, to hear the glorious *Emmanuel* is riding on in the chariot of his goſpel, from conquering to conquer? Every day people flock to hear the word, like doves to their windows. I have preached about thirty times in *Yorkſhire*, and at the deſire of many am returned thither again. The latter end of next week I hope to ſee good Lady H——n. I ſuppoſe her Ladyſhip will detain me a

few

few days at *Ashby*, and then I purpose coming directly to *London*. Thanks be to GOD, all places are near alike to me, so that I can but be doing something for Him, who hath done and suffered so much for me. This I would have to be my meat and my drink. To me to live, let it be CHRIST; for life is no further desirable than as we can improve it to the promoting his glory. *Mary* thought so, who in the days of his flesh sat at the Redeemer's feet and heard his words. This I believe is your Ladyship's daily employ; a glorious employ indeed. How sweet must his fruit be unto your Ladyship's taste! Surely it is sweeter than the honey or the honeycomb. And if the first-fruits are so delightful, how infinitely delightful must the full harvest be! Go on, honoured Madam, and whatever others may do, still keep pursuing after more and more of that better part, which shall never be taken away from you. JESUS is full of grace, and full of truth. Believers are welcome to him every moment. He is ready to water them continually with the dew of his heavenly blessing. It is our privilege to go on from grace to grace, till grace be swallowed up in endless glory. O that your honoured sister may march on with your Ladyship towards this blessed state! There she will have a house, not made with hands, eternal in the heavens. I send her Ladyship my most dutiful respects, and sincerely pray that she may be filled with all the fulness of GOD.—I hope your Ladyship is inclined to remember me at the throne of grace, your Ladyship knows my name, "The chief of sinners, less than the least of all saints;" but, for CHRIST's sake, honoured Madam,

Your Ladyship's most dutiful, obliged
and willing servant,
G. W.

LETTER DCCLXXXIII.

To Lady H——n.

Honoured Madam,   *Leeds, Oct.* 30, 1749.

ON *Saturday* evening I had the honour of your Ladyship's letter, and as it came before the *Manchester* post went out, I immediately sent the inclosed to Mrs. G——. If possible fible I am perfuaded fhe will comply. She feems to be quite in earneft. I converfed for about two hours with the Captain and fome other officers, upon the nature and neceffity of the new birth. He was affected, and I hope it was bleffed. Since I left them, I have preached to many thoufands at *Rofindale*, *Aywood*, and *Halifax*. I have alfo offered JESUS at *Burflal*, *Pudfy*, and *Armly*, and have had three precious feafons here. Congregations are exceeding large indeed, and both the eftablifhed and diffenting clergy are very angry. They thundered I hear yefterday heartily. But truth is great, and will prevail, though preached in the fields and ftreets. Indeed it begins to be cold abroad now; but the LORD JESUS is pleafed to ftrengthen me, and people flock from all quarters. This day fevennight, GOD willing, without fail your Ladyfhip may depend on feeing me. I thought to have been at *Afhby* next LORD's-day, but a door feems to be opened at *Nottingham*, and I have thoughts of trying what can be done there. This morning I fhall fet out for *Sheffield*. May the LORD give me a pilgrim heart for my pilgrim life, and then all will be well! I know I have your Ladyfhip's prayers.—I think your Ladyfhip judges right in refpect to the churches. I expect to meet with many rebuffs, but by the help of my GOD I fhall leap over every wall. That your Ladyfhip may ftand as a wall of brafs, is the hearty prayer of, honoured Madam,

Your Ladyfhip's moft dutiful obedient fervant,

G. W.

LETTER DCCLXXXIV.

To the Reverend Mr. H———.

Afhby-Place, Nov. 8, 1749.

My very dear Friend,

I Thank you heartily for your kind letter to me, and your kind benefaction to poor Mr. *C———*. That GOD, whom you both ferve, will plentifully reward and blefs you. I am in great hopes, enough will be raifed to pay his debts, and that a provifion will be made for his future fubfiftence. Rather than *Elijahs* fhall want, ravens fhall be fent to feed them.

them. Your present circumstances almost distress me, and at the same time make me ashamed. I think it requires more grace heartily to say, "Father, thy will be done," in such a situation, than to die a martyr forty times. But my dear friend, though your body is weak and confined at home, your pen hath been active, and your works walk abroad. I hear of them from all quarters. GOD hath blessed, and will bless them. Let that comfort you, and if health any way permits, pray write again. Fear not, my dear dear Man; let faith and patience hold out a little longer, and then the struggle shall be over. Yet a little while, and you shall join with that sweet singer Dr. *Watts*, who whilst on earth dragged a crazy load along, as well as you, for many years. As for my poor tabernacle, I wonder it is not dissolved every day; but we are immortal till our work is done. Now is my time for doing; my suffering time may come by and by. O for strength in a trying hour! Wherefore should we fear? Wherefore should we doubt? He that hath loved us, will love us to the end. This encourages me to hold on my way. Blessed be GOD, I have seen great things since I wrote last. The fields have been more and more white, ready unto harvest. I am now at *Ashby* with good Lady H——n. Her Ladyship has a great regard for you, and begs you would come and stay a week at her house. She will take great care of you. I think to remove hence on *Monday*, and should be very glad to see you in my way to *London*. However this be, we shall meet in heaven. There the wicked heart and wicked world will cease from troubling, and there the weary will enjoy an uninterrupted and eternal rest. This morning we have been remembering our blessed Redeemer's death, and I was enabled to pray earnestly for my dear Mr. H——. I beseech the Father of mercies and GOD of all consolations to excite you to do the same for my dear old friend.

Yours most affectionately in our common LORD,

G. W.

LETTER DCCLXXXV.

To Lady H——n.

Honoured Madam, London, *Nov.* 21, 1749.

YOUR Ladyship's letter greatly rejoiced me, and stirred me up to pray afresh that our blessed LORD would give you to see of the travel of his soul, in the salvation of many at *Ashby*. I am persuaded your Ladyship was not sent there for nothing.—But it is always darkest before break of day. I desire to be thankful that your honoured Sisters are pleased to approve of me. Thanks be to GOD, I feel myself unworthy; but unworthy as I am, my poor prayers I trust will reach heaven in their behalf. This day, both they and your Ladyship were remembered at the LORD's table. The Countess, Lady *G——* and Lady *F——* were there, and all I think are grown in grace and in the knowledge of our LORD and Saviour JESUS CHRIST. What encouragement is this for your Ladyship to go and speak for GOD? All send their best compliments, and Lady *F——* desired me to inform your Ladyship, that the man who was sent up has been taken care of. Blessed be GOD for putting it in your Ladyship's power to help the poor sufferers of *Cork*. Last night I received a letter from Mr. *L——*, and purpose this night or to-morrow to write to him about what your Ladyship desires; I think he will be a proper person. Mr. *W——* I believe is at his house. I pity those who have been persecuted in *Ireland*. The minister being taken so ill near your Ladyship, was an alarming providence. But who so blind as those that will not see? GOD honours your Ladyship, in making you instrumental to own and provide for those, who are cast out for his great name's sake. Great shall be your reward in heaven. I hope you and your honoured sisters will have great comfort in the perseverance of the poor baker. He is a *Jerusalem* sinner, a proper object for free grace to fix on. A woman of fourscore, and a boy about eleven, have been lately awakened, and it is hoped converted, in *Essex*. May JESUS feed them all with bread that comes down from heaven! We have blessed seasons here, and our LORD gives us to see his stately steps. GOD

God prepare me for a suffering hour! Mrs. C—— has met with a heavy trial in the death of her only daughter, aged twenty. I hear she behaves like a christian under it. Happy they who know that promise belongs to them, "All things work together for good to those who love God." How easy may *Isaacs* be given up by them? But I forget I am weary, when writing to your Ladyship. Pardon my taking up so much of your precious time. I wish your Ladyship, your honoured Sisters, and children, all the privileges of the new-born, heaven-born sons of God. This is the only return that can be made both to them and you, by, honoured Madam,

Your Ladyship's most obliged, dutiful,
and willing servant for Christ's sake,
G. W.

LETTER DCCLXXXVI.

To Mr. L————.

Very dear Sir, London, *Nov.* 22, 1749.

I Received your kind letter on *Monday* last, and to shew you how willing I am to carry on a correspondence, I take the very first opportunity of answering it. Yours found me just returned out of *Yorkshire, Lancashire,* &c. Since you heard of me last, I have been at *Sheffield* and *Nottingham,* and found the fields every where white ready unto harvest. I believe my particular province is, to go about and preach the gospel to all. My being obliged to keep up a large correspondence in *America,* and the necessity I am under of going thither myself, entirely prevents my taking care of any societies. Whether it will ever be my lot to come over to *Ireland,* I cannot say. I have some thought of being there next Spring; but I would not intrude on any one's labours. The world is large, and blessed be God, there is a range and work sufficient for all. As for my manner of preaching, I believe, was you to hear me, you would find it calculated to serve all, but intended at least to offend none. I profess to be of a catholic spirit; I am a debtor to all; I have no party to be at the head of, and through God's grace, I will have none; but as much as in me lies strengthen the hands of all, of every denomination, that preach Jesus Christ in sincerity. In this spirit I hope my dear Mr. L—— will find me, should he ever see me in *Ireland*; but whether I shall go there or to *America* in the Spring, is not yet determined. Future things belong to Him whose I am, and whom I desire to serve to my dying day, in the gospel of his dear Son. I earnestly beg an interest in your prayers, and in the prayers of all that love the Lord Jesus in sincerity. Pray how do the poor people at *Cork?* Lady H—— writes this concerning them. " I hope the poor persecuted people in *Cork* will be helped, and I should be glad if you could write in my name to any of them, and inform them that I would have written myself, but I know not how to direct. You may give them my kind assurance of serving them upon any occasion, and a hint that I believe they will meet with no more of the like rough usage." Thus far my good Lady. I have informed her Ladyship, that I should write to you, who I am persuaded will gladly and in a prudent manner communicate this to all concerned. And now, my dear Sir, have I not returned you a long letter? I love you, though I know you not, and the more so because I hear you breathe a catholic spirit. May the Lord increase it in your and all his children's hearts! I must now add no more, but subscribe myself, very dear Sir,

Yours most affectionately in our common Lord,

G. W.

LETTER DCCLXXXVII.

To Mr. N——.

Very dear Sir, *London, Nov.* 25, 1749.

FOR some few days I have been returned from my northern rout, in which the glorious *Emmanuel* gave me to see new wonders every day. It was no small concern to me to turn my back on *Scotland,* when so near. However it hath been greatly over-ruled for good. I have thereby been called to preach in many fresh places, and, glory be to God, I saw thousands flock to the hearing of the gospel, like doves to the windows. The generous offer made me by yourself and lady, I took exceeding kind, and gladly would I have embraced it, but——Well! what is, is best. " Father, not my will but thine

thine be done." Perhaps I may see you in the Spring; if not, ere long, dear Sir, we shall meet in heaven. My wife tells me, she answered Lady *I——*'s letter immediately. In this she joins, sending most grateful acknowledgments and cordial salutations. Blessed be GOD, we are both well, and surrounded with mercies on every side. — Only ungrateful, ill, and hell-deserving I, want a grateful and an humble heart. I am altogether an unprofitable servant, but our LORD I trust will purge me, that I may bring forth more fruit: for by this, and this only, I know our heavenly father is glorified. What I am most afraid of is, lest I should flag in the latter stages of my road. But he that hath loved and helped, will, dear Sir, love and help me to the end. I am persuaded your prayers and the prayers of christian friends will be very serviceable. O that you may be kept alive and warm in this cold declining day! Poor *Scotland*, I pity thee! I will pray for thy prosperity till I can pray no more! Be pleased to present our joint love and cordial respects to all friends in general, and we entreat you and yours to accept the same in a most particular manner from, very dear Sir,

Yours most affectionately in our common LORD,
G. W.

LETTER DCCLXXXVIII.

To Lady H———n.

Honoured Madam, London, Nov. 30, 1749.

I Think it is now a whole week since I had the honour and pleasure of writing to your Ladyship, and as your Ladyship was pleased to desire the prayers of GOD's people, I read that part of your letter. Thousands heartily united in singing the following verses for your Ladyship.

Gladly we join to pray for those,
 Who rich with worldly honour shine;
Yet dare to own a Saviour's cause,
 And in that hated cause to join:
Yes! we would praise Thee that a few
Love Thee, though rich and noble too.

Uphold this ſtar in thy right hand,
 Crown her endeavours with ſucceſs;
Among the great ones may ſhe ſtand,
 A witneſs of thy righteouſneſs!
Till many nobles join thy train,
 And triumph in the Lamb that's ſlain.

The verſes were made by T—— G—— who is now under my roof. He has grievouſly backſlidden, but I hope is now returning home to his heavenly Father. We had an uncommon ſcene when he firſt came to me. I find the LORD will be ſanctified in all them that come near him, and will not ſuffer thoſe who are concerned in his cauſe, and with his people, to continue in ſin long undiſcerned. O that I may be kept ſimple, and honeſt, and zealous unto the end! Mine eyes wait upon thee, O LORD, from whence alone cometh my ſalvation! I find he never fails thoſe that put their truſt in him. Bleſſed be his name, I have got ſufficient to pay off Mr. C——'s debts.—Poor, yet attempting at leaſt to make many rich, I would have my motto ſtill. Mr. L—— alſo writes word, that the glorious JESUS hath raiſed ſufficient for his charity ſchool, and that he is much bleſſed in his labours. The book that hath been given to me for your Ladyſhip, I purpoſe ſending next week, with one or two of the *Sundays Thoughts* for your Ladyſhip's honoured ſiſters. Indeed I honour them very much, and pray for them and all related to your Ladyſhip very earneſtly. I was glad to hear by Mr. R—— that your Ladyſhip and all were ſo well. May you proſper and be in health both in body and ſoul! *London* already begins to diſagree with my outward man, but the LORD's ſmiling upon my poor labours ſweetens all. I have begun to preach by ſix in the morning. We have large congregations even then. I truſt we ſhall have a warm winter. I have not been at the other end of the town this week, but I find all hold on: however a leader is wanting. This honour hath been put on your Ladyſhip by the great head of the church. An honour conferred on few, but an earneſt of a diſtinguiſhed honour to be put on your Ladyſhip before men and angels, when time ſhall be no more. That you may every day add to the ſplendor
of

of your future crown, by always abounding in the work of the LORD, is the fervent prayer of, honoured Madam,

Your Ladyship's most dutiful, and obliged,
though very unworthy servant,

G. W.

LETTER DCCLXXXIX.

To Mr. L———.

My dear Mr. L———,   *London, Dec.* 3, 1749.

I Thank you heartily for your kind Letter, and yet more heartily thank our glorious *Emmanuel* for succeeding your charity school, and smiling upon your public administrations. I have sent Lady H———n an account of it, and earnestly pray the blessed Redeemer to own and succeed you evermore. My winter quarters are made very agreeable; but so much business crouds in upon me, that I have not time to write long letters. I am looking out for some fresh sermons for you. Mr. H———, with whom I spent some agreeable hours lately at *Northampton*, would let you have some, but his are all in short hand. Here is a volume of one Mr. H———'s lately deceased that I guess will do for you. A friend to-day promises to send me *Gurnall's spiritual Armour*, of which I suppose you will highly approve. I will endeavour to bring or send it to you. I cannot think of stirring hence till after Christmas, but before the Winter is over, I shall long for the Spring to come, that I may enter on a fresh campaign. The encouragement given me this last fall, gladdens my poor heart, and makes me to long more than ever to spend and be spent for that JESUS, who hath shed his precious blood for us upon the cross. I know those last almost parting words of our ascending LORD, "Feed my lambs, feed my sheep," will be engraven upon the tables of your heart. Our obligations to do so, are very great, at least mine are. O that we may embrace all opportunities of shewing that we love our LORD more than every created thing. O for simplicity and godly sincerity unto the end of our race! Yet a little while, and we shall reach the goal and lay hold on the crown. Yonder our LORD stands holding it out. It has those words written upon it, *Vincenti dabo.* What is infinitely more, he will give us himself.

self. We shall behold, we shall partake of his glory. *O gloriam quantam et qualem!* You will urge all to press after it. Blessed be God, that you have so many around you that have a taste thereof. My hearty love attends them all. May the Lord Jesus be with your spirit, and give you to increase with all the increase of God! Nothing greater can be, nothing less shall be desired in your behalf by, my dear old friend,

Yours most affectionately,
G. W.

LETTER DCCXC.

To Mrs. K——.

Dear Madam,   *London, Dec.* 6, 1749.

I Thank you heartily for the acceptable favour of your letter, which came to my hand last night. It was quite welcome, as it bespoke the language of a heart panting after God, and desirous to be conformed to its great exemplar the blessed and holy Jesus. Go on, dear Madam, in his strength, who hath loved you and given himself for you. Confess him before men, and he will confess you before his holy angels in heaven. I am glad that Lady *H——* visits you often. Whenever you meet, may the glorious *Emmanuel* cause your hearts to burn within you. What you propose for the poor cast-out clergyman, will be accepted of and rewarded by our common Lord, as done to himself. God willing, I purpose waiting upon you next *Saturday* by eleven o'clock, and then I can receive your kind benefaction. Colonel *G——* being with me when your letter came, offered to accompany me. Perhaps Mr. *C——* will come too. I shall see him this day, and shall be sure to inform him and his wife of what you desire. Good Lady *H———n* would gladly make one in addressing the throne of grace. But she is happy in yonder dead place, and *Dorcas*-like is always employed for the poor. Glorious privilege! Blessed redemption! Jesus can make us happy any where and every where. You have a neighbour that dearly loves him. I mean the reverend Mr. *Z—,* the king's *German* chaplain. I believe, Madam, he would be glad to wait upon you; he has now three ministers with him, burning with the love of Christ, and going to preach

the

the gospel in the *East-Indies*. Have you seen a little piece entitled *Sunday Thoughts?* I think you would like it much. But I forget myself. I wish you the best of blessings, all the blessings of the everlasting covenant, and beg leave to subscribe myself, dear Madam,

Your most obliged and ready servant for CHRIST's sake,

G. W.

LETTER DCCXCI.

To Mr. W—— L——.

My dear Mr. L——, London, *Dec.* 9, 1749.

I Find by your last kind letter that the king's business requires haste. I therefore immediately dispatched it to good Lady H——, who I am persuaded will think it her highest privilege to serve the dear people of *Cork*. Whether your account of their sufferings has reached her Ladyship I cannot tell, but you will know soon. However this we know, that they have reached the ears of the blessed JESUS, who sitteth in heaven, and laughs all his enemies to scorn. He will take care that the bush, though burning, shall not be consumed, nay he will take care that it shall flourish even when in the midst of fire. In all our afflictions he is afflicted, and though the under shepherds be smitten, and his poor sheep for a while scattered, yet even this scattering shall be over-ruled for the propagation of the glorious gospel. It will be melancholy to have any preachers transported; but really the thoughts do not affect me so much, because I know what a field of action there is for them abroad. It has been my settled opinion for a long time, that CHRIST's labourers (at least some of them,) love home too much, and do not care enough for those thousands of precious souls, that are ready to perish for lack of knowledge in yonder wilderness. We propose having an academy or college at the Orphan-house in *Georgia*. Supposing the worst, hundreds may find a sweet retreat there. The house is large; it will hold an hundred. I trust my heart is larger, and will hold ten thousand. Be who or what they will, if they belong to JESUS, the language of my heart shall be, " Come in, ye blessed of the LORD." But perhaps this may not be the issue. The threatning storm

may

may blow over, and all may be at peace again. It is always darkeſt before break of day. May the glorious *Emmanuel* lighten the darkneſs of our minds! then we need not fear what men or devils can ſay of, or do unto us. Adored be his free grace for enabling you, dear Sir, to confeſs him before men, and to make *Moſes*'s choice your choice. Great ſhall be your reward of grace, though not of debt: he will confeſs you before his Father and his holy angels in heaven. When you write, be pleaſed to ſalute the dear confeſſors at *Cork*. I love them in the bowels of JESUS CHRIST, and pray the LORD of all lords to give them grace to quit themſelves like men, and be ſtrong. If any of my poor writings might be uſeful, I will ſend ſome to *Ireland* at any time. O free grace, that the adorable JESUS ſhould ever make uſe of ſuch a wretch as I am! This is free grace indeed. Help me, dear Sir, to adore it; and if at any time I can be ſerviceable, make no apologies, but write frequently, and command as well as pray for, my dear friend,

Your very affectionate brother and chearful ſervant,

G. W.

LETTER DCCXCII.

To Mr. G——.

My dear Mr. G——, *London, Dec.* 12, 1749.

I Thank you for your kind letter. It beſpoke the language of an honeſt heart. If I am not miſtaken, your name is *Nathaniel*. This is what I fain would be, an *Iſraelite* indeed, in whom is no allowed guile. Such will JESUS guide in his way. I therefore have no doubt of your receiving a bleſſing, a bleſſing, in what you intend doing next *Chriſtmas*. You have openly called JESUS and his diſciples to the marriage: and ſuch proceedings are always owned of GOD, whilſt contrary methods are as ſurely either blaſted or embittered by him, who loves a ſingle eye and an upright heart. You will remember me kindly to Mrs. *H——*, and all that love the bleſſed JESUS in ſincerity. I deſire to be thankful for the favour that was left behind a preached goſpel. It is the LORD's doings. Let us continue praying, and we ſhall yet ſee far greater things than theſe. You do well to meet at *Rotheram*. My cordial ſalutations

salutations, attend Mr. *C——*, Mr. *H——*, and their respective families. May the LORD bless them, as he did the house of *Obededom*, for the ark's sake! My advice is, quit yourselves like men, and be strong. If our LORD shall open a door, I fully purpose to have another stroke at Satan's strong-holds in *R——*. JESUS can and will make us more than conquerors over all. Blessed be his name for leading you, my dear friend, more and more into the knowledge of his divine, compleat, and everlasting righteousness. That is a rock against which the gates of hell shall never prevail. If we have a mind to go pleasantly to *Canaan*, we must lean, not on our frames, not on a stock received, but on our Beloved. Looking to him is the only way of being saved from every evil that annoys and disturbs us. It is his blood, sprinkled by the blessed Spirit upon the conscience, and that alone, which cleanseth from all sin. Whatever, therefore, you want, go to JESUS: that is his name. And why? Because he is to save his people from their sins. And what amazing grace is it, that we should be in the number of his people? Surely that GOD-exalting, that self-abasing expression, "Why me, LORD, why me?" should always be in the mouth of one redeemed of the Lamb. But I must stop, though with regret. Whilst I am writing the fire kindles. I beg all your prayers;—no one wants them more. My wife returns her love. I believe good Lady *H——* hath no place suitable for the person you mention. Why should she fly from her cross? Sometimes we do best when surrounded by enemies: they keep us upon our watch. JESUS is able to preserve us, though in a burning bush. To his never-failing mercy do I commend you all, and am, dear Sir,

Your affectionate friend and ready servant
for CHRIST's sake,

G. W.

LETTER DCCXCIII.

To Mr. *H——*.

My dear Mr. H——, London, *Dec.* 13, 1749.

YOUR kind letter almost made me to blush. I little thought, when I left *N——*, that you should have written first; but I have been so engaged since I came to town,

town, that I could not well write to you before now. However, you have generally been in my thoughts; and I have not failed to remember you before him, who is able to save to the uttermost all that come to the Father in and through him. I see you are still under the rod, and I trust are enabled to kiss the hand that holds it. These afflictions, at present are not joyous, but grievous; nevertheless, through these many tribulations, we shall at length enter into eternal glory. By doing, or suffering, or by both, our active and passive graces must be kept in continual exercise. Your sufferings are of a peculiar nature; peculiar grace shall be given under, and a peculiar conquest granted over them. Look, my dear Sir, not to the *Mysticks*, but to JESUS. Indeed, his righteousness is the only rock on which you can build any solid comfort. In this, and in this only are you compleat. This is the only breastplate; and faith in this, a true, living, operative faith in this, is the only shield whereby the believer will be enabled to repel all the fiery darts of the wicked one. Thanks be to GOD, who hitherto hath given you to triumph, hath raised you from a bed of sickness, and set you on a throne, I mean your pulpit again. May the glorious *Emmanuel* enable you to speak from thence both to him and his people, as becometh the lively oracles of GOD. I find Satan does all that he can to prevent your using your pen. The LORD will rebuke him in due time, and cause it yet to become the pen of a ready writer. I am glad you have opened a correspondence with our elect Lady. Keep it open I entreat you, my dear friend, and be not *nimis nullus*. Alas! if differences of every kind were to hinder any one, surely I must be the man. But in JESUS is my strength found; and as my day is, so he causes my strength to be. Thanks be to his holy name, we have seen his outgoings frequently of late in *London*. His glory hath filled the Tabernacle, and many have been brought under fresh concern for their souls. I shall be glad to hear that Dr. S—— hath begun to speak for the LORD. But what can be done, till we are delivered from worldly hopes and worldly fears? Perfect, unfeigned love to the blessed JESUS, can only expel these. That your dear soul may constantly overflow with it, and that

you

you may increase with all the increase of GOD, is the earnest prayer of, my very dear Mr. H——,

  Your most affectionate, though unworthy friend,
   and brother, and servant in our common LORD,

            G. W.

LETTER DCCXCIV.

To Mr. James B——.

My dear Friend,   London, *Dec.* 14, 1749.

IF you was rejoiced in hearing from me, I can assure you, I was delighted, when I received letters from my dear *Maryland* and *Bohemia* friends. Upon reading them, I hoped that our LORD was purging you, that you might bring forth more fruit to his glory. I hope you have found it a sanctifying rod, and that it hath only whipped you so much nearer to the ever-blessed Lamb of GOD. Now, my dear Sir, now is the time to shew your gratitude; now is the time to begin steadily to pursue the one thing needful. What avail the many things of this poor transitory world, in a sick and dying hour? Alas! they are nothing, and less than nothing. JESUS alone is all in all. He is the pearl of great price, which a wise merchant will gladly sell all to purchase. It is worth all, or worth nothing. O when shall it once be, that the children of this world shall not be wiser in their generations than the children of light! I trust my dear Mr. *B——* will labour to fulfil this wish, and with full purpose of heart 'cleave unto his once dying, but now risen, ascended, and interceding LORD. When shall I love him more; when shall unworthy I serve him better? My obligations to do so, are increasing every moment. This last fall has been a glorious seed-time indeed. I have been in six or seven *Northern* counties, and thousands and ten thousands flocked to hear the word. I am now in my Winter quarters. Our LORD is pleased to bow the heavens, and come down amongst his people. His glory fills the Tabernacle, and the shout of a king is heard in our camp. I wish I could hear of the revival of GOD's work among you. Let us pray, and not faint. You know who has commanded us to let him have no rest till *Jerusalem* be made a praise through the earth. Methinks I wish the months may fly away, wherein

wherein I am detained from coming to my dear *America* again. I entreat you to pray me over, and then I shall come in the fulness of the blessing of the gospel of peace. The glorious JESUS deals bountifully with me here. I am better in health, than I have been some years.—My wife hath much improved in hers, since her arrival in her native country. She joins in sending most affectionate respects. Pray remember us to all in the tenderest, and most endearing manner; and believe me to be, my very dear Mr. *B*———,

   Yours most affectionately in our common LORD,
               G. W.

LETTER DCCXCV.

To Lady H———n.

Honoured Madam,   *London, Dec.* 14, 1749.

YOUR Ladyship's letter gave me uncommon joy. I cannot help being delighted, when any thing I write gives your Ladyship any peculiar satisfaction. The inclosed I immediately shewed to Colonel *G*———, who was very glad, but is still concerned because he does not hear from your Ladyship; and on *Saturday*, GOD willing, I shall read it to Lady *H*——— and Mrs. *K*———. At that time, I am to give them the holy sacrament. Last *Saturday* I prayed with them; and in conversation, an aged gentlewoman was struck: I shall see how the physic works next visit. Thanks be to GOD, the Holy Spirit has not done striving with sinners. I have had glorious accounts of the success attending the word in my last *Northern* circuit. Three or four fresh instances of conviction and conversion I have heard of here, within these few days. Whatever seems worthy of your Ladyship's notice shall be sent. I wish I knew how a parcel might be best conveyed to your Ladyship. If your Ladyship remembers, last Winter application was made in behalf of one *Hill*, a Corporal. O that I could do any thing to express my gratitude to your Ladyship and honoured sisters. In public and private you have my prayers, which I trust will enter into the ears of the LORD of Sabaoth. I think your Ladyship hath great encouragement to go on, striving to win souls to the blessed JESUS. Mrs. *T*——— is another jewel in your Ladyship's crown. May the glorious
                Emmanuel

Emmanuel add daily to the number of them! We have golden seasons here. Poor Mr. H——— was quite revived with your Ladyship's letter. He is under the cross indeed. I am ashamed to think how little I do or suffer for JESUS CHRIST. Next *Saturday* I am thirty-five years old; fy upon me, fy upon me! I beg the continuance of your Ladyship's prayers, that I may now begin in earnest to glorify my blessed Master. Nothing else can satisfy, honoured Madam,

Your Ladyship's most dutiful, obliged,
and ready servant for CHRIST's sake,

G. W.

LETTER DCCXCVI.

To the Old Mrs. B———.

Dear Madam, London, Dec. 14, 1749.

IF this finds you in the land of the living, or rather this land of the dying, it comes to assure you that your dear letter and the other letters received from your dear family, gave me great satisfaction. Blessed be GOD, even the God and Father of our LORD JESUS CHRIST, for wounding and healing. This is his way. He wounds, in order to heal, and in the midst of judgment remembers mercy. Surely he is good in holding your soul in life, and being so much a staff to you in your old age. He has been a promise-keeping GOD. He has not forsaken you when grey-headed, and when your natural strength must necessarily begin to fail you. Though it is cruel to hope you will be kept out of heaven so long, yet who knows, but I may see you, dear Madam, on this side eternity. GOD willing, I purpose to embark some time next year without fail. The infinitely condescending Redeemer vouchsafes to crown my labours with great success; but in the midst of all, *America*, dear *America*, is not forgotten by me. Your family is peculiarly dear. I look upon you as my mother, and on your children as my brethren and sisters. I have lately been in *Yorkshire*, where I saw a widow, whose husband lately died in triumph, and who has five sons and one daughter all walking in the love of GOD. Let this strengthen your faith, dear Madam, and encourage you to hope that you shall still see the travail of the Redeemer's soul in the salvation of all your children,

and

and be satisfied. The Lord's Spirit seems still to be striving with them; and I trust he will not let them go, till they are enabled to give him spirit, soul, and body to be sanctified throughout. My poor prayers shall not be wanting. We often think and talk of you. My wife, with me, sends you and yours a thousand thanks for all your kindnesses. We are both pretty well, and have the satisfaction of seeing the glory of the Lord manifested in the great congregation. O what a blessed master is Jesus Christ. I am just now come to my thirty-fifth year of age. I blush and am confounded, when I think for what little purpose I have lived. It is time now to begin to do something for Him, who has done and suffered so much for me. I beg, dear Madam, you will pray for me while life lasts. I am the chief of sinners, less than the least of all saints; but for Christ's sake under manifold obligations to, and am, dear Madam,

Your most affectionate, obliged friend
and ready servant,
G. W.

LETTER DCCXCVII.

To Mrs. L——.

London, Dec. 15, 1749.

My dear and honoured Mother,

I Have been quite uneasy because your things have not been sent. The woman that was to procure them disappointed me. I hope you will not miss of them another week. Pray be not uneasy. I should never forgive myself, was I by my negligence, or any wrong conduct, to give you a moment's needless pain. To-morrow will be thirty-five years since you brought unworthy me into the world. Alas! how little have I done for you, and how much less for Him who formed me, and has heaped innumerable mercies upon me ever since I was born. O that my head was water, and mine eyes fountains of tears, that I might bewail my barrenness and unfruitfulness in the church of God! By his grace, I hope now to begin to work for Him, who stretched himself on the cross, and groaned and died for me. His care for his tender mother, excites me to wish I could do any thing for you. This is my comfort,

comfort, I hope you want for nothing. Thanks be to the LORD of all lords for his goodness to you in your old age! I hope you comfort yourself in him, who I trust will be your portion for ever. After Christmas I hope to see you. My wife sends you her most dutiful respects. If you would have any thing brought more than you have mentioned, pray write to, honoured mother,

    Your ever dutiful, though unworthy son,
               G. W.

LETTER DCCXCVIII.

To Dr. B——.

London, Dec. 15, 1749.

AND shall I forget my dear Dr. B——? I cannot, though I have received no letter from him. I remember his labours of love, I have heard of the sickness of his dear yoke-fellow, I must not, I cannot withhold my pen from writing. And what shall I say? I trust your soul prospers, and that you can cry out with dear Mrs. B——, now in heaven,

    ————*O happy rod,*
 That brought me nearer to my GOD.

Surely my dear friend has long ere now been convinced that good desires will not carry us to heaven. There must be a closing with CHRIST, a vital union of the soul with GOD, or, in other words, "CHRIST formed within us." This was the expression that first convinced me of the new birth. Since that, I hope It has been in a degree fulfilled in my heart. I want it to be more and more so, and to have the image of GOD stamped in more lively characters upon my soul. My dear Doctor, let you and I begin to strive, not by way of contention, but in a way of holy emulation, which shall love CHRIST most, and live most to his glory. I hope that Dr. *W*—— will join in this strife. Pray my love to him, to Mr. S—— and family, and to all *Bohemia* friends. I refer you to other letters for news, and beg leave to assure you that I am, my dear Doctor,

    Yours most affectionately in our blessed LORD,
               G. W.

LETTER DCCXCIX.

To Mr. N——.

My dear Mr. N——, London, *Dec.* 19, 1749.

IT is now almoſt an age ſince I wrote to you. Providence prevented my ſeeing you when laſt in the *North*, and ever ſince, buſineſs has kept me from writing. However, bleſſed be GOD, I can ſend you good news now I do write. For near three months I have preached in many places, and thouſands and ten thouſands flocked to hear the glorious goſpel. I have ſince had repeated letters of the impreſſions abiding upon the heart of many. Not unto me, not unto me, O LORD, but unto thy free grace be all the glory! At *Howarth* I met with *William Davy*, who has ſince been impriſoned for preaching. Though he is ſeemingly unqualified, yet I meet with many that date their awakening from their firſt hearing him. What ſhall we ſay to theſe things? Even ſo, Father, for ſo it ſeemeth good in thy ſight! I think he belongs to our LORD's family; and therefore what is done for him, he will take as done to himſelf. I hope all things go on well at *Glaſgow.* We have golden ſeaſons here. Winter quarters are made very agreeable. Many are brought under freſh awakenings. You muſt remember us in the kindeſt manner to all dear friends. I commend them and you to the mercies of GOD through CHRIST JESUS, and am, my dear Sir,

Yours moſt affectionately in our common LORD,

G. W.

LETTER DCCC.

To Mrs. R——.

Dear Madam, London, *Dec.* 20, 1749.

I Received your letter, and had thoughts of writing to you before it came; but had forgotten your name, and knew not how to direct. I rejoice that any good impreſſions have been made upon your heart by the bleſſed Spirit, under my poor unworthy adminiſtrations. I hope this will find you coming up out of the wilderneſs, leaning upon your beloved. You know whom I mean. It is the ever-loving, altogether lovely

lovely JESUS, even he who hath loved and given himself for you. I know his love will constrain you to give yourself, even your whole self to him in return. This is all he requires, " Give me thy heart." Amazing! Who can help echoing back, " My heart, LORD JESUS, will I give." But we must give it him as it is. We must come as poor, to be made rich, naked, to be cloathed, and miserable, to be made happy. O glorious exchange! precious redemption! May the LORD JESUS shed a sense of it abroad abundantly in your heart by the Holy Ghost! It is he that must apply, and bring home what CHRIST has done and suffered for our souls; and when this is done, the kingdom of GOD is erected in our hearts, and it is our privilege to go on from strength to strength, till grace is swallowed up in endless glory. This I hope, dear Madam, you will find true by happy experience. Your business is to look up continually to the LORD JESUS, not only as the author, but also as the finisher of your faith. This will strengthen you under every weakness, and in the end make you more than conqueror over all. Your concern for Mr. B——, the Redeemer takes kind at your hand. Fear not, only believe. Press him with arguments, and GOD with prayers. And who knows but ere long your husband may draw in the same yoke, and you may live together as heirs of the grace of life. All things are possible to that JESUS, who is able to save to the uttermost all that come to the Father in and through him. To his tender never-failing mercy do I commend you, and am, dear Madam,

Your affectionate friend and ready servant
for CHRIST's sake,
G. W.

LETTER DCCCI.

To Lady Ann H———.

Honoured Madam,   *London, Dec.* 29, 1749.

WILL your Ladyship and honoured sister be pleased to accept, though late, my most hearty and grateful acknowledgments for all the kindnesses you conferred on me when at *A——* place. They are noted in his book, who has promised, " That a cup of cold water given in the name of a disciple, shall in no -wise lose its reward." What a beneficent master does the christian serve! Who would but be his disciple, whose service is perfect freedom here, and who hath reserved in heaven a crown of glory for those that love him hereafter? I thank him ten thousand times for calling unworthy me to embark in his blessed cause! It is indeed a cause worth embarking in. It gives me great Pleasure to think, that some poor souls at A—— are under awakenings, and seem inclined to list under the Redeemer's banner. Your Ladyship and honoured sister, I trust, will now have repeated opportunities of seeing not only how JESUS receives publicans and sinners, but also how the Spirit of GOD strips the Pharisee of his pitiful fig-leaves, hunts him out of the trees of the garden (I mean his own tinsel performances), brings him naked to the bar, makes him see himself on a level with the worst of sinners, and then sweetly reveals unto him a saviour. Thanks be to GOD, I have had some blessed instances of this very lately; especially a boatswain of a ship, who a few weeks ago knew no more of the corruption of his nature, and the righteousness of CHRIST, comparatively speaking, than the whistle he used to make use of on board ship; but now hath undergone a wonderful change. What cannot grace do? Honoured Madam, I could say much of it, was I not afraid of being tedious. I hope your Ladyship will not be offended at my presenting you with Bishop *Hall*'s works. I thought your Ladyship and honoured sister might now and then like to read one of the contemplations, which, in my opinion, are very delightful. That both you and her Ladyship, and every branch of your noble family, may be every moment under the guidance and direction of the great Shepherd and Bishop of souls, is the earnest prayer of, honoured Madam,

Your Ladyship's most obliged humble servant,

G. W.

LETTER DCCCII.

To Mr. S——.

My dear Mr. S——,   *London, Jan.* 2, 1750.

THOUGH I am really very much busied, yet I cannot help complying with your request, lest it should be any disappointment. I love you in the bowels of JESUS CHRIST, and

and earnestly pray our common Head, that you may be a scribe more and more instructed to the kingdom of GOD, and out of the good treasure of your heart, bring forth things new and old, for the Redeemer's people. The more you are acquainted with, and see your compleatness in him, the more you will long after an entire conformity to him, and apply with greater boldness for fresh supplies of life and strength. His faithfulness must make us faithful. He must be the *Alpha* and *Omega*, the first and the last. When we are once taught this, not notionally, but by the Spirit of GOD, then we shall go on our way rejoicing, and experience the glorious liberty of the children of GOD. Thanks be to his name for enlightening you into these truths; but I love to see the LORD JESUS bringing this about in his own way and time. He gives us glorious seasons here. Yesterday was a blessed Letter day. These verses were sung for you, &c.

> *Thy work in the North,*
> *O* SAVIOUR, *increase;*
> *And kindly send forth*
> *The preachers of peace.*
> *Till throughout the nation,*
> *Thy gospel shall ring;*
> *And peace and salvation*
> *Each village shall sing.*

Thousands said, "Amen, and Amen." I have had brave news from *Virginia* and *Scotland*. O for a disinterested spirit! O to be willing to be poor, that others may be rich! O to be nothing, that JESUS may be all! I must not enlarge. Let me know when you set out for *Newcastle*, and whether the books shall be sent by land or water. I get very little by them. I do not desire it should be otherwise. I believe that as many are given away, as answers to the profits of what are sold. If souls are profited, I desire no more. Troubles increase in *Ireland*. You must remember me to all, and let them demonstrate their love by praying for, dear Sir,

Yours, &c.

G. W.

LETTER DCCCIII.

To the Reverend Mr. G———.

Reverend and very dear Sir,   London, *Jan.* 2, 1750.

WITH great pleasure did I receive yesterday a letter from Mr. *N———*, informing me of your boldness and success in the glorious gospel of the ever-blessed GOD. It came just as I was going to read an account of the LORD's doings in our parts to multitudes of souls. These lines were sung for you,

> *Thanks to the* LORD, *our souls give praise,*
> *Because he makes his vineyard thrive;*
> *Ten thousand thanks that still he rears,*
> *In answer to our daily prayers,*
> *Some faithful servants bold for* GOD:
> *Uphold them by thy chearing blood!*

GOD will hear our prayer; our cry shall come unto him. Go on, my dear Mr. *G———*. The more you do, the more you may do for the ever-blessed JESUS. Be instant in season and out of season, and boldly say,

> *For this let men revile my name,*
> *No cross I'll shun, I'll fear no shame;*
> *All hail reproach, and welcome pain,*
> *Only thy terrors,* LORD, *restrain.*

May GOD bless you among the students! Their names are *Legion*. He that catches one of them, catches many at once. We have blessed seasons here. I have good news from *Virginia*. I hear every day of fresh persons lately brought under conviction. A learned gospel minister, who was lately turned out for the sake of JESUS, I believe will be up here soon. Grace! grace! The more we are cast out, the more will JESUS come in unto us. You must remember me to all. Want of leisure, not of love, prevents my writing. I have frequently scarce time to eat bread: and little of that serves me. But JESUS is the bread of life. Whilst his servants feed others, he feasts them. Do you not find this true by

happy

happy experience? I know you do. Go on, prefs forward, dear Sir, and you shall find it more and more. Excuse this hasty scribble. I hope to answer Mr. *N——* shortly. My wife joins in cordial salutations to all, with, reverend and dear Sir,

Yours, &c.
G. W.

LETTER DCCCIV.

To the Rev. Mr. C————.

My dear Friend, London, *Jan.* 3, 1750.

YOUR letter surprized me; but *benefacere & male pati hic vere christianus est.* If your friend does not hurt himself, he is in no danger from me. I think sometimes of *Joseph*; He that appeared for him, will in time appear for me, and plead my injured cause. But all is well. The returns I have hitherto met with, shall not discourage me, or at least make me to give over and cease from serving you and yours. Mr. *L——* sends me dreadful news from *Cork.* *B———* is there again, making havock of the people. Mr. *H——* expected to be murdered every minute some time ago. I have been with some, who will go to the Speaker of the House of Commons, and represent the case. I hope I have but one common interest to serve; I mean, that of the blessed JESUS. O for simplicity, and godly sincerity! Our LORD abhors guile in all shapes, and sooner or later it will meet with its own reward. I am glad you are supported—Our LORD is a ready help in time of need. We have golden seasons here. Grace! grace! I wish you and yours a happy new year, and am,

Yours most affectionately in our common LORD,

G. W.

LETTER DCCCV.

To Lady H———n.

Honoured Madam,   London, *Jan.* 6, 1759.

THE inclosed letters came to hand on *Monday* last, as a new-year's-gift. As they bring such good news, I must communicate them to your Ladyship. The first writer is a *Virginia* planter, at whose house I lay, and who with some other gentlemen asked me to play a game at cards: I refused, and retired to pray for him. His present wife is my spiritual child. The letters will shew how GOD was pleased to answer our prayers. This, and other things I meet with, more and more convinces me, that a liberty to range and publish the gospel wherever providence shall call me, is what I am to maintain and preserve. Mr. *A———* abides still, and as far as I can judge, disinterested. Blessed be GOD for stripping seasons! I would not lose the privilege of leaning only upon the LORD JESUS for thousands of worlds. He alone can make me happy, and he alone without foreign assistance can bless; and blessed be his name, he daily makes me so. He has been pleased to remove in some degree the pain of my breast, and gives me to determine more and more, that every breath I draw by divine assistance shall be his. I thank him ten thousand times that your Ladyship is so well pleased with Mr. *B———*. He expresses the strong sense he has of the obligations he lies under to the LORD JESUS CHRIST, and under Him, to your Ladyship. O that neither of us may prove ungrateful in any respect! Next week I hope to let your Ladyship know how affairs go at Mrs. *K———*'s. I expect to see her then. Lately his Majesty seeing Lady *Chesterfield* at court with a grave gown, pleasantly asked her, "whether Mr. *Whitefield* advised her to that colour." O that all were cloathed in the bright and spotless robe of the Redeemer's righteousness! How beautiful would they then appear in the sight of the King of kings! This, honoured Madam, through free grace, is your dress. That your honoured sisters, and all your children, may be

adorned

adorned in like manner, is the earnest prayer of, honoured Madam,

> Your Ladyship's most obliged and ready servant
> for CHRIST's sake,
>
> G. W.

LETTER DCCCVI.

To the Reverend Mr. H———.

London, Jan. 8, 1750.

My very dear Mr. H———,

YOUR letter must not any longer lie by unanswered. It is a pleasure to me to steal a few minutes to keep up a correspondence with one I so dearly love, and with whom I am persuaded I shall live in the regions of peace and joy, through the endless ages of eternity. This the glorious *Emmanuel* hath purchased for us, and of this, (for ever adored be his free grace) he hath given us an earnest! Supported with this, I am still enabled to pursue my delightful work of preaching to poor sinners the unsearchable riches of redeeming love. Thousands and thousands flock to hear, and we have had a blessed Christmas and new year's season indeed. In the midst of all, I want more retirement. I want to read, meditate, and write. But I despair of getting much time for these things, till I get upon the mighty waters. In the mean while, I thank the Redeemer for letting my hands be full of work. These words lately have followed me, "Dwell in the land, be doing good, and verily thou shalt be fed." These words embolden me to inform you of two that love CHRIST, and therefore I believe you love them, and I think they want assistance; G—— F—— and I—— H——. The former I think has about eleven children, and scarce a crown a week to maintain them; and the latter writes me word, "He is about a guinea behind hand." I am doing what I can for them, and if you would send them a small token, or now and then let me have a little to give to the many christian objects that apply to me, I know not how your generous heart could lay out a little to more advantage. You know the pleasure of doing for CHRIST's disciples. I labour to contract every expence, and to save all I can for the good of others. Ought
I not

I not to do so, to express my gratitude to him, who for my sake had not where to lay his head, and though he was rich, yet he became poor, that we through his poverty might be made rich. Much, yea very much of his divine unction do I pray may be given to my dear Mr. H—— in his present plan. May the LORD make your pen the pen of a ready writer, and after death may your writings be blest to thousands yet unborn! I believe they will. O my dear friend, whilst I am writing the fire kindles. Blessed be GOD for JESUS CHRIST! Blessed be GOD for all the mercies he hath conferred upon us! O that this new year may be filled with good works, flowing from a principle of love and a new nature! That the LORD may bless and keep you, and fill you with all his divine fulness, is the continual earnest prayer of, my dear, dear old friend,

Yours most affectionately in our common LORD,

G. W.

LETTER DCCCVII.

To the Reverend Mr. B———.

My very dear Sir, London, *Jan.* 12, 1750.

LEST I should be hindered to-morrow, or in the beginning of the week, I now sit down to answer your kind letter. O that I may be helped to write something that may do you service, and be a means of quickening you in that delightful cause in which you are embarked. I see, my dear Sir, you are like to have hot work, before you quit the field:—For I find you have begun to batter Satan's strongest hold, I mean the self-righteousness of man. Here, Sir, you must expect the strongest opposition. It is the *Diana* of every age. It is the golden image, which that apostate *Nebuchadnezzar*, Man, continually sets up; and the not falling down to worship it, but much more for us to speak, write, or preach against it, exposes one immediately to the fury of its blind votaries, and we are thrown directly into a den of devouring lions. But fear not, Mr. B———, the GOD whom we serve, the captain under whose banner we are listed, is able to deliver us. He knows how to train us up gradually for war, and is engaged to bring us off more than conquerors from the field of battle. If any one need give way, it must be the poor creature that is writing to you, for I believe there is not a person living, more timorous by nature. But I trust in a degree, JESUS hath delivered me from worldly hopes and worldly fears, and by his grace strengthening me, he makes me often bold as a lion. But O, my dear Sir, this pretty character of mine I did not at first care to part with; 'twas death to be despised, and worse than death to think of being laughed at by all. But when I began to consider Him who endured such contradiction of sinners against himself, I then longed to drink of the same cup, and blessed be GOD, contempt and I are pretty intimate, and have been so for above twice seven years. JESUS's love makes it a very agreeable companion, and I no longer wonder that *Moses* made such a blessed choice, and rather chose to suffer affliction with the people of GOD, than to enjoy the pleasures of sin for a season. May the LORD JESUS make us thus minded! For there is no doing good without enduring the scourge of the tongue; and take this for a certain rule, " The more successful you are, the more hated you will be by Satan, and the more despised you will be by those that know not GOD." What has the honoured Lady suffered under whose roof you dwell! Above all, what did your blessed master suffer, who hath done such great things for you? O let us follow him, though it be through a sea of blood. I could enlarge, but time will not permit. I am ashamed of my unprofitableness, and must retire, after begging that you will not forget, reverend and dear Sir,

Yours, &c.

G. W.

LETTER DCCCVIII.

To Lady H——n.

Honoured Madam, London, *Jan.* 12, 1750.

THOUGH I have missed two posts, yet the only cause of my not writing was a fear of being troublesome, and too particular and prolix in the accounts sent your Ladyship in my last letters. Your Ladyship's kind letter this afternoon, together with the inclosed, which I received yesterday, give me fresh occasion to renew that pleasing employ of acquainting

ing your Ladyship with some more particulars. Every day we have new hearers, and I find some or another are almost continually brought under convictions, or are edified at the tabernacle. I have offered Mr. *W*—— to assist occasionally at his chapel, and I don't know but it may be accepted. Your Ladyship will hear soon. O that I may learn from all I see, to desire to be nothing! and to think it my highest privilege to be an assistant to all, but the head of none. I find a love of power sometimes intoxicates even God's own dear children, and makes them to mistake passion for zeal, and an over-bearing spirit for an authority given them from above. For my own part, I find it much easier to obey than govern, and that it is much safer to be trodden under foot, than to have it in one's power to serve others so. This makes me fly from that, which at our first setting out we are too apt to court. Thanks be to the Lord of all Lord's for taking any pains with ill and hell deserving me! I cannot well buy humility at too dear a rate. This is a grace after which your Ladyship pants, and with which our Lord will delight to fill you more and more. Your Ladyship's letter convinces me, that those who know and do most, think they know and do least. If it were not so, grace itself would prove our bane, and goodness and zeal, through the pride and corruption of our hearts, be our destroyers. Honoured Madam, my hands and heart are continually lifted up for you, that you may abound evermore in every good word and work, and be cloathed with that humility which your Ladyship delights to wear every day; I mean that humble mind which was in Christ Jesus. I rejoice exceedingly in the comfort which your Ladyship has in Mr. *B*——. I shall take care to cultivate our acquaintance, and earnestly pray that it may be blessed to our mutual improvement. I trust he will be a good soldier of Jesus Christ, and doubt not ere long I shall hear of his receiving some wounds and scars of honour in the field of battle. After I left Mr. *Z*——, by appointment I went to Mrs. *K*——, to whom with the Countess, Lady *G*——, Mr. *C*——, and one Mrs. *B*——, I gave the blessed sacrament, and afterwards a word of exhortation. Our Lord was there, and your Ladyship &c. were remembered before him. On *Tuesday* next the blessed feast is to be repeated at

the

the Countess's house, and on *Wednesday*, GOD willing, I shall leave town for about five weeks. All I think are as hearty as ever, and I trust some will take deep root downwards, and bear fruit upwards. His Majesty seems to have been acquainted with some things about us, by what passed in his discourse with Lady *Chesterfield*. The particulars are these; her Ladyship had a suit of cloaths on, with a brown ground and silver flowers, which was brought from abroad. His Majesty coming round to her, first smiled and then laughed quite out. Her Ladyship could not imagine what was the matter. At length his Majesty said, "I know who chose that gown for you: — Mr. *Whitefield*; and I hear that you have attended on him this year and half." Her Ladyship answered, "Yes I have, and like him very well;" but after she came to her chair, was grieved she had not said more; so that I find her Ladyship is not ashamed. O that she and all that have heard the gospel, may have grace given them to speak of their dear Redeemer, even before kings, when called to it, and not be daunted! I have also been with the Speaker about the poor people in *Ireland*. Mr. G—— introduced me, and opened the matter well. His honour expressed a great regard for your Ladyship, and great resentment at the indignities the poor sufferers underwent; but said, "Lord H—— or the secretary of state, were the properest persons to be applied to, and he did not doubt but that your Ladyship's application would get their grievances redressed." I wished for a memorial to acquaint him with particulars. He treated me with great candour, and assured me no hurt was designed us by the state. Mr. G—— was quite hearty, and has the utmost respect for your Ladyship. To-morrow I am to preach at Mr. *W*——'s chapel, and I suppose on *Sunday* also. O that I may be a freed-man, and ready to help all that preach and love the LORD JESUS in sincerity! I bless GOD for Mr. B————, and am exceedingly obliged to good Lady A————. I am ashamed of the length of this, but as it is on business, your Ladyship will excuse, honoured Madam,

Your Ladyship's most obliged, ready servant,

G. W.

LETTER DCCCIX.

To Mr. L———.

Very dear Sir, London, *Jan.* 18, 1750.

LAST *Monday* I waited upon the Speaker of the House of Commons, with one Mr. G———, a dissenting minister, who opened our poor suffering brethren's case in a proper manner.—The Speaker expressed great resentment upon hearing of the indignities they had met with, and said, that if it did properly belong to him, he would make a thorough search into the affair. But he wondered application had not been made to Lord H———, who was the King's representative in *Ireland.* He at the same time wanted to be informed of more particulars. For want of a memorial, I could only shew him the contents of your letter. Two things therefore seem necessary. Be pleased to send a well-attested narrative of the whole affair, and wait upon Lord H——— yourself. A friend of mine intends writing to Lord Baron B———. Is he in *Dublin?* As soon as ever I hear from you, more may be done. In the mean while, the dear souls have my constant prayers, and shall have my utmost endeavours to serve them. I count their sufferings my own. Pray let me hear how they do. We have great peace here. The blessed JESUS manifests himself among us, and you know that his presence is all in all. Hearty *Amens* are given, when our friends are mentioned in prayer at tabernacle. To-morrow I am to preach at Mr. *W———'s* chapel. O that it may be for the Redeemer's glory and his people's good! I am a debtor to the *Greek* and to the *Barbarian,* to the wise and to the unwise, and think it my highest privilege to preach CHRIST and him crucified to all. I know you wish me prosperity. Strange! that the love of JESUS should unite hearts at such a distance, persons who never conversed with each other. But thus it is. Blessed be GOD, we belong to one family, are travelling to one country, are redeemed by the same blood, and are heirs of the same glory. O glorious prospect! How happy are all they that put

their

their trust in the LORD JESUS! I commend you and yours to his everlasting mercy, and am, my very dear Sir,

Yours most affectionately in our Great High Priest,

G. W.

LETTER DCCCX.

To Mr. H———.

London, Jan. 18, 1750.

My very dear Mr. H————,

A Few days ago I received your welcome letter dated *November* 1, at a time I was wondering that I did not hear oftener from you. Blessed be GOD for dealing so favourably with my dear families, and for giving the prospect of such a plentiful crop! I take it as an earnest that, the LORD JESUS will be the LORD GOD of *Bethesda*, and let the world see that designs founded on him shall prosper. I shall not wonder to hear by and by that you are P———t. O that you and I, my dear man, may be cloathed with humility, and the more we are exalted by others, the more may we be abased in our own eyes! Then will the high and lofty One delight to dwell in us, and prosperity itself, that dangerous thing, shall not destroy us. O that something may now be done for the poor negroes. A good beginning now is of vast consequence. Pray stir in it, and let us exert our utmost efforts in striving to bring some of them to the knowledge of our LORD and Saviour JESUS CHRIST. Mr. Z—— will readily concur in any proper measures for promoting so blessed a work. I sent him a copy of your letter, and the original to good Lady H——. This night I have agreed to take little *Joseph* and his sister. Mr. H—— A—— hath been with me, and I find he is desirous, as are all their relations, that I should take them, for they will be but poorly provided for here. I think they have a kind of natural right to be maintained at *Bethesda*, and I have written to Mr. B—— about it. I suppose in your next, you will acquaint me with particulars concerning their father, and how he hath left his affairs. I hear there is a very little infant, besides the other two. I would willingly have that likewise, if it could be kept till it is about three years old. I hope to grow rich in heaven, by taking care of orphans on

earth

earth. Any other riches, bleſſed be GOD, are out of my view. If the crop anſwers expectation, I would have Mrs. *V——* and the other poor of *Savannah* reap the benefit. Pray let one barrrel of rice be reſerved for them. O what cannot, and what will not GOD do, if we put our truſt in him! O for faith! O for humility! May I learn of JESUS more and more! He deals bountifully with us here. We have had a bleſſed Winter indeed!—I am pretty well in health, but my wife at preſent is ill. We ſalute you and yours, and all friends, and wiſhing you the beſt of bleſſings, I ſubſcribe my-ſelf, my very dear Friend,

Yours moſt affectionately in our deareſt LORD,

G. W.

LETTER DCCCXI.

To Lady H——n.

Honoured Madam, *London, Jan.* 23, 1750.

THOUGH I am wearied in walking to and from *South-Audley-ſtreet*, yet I muſt not omit ſending to your Ladyſhip this night. I would have written on *Saturday*, but I waited to ſee the event of things. On *Friday* I preached at the chapel to a very crowded and affected auditory; Mr. *W——* read prayers. On *Sunday* I read prayers, and he preached, and afterwards the ſacrament was adminiſtred to about twelve hundred. More attended at the tabernacle than ever. Was it as big again, I believe on *Sunday* evenings it would be filled. This day hath been ſpent with the Counteſs, Mrs. *K——*, Lady *G——*, Colonel *G——*, Mr. *H——*, and Mr. *G——*. I gave them the communion, and afterwards preached. The public miniſter from *Genoa* came to hear me, and I believe it was a profitable ſeaſon. Lady *F——*, I hear, holds on, and writes word to the Counteſs, that ſhe wiſhes all were as happy as ſhe hath been in reading Biſhop *Hall*'s contemplations. Since I came home, I have received the incloſed paragraph that was ſent to a friend from *Portſmouth*. O that it may humble and quicken me! Surely ranging is my province. Methinks I hear a voice behind me ſaying, " This is the way, walk in it." My heart echoes back, " LORD, let thy preſence go along with me, and then ſend me where thou pleaſeſt."

Even

Even so Lord Jesus, Amen and Amen! O that I had strength equal to my will. But indeed, honoured Madam, this body is a daily trial to me. Sometimes I can scarce drag the crazy load along. At present, I am too fatigued to enlarge. However, I would inform your Ladyship, that I do not leave town till *Tuesday* next. My wife hath been confined to her bed some days, but is now, blessed be God, upon the recovery. God willing, I hope to write to Mr. *L*—— and the poor baker soon. If your Ladyship wants any more books to dispose of, I hope your Ladyship will mention it in your next. Your Ladyship, Lady *Ann*, &c. were remembered heartily to-day. May the prayer enter into the ears of the Lord of Sabaoth! I believe it will. I can only now commend your Ladyship and honoured relations to the God of all grace, and hasten to subscribe myself, honoured Madam,

  Your Ladyship's most obliged and very
    chearful servant for Christ's sake,
        G. W.

LETTER DCCCXII.

To Mr. H——.

London, Jan. 26, 1750.

My dear Mr. H——,

I Wrote to you not long ago, but that is no reason why I should not drop you a few lines now. I hope they will find you and your dear yoke-fellow resigned to the dispensations of providence, and chearfully saying, " It is well." I write thus, because Mr. *H*—— informed me in his last, that old Madam *W*—— was like to die. If she is yet alive, you will present to her my sincere love and service. I am endeavouring to prepare for my great change every day, by looking up to Jesus, and spending and being spent for the good of those souls for whom he shed his precious blood. Glory be to his great name, my labour is not in vain in the Lord. My work increases on my hands, and the prospect of being serviceable widens continually more and more. I beg the continuance of your prayers, and assure you that mine, such as they are, always attend you and yours and all my dear *Carolina* friends. O that the *Indian* land may become indeed wholly chriſtian land! Is there any thing too hard for the LORD?—Ere long I hope to come and ſow a little ſeed in your ground. May the LORD JESUS make my way plain before me! The bearer of this is named G――; he once preached, but has (ſome time paſt) greatly backſlidden. To ſave him from ruin I have taken him in, and have now ſent him to *America*. If he keeps cloſe to GOD and his book, he may yet do well. If not —he has good parts, and is of a good family. You will take no notice of what I write concerning him. I write to you as a friend. I mention it, that if he ſhould turn out wrong, as I pray GOD he may not, you may ſee I was not deceived. I hope you viſit *Betheſda*, which I truſt will be yet brought to ſomething. May the LORD haſten the time, when we ſhall arrive at the *Betheſda* that is above, even that houſe not made with hands, eternal in the heavens! I can now add no more, but my moſt cordial ſalutations to you, yours, and all, and ſubſcribe myſelf, dear Sir,

Yours moſt affectionately in our common LORD,

G. W.

LETTER DCCCXIII.

To Mr. L――.

Very dear Sir,   London, *Jan.* 27, 1750.

I Received your kind letter, and am glad to find the ſtorm is a little abated at *Cork*. I always thought it was too hot to hold long. I ſee by Mr. H―― that ſuffering grace is always given for ſuffering times. If they have honoured him ſo far as to give him ſome laſhes, for preaching the everlaſting goſpel, I ſhall rejoice. Such an inſtance of perſecution, I am perſuaded will ſtir up the reſentment of perſons in power on this ſide the water. I beg for the dear people's ſake, you would continue your accounts. They direct me in my prayers, and excite alſo the prayers of others. On *Monday,* GOD willing, your letter ſhall be read, and in the ſtrength of JESUS CHRIST, we will beſiege the throne of grace once more, in our dear brethrens behalf. Surely we ſhall prevail. Neither will I ſtop, but uſe all endeavours to extricate our friends out of their troubles. Incloſed you have a letter to the Judge. You may ſend or deliver it as you think proper. I hope you will wait on Lord H——, and let me hear what he says. The Duke was spoke to, and last post I wrote to Lady H—— for the memorial, which if sent, shall be put into the hands of some that are very near his Majesty. Some honourable women are much your friends; JESUS makes them so, and when his people are distressed, if needful, a thousand *Esthers* shall be raised up. What are all these mountains in the sight of our great *Zerubabel?* Let him but speak the word, and they shall become a plain. I am glad my dear Mr. L——'s hopes begin to brighten. O for faith to look through every cloud! Ere long the sun of righteousness will shine upon us, and not one cloud be seen to intercept his blessed rays. I trust I can say, that we have lately felt many of his benign influences warming our souls, and the prospect of future usefulness increases daily. O for humility! O for gratitude and love! I have now preached three times in Mr. W——'s chapel, and each time the LORD was with us of a truth. Next week I leave town for about five weeks, but if you write, your letters will be sent to me. In the spring, I am apt to believe the cloud will move towards *Ireland*; but future things belong to him, before whom things past, present, and to come, are one *eternal Now*. Mr. C—— is much obliged to you for your kindness to his friend. He writes word, that you are a father to him. The LORD will reward you for all your works of faith, and labours which proceed from love. Perhaps it may do no harm, to let some know that application has been made, and is making to several in power here, and that they all express great resentment at the *Cork* proceedings. I find their afflictions are my own, and I pray GOD when they have gotten rest, they may not grow lukewarm, but like the churches of old, walk in the comforts of the Holy Ghost and be edified. O for that rest which remains for the people of GOD! It is just at hand. We have a blessed foretaste of it here: We shall have a full fruition in the Redeemer's kingdom hereafter. I wait for thy salvation, O LORD! I can now only add my most cordial salutations, and beg the continuance of your prayers for, very dear Sir,

Yours most affectionately in our blessed I AM,

G. W.

Dear Tommy,   *Gloucester, Feb.* 6. 1750.

THOUGH I left *London* in a very weak condition, and the weather was but bad in coming down, yet the Angel of the everlasting covenant preserved and strengthened me, and I came to *Gloucester* last *Friday* evening. On *Saturday* evening I preached, and likewise on *Sunday* evening, and twice the same day in the country,—at the new house, and at *Hampton*. Hundreds attended that could not come in; and at *Hampton* all was still and quiet. I like that place very well. Yesterday morning I preached at Mr. *Fowler's*, and our LORD gave us a blessed season from those words, "I am the bread of life." On *Wednesday* I am to preach at the *New-house*, and on *Thursday* at Mr. *Fowler's* again. From thence I think to go once more to *Hampton*, but am not yet determined. More come here than can enter, and some young fellows behave rudely; but that is no wonder; the carnal mind is enmity with GOD. C———— was rejoiced much with the guinea. How thankful are some only with the crumbs that fall from others tables! Blessed be GOD, our branch of work is a poor branch; but if we are honest and disinterested, dead to parties, and aiming only at the Redeemer's glory, and the good of souls, the LORD will appear for us in a manner that shall even make his children astonished. I never was easier about his work than now. I see every thing in CHRIST's hands, and therefore every thing must end well. Go on then, my dear Sir, and let us be all heart. Remember me to your wife and all enquiring friends; and cease not praying for, my dear Sir,

Yours most affectionately in our common LORD,

G. W.

LETTER DCCCXV.

To Colonel G————.

My very dear C————,   *Feb.* 8, 1750.

YOUR kind letter reached me this day, just as I came out of the country from preaching the everlasting gospel, and where the blessed Redeemer was pleased to visit and greatly

greatly refresh his people. Last *Monday* we had a like feast; and in this place the word has been attended with an alarming and quickening power. Contrary to my intentions, I have been prevailed on to stay all this week; so that I do not expect to be at *Bristol* till *Monday* or *Tuesday* next. A letter, if you are pleased to favour me with another, may find me there next week. I am sorry to hear you are ill of an ague; but this, and every thing we meet with here, is only to shake and free us of our corruptions, and to fit us more and more for a blessed hereafter. As long as we are below, if we have not one thing to exercise us, we shall have another. Our trials will not be removed, but only changed. Sometimes troubles come from without, sometimes from within, and sometimes from both together.—Sometimes professed enemies, and sometimes nearest and dearest friends, are suffered to attack us. But CHRIST is the believer's *hollow square*; and if we keep close in that, we are impregnable. Here only I find my refuge. Garrisoned in this, I can bid defiance to men and devils. Let who will thwart, desert, or over-reach, whilst I am in this strong-hold, all their efforts, joined with the prince of darkness, to disturb or molest me, are only like the throwing chaff against a brass wall. O my dear Sir, what did I experience on the road this day! How did I rejoice at the prospect of a judgment to come, and in the settled conviction, that, to the best of my knowledge, I have no designs, no views, but to spend and be spent for the good of precious and immortal souls. O that I may be content to be poor, to make others rich! O that I may never be suffered to seek my own things, but the things of the LORD JESUS! His hand, without adding our carnal policy to it, will support his own cause, and make it more than conqueror over all. When fleshly wisdom, carnal reason, or human cunning is made use of, what is it, but, like *Uzza*, to give a wrong touch to GOD's ark, and in the end provoke GOD to smite us? I love you, dear Sir, because I hope and believe you have a tenderness for all that belong to JESUS. I pray GOD to increase this spirit in you. For what we lose of this, so much we lose of heaven, and so far are we destitute of the mind that was and is in JESUS. A bigotted, sectarian, party spirit cometh not from above, but is sensual, earthly, devilish. Many of GOD's children are infected with it; but then they are sick of a bad distemper. May the Spirit of GOD convince and cure them! But whither am I running? Excuse, dear Sir, the overflowings of a heart, at present, I hope, filled with the love of GOD. It is free, unmerited, distinguishing, infinite love, or it would never flow into my ungrateful soul. As our LORD enables, I shall remember all you desire. The King and his family I always remember in the most explicit manner. I hope you will succeed for *Miles*, and for the poor sufferers in *Ireland*. Learn of *Esther*, and go in the name of JESUS of *Nazareth*. Your relations are in the same condition as mine. Are we not as brands plucked out of the burning? Free grace! free grace! I hope to spend an eternity with you in praising the LORD of all lords for it. You will remember me to all, chiefly to the friend of all. You know my name, "The chief of sinners;" but for CHRIST's sake, very dear Sir,

Your most obliged, affectionate friend,
and very chearful servant,
G. W.

LETTER DCCCXVI.

To Lady H———n.

Honoured Madam,   *Bristol, Feb.* 12, 1750.

WITH great pleasure (on my coming to *Bristol* last night) I heard of your Ladyship's recovery from your late indisposition. May the LORD of all lords perfect the begun blessing, and give you to live many years to be an ornament to his church, and a blessing to his people. Since I wrote last, we have been favour'd both in *Gloucester* city, and in the country, with very pleasant and delightful seasons. I have preached about twenty times within these eight or nine days; and though frequently exposed to rain and hail, thanks be to the ever-loving, ever-lovely JESUS, am much better than when I left *London*. I hear that they go on well in *London*; and if we can be helped to keep a single eye, I am persuaded in the end we shall see greater things than ever. Every thing I meet with seems to carry this voice with it, "Go thou and preach the gospel; be a pilgrim, be a stranger here on earth; have no party, or certain dwelling-place; but be continually

preparing

preparing for, and labouring to prepare others for, a house not made with hands, eternal in the heavens." My heart at present echoes back, " LORD JESUS, help me to do or suffer thy will; only let me be kept by thy mighty power, and when thou seest me in danger of nestling, in pity, tenderest pity, put a thorn in my nest to preserve me from it." Hitherto he has in mercy answered my prayer; and though sometimes painful to the flesh, I thank him for it with my inmost Spirit. But surely no one's heart requires so much pains to be taken with it, as doth mine. Surprizing, that the friend of sinners should yet regard me! I must still cry, " Grace! grace!" At present, honoured Madam, I am lost in wonder. May the LORD JESUS be with your spirit, and with the spirit of your honoured sisters, whom I always remember. I doubt not but they were much concerned at your Ladyship's illness. May they long live with you, to be fellow-helpers of each others faith, and to shine as lights in the world! I hope the work goes on at *Ashby*. How matters go on here, your Ladyship shall know hereafter. I purpose continuing at *Bristol* till *Monday* next. I believe my brother thinks it best to have your little orphan-boy as soon as possible. May the blessing of many ready to perish descend on your Ladyship! I must now add no more, but my most dutiful respects, and my sincere acknowledgements of being, honoured Madam,

Your Ladyship's most dutiful and ready servant,

G. W.

LETTER DCCCXVII.

To Mr. W———.

My dear Mr. W———, *Bristol, Feb.* 15, 1750.

WHAT shall I say? Really I can scarce tell what to say, because I have been so long silent to my dear *New-England* friends. But indeed were they to know my circumstances, they would pity me; for my hands have been continually so full of work, and my removes from place to place so frequent, that I often had scarce time to eat bread. However, I must now break through all restraints, and snatch a few moments to inform my dear Mr. *W———*, that I can set up my *Ebenezer*, and say, " Hitherto hath my has helped me." Words cannot well express how bountifully he has been pleased to deal with me. The prospect of doing good in my native country, is more and more promising every day. Last fall, the LORD of the harvest was pleased to give us a most delightful seed-time in many places in the North of England;—in *Lancashire, Cheshire, Yorkshire, Nottingham, Newcastle*, &c. the word of the LORD ran and was glorified, and I hear of fruit remaining in every place. At *London* this Winter, the glory of the LORD filled the Tabernacle, and since I have been in the country, we have had delightful seasons. I am now going *Westward*, and in about two months time purpose going to *Scotland* and *Ireland*, and then shall embark for my dear *America* once more. My health is much restored to me, and I only want an humble and thankful heart. O my dear friend, what cannot GOD do? Ought I not to spend and be spent for the good of souls? Ought I not to be always upon the full stretch for Him, who was stretched upon the accursed tree for me? Yes, the LORD being my helper, I will now begin to be in earnest. And O that I may hear that a prayer-hearing GOD has revived his work in dear *New-England!* You must let this serve as an historical letter, to be read to my dear friends. I would write to many, but indeed I have not time. I long as much to see them, as they can do to see me. I begin to count the days, and to say to the months, "Fly fast away, that I may once more spread the gospel net in dear *America*." But my time and seasons are in thy hands, O LORD; do with me as seemeth good in thy sight, only let me love thee, and continue faithful unto death! You will remember me to my honoured friends and brethren in the ministry, and to all others as they come in your way. That grace, mercy, and peace may be multiplied upon you all, is the hearty prayer of, very dear Sir,

Yours most affectionately in our common LORD,
G. W.

LETTER DCCCXVIII.

To Lady H———n.

Honoured Madam, Briſtol, Feb. 17, 1750.

BLESSED be the GOD and Father of our LORD JESUS CHRIST, who, in mercy to his church and people, is pleaſed yet to hold your ſoul in life, and make your Ladyſhip inſtrumental in plucking ſinners as brands out of the burning. All theſe things I look upon only as the earneſts of good things to come. Goodneſs and mercy will follow your Ladyſhip all the days of your life, and you ſhall dwell in the houſe of the LORD for ever. Lady *Ann*'s ſudden ſhock proves that the old obſervation is true, " Seldom one affliction comes alone," I rejoice to hear that her Ladyſhip is recovered, and pray the LORD of all lords ſo to ſanctify it to her Ladyſhip's better part, that ſhe may be ready at a moment's warning to go forth and meet the heavenly bridegroom. O to be always ready! to have nothing to do, but to die! Surely the Redeemer hath purchaſed this bleſſing for us. Doth not your Ladyſhip find it difficult to be reſigned to live, and to continue ſo long abſent from the LORD? But there is one conſideration which may make life deſirable to the greateſt ſaint on earth; he may here do and ſuffer for JESUS, and call ſinners to him; but in heaven all this will be over. Come life then, come death, JESUS may thy will be done in, by, and upon thy people! I know your Ladyſhip's heart echoes back, Amen. But what ſhall I ſay to the oppoſition ariſing at *Aſhby?* I truſt it is a ſign that good has already been done, and that more is ſtill doing. The Searcher of hearts knows how highly I value your Ladyſhip's letters; yet I think it honour enough to have leave to write to your Ladyſhip, without expecting punctual anſwers. O that I may gladden your Ladyſhip's heart with glad tidings from the *Weſt!* I believe I ſhall. I have been much helped in preaching here, and have heard of two that were thoroughly awakened when I was here laſt. Mr. *H———,* I think, does not loſe ground. The perſons that ſeem calculated to do him ſervice, muſt be ſuch as have a knowledge of themſelves, of the world, and of GOD, whoſe practice proves their eye to be ſingle, and their minds diſintereſted,

rested, and who have gone several stages before him to heaven. These would command respect from him; these he would hear, and to their judgment he would pay a great deference. The Captain, blessed be GOD, begins to be weary of his fine house; and I hope will be so uneasy in every worldly state, as to find no rest for the soles of his feet. May the glorious JESUS reach out the hand of his mercy, take him into the ark, and shut the door fast upon him! But I forget that your Ladyship is yet confined to your room. May the LORD JESUS make it a *Bethel*, a house of GOD, and a gate of heaven to your soul! He will, he will. I hear that the Tabernacle people are blessed in *London*. I am quite easy about that, and every other public concern, and desire nothing but to approve myself upright and disinterested in the sight of GOD and man. I hope your Ladyship will never find any thing to the contrary in, honoured Madam,

Yours, &c.
G. W.

LETTER DCCCXIX.

To Mr. J—— B——.

My dear Mr. B——,   *Exon, Feb.* 22, 1750.

I Received your kind letter a few days ago at *Bristol*, and embrace this first opportunity of answering it. In *London* I was so continually busied with a multiplicity of avocations, that I could not possibly write to you from thence. However, it has pleased him, whose mercy endureth for ever, to give me and his dear people a very pleasant and warm Winter; and I trust much real good hath been done to precious and immortal souls. Just before I left town, I preached four or five times in Mr. *W——*'s chapel, and administred the sacrament twice or thrice. Congregations were very large, and the Redeemer caused much of his glory to pass before us. At *Bristol*, and in *Gloucestershire*, we have had delightful seasons. At the former I saw and dined with Mr. *C—— W——y*, who talked about my preaching in their new room. I said but little, having, as the Searcher of hearts knows, to the best of my knowledge, no view to head or gather a party, but only to preach CHRIST crucified to all. In this I am blessed, in this I find
un-

unspeakable freedom, and to this, the necessity I lie under of labouring on both sides the water, evidently calls me. I am now going *Westward*. Some time in *April* I purpose, GOD willing, to visit your parts again in my way to *Scotland*, and then we can talk over many things. I think it is high time that all reasonings *pro* and *con* about what is past, should be buried in utter oblivion. But I fear——However, this is my comfort—" The LORD reigneth." Our business is to be guileless, and to go forwards, looking continually to that JESUS, in whose cause we are embarked. He will order all things well. I cannot do any thing at present for *W—— D——*. I tried my utmost for Mr. *C——*. If he turns out bad, woe be to him, after such providential interpositions. I have no intimate correspondence with Mr. *S——*, but hear by Mr. *B——*, that he is blest in the parts round about him. I see that he and all young preachers need the Apostle's caution, to " Take heed, lest being puffed up with pride, they fall into the condemnation of the devil."— And this I know, that no one will stand long in this work, unless he is disinterested, and looks for nothing but poverty, disgrace, and death. Whosoever is willing thus to lose his life shall find it; and, on the contrary, whosoever by sinister ends or practices seeks to save his life, the same (mark the end) shall lose it. For the present adieu! The LORD be with you and yours! Be pleased to remember me to all as they come in your way. Direct as usual; and cease not to pray for, dear Sir,

Yours, &c.
G. W.

LETTER DCCCXX.

To Mrs. G——.

Dear Madam, *Exon, Feb.* 22, 1750.

I Rejoice to hear by your last kind letter, that the seed sown at *Manchester* begins to spring up. More especially, I desire to be thankful, that you have grace given you, Madam, to confess the LORD JESUS and his gospel before men. A blessed earnest this, of your being confessed by him before his Father and the holy angels in the kingdom of heaven. The inward peace and satisfaction you enjoy by so doing, I am persuaded

suaded far surpasses all you ever enjoyed, or could possibly enjoy in the polite world. With what unspeakable comfort can you now sing,

> *Be gone, vain world, my heart resign,*
> *For I must be no longer thine;*
> *A nobler, a diviner guest,*
> *Now claims possession of my breast.*

And if the beginning of the divine life be so sweet, what must the end be, when this mortal puts on immortality, and the soul rises to all the fulness of GOD. Blessed be GOD, who has given you to choose that better part, that shall never be taken from you! What have you to do now, but daily to sit at the dear Redeemer's feet and hear his word; I mean, search the scriptures, which testify of him: and for His great name's sake, let your remaining life be one continued sacrifice of love to GOD and man. This is true faith, even a faith that works by love, and overcomes this wicked world. Well may it be stiled *precious faith*. It is precious in itself, and precious in its fruits. It lays hold on, and unites to CHRIST, and carries out the soul day by day after a nearer conformity to him. It goes on from strength to strength, and conducts the soul at length to the perfect and uninterrupted vision of the ever-blessed GOD. Methinks I hear you say, " LORD, evermore give me this faith." He will, Madam, he will: for he giveth liberally, and upbraideth not. Be not afraid of asking too much. Lay your foundation deep in the knowledge of yourself, and you cannot build too high. O that the worthy Captain may bear you company to heaven! I trust he will. Perhaps some time in the Spring, I may have the pleasure of waiting upon you. I am now in the *West*, and have had blessed seasons in my way hither. Good Lady *H———n* hath been ill, but is recovering. There hath been an awakening at *Ashby*; but opposition begins to shew itself in these parts by the instrumentality of a dissenting minister. That the number may daily increase among you, and that you and yours may be watered every moment, is the hearty prayer of, Madam,

Your most obliged and ready servant for CHRIST's sake,

G. W.

LETTER

LETTER [DCCCXX.]

To Lady H———.

Honoured Madam,   *Plymouth, Feb.* 25, 1750.

THE day after I wrote to your Ladyship my laſt letter, I preached three times, once at *Kingſwood*, and twice at *Briſtol*. In the evening I ſtood at *Smith*'s hall window and preached. It was a bleſſed day. The next morning our aſcended Saviour gave me much of his preſence, and I came on my way rejoicing. At *Taunton* I met with Mr. *Pearſall*, a Diſſenting miniſter, a preacher of righteouſneſs before I was born. At *Wellington* I lay at the houſe of one Mr. *Darracott*, a flaming ſucceſsful preacher of the goſpel, and who, I think, may juſtly be ſtiled (what Mr. *Hieron* was ſome years ago) the ſtar in the *Weſt*. He hath ſuffered much reproach; the common lot of all that are owned in the LORD's vineyard: and in the ſpace of three months, he hath loſt three lovely children. Two of them died the *Saturday* evening before the ſacrament was to be adminiſtred; but weeping did not hinder ſowing. He preached the next day, and adminiſtered as uſual. Our LORD ſtrengthened him; and for his three natural, hath given him above thirty ſpiritual children: and he is in a likely way of having many more. He has ventured his little all for CHRIST; and laſt week a ſaint died who left him and his heirs two hundred pounds in land. Did ever any one truſt in the LORD and was forſaken? At his place I began to take the field for this *Spring*. At a very ſhort warning, a multitude of ſouls aſſembled, and the bread of life, that cometh down from heaven, was diſpenſed amongſt them. The following evening I preached at *Exeter*, where there is a little flock, and laſt night and this morning I have preached here: I humbly hope to the comfort of many. This afternoon, GOD willing, I am to take the field again. What ſucceſs I meet with here, and in *Cornwall*, your Ladyſhip ſhall know by another opportunity. I am now waiting for a letter from Mr. *B———*, which I hope will bring me the wiſh'd-for news of the confirmation of your Ladyſhip's health. This is what I continually pray for from my inmoſt ſoul. I am ſorry to inform your Ladyſhip (if it has not reached you before) that Mr. *A———* of *London* is dead.

dead. I think he was one of the moſt lively, and like to have been the moſt ſucceſsful Diſſenting preacher in that great city: but our LORD orders all things well. The reſidue of the Spirit is in his hands. Bleſſed Redeemer, quicken my tardy pace, and make me alſo ready! Good Lady *Ann* I hope is now perfectly recovered. But why do I talk of a perfect recovery in this dying life? Then only ſhall we be perfectly recovered, when we awake in the morning of the reſurrection after our Redeemer's likeneſs; then, and not till then, will my poor ſoul be fully ſatisfied; then, and not till then, will your Ladyſhip fully know how much the temporal and eternal welfare of your Ladyſhip is deſired and prayed for by, honoured Madam,

Your Ladyſhip's moſt humble, dutiful,
and ready ſervant for CHRIST's ſake,
G. W.

LETTER DCCCXXI.

To the Rev. Mr. H——.

Reverend and dear Sir,   *Plymouth, Feb.* 25, 1750.

YOUR letters always fill me with ſympathy. Your laſt I have juſt been reading; and in reading breathed out this ejaculation, " LORD, when will the days of his mourning be ended." Surely you are not always thus to ſtick faſt in the mire and clay. Certainly the time will come, when the dear Redeemer will put your feet upon a rock, and a ſong into your mouth, and order your going for the promoting his glory and his people's good. *Satan* hath indeed deſired to have you, that he may ſift you as wheat; but CHRIST, a ſympathizing, compaſſionate high-prieſt, prays for you, and your faith ſhall not fail. Look up then, my dear Mr. *H*——; you ſhall find grace to help in time of need.

> *Leave to his ſovereign ſway*
>   *To chooſe and to command;*
> *So ſhalt thou wond'ring own his way,*
>   *How wiſe, how ſtrong his hand.*
> *Far, far above thy thoughts,*
>   *His counſel ſhall appear,*
> *When fully he the work hath wrought,*
>   *That caus'd thy needleſs fear.*

This

This is the advice I give you. I know you will pray that I may take it myself. For I find, that sufficient for every day is the evil thereof. But the LORD causes me to renew my strength, and blessed be his name, enables me to go on my way rejoicing. In *London* we have had a blessed Winter. In the country we have seen a Spring time. Hither I came last night, and have preached twice since my coming. Thus I live a moving life. O that I may be a pilgrim indeed, and desire no continuing city till I come to the *New Jerusalem*, which is above, and the mother of us all. There, all that are born of GOD, whether *Mysticks*, *Calvinists*, &c. shall join in one common song, even the song of *Moses* and of the LAMB. Your hymn, for which I thank you, is a preparative for this. I sent it to good Lady H———n, who has been ill, but is now, I hope, recovered. Pray write to me often. Sorrows grow less, and joys greater, by being communicated. Load me as much as you will with all your grievances, and I will lay them before Him, who came to bear our sicknesses, and heal our infirmities. Pray what is become of Mr. S———? Will he preach, now he is sure of something in hand? But alas! the disease is in the heart. When the love of GOD reigns there, then and not till then will the love and fear of the world flee away. Blessed freedom, wherewith JESUS CHRIST makes his servants free! Remember me when at his footstool, and write long and often to, reverend and dear Sir,

Your's, &c.
G. W.

LETTER DCCCXXII.

To Mr. F———.

My dear Mr. F———, *Plymouth, Feb.* 26, 1750.

EVER since I received your last kind letter, I have been endeavouring to redeem some time to answer it, but till now have not had opportunity. Indeed even now a multiplicity of business obliges me to be much more brief than otherwise I should. However, I cannot help informing you, that I am glad that the gentlemen of *Philadelphia* are exerting their efforts to erect an academy. I have often thought such an institution was wanted exceedingly; and if well-conducted, am persuaded perfuaded it will be of public fervice. Your plan I have read over, and do not wonder at its meeting with general approbation. It is certainly well calculated to promote polite literature; but I think there wants *aliquid Chrifti* in it, to make it fo ufeful as I would defire it might be. It is true, you fay, " The youth are to be taught fome public religion, and the " excellency of the chriftian religion in particular:" but methinks this is mentioned too late, and too foon paffed over. As we are all creatures of a day; as our whole life is but one fmall point between two eternities, it is reafonable to fuppofe, that the grand end of every chriftian inftitution for forming tender minds, fhould be to convince them of their natural depravity, of the means of recovering out of it, and of the neceffity of preparing for the enjoyment of the fupreme Being in a future ftate. Thefe are the grand points in which chriftianity centers. Arts and fciences may be built on this, and ferve to embellifh and fet off this fuperftructure, but without this, I think there cannot be any good foundation. Whether the little *Dutch* book I have fent over, will be of any fervice in directing to fuch a foundation, or how to build upon it, I cannot tell. Upon mentioning your defire to the King's *German* chaplain, a worthy man of GOD, he fent it to me, and thought, if tranflated, it might be of fervice. Glad fhould I be of contributing, though it was but the leaft mite, in promoting fo laudable an undertaking; but the gentlemen concerned are every way fo fuperior to me, both in refpect to knowledge of books and men, that any thing I could offer, I fear, would be of very little fervice. I think the main thing will be, to get proper mafters that are acquainted with the world, with themfelves, and with GOD, and who will confequently naturally care for the welfare of the youth that fhall be committed to their care. I think alfo in fuch an inftitution, there fhould be a well-approved chriftian Orator, who fhould not be content with giving a public lecture in general upon oratory, but who fhould vifit and take pains with every clafs, and teach them early how to fpeak, and read, and pronounce well. An hour or two in a day, I think, ought to be fet apart for this. It would ferve as an agreeable amufement, and would be of great fervice, whether the youth be intended for the pulpit, the bar, or any other profeffion whatfoever. I wifh alfo, that

the

the youth were to board in the academy, and by that means be always under the master's eye. And if a fund could be raised, for the free education of the poorer sort, who should appear to have promising abilities, I think it would greatly answer the design proposed. It hath been often found, that some of our brightest men in church and state, have arisen from such an obscure condition. When I heard of the academy, I told Mr. B——, that the new building, I thought, would admirably suit such a proposal; and I then determined in my next to mention some terms that might be offered to the consideration of the Trustees. But I find since, that you have done this already, and that matters are adjusted agreeable to the minds of the majority. I hope your agreement meets with the approbation of the inhabitants, and that it will be serviceable to the cause of vital piety and good education. If these ends are answered, a free-school erected, the debts paid, and a place preserved for public preaching, I do not see what reason there is for any one to complain. But all this depends on the integrity, disinterestedness, and piety of the gentlemen concerned.—An institution, founded on such a basis, GOD will bless and succeed; but without these, the most promising schemes will prove abortive, and the most flourishing structures, in the end, turn out mere *Babels*. I wish you and the gentlemen concerned much prosperity; and pray the LORD of all lords to direct you to the best means to promote the best end; I mean, the glory of GOD, and the welfare of your fellow-creatures. Be pleased to remember me to them and all friends as they come in your way, and believe me, dear Sir,

Yours, &c.

G. W.

LETTER DCCCXXIII.

To Governor B———.

Honoured Sir, *Plymouth, Feb. 26, 1750.*

I Was much rejoiced to hear, by a letter lately received from Mr. *Bradford*, that your Excellency was pretty well, and am very thankful that you was pleased to enquire so cordially after unworthy me. I take this first opportunity of returning my most grateful acknowledgements, and to assure your Excellency, you are not forgotten by me at the throne of grace. Ere now, I thought to have waited upon you in person, but it hath pleased Him, whose I am, and whom I desire to serve in the gospel of his dear Son, to detain me longer than I expected in my native country. The door for usefulness opens wider and wider. The seed sown among the rich, springs up and bears fruit in some; and the poor in various places receive the gospel more gladly than ever. Last fall was a glorious seed-time in the *North* of *England*. In *London* we had a warm winter; and in the country we have had reason to sing, that "the voice of the turtle is again heard in the land." GOD willing, I purpose ranging this Summer, and then to embark for my beloved *America* once more. Whether I shall see your Excellency is uncertain. You are upon the decline of life; and for my own part, I wonder that I live so long. But I trust I shall meet your Excellency in heaven, where the wicked heart, the wicked world, and wicked devil will cease from troubling, and every soul enjoy an uninterrupted and eternal rest. This I am waiting for every day; and according to the present frame of my soul, desire no continuing city, till I arrive at and take possession of the *New-Jerusalem* above. My Master makes ranging exceedingly pleasant; and I hope in his strength to begin now to begin to spend and be spent for him, who shed his own dear heart's blood for sinful, ill, and hell-deserving me. O that death may find me either praying or preaching! I hope your Excellency will increase my obligations, by continuing to pray for me. My prayer for you is, "That your Excellency may bring forth much fruit in old age; and that whensoever you go off, you may be gathered like a ripe shock of corn into the Redeemer's heavenly garner!" That you may till then go on from strength to strength, and increase with all the increase of GOD, is the earnest desire of, honoured Sir,

Your Excellency's most obliged, dutiful,
and ready servant for CHRIST's sake,
G. W.

LETTER

LETTER DCCCXXIV.

To Lady H———n.

Saint-Ginnys, March 5, 1750.

Honoured Madam,

I Was afhamed to fend your Ladyfhip fo fhort a letter from *Plymouth,* but it was unavoidable. I was obliged to take horfe, and therefore could only promife your Ladyfhip to fend you particulars afterwards. At *Plymouth* I preached twelve times in fix days, and the longer I preached, the more hearers, and the power that attended the word increafed alfo. Friends grew more hearty, and enemies more foftened. Mr. *T———* and Mr. *G———* came to *Plymouth* to meet me. I preached at *Taviftock* in my way hither, and yefterday was a glorious day of the Son of man. Our LORD gave us to fee his ftately fteps and out-goings in the fanctuary. Four of Mr. *Wefley*'s Preachers were prefent, and alfo four Clergymen in their gowns and caffocks.—Mr. *Bennet* aged fourfcore, Mr. *Thompfon*, Mr. *Grigg*, and myfelf. It was a day of fat things. By the advice and defire of friends, I am going further Weftward, and fhall take care to let your Ladyfhip know, how the LORD is pleafed to deal with me and his dear people.

Redruth, March 10.

Though the above was begun at *St. Ginnys*, yet I have not been able to go on with it till now. Every day I have been travelling and preaching, and could I ftay one month, it might be fpent to great advantage. At a place called *Port-Ifaac* the Redeemer's ftately fteps were feen indeed, and his people were filled as with new wine. At *Camelford* I preached with great quietnefs in the ftreet. At *St. Andrews* we had a very powerful feafon, and yefterday at *Redruth* feveral thoufands attended, and the word was quick and powerful. Invitations are fent to me from *Falmouth,* and feveral other places. I want more tongues, more bodies, more fouls for the LORD JESUS. Had I ten thoufand, he fhould have them all. After preaching, about noon I am to go to *St. Ives,* and in about nine days I hope to be at *Exeter.* Your Ladyfhip fhall be fure to hear how the LORD profpers the gofpel plough. Mr. *T———* is mighty hearty, and gone to his parifh in a gof- pel

pel flame. The people here want it much. Surely, GOD will some time or another turn their captivity. Mr. T—— desired his most dutiful respects might be presented to your Ladyship. Blessed be GOD, that you are better. I am not forgetful of your Ladyship by night or by day. I hope the souls of your honoured sisters do prosper, and that you will yet live to see JESUS CHRIST formed in all your relations hearts. That every thing your Ladyship writes, says, or does, may be mightily blessed and owned of the dear Redeemer, is the continual prayer of, honoured Madam,

Your Ladyship's most dutiful, obliged, and
ready servant for CHRIST's sake,
G. W.

LETTER DCCCXXV.

To Lady H————.

Honoured Madam,   *Exeter, March,* 21, 1750.

I Think it is now almost an age since I wrote to your Ladyship, but travelling and preaching have prevented me. Immediately after writing my last, I preached to many thousands, at a place called *Gwinnap*. The rain dropped gently upon our bodies, and the grace of GOD seemed to fall like a gentle dew and sprinkling rain upon our souls. It was indeed a fine spring shower. In the evening I rode sixteen miles to *St. Ives,* and preached to many that gladly attended to hear the word; a great power seemed to accompany it. On the morrow, being LORD's day, I preached twice to large auditories, and then rode back again rejoicing to *Gwinnap.* In my way, I had the pleasure of hearing that good was done, and had fresh calls to preach elsewhere. In the morning I went to church, and heard a virulent sermon from these words, " Beware of false prophets." On *Saturday* the preacher was heard to say, " Now *Whitefield* was coming, he must put on his old armour." It did but little execution, because not scripture proof, and consequently not taken out of GOD's armory. On *Monday* I preached again at *Redruth,* at ten in the morning, to near (as they were computed) ten thousand souls. Arrows of conviction seemed to fly fast. In the evening I preached to above five hundred, at twelve miles distant,

and

and then rode about sixteen miles to one Mr. B——'s, a wealthy man, convinced about two years ago. In riding, my horse threw me violently on the ground, but by GOD's providence, I got up without receiving much hurt. The next day we had a most delightful season at *St. Mewens*, and the day following a like time, at a place called *Port-Isaac*. In the evening, I met my dear Mr. *Thompson* again at Mr. *Bennet*'s, a friendly minister aged fourscore, and on *Thursday* preached in both his churches. Blessed seasons both! On *Friday* we went to *Biddeford*, where there is perhaps one of the best little flocks in all *England*. The power of GOD so came down while I was expounding to them, that Mr. *Thompson* could scarce stand under it. I preached twice; a commanding, convincing influence went forth a second time, and one came to me the next morning under awakenings. The LORD JESUS has here brought home a lawyer; and one of the youngest but closest reasoners that ever I met with, is now under deep convictions. On *Monday* evening I came to *Exeter*, and with great regret shall stay till *Friday*. For I think every day lost, that is not spent in field preaching. An unthought of and unexpectedly wide door is opened in *Cornwall*, so that I have sometimes almost determined to go back again. I beg the continuance of your Ladyship's prayers, and hope Mr. B—— will let me know of your Ladyship's welfare. You will not be forgotten by, honoured Madam,

Your Ladyship's most dutiful, obliged, and
chearful servant for CHRIST's sake,
G. W.

LETTER DCCCXXVI.

To the Countess D———.

Honoured Madam, *Exeter, March* 21, 1750.

I Did not think of being so long out of *London*, without sending your Ladyship a letter; but I have been so employed in travelling and preaching and answering letters, that I have scarce had any time at all. However, I bless the glorious Redeemer, that I can now send your Ladyship good news. Every where the word of GOD has ran and been glorified. I am just returned from near the land's end, where thousands and thousands heard the gospel gladly. I have generally

nerally preached twice a day, and rode several miles; but my greatest grief is, that I can do no more for the blessed JESUS. Wherever I am, your Ladyship and honoured sister, with the other honourable ladies, are continually remembered by me at the throne of grace. I hope all are determined with full purpose of heart to cleave unto the LORD. The earthquake hath been an alarming providence. Happy they, that have an interest in CHRIST, and are always ready! On Him alone is my strength and safety founded. Did not this support and comfort your Ladyship under the awful alarm? Go on then, honoured Madam, and by a constant looking to JESUS, make continual advances in the divine life, which I believe hath been communicated to you from above. The more you see of his excellencies, the more will all created things sicken and die in your view and taste. I commend your Ladyship to his never-failing mercy, and beg leave to subscribe myself, honoured Madam,

Your Ladyship's most dutiful,
and obliged humble servant,
G. W.

LETTER DCCCXXVII.

To Lady H———.

Honoured Madam,   *Exeter, March* 24, 1750.

AS I am persuaded your heart's desire and prayer to GOD is, that the kingdom of the LORD JESUS may be set up on earth, I cannot return to *London* without informing your Ladyship, that the gospel has been most gladly received in these western parts. I have been very near the land's end, and every where souls have fled to hear the word preached, like doves to the windows. The harvest is great, yea very great; but the labourers are few. O that the LORD of the harvest would thrust out more labourers! Something out of the common road must be done, to awaken a thoughtless world. GOD has been terribly shaking the metropolis. I hope it is an earnest of his giving a shock to secure sinners, and making them to cry out, "What shall we do to be saved?" I trust, honoured Madam, you have been brought sweetly to believe on the LORD JESUS, and have experienced the beginnings of a real salvation in your heart. What a mercy

mercy is this! To be plucked as a brand out of the burning, to be one of those few *Mighty* and *Noble* that are called effectually by the grace of GOD; what consolation must this administer to your Ladyship under all afflictions! What can shake a soul whose hopes of happiness, in time and eternity, are built upon the rock of ages? Winds may blow, rains may and will descend even upon persons of the most exalted stations; but they that trust in the LORD JESUS CHRIST never shall, never can be totally confounded. That your Ladyship may every day and hour experience more and more of this blessed truth, is the earnest prayer of, honoured Madam,

Your Ladyship's most dutiful, obedient humble servant,

G. W.

LETTER DCCCXXVIII.

To Mr. L——.

Very dear Sir, London, *April* 3, 1750.

LAST *Friday* evening I came to town, and would have answered your kind letters (which I found waiting for me here) last post, had not fatigue and a multiplicity of business prevented me. Surely the distress of our suffering friends is great, but he that dwelleth on high is greater. I have already laid your account before some particular persons, and shall use all possible means to have our dear friends grievances redressed. In the interim, let us besiege the throne of grace, and by earnest prayer engage his assistance, who has promised that the gates of hell shall never prevail against his Church. As I hear Mr. *John W——* is now in *Ireland*, I suppose he will best answer your question about "coming out from amongst them." For my part, I think my business is to preach the gospel unto all, without setting up any particular party. The acceptance which the glorious *Emmanuel* is pleased to give to me, and the various calls sent, as well as the freedom I find in complying with them, confirm me more and more that this is my province. I am just returned from the West, where I have seen the fields every where white ready unto harvest. Though thousands flock to hear the word in town, yet I almost think every day lost in which I am not preaching about the country, now the summer is coming on. GOD only knows whether I shall reach as far as *Ireland*. Pray continue your accounts. I cannot help thinking, but that this opposition is a blessed presage of a future glorious harvest in the kingdom of *Ireland*. Yet a little while, and he that will come, shall come, and will not tarry. That your soul may be filled with all the divine fulness, is the hearty prayer of, dear Sir,

Your affectionate friend and servant for CHRIST's sake,
G. W.

LETTER DCCCXXIX.

To Governor B———.

Honoured Sir,   *Portsmouth, April* 27, 1750.

I Wrote to your Excellency last from *Plymouth*, where, as well as in many other places in the west, the LORD of all lords has been pleased greatly to bless my poor unworthy ministrations. I am now (after having seen much of the Redeemer's power in *London*) making a short elopement to *Portsmouth*, and from thence I purpose to go into the North, where I trust thousands are already awakened to seek after the things which lead to life eternal. The harvest in *England* is exceeding great. I know that your Excellency will pray, that the LORD of the harvest may thrust out more labourers into his harvest. I am glad your Excellency hath been honoured by providence, to put *New-Jersey* college on such a footing, that it may be a nursery for future labourers. I have had the pleasure of seeing Mr. *A———* and Colonel *W———*, and have introduced them to such of my friends, as I believe, under GOD, may serve the interest in which they are engaged. Glad shall I be of every opportunity offered me, of promoting the Redeemer's cause in *New-England* or *New-Jersey*. By the divine blessing, I hope that something considerable will be done in *England* and *Scotland* for *New-Jersey* college. I wish your Excellency joy of the relation into which I hear you have lately entered. I hope my dutiful respects will find acceptance with Madam *Bel———*, and I earnestly pray that you may live together as heirs of the grace of life. May GOD honour you both to bring forth much fruit in old age! Here I would end; but the love I owe to the bearer, Mr. *S———*, for CHRIST's sake, constrains me to recommend him to your Excellency. He is I think an *Israelite* indeed. I

pray

pray the LORD JESUS to succeed and bless him. He can give your Excellency an account, how the work prospers on this side the water. That every wilderness in *America* may blossom like a rose, and that your Excellency's province may be like the garden of the LORD, is the hearty prayer of,

Your Excellency's most dutiful
but obliged humble servant,
G. W.

LETTER DCCCXXX.

To the Reverend Mr. H———.

Portsmouth, April 28, 1750.

My very dear friend and Brother,

YOUR letter should have had an immediate answer, if the least leisure had offered when in town. But there I am continually hurried, and had scarce time to eat bread. However, our LORD gave me meat which the world knows not of, and enabled me to preach three or four times a day to great multitudes, and I trust with great blessings. Fear not your weak body; we are immortal till our work is done. CHRIST's labourers must live by miracle; if not, I must not live at all; for GOD only knows what I daily endure. My continual vomitings almost kill me, and yet the pulpit is my cure, so that my friends begin to pity me less, and to leave off that ungrateful caution, " Spare thyself." I speak this to encourage you. Persons whose writings are to be blessings, must have some thorns in the flesh. Your disorders, like mine, I believe are as yet only to humble, not to kill us. Though I long to go to heaven, yet I am apt to think we are not to die presently, but live and declare the works of the LORD. You by your pen, I by my tongue. May the glorious *Emmanuel* bless us both ! I believe he will. Courage, my dear, very dear Mr. *H———*; Courage. When we are weak, then are we strong. — But to your letter. I am glad Dr. *S———* preaches, and that Mr. *H———*, is at work. In working we shall be blessed. To him that hath, shall be given. How shall we contrive to meet. I purpose being at *Oulney* next *Sunday* sevennight, and in a day or two after at *Northampton*. I wish I could have a line from you. In the mean while I shall endeavour to get Dr. *W———*. There is a glorious plan set on foot

by

by the Great and Good, for a college in the *New-Jersies*; the particulars will ere long be published. I wish it much prosperity. Your Meditations are now printing in *Philadelphia*. Why do you not sit for your picture?—The seed sown here months ago, hath sprung up. People hear with great attention. What cannot God do? The Lord be with you! I love you most tenderly. I thank you ten thousand times for all favours, and am, very dear friend,

Yours most affectionately and eternally
in our dear Lord Jesus,
G. W.

LETTER DCCCXXXI.

To the Reverend Mr. D————.

My very dear Friend, London, *May* 1, 1750.

THOUGH I am somewhat fatigued with my journey, yet I cannot help answering your very kind and wished-for letter. Blessed be the God and Father of our Lord Jesus Christ, who delights to multiply his benefits upon us! I wish you and dear Mrs. D—— joy of your twins. May Jesus sanctify them from the womb, and spare them with their tender mother, to be lasting blessings to yourself and others! What shall I render unto the Lord for removing prejudices from *Taunton* people? It is his doing; and the same grace was shewn at *Portsmouth*, from whence I am just now come. I was there this time twelvemonth, and now had the pleasure of hearing that many were then awakened, who hold on their way. Thousands came to hear, and the word seemed to strike like a pointed arrow. You have been misinformed about *Moor-fields*. I have preached there twice lately to many thousands, but without molestation. A blessed power attended the word, and we have had most delightful seasons in *London*. Help me to cry Grace! grace! I am now going Northward, and hope next week to have another interview with Messrs. H——, H——ly, Dr. D——, and Dr. S——. I rejoice in the success of the Doctor's books, and pray the Lord earnestly to bless all his labours more and more. Poor Lady H——n is ill. I say of her, as I would to you, *serius in cælum redeas!* You may direct to her Ladyship at *Ashby-place*. I am glad to hear that your brethren begin to envy you;

you; It is a good sign. You have heard of the viper and the file. Their biting will only make their own teeth to bleed. We are to go on. I pray GOD you may, and increase with all the increase of GOD. I salute you and all your family. My wife joins, very dear Mr. D——, with

   Yours most affectionately in our common LORD,
              G. W.

LETTER DCCCXXXII.

To Mr. C——.

Very dear Sir,   *Ashby, May* 11, 1750.

AS you talked when I left *London* of setting out on your journey in about a fortnight, I cannot help sending you these few lines. I believe they will be acceptable, because they acquaint you with the continuance of the Redeemer's loving kindness to the very chief of sinners. At *Oulney*, where I preached last LORD's day, we had two sweet seasons. A great multitude attended, and I had the pleasure of seeing some, that were wrought upon when I was there last. On the *Monday*, about six miles from *Northampton*, I had a private interview with Dr. S——, Dr. D——, Messrs. H—— and H——*ly*. On the *Tuesday* I preached in the morning to Dr. D——'s family, and in the afternoon to above two thousand in the field. Dr. S——, Mr. H——, &c. attended me, and walked with me afterwards along the street; so that I hope the physician will now turn his back on the world, and be content to follow a despised crucified Redeemer without reserve. I expounded at his house in the evening, and amhereafter to come to it as my own. On *Tuesday* I preached twice at *Kettering* to several thousands. The people gladly received the word, and the Inn-keeper where I put up, I hope is a real christian. On *Wednesday* I came hither, and found good Lady H——, though very weak, yet better than I expected. I hope you will beg Mr. G——, and all GOD's people, to strive together in their prayers, to keep her out of heaven as long as they can, that she may do more good on earth. I greet you and Mrs. *C*—— most heartily, and wishing you a very prosperous journey, by the will of GOD, I am, very dear Sir,

   Yours most affectionately in our common LORD,
              G. W.

To Doctor S——.

My Dear Doctor,   *Ashby, May* 11, 1750.

HOW do you? I have thought of, and prayed for you much, since we parted from *Northampton.* Now I believe is the time in which the ax is to be laid at the very root of the tree. How wonderfully doth the LORD JESUS watch over you? How sweetly does he lead you out of temptation! O follow his leadings, my dear friend, and let every, even the most beloved *Isaac,* be immediately sacrificed for GOD. Kindness is cruelty here. Had *Abraham* consulted either *Sarah* or his affections, he never would have taken the knife to slay his son. GOD's law is our rule, and GOD will have all the heart or none. *Agags* will plead, but they must be hewn in pieces. May the LORD strengthen, stablish, and settle you! Good Lady *H*——*n* was much rejoiced to hear that you had been without the camp. May you quit yourself like a man, and in every respect behave like a good soldier of JESUS CHRIST! Her ladyship is very weak, but I hope will yet be spared to do much good on earth. O the happiness of giving up all for CHRIST, who hath given himself for us. The LORD be with you!

    I am yours to command,

        G. W.

LETTER DCCCXXXIV.

To the Reverend Mr. M——.

Ashby, May 14, 1750.

Reverend and very dear Sir,

I Have desired to write you a long letter for a considerable time, but was so hurried when at *London,* that I could not be so explicit as the affair I wanted to write about, necessarily required. It is concerning the Presbyterian College in the *New Jersies*; the importance and extensive usefulness of which, I suppose you have long since been apprized of. Mr. *A*——, a friend of Governor *B*——, is come over with a commission to negotiate this matter; he hath brought with him a copy of a letter, which Mr. *P*—— sent to you some months past.

This

This letter hath been shewn to Doctor D——— and several of the *London* ministers, who all approve of the thing, and promise their assistance. Last week I preached at *Northampton*, and conversed with Doctor D——— concerning it. The scheme that was then judged most practicable was this, "That Mr. P———'s letter should be printed, and a recommendation of the affair, subscribed by Doctor D——— and others, be annexed; that a subscription and collections should be then set on foot in *England*, and afterwards that Mr. A——— should go to *Scotland*." I think it is an affair that requires dispatch. Governor B——— is old, but a most hearty man for promoting GOD's glory, and the good of mankind. He looks upon the college as his own daughter, and will do all he can to endow her with proper privileges. The present President Mr. B———, and most of the Trustees, I am well acquainted with. They are friends to vital piety, and I trust this work of the LORD will prosper in their hands. The spreading of the gospel in *Maryland* and *Virginia* in a great measure depends upon it, and therefore I wish them much success in the name of the LORD. But more of this when we meet. As I am going further northward, I know not but I may go as far as *Glasgow*. Indeed there are so many doors opened in *England*, that I know not well where to go first. I have lately been in *Cornwall*, at *Portsmouth*, and *London*.—Since that I have preached at *Oulney*, *Northampton* and *Kettering*. For a few days I have been at good Lady H———n's, who though weak in body, is always abounding in the work of the LORD. She sends you her kind compliments, and ordered me to beg the favour of you to acquaint Mr. R———, that she will answer his kind letter as soon as ever her strength will permit. I preach daily at her Ladyship's, and this week, GOD willing, I shall preach in two or three churches. My bodily health is better than usual, and I long to be on the stretch for Him, who was stretched upon a cursed tree for ill and hell-deserving me. I beg a continued interest in your prayers. I salute you and yours, Mr. G——— and his wife, and all dear friends, in the heartiest manner, and am, reverend and very dear Sir,

Your most affectionate brother, &c.

G. W.

LETTER

LETTER DCCCXXXV.

To Doctor D——.

Ashby, May 19, 1750.

Reverend and very dear Sir,

YOUR kind letter found me happy at our good Lady H——n's, whose path shines more and more bright unto the perfect day. She is strangely employed now.—Can you guess? The kind people of *Ashby* stirred up some of the baser sort to riot before her Ladyship's door, while the gospel was preaching; and on *Wednesday* evening, some people in their return home, narrowly escaped being murdered. Her Ladyship has just received a message from the Justice, in order to bring the offenders before him. I hope it will be over-ruled for great good, and that the gospel for the future will have free course. This week I have preached in three churches, and to-morrow morning, GOD willing, I am to preach at a fourth. In the evening I shall preach at *Nottingham*, and purpose lying at the house of Mr. S——. Thus, reverend and dear Sir, you see I lead a pilgrim life. Blessed be GOD, it is quite pleasant, and I humbly intreat you to pray, that I may have a pilgrim heart, and be kept from trimming or nestling even to my dying hour. I rejoice, dear Sir, that you was blest at *Kettering*. Gladly shall I call upon you again at *Northampton*, if the LORD spares my life; and in the mean while shall not fail to pray, that the work of our common LORD may more and more prosper in your hands. I thank you a thousand times for your kindness to the very chief of sinners, and assure you, reverend Sir, that the affection is reciprocal. Good Lady H—— greatly esteems you. I go with regret from her Ladyship. Her Ladyship intends writing to you this evening. Do come and see her soon. I shall not be unmindful of your sick student. May the LORD JESUS sanctify all pain, and through his sufferings make him perfect. I would enlarge, but cannot. I write in great haste, but with greater love subscribe myself, reverend and dear Sir,

Your most affectionate, obliged, though unworthy younger brother and servant, for CHRIST's *sake,*

G. W.

LETTER DCCCXXXVI.

To Lady H———n.

Honoured Madam,   *Nottingham, May* 21, 1750.

WITH regret I left your Ladyship; but I hope it was for the furtherance of the gospel. At *Radcliff* church, the divine influence was greater than at *Millburn*. I preached on these words, " But one thing is needful." Many were impressed deeply. After sermon I conversed with Mrs. *B——* and Mr. *Law*'s sister. The latter seems to be under awakenings, and the former in her first love. She carries high sail; our LORD knows how to put in proper ballast. In the morning I preached here to many thousands. I had a great cold, but the LORD strengthened me. This evening, GOD willing, I preach again, and to-morrow shall set off for *Mansfield*, where a friend has invited me to his house. What care does our LORD take of his poor pilgrims! As I go on, your Ladyship shall hear how I am dealt with. I know it will be bountifully, because I have got such a bountiful master. He will bless your Ladyship more and more. When Mr. *B——* comes, I shall be glad to hear what becomes of the rioters. A line may be sent to *Manchester*. O that your Ladyship may live to see many of those *Ashby* stones become children to *Abraham!* I trust you will. I write in great haste, but with respect and gratitude greater than I can express; and beg leave to subscribe myself, very honoured Madam,

                      Your Ladyship's, &c.

                             G. W.

LETTER DCCCXXXVII.

To Dr. S———.

My dear Doctor,   *Mansfield, May* 24, 1750.

YOURS found me just as I was about to leave good Lady H———. Ever since, I have been engaged in travelling and preaching the everlasting gospel. In *Radcliff* church, at *Nottingham*, and *Sutton*, our LORD's Spirit hath accompanied the word preached. This morning I preached here, and, GOD willing, purpose to do so again in the evening, and to-morrow.

to-morrow morning. Little was expected here but rudeness; however the auditory was large and attentive. What cannot the Redeemer do? I am quite sorry that Mr. *H*——'s letter was printed:—But it was no Methodist that published it. *Felix quem faciunt aliena pericula cautum.* I pray GOD to give my dear friend prudence and courage whilst he is in *London.* Remember, if thy right hand offend thee, cut it off;—if thy right eye offend thee, pluck it out and cast it from thee. Now is your time to sacrifice your *Isaac.* CHRIST will have all the heart or none. I write thus, because I love you dearly. I pray for you from my inmost soul. O that you may be kept as in a garrison, by GOD's mighty power, through faith unto salvation! Without CHRIST you can do nothing. *Nil desperandum Christo duce.* That he may strengthen you to do what you know to be his will, is the hearty prayer of, very dear Sir,

Yours most affectionately in our common LORD,

G. W.

LETTER DCCCXXXVIII.

To Lady H———*n.*

Honoured Madam, *Mansfield, May* 24, 1750.

I Beg leave on my journey, to trouble your Ladyship with a few lines. They bring your Ladyship good news. I have been quite sick ever since I have left *Ashby*; but the glorious *Emmanuel* has been pleased to work by my unworthy ministry. At *Nottingham* several came to me, enquiring what they should do to be saved. I preached there four times. One evening Lord *S*—— and several gentlemen were present, and behaved with great decency. Many thousands attended. Yesterday morning I breakfasted with three dissenting ministers and Mr. *P*——'s, who told me that Lady *P*—— desired he would press me to preach at *B*—— church. Yesterday in the afternoon I preached at *Sutton*, and this morning I lifted up the gospel standard here. All was quiet; and this evening and to-morrow morning I am to preach again. As I travel on, your Ladyship shall hear. I must lie down to refresh this weary body: my soul, through grace, smiles at bodily weakness, and longs to take its flight. I doubt not but your Ladyship

Ladyship is happy in him, who alone killeth and maketh alive. Night and day do I look up to him in behalf of your Ladyship, as being, ever-honoured Madam,

Your Ladyship's most obedient, obliged, and chearful servant for CHRIST's sake,

G. W.

LETTER DCCCXXXIX.

To the Countess D——.

Honoured Madam,   *Leeds, May* 30, 1750.

I Heard about a week ago, that your Ladyship was exceeding ill. I have been much concerned ever since, and have attempted to write more than once, but travelling and preaching twice a day prevented me. Ere now I trust the great physician has rebuked your Ladyship's indisposition, and given you to rejoice in his great salvation. If not, his grace will be sufficient for you. He will not suffer you to be tempted above what you are able to bear, but will with the temptation make a way for you to escape. Sanctified afflictions are signs of his especial love. Love holds the rod, love strikes, love wounds, and love heals again. " Strike, LORD; (says *Luther*) now I know thou art my father."—And, says that sweet singer Mr. *Mason*,

> —— *O happy rod,*
> *That brought me nearer to my* GOD.

This, I believe, will be the language of your Ladyship's heart. Look, therefore, honoured Madam, to JESUS, the author and finisher of your faith. In all your afflictions, he is afflicted. He will bring you out of this furnace, like gold purified seven times in the fire. Good Lady H—— is weak too, but I trust will yet live to declare the works of the LORD. *Ashby* is not worthy of so rich a pearl. Was I not afraid of hurting your Ladyship, I would give you some particulars of my circuit. Let it suffice to inform your Ladyship, that the gospel plough seems to prosper. New ground has been broken up, and seed sown, that I trust will bear fruit to life eternal. I am here amongst a multitude of souls that seem to love the

LORD JESUS in sincerity. To-morrow I move *Northward*; and if I hear that your Ladyship is recovered, I shall take the freedom of writing now and then. I purpose sending a few lines also to Lady F—— and Lady H——. All were constantly remembered at *Ashby* at the holy table. All shall still be remembered, as our LORD enables, by, honoured Madam,

Your Ladyship's most obliged and ready servant,
for CHRIST's sake,

G. W.

LETTER DCCCXL.

To Lady H——n.

Honoured Madam,   Leeds, *May* 30, 1750.

I Cannot travel far without sitting down to refresh myself by writing to your Ladyship. *Mansfield* I hope was taken. After leaving that place, I went to *Rotheram*, where *Satan* rallied his forces again. However, I preached twice, on the *Friday* evening, and *Saturday* morning. The cryer was employed to give notice of a bear-baiting. Your Ladyship may guess who was the *Bear*. About seven in the morning the drum was heard, and several watermen attended it with great staves. The constable was struck, and two of the mobbers were apprehended, but rescued afterwards. But all this does not come up to the kind usage of the people of *Ashby*. I preached on those words, "Fear not, little flock."—They were both fed and feasted; and after a short stay I left *Rotheram*, when I knew it was become more pacific. In the evening I preached at *Sheffield*, where the people received the word gladly. A very great alteration was discernable in their looks since I was there last. On *Sunday* great multitudes attended, and in the evening many went away that could not come near enough to hear. On *Monday* we had a parting blessing; and in the evening the LORD JESUS fed us plentifully, with the bread that cometh down from heaven, at *Barly-Hall*. Last night I preached to many, many thousands, and this morning also at five o'clock. Methinks I am now got into another climate. It must be a warm one, where there are so many of GOD's people. Our Pentecost is to be kept at Mr. G——'s. I have seen him and Mr. J——, and

hear

hear that Mr. B—— died comfortably, being fully aſſured, "That not only all his ſins before, but after converſion were forgiven him." To-morrow, GOD willing, I move hence, and expect to-morrow evening to ſee Mrs. H——, and to reach *Mancheſter* next week. From thence I purpoſe writing to your Ladyſhip again. O that any thing I write, ſay, or do, may afford the leaſt comfort to your Ladyſhip's ſoul! This is my deſire and hearty prayer: and I earneſtly entreat the LORD, that you may live long, and proſper in ſoul and body. I ſend my uſual and moſt dutiful reſpects to the honourable ladies, and am, ever-honoured Madam,

Your Ladyſhip's moſt obliged and ready ſervant
for CHRIST's ſake,

G. W.

LETTER DCCCXLI.

To Lady H————.

Honoured Madam, *Mancheſter, June* 8, 1750.

I Thought to have troubled your Ladyſhip with a letter long before this time, but travelling, and preaching twice every day, prevented. Bleſſed be GOD, it is pleaſant work, and I truſt it hath proſpered in my unworthy hands. Thouſands and thouſands for ſome time paſt have flocked to hear the word twice every day, and the power of GOD has attended it in a glorious manner. Good Lady H————n I left ſome time ago weak in body, but ſtrong in the grace which is in CHRIST JESUS. The good people of *Aſhby* were ſo kind as to mob round her Ladyſhip's door, whilſt the goſpel was preaching. Alas! how great and irreconcileable is the enmity of the ſerpent! This is my comfort, "The ſeed of the woman ſhall at length be more than conqueror over all." I hope that your Ladyſhip every day experiences more and more of this conqueſt in your heart. This is the chriſtian's daily employ; this the believer's daily triumph, to die to ſelf and ſin, and to riſe more and more daily into the image of the bleſſed JESUS. As it is our duty, ſo it is our unſpeakable privilege. All the croſſes we meet with, all the afflictions with which we are viſited, are all intended by the good phyſician, to beat down, and keep under, and weaken the old man, and to raise up, strengthen, and give fresh vigour to the new man, which is created after GOD in righteousness and true holiness. Our business is to look continually to JESUS, and to lean on him hourly, nay every moment. May this be your Ladyship's continual employ! May the LORD JESUS strengthen, stablish, and settle you more and more in his love. May he give you to see your honoured Relations partakers of a divine nature in this world, and grant you mansions of eternal bliss in the world to come! No less mercies shall, no greater can be desired for your Ladyship and family by, honoured Madam,

Your Ladyship's most obliged and ready servant
for CHRIST's sake,

G. W.

LETTER DCCCXLII.

To Mr. C———.

Rosindale (Lancashire), June 14, 1750.

Very dear Sir,

EVER since that I heard your journey into the country was deferred, I have been impatient to write you a line. Till now, I cannot say I have had a proper opportunity. Travelling, and preaching twice a day, as I generally do, is almost too much for my frail tabernacle. But he is faithful who hath promised, "That as our day is, so our strength shall be." Though faint, I am yet pursuing, and, glory be to GOD, hitherto I have had a most delightful and successful circuit. I suppose you have heard of my reception at *Northampton* and *Ashby*, and of that people's unkind treatment of good Lady H———. At *Nottingham* I lodged with Mr. S———, and in that place and several others found great success. In *Yorkshire* the work hath advanced most. In about a week's time, within the compass of twenty miles, I preached, I believe, to above six thousand souls. This last week I have been beating up for recruits in and about *Manchester*, and I trust some have listed. Mrs. G——— behaves like a good soldier; and if I am not mistaken, her husband will follow her good example. I am now going towards *Kendal*, then to *Whitehaven*, and it may be to *Scotland*. I know you will pray, that the hand of the LORD may be with me. That is all in all! I hope this will find

my

my dear friend quite busy for his GOD, even his GOD in
CHRIST. We have not a moment to be idle here; the Judge
is before the door. I want to have my lamp trimmed, and
my loins girt, and to be always habitually and actually ready
to meet the blessed Bridegroom. Then do we begin to live
like ourselves, and to act like those who are redeemed unto
GOD by the precious blood of JESUS CHRIST, and made
kings and priests unto GOD and his Father; to him be glory
and dominion now and for evermore. My dear Sir, my cold
heart is warmed when I think of this. O why am I not a
flame of fire? Why am I not all life, all love, all humility,
all zeal? O my naughty heart! May JESUS sprinkle it
afresh with his precious blood, and help me this morning to
begin to hunt for souls. Though aged, I wish you may be
employed in the same work before you die. But future things
belong to GOD. I must now bid you adieu. My cordial
love and respects await Mrs. C——, Mr. G——, and all enquiring friends. Continue to pray for, very dear Sir,

   Yours most affectionately in our common LORD,

              G. W.

LETTER DCCCXLIII.

To Lady H———n.

Honoured Madam,   *Newby-Cote, June* 16, 1750.

IT is late, and I am somewhat fatigued, but I cannot rest
without finishing my week's work in writing to your Ladyship. Blessed be GOD, I have still good news to send to
your Ladyship. All was quiet at *Manchester*; and I humbly
hope the Redeemer will gather to himself a people there.
Kind Captain G—— and his lady will acquaint your Ladyship with particulars. I hope he will prove a good soldier of
JESUS CHRIST. I advised him to send your Ladyship word
of their coming to *Ashby*, that they might be directed the best
road from *Derby*. We had sweet seasons at the places adjacent to *Manchester*. Only at *Balton* a drunkard stood up to
preach behind me, and a woman attempted twice to stab the
person that was putting up a stand for me to preach on, in her
husband's field. However, the LORD got himself the victory.
Since that, we have had very large and powerful meetings,

where formerly were the most violent outrages. Perhaps within these three weeks, sixty-thousand souls or upwards have heard the gospel. I am now in Mr. *J——*'s circuit, and purpose being at *Kendal* next *Thursday*. I hope that there, or at *Whitehaven*, where I am to preach to-morrow se'nnight, I shall hear from Mr. *B——* concerning your Ladyship's welfare.—His letter I received to night, and will answer it the first opportunity. Nature now calls for rest. I shall retire, praying that your Ladyship and honoured relations may be blessed with all spiritual blessings. I am a sink of sin and corruption; but JESUS comforts and supports me, and, I believe, will hear your Ladyship's prayers in behalf of one, who, next to being a poor despised minister of the glorious *Emmanuel*, thinks it his highest honour to subscribe himself,

Your Ladyship's most dutiful, obliged, and very ready servant for CHRIST's sake,

G. W.

June 17th, seven in the morning.

Honoured Madam,

THIS last night Satan hath shewed his teeth. Some persons got into the barn and stable, and have cut my chaise, and one of the horse's tails. What would men do, if they could? The LORD be with your spirit. *Amen.*

LETTER DCCCXLIV.

To the Rev. Mr. H——.

Kendal, June 21, 1750.

Reverend and very dear Sir,

I Guess this will find you returned from good Lady *H———n*, with whom undoubtedly you have taken sweet counsel, and been mightily refreshed in talking about the things which belong to the kingdom of GOD. This leaves me at *Kendal*, where I arrived this morning, and where, GOD willing, I shall preach the everlasting gospel this evening. An entrance is now made into *Westmoreland*; and pen cannot well describe what glorious scenes have opened in *Yorkshire*, &c. Perhaps since I saw you, seventy or eighty thousand have attended the word preached in divers places. At *Howarth*, on *Whitsunday*,

the

the church was almost thrice filled with communicants, and at *Kirby-Steven* the people behaved exceedingly well. It was a precious season. In my way I have read Mr. *Law*'s second part of *The Spirit of Prayer*. His scheme about the Fall, &c. I think is quite chimerical; but he says many things that are truly noble, and which I pray GOD to write upon the tables of my heart. Several things at the end of his treatise on regeneration, in my opinion, are entirely unjustifiable: but the sun hath its spots, and so have the best of men. I want to see my own faults more, and others less. It will be so, when I am more humble. If mercies would make a creature humble, I should be a mirror of humility. But I am far from the mind that was in JESUS. You must pray, whilst I go on fighting. Though faint, I would yet pursue. Next week I hope to reach *Edinburgh*. GOD willing, you shall have notice of my return. Glad shall I be to meet such a friend upon the road. May the friend of sinners bless and support you, and give you always an heart to pray for, reverend and very dear Sir,

Yours most affectionately in our common LORD,

G. W.

LETTER DCCCXLV.

To the Rev. Mr. B———.

Kendal, June 21, 1750.

Reverend and very dear Sir,

ON *Saturday* last I received your kind letter, but have not had an opportunity of answering it till now. I have been preaching the gospel amongst the poor knitters, whose simple manner of life pleased me much. I am glad you have founded the silver trumpet in *London*; *crescit eundo* must be your motto, and mine. There is nothing like keeping the wheels oil'd by action. The more we do, the more we may do; every act strengthens the habit: and the best preparation for preaching on *Sundays*, is to preach every day in the week. I am glad you have peace at *Ashby*. What a fool is Satan always to overshoot his mark! I hope that Mr. G———, as well as Mr. S———, will hold on. They will be glorious monuments of free grace indeed. I am like-minded with you in respect to the Doctor's comment; he is indeed a glorious writer. May the LORD JESUS strengthen him to finish the work! My dear Mr. B——, what blessed opportunities do you enjoy for meditation, study, and prayer! Now is your time to get rich in grace, to search into the depths of divine love, and the mystery of iniquity hid in your own heart. Such an example, and such advantages no one in *England* is favoured with but yourself. I do not envy you; but I pray the Redeemer, from my inmost soul, to sanctify your situation, and give you to increase with all the increase of GOD. I am called forth to battle; remember a poor cowardly soldier, and beg the Captain of our salvation, that I may have the honour to die fighting. I would have all my scars in my breast. Methinks I would not be wounded running away, or skulking into an hiding-place. It is not for ministers of CHRIST to flee or be afraid.—And yet alas!—Well—*Nil desperandum Christo duce.* For his great name's sake, I subscribe myself, reverend and very dear Sir,

Your most affectionate, obliged friend and brother,

G. W.

LETTER DCCCXLVI.

To the Countess of H———n.

Honoured Madam,   Kendal, *June* 26, 1750.

STILL (O amazing love!) the LORD of all lords vouchsafes to prosper the gospel plough. Such an entrance hath been made into *Kendal*, as could not have been expected. I preached twice to several thousands last week, and the people were so importunate, that I was prevailed on to return hither again last night. The congregation was greatly increased, and the power of the LORD was displayed in the midst of them. On *Saturday* evening, and on the Lord's-day, I preached at *Ulverston,* a town about sixteen miles distant from this. There Satan made some small resistance; a clergyman, who looked more like a butcher than a minister, came with two others and charged a constable with me; but I never saw a poor creature sent off in such disgrace. Good I believe was done in the town. To the giver of every good gift be all the glory! Thus, honoured Madam, a poor pilgrim goes on. How I am to succeed at *Whitehaven,* your Ladyship shall know here-

hereafter. GOD willing, I set forward after preaching this evening. I hear Mr. *W*——— has been much abused in *Ireland*, but that the Mayor of *Cork* hath quite overshot himself. I have some thoughts of seeing *Ireland* before my return. May the LORD direct my goings in his way! I am persuaded that this will find your Ladyship travelling apace towards *Canaan*, and increasing your reward daily. Great shall it be indeed in heaven.—I shall be extremely glad of the honour of a line when at *Edinburgh*. In the mean while, your Ladyship shall not fail, with your honoured sisters and family, of being prayed for, and hearing from, ever-honoured Madam,

Your Ladyship's most dutiful, obliged,
and very chearful servant for CHRIST's sake,

G. W.

LETTER DCCCXLVII.

To Mr. K———.

My dear Mr. K———,   Kendal, *June* 26, 1750.

YESTERDAY I read in the public papers, that you was married. This morning I sit down to wish you joy. GOD hath given you a choice help-mate. May you love her as JESUS CHRIST loveth the church; and may both of you be enabled to live together as heirs of the grace of life! The LORD of all lords has been daily pouring down his benefits on you and me. O that his goodness may lead us to repentance, and his love constrain us to obedience! You have now another blessing given you; one who, I believe, will strengthen your hands in the LORD, and stir you up in the good ways of GOD. Now for *Joshua*'s resolution, "As for me and my house, we will serve the LORD." You are now entered on a new state; you will want new supplies of grace. It is hard to govern; it is much easier to obey. To come into a flow of business, and at the same time to keep the heart near to GOD, what a task is this? JESUS alone can make you sufficient for it. Look then, my dear friend, continually to him, and take heed that nothing drowns the sound of this small still voice speaking in your heart. When I come to town, GOD willing, I will pay you a visit. In the mean while let us meet at the throne of grace. I am travelling, and

you

you trading, for JESUS CHRIST. His strength is my joy. Every where the gospel plough hath prospered. These *Northern* parts promise well. Adieu! The LORD be with you both! Pray remember me in the kindest manner to your mother and brothers. You are come into a family that I dearly love. That you all may sit down with the glorious family of the first-born, whose names are written in heaven, is the earnest prayer of, my dear friend,

Yours most affectionately,

G. W.

LETTER DCCCXLVIII.

To Mr. B———.

Whitehaven, June 29, 1750.

My dear Mr. B———,

YESTERDAY, upon my arrival hither, I received your kind letter, and am now seated to send you an answer. May the LORD JESUS cause it to be an answer of peace! You need make no apology for your openness and freedom; reserves to me are odious. I would willingly be a father, brother, and friend to all concerned with me; and consequently I would gladly bear a part with them in their sorrows and their joys. Your suspicions about Messrs. S———, G———, and N———, were groundless. The sole cause of your not hearing from me, was my not knowing where to direct to you. As I am utterly unconcerned in the discipline of Mr. W———'s societies, I can be no competent judge of their affairs. If you and the rest of the preachers were to meet together more frequently, and tell each other your grievances, opinions, &c. it might be of service. This may be done in a very friendly way, and thereby many uneasinesses might be prevented. After all, those that will live in peace must agree to disagree in many things with their fellow-labourers, and not let little things part or disunite them. I know not well, what my dear Mr. B——— means, about concealing the gospel privileges. There is no doubt but milk must be given to babes, and meat to strong men; but this all depends on the skilfulness of the preacher, and his being taught of GOD rightly to divide the word of truth. In general, gospel privileges may be

spoken

spoken of to encourage awakened sinners and quicken saints. If by gospel privileges you mean *love-feasts*, *bands*, &c. these I think are only prudential means, and therefore no doubt prudence should be exercised in the use of them. I am of your opinion, that too much familiarity in these things is hurtful. But it is hard to keep a medium, where a multitude is concerned. As ill effects are discovered, they should be corrected and avoided. The question and answer you refer to, I do not like. I know nothing of CHRIST's righteousness being imputed to all mankind. It is enough to say with the scriptures, " That it is imputed to all believers." What does my dear Mr. B—— think of that assertion of the Apostle, " He made him sin for us, who knew no sin, that we might be made the righteousness of GOD in him." And again, " Who of GOD is made to us, wisdom, righteousness, &c." *cum multis aliis*, vide Romans, ivth and vith.—Is it not as express as can be, that CHRIST's righteousness is imputed to believers? Consequently, it is sufficient for us, as preachers, to declare, " That all believers are actually delivered from the guilt of both actual and original sin, from the power of their corruptions here, and that at the hour of death they shall be delivered from the very in-being of sin, and be admitted to dwell with the glorious JESUS, and the spirits of just men made perfect, hereafter." Another seven years experience, will teach some to handle the word of life in a better manner. Our business is to shew believers their compleatness in CHRIST, and to point them to Him for strength for every good word and work; and all to be done out of gratitude and love for what he hath done and suffered for them. But you know my sentiments; you have heard them all in my sermons. I have no reserves. What Mr. S—— says, I know not; I believe CHRIST's redemption will be applied to all that shall believe. Who these are, we know not, and therefore we are to give a general offer and invitation; convinced of this, that every man's damnation is of himself, and every man's salvation all of GOD. You would do well to read more; but whether it would be best for you to pursue, or re-assume your old studies, unless you are determined to settle, I cannot tell. Reading a *Latin* author, a little every day, to be sure could do you no hurt. *Terentius Christianus*, *Castalio*'s Scripture Dialogues, and *Selectæ Prælectiones Veteri Testamenti*

Testamenti, would both delight and profit you. It has long since been my judgment, that it would be best for many of the present preachers to have a tutor, and retire for a while, and be content with preaching now and then, till they were a little more improved. Otherwise, I fear many who now make a temporary figure, for want of a proper foundation, will run themselves out of breath, will grow weary of the work, and leave it. May the LORD JESUS direct! This is the plan I purpose to pursue abroad. Whether GOD will be pleased to succeed it, I know not. All I can say is, that I am willing to lend an helping hand wherever I see the interest of CHRIST promoted. This is my motive, dear Sir, in answering your last. I hope it is satisfactory. If not, let me know. You may direct for me at Mr. T——'s, *Edinburgh*. I hope to be there next week. We have had good seasons since I parted from you. At *Kendal* a most promising door is opened. Follow me with your prayers. — Look up to JESUS, and let not little things disappoint and move you. If this be your foible, beware, and pray that Satan may not get an advantage over you. He will be always striving to vex and unhinge you. " The LORD reigneth." Let this consideration support and comfort you, under the various changes you must necessarily meet with in the church. She is now militant, ere long she shall be triumphant. Till then, as the elect of GOD, let us put on bowels of compassion, meekness, long-suffering and humbleness of mind. But what am I doing? Adieu. The LORD be with you and yours, and give Mrs. B—— faith and courage in her approaching hour! All with me salute you. I must hasten to subscribe myself, my dear Mr. B——,

Yours most affectionately in our common LORD,

G. W.

LETTER DCCCXLIX.

To Mr. T—— A——.

Very dear T——, *Edinburgh, July* 7, 1750.

I Thought it long, yea very long since I heard from you; but as I believe your heart is upright towards the LORD JESUS, and to me your unworthy friend, for his great name's sake, I have been quite easy. The news of your success, rejoices me. May the LORD increase it more and more! Pen cannot well exprefs what hath been done in the North. I have preached above ninety times fince I left *London*, and perhaps to a hundred and forty thoufand people. It is amazing to fee how people are prepared, in places where I never was before. What fhall I render unto the LORD? I will beg him to make me humble and thankful. Here, I am received with as much affection as ever. Still I will cry, Grace! grace! Ere this reaches you, I fuppofe you will be thinking of *London*. Mr. C—— I believe wants a breathing. I hear he hath been bleft much. You and Mr. C—— are the only perfons I chufe to have at the tabernacle, as heads in my abfence. Several of —— have offered to join me; but you know I hate taking other perfons as helpers, and as I defire no party, I give no encouragement. But future things belong to Him, on whofe fhoulders the government is put. You muft ftill remember me before Him. His word is indeed running, and like to be glorified day by day. How matters go on here, you will know hereafter. In the mean while pray for, and write to, my very dear *Tommy*,

Yours moft affectionately in our common LORD,

G. W.

LETTER DCCCL.

To Lady H——.

Edinburgh, July 7, 1750.

Ever-honoured Madam,

AFTER preaching at *Cockermouth*, and near *Wigton*, with great acceptance, laft night I came here, and was received in a moft loving and tender manner. At noon, I dined with a family that honours your Ladyfhip very much, and this evening I have been preaching to a great multitude of very attentive and affected hearers. At my return to my lodgings, I had the wifhed-for pleafure of your Ladyfhip's two letters. They both led me nearer to, and laid me lower before Him, at whofe throne I am daily pleading for the welfare of your Ladyfhip, both in temporals and fpirituals. Indeed, ever honoured Madam, I have confidence with you that your Ladyfhip fhall have all the deliverance you long for. By divine grace, I will let the LORD have no reft, till he fulfils all your defires. I quite forget myfelf, when I think

of

of your Ladyship. Ever honoured Madam, the LORD as yet hath but begun to bless you; you shall, you shall, you will be made a greater blessing indeed. If dear Mr. H—— gets A——y, that will be making your Ladyship a blessing. He is a dear soul; I am glad that both he and Dr. D—— have been with your Ladyship. I would have all the good ministers come and visit your Ladyship. There are numbers would go scores of miles willingly for that purpose. I hope soon to send your Ladyship some pleasing particulars. I have heard from my family. May the blessing of many ready to perish descend on your Ladyship. I pity poor A—— B——. Your Ladyship I believe will soon get the better of him. Your Ladyship hath acted like yourself in forgiving the offenders. Such offences come, that CHRIST's followers may give evidence of his blessed temper being wrought in their hearts. In my return, without fail your Ladyship may expect me at ungrateful *Ashby*. Out of those stones may the LORD JESUS raise up children unto *Abraham!* However GOD is pleased to deal with me, your Ladyship may be assured of hearing from me. In the mean while, your Ladyship and honoured relations and family will be continually remembered by, ever-honoured Madam,

Your Ladyship's most dutiful, ready, obliged,
though unworthy servant for CHRIST's sake,
G. W.

LETTER DCCCLI.

To Lady H——.

Edinburgh, July 12, 1750.

Ever-honoured Madam,

THOUGH I am really burning with a fever, and have a violent cold, yet I must send your Ladyship a few lines by this post. They bring good news. People flock rather more than ever, and earnestly entreat me not to leave them soon. I preach generally twice a day,—early in the morning, and at six in the evening. Great multitudes attend. Praise the LORD O my soul! Your Ladyship's health is drank and enquired after every day. Mr. N——, who married Lord ————'s sister, has given me three franks, and his family are in the number of those who are left in *Sardis*, and
have

have not defiled their garments. Enclosed your Ladyship hath my last from *Carolina*, and an account of the affair mentioned by the Bishop of *Cork*. I fear I cannot reach *Ireland* this season. Your Ladyship's message to Mr. *Robe*, I sent last post; he will think himself highly honoured. Some time next month I hope to see your Ladyship. In the mean time, whether sick or well, your Ladyship shall be sure to hear how the LORD of all Lords is pleased to deal with me and his people. His presence makes me to smile at pain, and the fire of his love burns up all fevers whatsoever. This your Ladyship knows by happy experience. That you may know it more and more every hour, and every moment, is the continual prayer of, honoured Madam,

Your Ladyship's most dutiful, obliged and
chearful servant for CHRIST's sake,
G. W.

LETTER DCCCLII.

To Mr. C——.

Dear Jemmy,   *Glasgow, July* 21, 1750.

I Have nothing but good news to send you. The entrance GOD has been pleased to give me into *Scotland*, demands the highest tribute of gratitude and love. I preached twenty times at *Edinburgh*, and thousands attended morning and evening. Many I hope got good. To the giver of every good gift be all the glory! Last night I came hither, and was most lovingly received, and this morning the LORD of all Lords hath given us a delightful meeting. Blessed news is sent from *Kendal*. Enclosed you have the marks of my friends bounty, who love me for JESUS sake. Be pleased to receive the bill, and as you live near Mr. *S———*, be so kind as to pay him the remainder of what is due for printing my last sermons. Take his accompt, and a receipt under; what is left, pray give to my wife to pay *Wr———* the book-binder. For I would fain owe no man any thing but love.—I would have my worldly affairs so ordered, that let death come when it will, I may have nothing to do but to die. That is a blessed word to me; the thoughts of death gladden my heart, and cause me often almost to leap for joy. But perhaps our LORD has more work for me to do. His will be done in, by, and upon me, in time, and to all eternity. Pilgrims must not expect much rest here. In heaven we shall have enough. There I shall meet you and yours. I salute you both most tenderly, and beg you would all pray for, my dear friend,

   Yours most affectionately in our common Lord,
              G. W.

LETTER DCCCLIII.

To Mr. R——.

Glasgow, July 23, 1750.

My very dear Friend,

WITH pleasure I sit down to perform my promise, and to thank you for all favours. The Lord is still adding to my obligations, to love and serve him. Friends here received me most kindly, and the congregations I think are rather larger than ever. Yesterday, besides preaching twice in the field, I preached in the college *Kirk*, being forced by Mr. G——. 'Twas a blessed season. Mr. R—— and Mr. E—— were very affectionate. I have met, and shaken hands with Mr. R—— E——. O when shall God's people learn war no more! God willing, I shall leave *Glasgow* on *Thursday* next, and if you please, will sup quietly with you and your lady, or with Mr. G——, on *Friday* evening. I hope to be in early, because I intend lying at Mr. E——'s house, or at *Kylsyth* on the *Thursday*. Letters this post make me resolve not to visit *Ireland* this summer; Mr. H'—— is there, and persecution increases. I send the inclosed open. A copy might be put into my wife's, lest the other should miscarry. My stay in *Edinburgh* at my return must be very short. May the Lord Jesus make it sweet! You must remember me in the kindest manner to your dear lady, the other ladies, and all enquiring friends, and accept of most hearty love from, my very dear Sir,

         Yours, &c.
             G. W.

LETTER DCCCLIV.

To Mr. W——.

Dear Sir, Glasgow, July 23, 1750.

I Received your kind letter laſt week, but till now had not time to anſwer you: Bleſſed be GOD, it brought glad tidings. Thanks be to the ever-loving ever-lovely JESUS, for cauſing his arrows to ſtick faſt in any ſinners hearts! May he that hath wounded, in his own due time and way heal and eaſe them!—He is the awakened ſinners only refuge. To Him the weary and heavy laden are invited. Let them but come to him, and he will, indeed he will give them reſt. O that thoſe who have begun to put their hands to the plough, may be kept from looking back! Awakening times are like ſpring times. Many bloſſoms, but not always ſo much fruit. However, glory, glory be to GOD, that the Winter of deadneſs is in ſome degree over, and that a Spring time of grace is ſeen at *Kendal*. Pray remember me in the kindeſt manner to all under awakenings, and exhort them all with full purpoſe of heart to cleave unto the LORD. Whether I can ſee you again in my return, is uncertain. If it be any way practicable, I ſhall comply with your earneſt ſolicitation. Next week, GOD willing, I leave *Scotland*, and if I can come, you ſhall hear from me. In the mean time, as the LORD enables, I ſhall not ceaſe to pray for all that are ſetting their faces Zionward. You know the many turnings that lie in the way thither, and therefore can direct young travellers. It is pretty work for you in the decline of life. Methinks you may be ſurprized like *Sarah*, who ſaid, " who would have thought that *Sarah* ſhould have given ſuck!" But is there any thing too hard for the LORD? O for faith, patience and humility! Theſe are graces my ſoul thirſts after. How humble, how thankful ought I to be! After leaving *Kendal*, the word of the LORD ran and was glorified in ſeveral places, and in *Scotland* I think congregations are rather greater than ever. You muſt exhort all to pray for me, that I may be kept from flagging in the latter ſtages of my road. My love to Mr. G——. I ſhall take care to anſwer his letter when it comes to hand. I have ordered ſome volumes of my ſermons to be ſent to him. May GOD ſanctify the reading of them to the carrying on his blessed work. I can now no more. The LORD be with you. I am, dear Sir,

Yours, &c. in JESUS CHRIST,

G. W.

LETTER DCCCLV.

To Lady H———.

Edinburgh, July 29, 1750.

Ever-honoured Madam,

WHAT shall I say? Your Ladyship's condescension in writing to unworthy me, lays me low before Him, who continues to follow me with his goodness and mercy every hour of my life. Ungrateful *Ashby*! O that thou knewest the day of thy visitation! Surely your Ladyship may shake off the dust of your feet against them. This was the command, that the meek and lowly JESUS gave to his apostles, when the gospel was not received. And he himself departed, when the *Gadarenes* desired him to go out of their coasts. This justifies your Ladyship in removing Mr. *B———*. What avails throwing pearls before swine, who only turn again and rend you? However, I bless GOD that your Ladyship's house is made a *Bethel*. Glad would I be of the honour of joining your Ladyship's little select company, but our Redeemer appoints me other work.—Indeed it is very pleasant work. No one can well describe the order, attention, and earnestness of the *Scotch* congregations. They are unwearied in hearing the gospel. I left thousands sorrowful at *Glasgow*, and here I was again most gladly received last night. By preaching always twice, and once thrice, and once four times in a day, I am quite weakened; but I hope to recruit again, and get fresh strength to work for Him, who shed his precious blood for ill and hell-deserving me. On *Thursday* next, GOD willing, I shall leave *Scotland*. Your Ladyship shall know whither I go. In the mean while, I send your Ladyship some *Georgia* letters, which I hope will afford you satisfaction. I have been upon the enquiry for some proper persons, for dear Captain *G———* and his Lady to converse with at *Dumfries*, and last night I hear I have succeeded. Particulars they shall know hereafter. I can now only send them my most grateful and cordial respects, being obliged to stop to get strength even whilst I write

write this. O this mortal body! How does it weigh down my precious and immortal soul! Ere long it will be set at liberty, and body and soul shall be for ever with the LORD. I cannot enlarge. Your Ladyship is remembered every day by many here. I hope your Ladyship's honoured sisters are prospering in soul and body. The searcher of hearts can tell how much I count it my honour to subscribe myself, ever-honoured Madam,

Their and your most obliged, dutiful, and chearful
servant for JESUS CHRIST's sake,
G. W.

LETTER DCCCLVI.

To Lady H———.

Honoured Madam,   *Berwick, Aug. 4, 1750.*

AT length I have taken a very sorrowful leave of *Scotland*. The longer I continued there, the more the congregations, and the power that attended the word, increased. I have reason to think that many are under convictions, and am assured of hundreds having received great benefit and consolation. The parting was rather more affectionate than ever, and I shall have reason to bless GOD to all eternity for this last visit to *Scotland*. Not a dog moved his tongue all the while I was there, and many enemies where glad to be at peace with me. Who is like our GOD, glorious in holiness, fearful in praises, continually doing wonders! Preaching so frequently, and paying so many religious visits, weakened me very much; but I am already much better for my riding thus far, and I trust the LORD will cause me to renew my strength. My obligations to spend and be spent for the blessed JESUS, are greatly increased. O that I may spring afresh, and soar aloft till I fly into the embraces of a sin-forgiving GOD! He hath prepared my way at *Berwick*. One of the ministers hath sent me an offer of his pulpit, and I hear of about ten more round this town that would do the same. I came hither this evening, and purpose, GOD willing, to set out for *Newcastle* on *Monday* morning. What success I meet with, your Ladyship shall hear in my next. Was it not so late in the year, I think I would go to *Ireland*. May the LORD direct my goings in his way! *Kendal*, I believe, must have another visit.

The enclosed is from one of Mr. *W*——'s preachers. The contents I believe will please your Ladyship. Honoured Madam, what shall I say? The Redeemer's goodness quite amazes me. " Less than the least of all," shall be my motto still. With regret, I send your Ladyship Mr. *H*——'s too, too much embellished and extravagant character of ill and hell-deserving me. It came from *Plymouth* last post. Your Ladyship desired to see it, or otherwise I could not bear to send it. To me, O blessed JESUS, nothing belongs, but shame and confusion of face. O that praise as well as contempt may humble this proud heart of mine! Then I shall never be hurt by having the honour to subscribe myself, honoured Madam,

Your Ladyship's most dutiful, obliged, and
very ready servant for CHRIST's sake,
G. W.

LETTER DCCCLVII.

To Mr. L——.

Newcastle, Aug. 9, 1750.

My dear dying Friend,

THOUGH absent in body, yet I am present with you in spirit; and whilst you are in this tabernacle of clay, as our LORD enables, you shall not be forgotten before his throne. Ere long you will be called to sit upon it; JESUS himself will rise and take you in.—And why? He hath redeemed you unto GOD by his blood, and given you the first fruits of heaven already in your heart. Fear not therefore, my dear friend, to go through *Jordan*. The great High Priest stands ready to guide you, and will land you safe in *Canaan. I præ, sequar.*—Yet a little while, and my turn will come. In heaven we shall part no more. Till then, my dear dying friend, farewel! O that I may hear that you go off in triumph. But whether this be vouchsafed or not, I know you will die in peace. To the GOD of peace and love do I most earnestly commend you. Let this be your joyful language,

> *A guilty, weak and helpless worm,*
> *Into thy arms I fly:*
> *Be thou my strength and righteousness,*
> *My* JESUS *and my all.*

I send

I send affectionate respects to both your sisters, and to Mr. B——. I pray that the LORD JESUS may love them as he loved *Lazarus*, *Mary*, and their sister *Martha*, and I entreat you to accept this as a token of unfeigned christian love, from, my very dear Sir,

Yours most affectionately in our common LORD,

G. W.

LETTER DCCCLVIII.

To Mr. P———.

My dear Mr. P——,   *London, Sept.* 4, 1750.

I Received your kind letter yesterday, which was like the prophet's roll, full of lamentation, and mourning, and woe. But what shall we say? It must needs be that offences come.—Wo to the inhabitants of the earth, and of the sea, for the devil is come down in great wrath, knowing he hath but a short time to reign; but let us look upwards. Every plant that our heavenly father hath not planted, shall be rooted up; only let him that standeth take heed lest he fall. You must salute dear Mr. R—— and the rest of the brethren in my name. As far as I know, we are like-minded as to principles, and I shall be glad to do all that I can to strengthen their hands, only let nothing be done through strife and vain-glory. Blessed be GOD, my poor labours never met with greater acceptance in *England* and *Scotland* than now, and I would gladly fly to *Wales*, but perhaps my coming had better be deferred to the cool of the day. Let us not fear. This storm will blow over.—Truth is great, and though driven out of doors for a while, will prevail at the last. Alas, what are we when a party spirit lays hold on us! I suspect the principles that are productive of such practices.—O that these things may lead us nearer to CHRIST, keep us closer to his blessed word, and be sanctified to the moulding us into a nearer conformity to his divine image. The meekness and lowliness of JESUS, I want to be a large partaker of. You must pray for me, and let me know how affairs stand. My tender love to all. I am, dear Sir,

Yours, &c.

G. W.

To Lady H———n.

Honoured Madam,   *Portsmouth, Sept. 8, 1750.*

TO day my wife sent me the melancholy news of the death of your Ladyship's eldest daughter, but withal wrote me that she died very comfortably. Indeed when I left her, GOD's spirit seemed to be working so strongly upon her heart, that I thought she would soon go to heaven, or shine as a glorious saint on earth. It hath pleased a sovereign GOD to cut short his work in righteousness, and call her home. A trial this indeed, for your Ladyship! but a trial, in which I hope your Ladyship will have grace given to acquiesce. O that with *Aaron* you may be enabled to hold your peace, and with the bereaved *Shunamite* to say, "It is well." And if the Redeemer should call your Ladyship to part with another daughter (hard trial for flesh and blood) may you be strengthened chearfully to give her up, and hear the LORD of all Lords saying unto you, "Now know I that thou lovest me, since thou hast not with-held two dear daughters from me." Now is the time, honoured Madam, to prove the strength of JESUS to be yours. Now is the time to be strong in faith, and give glory to GOD. The Redeemer will be better to you than seven daughters. What a comfort is it, honoured Madam, for you to think that Miss C—— gave such comfortable evidences of her dying in the LORD. She is blessed indeed, and the language of her departed soul is, "weep not for me." Comfort yourself, honoured Madam, with this thought, and say like *David*, "I shall go to her, but she will not return to me." May this trial be sanctified to your Ladyship's whole household, and may your surviving children learn to die betimes! I could enlarge, but am afraid of being troublesome. On *Tuesday*, GOD willing, I hope to be in *London* for one day, and shall be impatient to know how the all-wise GOD is pleased to dispose of your Ladyship's other daughter. In the mean while, my poor prayers shall be put up night and day, that your Ladyship may have grace given you to glorify CHRIST in this time of need. I commend your Ladyship to his never-failing mercy, as being, honoured Madam,

  Your Ladyship's most dutiful, sympathizing,
   obliged, and ready servant for CHRIST's sake,
              G. W.

LETTER DCCCLX.

To Mr. R——.

London, Sept. 14, 1750.

My very dear Mr. R——,

GLAD was I, yea very glad, to receive your kind letter about two days ago. I send you this in return, with ten thousand thanks for all favours conferred upon me, by you and yours. They are all numbered, and not one of them shall be forgotten before the LORD of all Lords, whose mercy endureth for ever. Surely, his goodness and mercy have followed me all the days of my life, and blessed be his holy name, I shall ere long dwell in his house for ever. At my return to town, I was received, though utterly unworthy, with great joy, and our LORD has manifested forth his glory in the great congregation. I have preached in Mr. *W——*'s chapel several times, and I trust a young lady of high rank was truly awakened about a fortnight ago, and who is since gone triumphantly to heaven. Mr. *W——* breakfasted and prayed with me this morning, and Mr. *H——y* was so kind as to come up and be with me in my house. He is a dear man, and I trust will yet be spared to write much for the Redeemer's glory. I have prevailed on him to sit for his picture, and it will be published in a short time. Two dozen of my pictures, as my friends so earnestly desired them, are sent directed to you. Be pleased to let them be disposed of, as shall be judged most proper. O that my heart might in some measure resemble the image of my dear LORD! You and yours will not fail to pray, that it may be written in lively characters, and that I may go on my way rejoicing. I never forget you or any other of my dear *Scotch* friends. Just now I have good news from *Kendal*; a young woman, whom GOD was pleased to awaken when I was there, went off lately (as my friend expresses it) " with flying colours." Grace! Grace! LORD, make me humble! LORD JESUS, make me truly thankful!

ful! I am just now going for *Chatham*. Last LORD's day I was at *Portsmouth*. Next week, GOD willing, I go to *Gloucester*. I hope good Lady D—— and her beloved son and daughter, &c. are prospering in soul and body. I send them my most dutiful respects, and ten thousand thanks, and beg you, my very dear Sir, to accept the same from,

Yours most affectionately in our blessed LORD,

G. W.

LETTER DCCCLXI.

To Lady H——.

Ever-honoured Madam,   London, Sept. 17, 1750.

THOUGH it is a cross to me to be detained so long from coming to *Ashby*, yet I trust hitherto my steps have been guided by an over-ruling providence for good. Yesterday afternoon I returned from *Chatham*, where I think there is as promising a work begun as almost in any part of *England*. Last night the Redeemer's glory was seen in the tabernacle, and your Ladyship's letter revived my heart, and gave me some fresh hopes for ungrateful *Ashby*. My heart's desire and prayer to the LORD of all Lords is, that your Ladyship may live to see much of the travail of the Redeemer's soul. I am glad Mr. *M——* is ordained, and hope Mr. *B——* will be the next, soon. By Mr. *L——*'s letter to him, I find your Ladyship has acted in the affair like yourself. Your Ladyship shall have a copy of it, and you will then see how matters go. Mr. *B——* is much for embarking in CHRIST's cause, and if the D—— would but help him at this juncture, he might be a useful and happy man. Both he and Mr. *H——* have the most grateful sense of your Ladyship's great kindness. The latter I believe intends to winter with me in *London*. If possible, I will prevail on Mr. *H——ly*, at my return, to come and pay him a visit. To-morrow morning, GOD willing, I set out for *Gloucester*, and intend coming to *Birmingham*, and so to your Ladyship's. In my way I hope to write to Lady *B——*, and be as particular as circumstances will admit. I am surprized at your Ladyship's doing and going through so much. But what cannot a believer do, when strengthened by the blessed JESUS? Your Ladyship will be remembered most heartily before him this afternoon, it being our letter-

day.

day. That you may long live to shine in his church below, and after death be translated to shine with distinguished lustre in the realms of light and love above, is the continual prayer of, ever, ever-honoured Madam,

   Your Ladyship's most dutiful, obliged, and
    most cheerful servant for CHRIST's sake,
              G. W.

LETTER DCCCLXII.

To Lady B—— H——.

Madam,   *Gloucester*, Sept. 22, 1750.

AS I know your Ladyship had a great esteem for the late honourable Miss H——, I cannot but think a short account of her behaviour, under her last sickness, must not only alleviate the concern your Ladyship must necessarily have for so intimate a friend, but also excite you to pray, that your latter end may be like hers. I think it is now near three weeks since good Lady G—— desired me to visit her sick daughter. She had been prayed for very earnestly the preceding day after the sacrament, and likewise previous to my visit in Lady H——'s room. When I came to her bed-side, she seemed glad to see me, but desired I would speak and pray as softly as I could. I conversed with her a little, and she dropped some strong things about the vanity of the world, and the littleness of every thing out of CHRIST. I prayed as low as I could, but in prayer (your Ladyship has been too well acquainted with such things to call it *enthusiasm*) I felt a very uncommon energy and power to wrestle with GOD in her behalf. She soon broke out into such words as these, " what a wretch am I?" She seemed to speak out of the abundance of her heart, from a feeling sense of her own vileness. Her honoured Parent and attending servants were affected. After prayer, she seemed as though she felt things unutterable, bemoaned her ingratitude to GOD and CHRIST; and I believe would gladly have given a detail of all her faults she could reckon. Her having had a form of godliness, but never having felt the power, was what she most bewailed. I left her; she continued in the same frame; and when Mrs. S—— asked her whether she felt her heart to be as bad as
                she

she expressed herself, she answered, " yes, and worse." At her request, some time after this, I gave her the holy communion; a communion indeed it was. Never did I see a person receive it with seemingly greater contrition, more earnest desire for pardon and reconciliation with GOD through CHRIST, or stronger purposes of devoting her future life to his service. Being weak, she was desired to keep lying on her bed. She replied, " I can rise to take my physic; shall I not rise to pray?" When I was repeating the Communion Office, she applied all to herself, and broke out frequently aloud in her applying. When I said, the burden of them is intolerable, she burst out—" yea very intolerable," with abundance of such like expressions. When she took the bread and wine, her concern gave her utterance, and she spake like one that was ripening for heaven. Those around her, wept for joy.— My cold heart also was touched, and I left her with a full persuasion, that she was either to be taken off soon, or to be a blessing here below. I think she lived about a week afterwards: she continued in the same frame as far as I hear, and I trust is now gone, where she will sing the song of *Moses* and of the Lamb for ever. The thoughts of this, comforts good Lady G——, and the same consideration, I am persuaded, will have the same effect upon your Ladyship. Only methinks I hear your Ladyship add, " No, I will not stop here. By divine grace I will devote myself to JESUS CHRIST now, and give him no rest, till I see the world in that light as dear Miss H—— did, and as I myself shall, when I come to die. I will follow my honoured mother as she follows JESUS CHRIST, and count the Redeemer's reproach of more value than all the honours, riches and pleasures of the world. I will fly to CHRIST by faith, and through the help of my GOD, keep up not only the form, but also the power of godliness in heart and life." That the glorious *Emanuel* may enable your Ladyship to put all this into practice, is the earnest prayer of, Madam,

Your Ladyship's most ready servant for CHRIST's sake,

G. W.

LETTER DCCCLXIII.

Dear Miſs B——, *Everſham, Sept.* 28, 1750.

I Thank you for your kind letter, and thank our heavenly Father for bleſſing the ſeed ſown to any of my hearers. Not unto me O LORD, not unto me, but unto thy free unmerited mercy, be all the glory!

If thou excuſe, then work thy will,
By ſo unfit an inſtrument;
It will at once thy grace diſplay,
And prove thy power omnipotent.

Hitherto our LORD continues to help me. Since my return from *Scotland*, I have been brought very low; but as my day is, ſo is my ſtrength. At *London*, *Portſmouth*, *Chatham*, and lately in *Glouceſterſhire* we have had many pleaſant ſeaſons. I am now going to *Birmingham*, *Coventry*, &c. GOD only knows when I ſhall ſee my beloved *Scotland* again. Gladly could I live and die with my dear friends there. It is my comfort, that thoſe who are friends to JESUS, ſhall live eternally together hereafter. I know ſeveral of late that went off triumphantly. O that we may be kept from being cumbered! O that nothing may draw us from the feet of JESUS! There, and there alone is ſolid peace to be found. Every thing is good that drives us thither. That this may be always your abiding place, is the earneſt prayer of, dear Miſs *B——*,

Your affectionate friend, and
ready ſervant for CHRIST's ſake,

G. W.

LETTER DCCCLXIV.

To the Reverend Mr. Z——.

Aſhly, Oct. 9, 1750.

I Should have written to you long before now, but I waited for the arrival of Mr. *Haberſham*'s ſhip, in which I expected letters of conſequence. They are now come, and two of the chief I ſend encloſed in this, and ſhall omit ſaying any thing further, till I have the pleaſure of ſeeing you, which I hope will be ſome time next week or the week after. Immediately

diately after I left you, I have reason to think that the glorious Redeemer (O infinite condescension!) vouchsafed to make me instrumental in the conversion of Lady H———'s eldest daughter, who I hope is gone to rest. I am now at her Ladyship's house with four other clergymen, who I believe love and preach CHRIST in sincerity: but *Ashby* people reject the kingdom of GOD against themselves. At *Portsmouth, Chatham, Gloucestershire, Birmingham, Wednesbury, Evesham, Nottingham,* &c. our infinite High-priest has given us pleasant seasons. I am now waiting every day for my wife's being delivered of her present burden, and hope ere long to rejoice that a child is born into the world. O that it may be born again and made an heir of the Redeemer's kingdom. This is all my desire. Honoured Sir, you see how freely I open myself unto you. I count it a great privilege that you allow me this liberty, and I earnestly pray our blessed LORD to reward you ten thousand fold. He has been pleased frequently to comfort and encourage my heart this circuit, and in the midst of all, lets me know he is my GOD. O that he may be my glory! O that I may be never left to dishonour him! Reverend Sir, for JESUS's sake continue to pray for me, who, with grateful acknowledgments for all favours, beg leave to subscribe myself, honoured Sir,

Your most obliged, affectionate, though unworthy younger brother, and fellow-labourer in the kingdom of CHRIST,

G. W.

LETTER DCCCLXV.

To the Countess D———.

Honoured Madam, *Ashby, Oct.* 11, 1750.

IT would give me concern, was I to return to *London*, though from ever so short an excursion, without letting your Ladyship know that you are always remembered by me at the throne of grace. Upon such a throne the Redeemer sits, holding out his golden sceptre, and asking us, "What is your petition? And what is your request?" My request for your Ladyship is, that you may increase with all the increase of GOD. This I trust your Ladyship is daily doing, and consequently increasing in inward happiness, peace and joy. The riches of the divine life are indeed unsearchable. May your Ladyship

Ladyship dig for them as for hid treasure, till faith be turned into vision, and hope into the endless fruition of the ever blessed GOD! That time will shortly come. I have been labouring at *Birmingham*, in *Gloucestershire*, at *Nottingham*, &c. to awaken a sleepy world to a sense of it, and I trust not without success. On last *Thursday* I came here, and next *Monday*, GOD willing, shall set out for *London*. Good Lady H—— goes on acting the part of a mother in *Israel*, more and more. For a day or two she has had five clergymen under her roof, which makes her Ladyship look like a *good Archbishop* with his Chaplains around him. Her house is indeed a *Bethel*. To us in the ministry, it looks like a college. We have the Sacrament every morning, heavenly conversation all day, and preach at night. This is to *live at Court*, indeed. Last night I had the pleasure of seeing a little flock that seemed to be awakened by the grace of GOD; so that even out of ungrateful *Ashby*, I trust there will be raised up many children unto *Abraham*. Your Ladyship, and the other elect Ladies, are never forgotten by us. I would write to good Lady F——, but I hear she is out of town. That the choicest of divine blessings, even the sure mercies of *David*, may follow you both all the days of your lives, is the hearty prayer of, honoured Madam,

Your Ladyship's most dutiful,
obliged, and ready servant,
G. W.

LETTER DCCCLXVI.

To Lady H———m.

Honoured Madam,   *Ashby*, *Oct.* 11, 1750.

IT is with great pleasure that I have heard of your Ladyship's being so supported under your late bereavement, and of the good impressions made on surviving relations by it. Thus the Redeemer delights to magnify his strength in his people's weakness, and causes the death of one, to be the life, as it were, the resurrection of another. O what amazing mysteries will be unfolded, when each link in the golden chain of Providence and Grace, shall be seen and scanned by beatified spirits in the kingdom of heaven! There all will appear symmetry and harmony, and even the most intricate and seemingly

ingly moſt contrary diſpenſations, will be evidenced to be the reſult of infinite and conſummate wiſdom, power, and love. Above all, there the believer will ſee the infinite depths of that myſtery of godlineſs, "GOD manifeſted in the fleſh," and join with that bleſſed choir, who with a reſtleſs unweariedneſs are ever ſinging the ſong of *Moſes* and the Lamb. There your Ladyſhip I believe will ſee your departed daughter, not ſtruggling with a burning fever, but burning with love extatic, and with ſeraphic ſweetneſs adoring that Redeemer, who at the eleventh hour, even on a dying bed, ſnatched her as a brand out of the fire. But what am I doing? I fear, making your Ladyſhip's wounds to bleed afreſh.—But, honoured Madam, is it not a pleaſant bleeding, to think of bearing children for heaven? To ſee thoſe neareſt and deareſt parts of ourſelves go before us thither—O what a favour is this! May your Ladyſhip be always thus highly favoured: may you live to ſee all your ſurviving children taught and born of GOD. I muſt not enlarge. Neither have I room to acquaint your Ladyſhip, how that mirror of piety, good Lady *H——*, adorns the goſpel of her LORD in all things. I wrote ſome particulars of our ſituation to the good Counteſs. I can now only add, that when I come to town, your Ladyſhip may at any time command, honoured Madam,

Your Ladyſhip's moſt dutiful, obliged,
and ready ſervant for CHRIST's ſake,
G. W.

LETTER DCCCLXVII.

To Mr. T——.

My very dear Mr. T——, *Aſhby, Oct.* 13, 1750.

YOUR kind letter did not reach me till about two days ago. I embrace the firſt opportunity of anſwering it. If you write often, GOD willing, you ſhall hear oftener from me. You are peculiarly dear to me, and therefore I heartily wiſh you was thruſt out into our LORD's harveſt. *Vox populi,* much more *vox amicorum,* is frequently *vox Dei.* I ſay to you, as a good old miniſter did to one whom you know, and who was as unwilling to go into the vineyard, as you can be, "I believe if St. *Paul* was alive, he would ordain you." You have a moderate ſhare of learning, an agreeable addreſs, a

good

good elocution, a little knowledge of mankind, and of yourself, and above all an experimental acquaintance with the LORD JESUS CHRIST, with a door of usefulness immediately opening; and what would you more? I wish some latent pride may not be at the bottom. Lose no more time, my dear man. The voice of CHRIST to you now is, "Follow me, and I will make thee a fisher of men." The harvest is great, the labourers are few. Thousands are perishing for lack of that knowledge, which you have already. The world wants more heat than light. *Crescit eundo, crescit agendo*, is a young minister's motto. I think the Itinerancy abroad would suit you well. By travelling before you take on you a settled charge, you will get a deeper insight into the world and the church; you will insensibly acquire larger and more sublime thoughts of GOD's providence and grace, and consequently be more fit to serve whatever flock the Holy Ghost shall hereafter place you over. I believe that your honoured father loves CHRIST too well, to stand out long against a rational scheme for the extensive usefulness of his son. He is a dear man, whom I love in the bowels of JESUS CHRIST. Pray remember me to him in the kindest manner, and tell him I purpose writing to him as soon as possible. This leaves me at *Ashby*, at good Lady *H——n*'s, whose house is indeed a *Bethel* to those who are willing to follow her, as she follows JESUS CHRIST. One of high rank, I really believe, was converted lately on a dying bed, and her death I trust hath proved the life of one or two more. One of the *Kendal* converts is gone off in flying colours, and our blessed LORD has given us sweet seasons at *Portsmouth, Chatham, Gloucestershire, Birmingham, Eversham, Wednesbury, Nottingham*, &c. Next *Monday*, GOD willing, I go for *London*, in order to put into winter quarters. The LORD prepare me for a fresh campaign! Do you know any one fit for a Tutor at *Georgia?* I am glad that *New Jersey* college succeeds. I had lately a letter from Governor *Belcher*, which I suppose you have seen; it was sent to Mr. *N——*. Colonel *W——* proposes that Mr. *P——* shall come over with one of the *Indians*; I wish he may. I am sorry to hear that Mr. —— is likely to destroy himself by hard study. I had rather he would kill himself with hard working, and going about to do good. Mr. *G——* seems to me to have chosen the better part. How is

dear

dear Mr. R—— W——? I hope he is like a flame of fire. Pray salute him and all my dear, very dear friends in the tenderest manner. I could live and die with them. In heaven we shall live together. There we shall see our dear Mr. L——. I hope your little choir are every day learning more and more of the new song, in order to join him in the realms above.— You have all my hearty love and prayers. Accept the same yourself in a very particular manner from, very dear Sir,

Yours most affectionately in a precious CHRIST,

G. W.

LETTER DCCCLXVIII.

To Governor B——.

Honoured Sir, *Ashby, Oct.* 13, 1750.

I Had the favour of your Excellency's letter, and took the liberty of communicating it to good Lady H——n, who shines in the church of CHRIST on this side the water, as a star of the first magnitude. Her Ladyship will be very glad to open a correspondence with your Excellency; and seems to speak of *New-Jersey* College with great satisfaction. I rejoice to hear that it is in a prosperous situation. If Mr. P—— or Mr. B—— can be prevailed on to come over, I am persuaded liberal contributions will be raised both in *England* and *Scotland*. All was ready, if dear Mr. A—— had not been taken off by death; but even this our blessed LORD can and will over-rule for good. I think it forebodes good for *America*, that such a spirit is excited in so many provinces for promoting a learned and religious education. GOD only knows how much my heart is on that side the water. I should certainly have embarked about this time, did not my wife daily expect an hour of travail. I can only say, "It is the LORD; let him do what seemeth him good." Blessed be his name, fresh doors for usefulness are opened every week. We had a blessed scene this Summer in *Scotland*, and ever since I have been ranging about, to see who will believe the gospel report. O that I may die in the field! I am now at my good Lady's with three clergymen that love and preach JESUS CHRIST. Several souls have been awakened here. One of high birth was lately converted on her dying bed; and by that means I trust one or two more are put upon securing the one thing needful. On *Monday* I shall leave her Ladyship, to go for *London*, which is to be my Winter quarters. I shall long for *Spring*, that I may enter upon a fresh campaign. O that my soul may begin to spring indeed! spring for Him who was stretched upon the accursed tree to save my wretched soul. Blessed be his name, that your Excellency has got such a sweet retreat in the decline of life; where, free from noise and hurry, you and your consort may ripen for heaven, and consequently be more and more fitted for your last great change. That will now shortly come. Your Excellency is arrived to a good old age. You have by faith seen the LORD CHRIST. You have been instrumental in founding a christian college. Let death come when it will, with good old *Simeon*, you may say, " LORD, now lettest thou thy servant depart in peace," for my soul hath experienced thy great salvation! This I believe, honoured Sir, is all your desire. Our LORD will grant it to you. O that when you are near his throne, you may have a petition upon your heart for unworthy, ill-deserving, hell-deserving me! Your Excellency hath laid me under many obligations; let me entreat you by the mercies of GOD in CHRIST JESUS, to add to them by not ceasing to pray for me, that as I have had much forgiven me, I may, with *Magdalen*, love much; and being a brand plucked out of the burning, I may, in GOD's own time and way, be translated to dwell with JESUS in his kingdom. As our LORD enables, the favour shall constantly be returned in behalf of you and yours, by, honoured Sir,

Your Excellency's most dutiful, obliged,
and ready servant for CHRIST's sake,
G. W.

LETTER DCCCLXIX.

To Baron Z———.

Honoured Sir,   *London, Nov.* 9, 1750.

THE love of JESUS CHRIST constrains me to send you a few lines. They flow from a heart truly sympathizing with your beloved Baroness, under your present trials. O that patience may have its perfect work in your souls! O that with your tempted, afflicted, agonizing JESUS, you may be enabled to say, " The cup, which our heavenly Father hath given us, shall we not drink it?" I doubt not, but you find it sweetened with his love:—" for he will not suffer us to be tempted above what we are able to bear; but will with the temptation make a way for us to escape." The sacrificing our relations to his sovereign good will and pleasure, is no small trial, especially when unconverted. But what says the scripture? " Neither did his brethren believe on him." Your LORD can sympathize with you under your present circumstances;

> *He knows what this temptation means,*
> *For he has felt the same.*

Look up, therefore, to him, honoured Sir, who has promised never to leave nor forsake you. He hath helped you out of six, he will also help you out of seven troubles. I write this out of the fulness of my heart. My poor prayers are continually ascending to the throne of grace in your behalf. I hope you will not be offended at my freedom in writing. Love and gratitude are my only motives. Good Lady H———n will sympathize with you, when she hears how you are situated. I left her some little time past abounding in the work of the LORD. I had a pleasant excursion into the country, and my Winter quarters are made very agreeable in town. What shall I render unto the LORD? Honoured Sir, I beg a continued interest in your prayers, and those of your honoured Baroness.—You know my name,—I am the chief of sinners, less than the least of all saints, but for JESUS CHRIST's sake,

Your sympathizing ready servant,

G. W.

LETTER DCCCLXX.

To Mr. S———.

My dear Mr. S———, *Canterbury, Nov. 20, 1750.*

BY that time yours reached *London*, I suppose my last will have reached *Dublin*, and find you on the full stretch for him, who was stretched upon the cross for you and me. As far as I can judge of the circumstances you related to me, settling as you propose, will not hinder, but rather further you in your present work. Only beware of nestling. If you do, and

and GOD loves you (as I believe he does) you shall have thorns enough put into your nest. O that I may be enabled, even to the end, to evidence, that nothing but a pure disinterested love to CHRIST and souls, caused me to begin, go on, and hold out, in pursuing the present work of GOD! I have seen so many that once bid exceedingly fair, and afterwards, *Demas* like, preferred the world to CHRIST, that I cannot be too jealous over myself, or others whom I profess to love. This is my motive in writing to you, love, even love unfeigned; love for CHRIST's sake, and the good of souls. O let no one take away your crown. If you marry, let it be in the LORD, and for the LORD, and then the LORD will give it his blessing. Only remember this, marry when or whom you will, expect trouble in the flesh. But I spare you. Seven years hence, if we should live and meet, we can talk better of these things. In the mean while, let us go on leaning on our Beloved. He, and He alone, can keep us unspotted from the world. Does the work prosper among you? It increases here. At *Canterbury* I find several souls are awakened. GOD willing, I leave it to-morrow. You must pray for me, and exhort all to continue their prayers also. I expect, one day or another, to see some glorious days in *Ireland*. I am called away.—For the present, adieu.

Yours most affectionately in our blessed LORD,

G. W.

LETTER DCCCLXXI.

To Mr. T——.

My dear Mr. T——,   *London, Nov.* 30, 1750.

AS I love you in the bowels of JESUS CHRIST, and look upon you as an aged friend of the blessed Bridegroom, and my friend for his great name's sake, I cannot help dropping you a few lines. They are lines of gratitude; lines of thanks for all favours conferred upon me when in *Scotland*. They leave me pleasantly sojourning in my Winter quarters, and longing for the Spring that I may enter upon a fresh campaign. Now and then I make little excursions, and can inform you, that there is a sweet work begun and carrying on at *Canterbury* and *Chatham*. I long to hear that your son

John has put his hand to the gospel plough, and am not without hopes that his lot will be to itinerate, at least for a while. He seems to be qualified for such an employ. I shall be glad to see him on the other side of the water. Had I the management of a thousand youths, if circumstances would allow, they should travel for one year at least, before they took upon them a settled charge. Methinks I hear you say, "What! will you take my *Benjamin* away?" This was old *Jacob*'s infirmity. You love CHRIST too well to refuse giving up the young lad, if it should appear in providence that the LORD hath need of him either at home or abroad. I pray GOD to direct and bless you both, and to establish his covenant with you and your seed for ever. You are now on the decline of life. I have been just reading about the year of jubilee. How joyful were the prisoners when they heard of the approach of that wish'd-for day! How much more joyful may those be, who having an interest in JESUS CHRIST, are waiting for the last trump, to proclaim our eternal jubilee in heaven! This, my dear friend, is your happy lot. Rejoice, and again I say, rejoice. The day of our complete redemption draweth nigh. Let us then lift up our heads, and let us lift up our hearts to praise him, from whom alone cometh our salvation. I could enlarge, but am called away. My hearty love to all enquiring friends. I think to write to your son soon. We had a happy day yesterday among the Great Ones. I am, my very dear Sir,

Yours most affectionately in our dear LORD,

G. *W*.

LETTER DCCCLXXII.

To Doctor W———.

My dear Doctor; London, *Dec.* 17, 1750.

I Received your kind letter, and would have answered it much sooner, had I not been prevented by sickness. For near a fortnight past, I have been confined to my room; but through the divine blessing, am now enabled to preached again. Praise the LORD, O my soul. My disorder was a violent fever: JESUS hath rebuked it. I am raised up once more. O may it be that I may minister unto him! For me to live is CHRIST. But alas! how little do I live to his glory! Yesterday I entered

tered upon my seven-and-thirtieth year. I am ashamed to think I have lived so long, and done so little, and yet every year, day, and hour of my life hath been crowned with the divine goodness. O my dear friend, let this be our motto, *Vivimus ut viviamus.* It is enough when we come to our last moments, to have nothing to do, but to die. Blessed be GOD, that you have courage given you to speak to the dying. A word spoken in such a season how good is it? May the great physician take you under his peculiar care, forgive you all your sins, and heal all your diseases! I purpose writing to my friend J—— T——, and others, as I get strength. At present, I must content myself with sending general, but cordial salutations, and begging the continual interest of your prayers in behalf of, my very dear Sir,

Yours, &c.

G. W.

LETTER DCCCLXXIII.

To Mr. T——.

London, Dec. 21, 1750.

I Have been lately near the gates of death, which has hindered my answering your kind letter as soon as I proposed. Accept a few, though loving lines now. I hope they will find you entered upon your trials, and longing to preach the gospel, which you have felt to be the power of GOD to the salvation of your soul. Every line of your letter seemed to have this call in it, " Rise, T——r, rise,—the harvest is great; the labourers are few: pray the LORD of the harvest to send thee, and many more like-minded, into the harvest." I cannot write much at present. Inclosed you have a few extracts. That from Lady H——n, came last week when she was dangerously ill. May the LORD continue her useful life! I am now entering upon my seven-and-thirtieth year. O that I may begin to live to him, who hath lived and died for me! I shall be glad to know your friend's answer about *Georgia.* If the LORD raises up a solid, heavenly-minded, learned young man for a tutor, I shall be glad. Nothing, I believe, but sickness or death, will prevent my going over next year. Methinks the winter is long; I want to take the field again.

again. Could you send me all Mr. G——'s weekly papers. We prayed heartily last *Monday* for the awakened *Hollanders*. I have heard of several lately awakened here. To the blessed and glorious JESUS be all the praise. My dear friend, my heart leaps at the very mention of his name. When I muse of him, the fire kindles. O that you and I may shew forth his praise while we have a tongue! Pray remember me to all in the kindest manner, and beg them not to forget unworthy me. Let not my being so slow in answering your last, prevent your writing speedily to, my dear Mr. T——,

Yours most affectionately in our dearest LORD,

G. W.

LETTER DCCCLXXIV.

To Lady S——.

Honoured Madam,   London, *Dec.* 25, 1750.

I Had the favour of your Ladyship's letter on *Saturday* afternoon, and immediately communicated what concerned him, to my ingenious and devout friend Mr. H——. With this, your Ladyship will receive a line from him. I persuaded him, that your Ladyship would not take it ill. Poor Mr. B—— is much obliged to your Ladyship for speaking in his behalf. He happened to be with me, when your Ladyship's letter came. The Reception that your Ladyship's kind motion met with, convinces me more and more, that " Be ye warmed, and be ye filled," without giving any thing to be warmed and filled with, is the farthest that most professors go. Words are cheap, and cost nothing; and therefore many can say, " they pity," and that extremely too, when at the same time, their practice shews it is only a verbal, and not a real compassion. I often told the poor man, that his dependance was too strong; and that I was afraid least help would not come from that quarter where he expected most. He sends ten thousand thanks for what your Ladyship hath done already. Surely he is worthy. He is a lover of CHRIST, and his outward circumstances very pitiable indeed. Your Ladyship will not be offended at the freedom I take. You love to help the distressed to the utmost of your power; and your Ladyship shall find that good measure, pressed down and running over, shall be returned into your

your bosom. That your Ladyship may experience the truth of this, in respect to temporals and spirituals, more and more every day, is the earnest prayer of, honoured Madam,

Your Ladyship's most obliged, dutiful,
and ready servant for CHRIST's sake,
G. W.

LETTER DCCCLXXV.
To Mr. S——.

My dear Mr. S——, London, *Jan.* 4, 1751.

IMMEDIATELY upon the receipt of your last from *Limerick*, I wrote you an answer, directed for you at *Limerick* post-office, as you desired. As you are going that way, ere this reaches you, I hope you will have received it. I pray the LORD of all lords to give you such grace, that all may see, that the doctrines of the gospel are indeed productive of righteousness, and true holiness in heart, lip, and life. Mind this, and then fear not. Continue as you are, until you are absolutely rejected. I want not to proselyte persons to myself; but to the glorious *Emmanuel*, my LORD and Master JESUS CHRIST. Perhaps He may send me to *Ireland*; though some weeks ago I hoped that he was about to take me to heaven. I kept my room near a fortnight, and still continue very weak. This obliges me to be brief. My wife is now expecting an hour of travail. Some time this month I trust she will be delivered. She desires to be remembered to you. GOD willing, Mr. Z—— shall hear from me. I do not yet hear who is to be the person. Unless you have thoughts of going abroad, I see no objection against your altering your condition. May the LORD direct and bless you and all in that important step! It is a change for life. We have had blessed seasons here; but methinks the Winter is very long. O that I was entering upon a Spring campaign! It is a new year. My dear Mr. S——, why should we not begin to begin to live to that JESUS, who has done and suffered so much for us! I trust this is the language of your heart,

> *A life that all things casts behind,*
> *Springs forth obedient at thy call;*
> *A heart, that no desire can move,*
> *But still t'adore, believe, and love,*
> *Give me, my* LORD, *my life, my all!*

I hear you say, *Amen, Amen. Hallelujah!* I must have done. Bodily strength fails me. My love to all that love CHRIST JESUS. Brethren, pray for us, is the earnest request of, my dear Mr. S——,

   Yours most affectionately in our dearest LORD,

           G. W.

LETTER DCCCLXXVI.

To Mr. L——.

Dear Mr. L——,   London, *Jan.* 13, 1751.

BEFORE I had the pleasure of your letter, I had heard some particulars of the late commotion at *Canterbury*. Ere now I hope you have been directed to the choice of such means, as may, under GOD, open the door wider than ever for preaching the everlasting gospel in your parts. Satan has done at *Canterbury* as he always does elsewhere; I mean, he has overshot his mark. Such proceedings are too violent to hold long. Exhort, therefore, my dear Sir, your fellow-soldiers, to quit themselves like men, and be strong. Put ye on the whole armour of GOD; and always remember, that through much tribulation we must enter into glory. Now is the time for you to prove the strength of JESUS to be yours. Your way to fight, is upon your knees. That weapon *all-prayer* will do wonders. The devil has lost some servants, and he is afraid of losing more. Therefore he rallies his forces as *Pharaoh* harnessed his chariots, and wants to bring you back to *Egypt*. Your business is to go on. Though *Pharaoh* is behind, and a red-sea before you,—ere long you shall pass through the one, and see the other totally destroyed. In patience possess ye your souls. GOD is able to bring the counsel of every *Achitophel* to nought. You know in whom you have believed. He never did, he never will, he never can fail those that put their trust in him. Think of those farewel words, which he spake in the days of his flesh to his dear disciples, "Let not your hearts be troub'ed; in the world ye shall have tribulation:—But I have overcome the world." That is enough to raise every drooping heart. He hath overcome for us; he will overcome in us, and ere long call us to reign with him for ever in glory. O blessed hope! Whilst I am musing on it, the fire kindles. Brethren, my heart is enlarged towards you. The LORD strengthen you, and give you to pray for

Your affectionate friend, brother, and servant

for CHRIST's sake,

G. W.

LETTER DCCCLXXVII.

To Mr. X—— Y——.

Dear Sir, London, *Jan.* 15, 1751.

YOUR letter came safe to hand. I pray GOD enable me to answer it agreeable to his will. Your call to enter into the ministry, seems to be pretty clear, and if your health would permit you to be a tutor, and courage be given you to act like a good soldier of JESUS CHRIST, you might do unspeakable good in residing at college. If a person's health will not admit of such a residence, I think by the laws of GOD and man, his absence may be dispensed with. Originally, *Fellows* were appointed to reside; but there is no general rule without an exception. Particular circumstances can only determine particular cases. Mr. *W——* I know hath been dispensed with many years:—and though I cannot say I have approved of this part of his conduct, yet as he is called elsewhere, and applies the college income to good purposes, I suppose he thinks he acts an honest and christian part. As for the difficulties you seem to place before you, I can only say, " *Nil desperandum Christo duce.*" Every new scene brings its new temptations; but faith in the Son of GOD, will make us more than conquerors over all. His love shed abroad in the heart by the Holy Ghost, is the best director and support in all circumstances whatsoever. For want of an establishment in this, and through the prevalency of an hypocondraical disorder, you seem to have particular scruples about particular things. It is what all persons, entering on the divine life, are more or less exposed to. " Meditation, prayer, reading, and temptation, (says holy *Luther*) make a minister." Your levity of spirit, and fickleness of temper, are your greatest diseases. These are to be watched and prayed against, and by divine grace will be overcome. Look up, therefore, dear Sir, to the blessed JESUS. Out of weakness he can and will make you to become strong, and turn your lightness of spirit into solid joy. Till then, be content rather to appear stupid, than by giving way to the luxuriancy of unsanctified wit, bring guilt upon your soul. Thus, dear Sir, I have endeavoured to answer your letter; though I must confess, as you are so near, I had rather converse with you personally. You may use freedom with me. I rejoice that the glorious JESUS hath in any degree blessed my poor administrations to you. I need not, therefore, remind you to give him all the glory, and entreat you to pray for me, who am the very chief of sinners, and less than the least of all saints, but for CHRIST's sake, dear Sir,

Your very ready servant,
G. W.

LETTER DCCCLXXVIII.

To Mr. B———.

My very dear Friend,   London, *Jan.* 18, 1751.

YOUR kind letter I received this morning. The love I owe you for CHRIST's sake, constrains me to send you an immediate answer. From the same motive I just now wrote to Mr. B———. Poor man! This is a home-stroke indeed! I hope he and his yoke-fellow will now take a large step to heaven. May GOD prepare us, my dear friend, for the finishing trials! We must all have them in our turns. But wherefore should we fear? Out of very faithfulness, our heavenly Father causes us to be troubled. Of his infinite mercy he hath lately been pleased to visit me with a threatening illness. I was just casting anchor;—but it seems I must put out to sea again. O that it may be to direct others to the way that leads to the haven of eternal rest! Who knows but I may found the gospel once more in *Scotland?* I have some thoughts of coming for a little while, before I embark for *America.* You will desire all the societies to pray, that the LORD would order my goings in his way. I rejoice that they hold on their way. May they hold on and hold out to the end! My constant prayer for them is, that they may increase with all the increase of GOD. Many in town have been awakened this Winter. O that I was humble! When shall that once be? O that

I was

I was thankful! Fain would I burn with love and gratitude like a seraph.

> *With arms of love, and wings of faith,*
> *I'd fly and take the prize.*

Well! Let faith and patience hold out a little longer, and all will be well. He is faithful, who hath promised, who also will do it. Believers should look more to JESUS. It is the only way to keep their hands from hanging down, and to strengthen their feeble knees. Exhort all to this: and pray salute every enquiring friend, every member of the societies, in the most endearing manner; for indeed I love my *Scotch* friends in the bowels of JESUS CHRIST. Whilst I am writing to and thinking of them, tears, but tears of love, are ready to gush from mine eyes. O that I may meet them all in the kingdom of our Father! O that their lamps may be always trimmed, and their loins girt! Behold JESUS comes quickly, and his reward is with him: let us not leave him. Let us not flag in the latter stages of our road. O our bleeding, agonizing, dying JESUS, how have we pierced thee! At least how have I! O that we may look and love, look and mourn, even as one that mourneth for a first-born or an only son. Dear Mr. B—— can now comment on this text. May the LORD comfort his heart, and be better to him than seven sons! I can no more. Affections of various kinds quite overflow. I long to begin to do something for JESUS. A sense of my vileness and unfruitfulness, quite breaks my heart. Surely I shall sing, free grace in heaven.—I write this to you as a friend. The LORD be with you, and reward you and all, for their sympathy with me and mine. Fail not to pray for me; and believe me to be, my very dear Mr. B——,

Yours in the best of bonds,

G. W.

LETTER DCCCLXXIX.

To Dr. W——.

My very dear Sir,   *Ashby-Place, Jan.* 29, 1751.

IT is high time to answer your kind letter. I am doing it at *Ashby*, whither I rid post, not knowing whether I should see good Lady H——n alive. Blessed be GOD, she is somewhat

what better, and I truſt will not yet die, but live and abound more and more in the work of the LORD. Entreat all our friends to pray for her. Indeed ſhe is worthy. Her ſiſter-in-law, Lady *Frances H*——, lies dead in the houſe. She was a retired chriſtian, lived ſilently, and died ſuddenly without a groan. May my exit be like hers! Whether right or not, I cannot help wiſhing that I may go off in the ſame manner. To me it is worſe than death, to live to be nurſed, and ſee friends weeping about one. Sudden death, is ſudden glory. Methinks it is falling aſleep indeed, or rather a tranſlation. But all this muſt be left to our heavenly Father. He knows what is beſt for us and others. Let it be our care to have all things ready. Let the houſe of our hearts, and our temporal affairs be put in order immediately, that we may have nothing to do but to obey the ſummons, though it ſhould be at evening, cock-crowing, or in the morning. Phyſicians that are always attending on the dying, one would imagine ſhould in a peculiar manner learn to die daily. May this be your daily employ! I believe it is; though, like me, you muſt complain that the old man dies hard. Well, has he got his deadly blow? Die then he ſhall, even that death to which he put our LORD: O that the language of our hearts may always be, " Crucify, crucify him." This is painful. But the Redeemer can help us to bear it.

> *Thou wilt give ſtrength, thou wilt give power;*
> *Thou wilt in time ſet free;*
> *This great deliverance let us hope,*
> *Not for ourſelves, but thee!*

I write this out of the fulneſs of my heart. You will receive it as ſuch, and remember me in the beſt manner to all friends. We have had good times. All glory be to JESUS through all eternity!

Yours, &c.

G. W.

LETTER DCCCLXXX.

To Lady M—— H——.

Honoured Madam, *Ashby, Jan.* 30, 1751.

LAST *Monday* evening, through the goodness of an everblessed Redeemer, I got safe to *Ashby*, where I found good Lady H———n very sick, though I trust not unto death. All advise her Ladyship to take a journey to *Bristol*, for the benefit of the waters, which her Ladyship seems determined to do. The death of Lady *Frances*, has not affected her Ladyship so as to hurt her. She rejoices at the thoughts of her sister's being so quickly translated out of this house of bondage, into the glorious liberty of the sons of GOD. Her death was a translation indeed. Her Ladyship died without a groan. She seemed as it were to smile at death; and may be said, I trust, truly " to fall asleep in JESUS." Ere long, she and all that sleep in JESUS, shall come with him. I hope it hath been a purging time in this family. Almost all have been sick in their turns. Lady *Selina* has had a fever, but is better. Lady *Betty* is more affected than ever I saw her. A letter now from one of the young ladies, I hope would do service. Lady *Ann* bears up pretty well, but Miss W———r is inconsolable. It is a house of mourning; that is better than a house of feasting. The corpse is to be interred on *Friday* evening. May all that follow it, look and learn! I mean, learn to live, and learn to die. This is a lesson which you and yours, honoured Madam, I trust are learning every day. We had need be careful to get our lesson perfect, since we know not when the Son of Man will come, whether at evening,—cock-crowing,—or in the morning. To be ready at that hour, is all in all. Good Lady H———n sends her sincerest compliments. If any thing extraordinary happens before my return, your Ladyship shall hear again from, honoured Madam,

Your Ladyship's most dutiful, obliged,
and ready servant for CHRIST's sake,

G. W.

LETTER DCCCLXXXI.

To Doctor S——.

My dear Doctor,   *Ashby, Feb.* 4, 1751.

YOUR letter distresses me. GOD hasten the time when you shall sing chearfully,

> *Be gone, vain world, my heart resign,*
> *For I must be no longer thine;*
> *A nobler, a diviner guest,*
> *Has got possession of my breast.*

Why will you not shake off your chains? Why will you be stricken any more? You must come back, or be undone for ever. What have you gained by running from your father's house? His servants have bread enough, whilst you are perishing with hunger. Say, say, I pray you, without delay, "I will arise and go to my Father." His love keeps you uneasy; his love hedges up your way; his love follows and pursues you with this mighty famine. The language of all is, "Give me thy heart." Be content to become a fool for CHRIST's sake. Your body as well as soul, will suffer even in this world, if you do not comply. You are half dead already. Faith in CHRIST, and the love of GOD shed abroad in your heart, can alone cure you. You know too much to be happy without it: and O that dreadful sentence, "It had been better for them never to have known ——— &c." For CHRIST's sake, remember *Lot*'s wife. You are almost become a pillar of salt already. Out of anguish I write this. May CHRIST's love so constrain you, that you may never rest till you find solid rest in him! Good Lady H———n is gone to take the air. Your message shall be delivered. She is but poorly; and my wife writes me word, that she is exceeding bad. This must hasten my remove from hence. I insist upon Mr. H———*y*'s coming directly to *Ashby*, if he has any regard for good Lady H———n. She ought always to have a christian friend with her. That you may have a feeling possession of CHRIST in your heart, is the hearty prayer of, my dear Sir,

Yours, &c. in great haste, but greater concern for you,

G. W.

LETTER DCCCLXXXII.

To Mr. B———.

Dear Sir, London, Feb. 8, 1751.

YESTERDAY I saw your letter to Mr. *V———*, which made me to think a line would not altogether be unacceptable to you. And what shall I say? Your case is affecting. O that your present confinement may be sanctified to the setting of your imprisoned soul at liberty, and bringing you home (after having so long fed on husks with swine) to feed upon the fatted calf! You know the father's behaviour to the returning prodigal. He saw him when he was yet a great way off.—He ran towards him,—filthy as he was, he fell upon his neck, and kissed him. Thus, if you resolve with the prodigal, to arise and go to your Father, will the ever-blessed GOD deal with you. He will embrace you in the arms of his love; he will also cloathe you with the righteousness of his dear Son, and cause joy to be in heaven even over you, on repenting and returning to him. Is not this enough to encourage you to lay hold on his golden sceptre? to resolve, in divine strength, to mortify and bid adieu to all those sins, by which you have dishonoured your glorious Maker? You see, Sir, what wages Satan gives; *death* even in this world, and alas! *eternal death* in the world to come. GOD keep you from this second death, and then temporal shame will be but little. The way you know; JESUS is the way, the truth, and the life. He is mighty, and willing to save to the uttermost all that come to the Father in and through him. Come then, dear Sir, and throw yourself at the feet of his mercy. He will not only pardon, but abundantly pardon you. In JESUS CHRIST there is a fountain opened for sin and for all uncleanness. " Wash ye, make ye clean," is the call of GOD to all, and now the particular call of GOD to you. May the Spirit of the ever-loving, ever-lovely JESUS, bring it home to your soul, and make it effectual to your thorough conversion! Let this be your sole care. For this and this only is the one thing needful. As for seeing Mrs. ———, if I was to advise (as it hath been hitherto deferred) I would have you both decline it a little longer. Wait and see the issue of your trial;

she

she can do you no good, and by coming may do herself harm. But this is a tender point. May Providence point out what is best! If we acknowledge the LORD, we have a promise, "that he will direct us in all our ways." I commend you to his never-failing mercy, and beg you to accept this from, dear Sir,

Your sympathizing friend and servant
for CHRIST's sake,
G. W.

LETTER DCCCLXXXIII.

To Lady H——n.

Ever-honoured Madam,   London, *Feb.* 26, 1751.

YOUR Ladyship's kind letter, which came to hand yesterday, was an unexpected as well as undeserved favour, and for which I return your Ladyship ten thousand thanks. Surely the LORD of all lords will at length answer the prayers of his people, and raise you up to the joy of many souls. It would rejoice your Ladyship much to see what has been doing here. I have not known a more considerable awakening for a long time. The LORD comes down as in the days of old, and the shout of a king is amongst us. Praise the LORD, O my soul! The inclosed, which came from abroad, I believe will give your Ladyship satisfaction. I think it is an earnest of good things to come. To-morrow I purpose to leave *London*; but whether the rain and wind will permit me is uncertain. I am at present quite feverish, by my late hurry and fatigue; but GOD is my portion and my confidence for ever. Underneath your Ladyship are his everlasting arms; you cannot sink with such a prop. Your Ladyship must be made conqueror, yea more than conqueror, through his love. That, is engaged to bring you through whatever sufferings may be yet before you. He is faithful, who hath promised, "that we shall not be tempted above what we are able to bear." This is my daily support. To explain GOD's providence by the promise, and not his promise by his providence, I find is the only way both to get and to keep our comforts. Above all, I find that looking unto JESUS, is an universal, never-failing antidote against every evil. This is what your Ladyship knows by happy experience. May you know it more and more so every day and hour! But I fear I weary your Ladyship, and therefore hasten to subscribe myself, ever-honoured Madam,

> Your Ladyship's most dutiful, obliged and ready servant for CHRIST's sake,
> G. W.

LETTER DCCCLXXXIV.

To Mr. ———.

Very dear Sir, London, *March* 1, 1751.

YOUR generous conduct much affects me; it hath drawn me to the throne of grace in your behalf. If any of my poor writings should be rendered either entertaining or beneficial to you, I hope it will make me more thankful to him, who is the father of lights, and from whom every good and perfect gift cometh. Mr. H—— writes me word, that his heart is knit to you. I wish the colony affairs may not lie too hard upon him. Whenever he dies, I believe he will die as it were a martyr for the welfare of *Georgia*. He mentions Mr. H—— for a magistrate in his stead; if I might advise, nothing should be denied, that might strengthen Mr. H——'s hands. I know him to be a tried friend, and one who has the good of that poor province exceedingly at heart. Young M——, he thinks, might be ordained for an itinerant preacher among the negroes. A good beginning amongst them might be of vast consequence. Mr. Z—— hath this affair much at heart. I give you these hints to be improved as you think proper. My views to serve *Georgia* are disinterested; so I believe are yours. Such intentions the great Redeemer will own and bless one way or another. I wish I could have my packet from *Westminster,* before I leave town. I think you do right to send the young gentleman to B——. If he inquires for Mr. J—— S—— a merchant, he will be taken care of. B—— is no good place however for young men, for there young B—— has been hurt. But alas, if people's hearts are not upright, change of place will avail but little. This consideration induces me to send the inclosed. I commit it to your care, and commend your better part to his mercy, who hath loved and given himself for us. That you may experience all the unsearchable riches of his superabundant grace, is the earnest prayer of, very dear Sir,

   Your affectionate friend, and very obliged
      and ready servant for CHRIST's sake,
             G. W.

LETTER DCCCLXXXV.

To Mr. ———.

Dear Sir,   London, *March* 1, 1751.

YOUR acknowledgment for my poor present, is more than it deserved. If it is made of use to your precious soul, I have my desired end. My heart's desire and prayer to GOD is, that his goodness may lead you to a thorough repentance, and that you may have no rest, till you truly believe on JESUS CHRIST. Reformation is not renovation: and unless the heart be totally and thoroughly changed, when the fear of hell and other outward restraints are gone, good impressions will gradually wear off, and the seeming convert return again to folly. The love of CHRIST therefore constrains me, dear Sir, to exhort you to make thorough work of it, and to give all diligence to make your calling and election sure. Now indeed is the accepted time! Surely you may say, "Am I not a brand plucked out of the burning?" Satan will not care that you should leave him without some attacks. When you are abroad, old habits, and old corruptions will strive to renew their ancient acquaintance with you: merry company will endeavour to redebauch you, and your grand adversary the devil will labour to render all the amazing mercies you have received, fruitless and abortive.—Be upon your guard. Distrust yourself. Be instant in prayer. Look continually to JESUS, and then as your day is, so shall your strength be. Be pleased to accept this in love. If I may judge of your aspect and letter, you will. Glad shall I be to find you a new creature in *Georgia*. My prayers shall follow you, and I hope ere long we shall meet with our brother and all the redeemed of the LORD in paradise. Be pleased to remember me to Mr. R———; and if you would mind me, as the chief of sinners and less than the least of all saints, when you get access to the throne of grace, you would oblige, dear Sir,

Your real friend for CHRIST's sake,

G. W.

LETTER DCCCLXXXVI.

To the Reverend Mr. H———.

Bristol, March 17, 1751.

My very dear Friend,

THIS comes with a summons from good Lady H———, for you to appear in *Bristol*, and abide for a month or two at my brother's house. You must not refuse. The GOD who has carried that elect Lady through such bad roads from *Ashby* hither, will take care of you, and I am persuaded you will not repent your journey. Her Ladyship made the motion to me, and intends writing herself. Blessed be GOD, she is much better, and I trust will do well. She will have nobody to give her the sacrament unless you come. I hope this will find you at the tabernacle house, and trust shall hear of your sister's safe delivery. My tender and cordial respects await her, your dear brother, and his whole houshold. I ventured the other day to put out a guinea to interest for you. It was to release an excellent christian, who by living very hard, and working near twenty hours out of four-and-twenty, had brought himself very low. He has a wife and four children, and was above two guineas in debt. I gave one for myself and one for you. We shall have good interest for our money in another world. O for a mind like his, who though he was rich, yet for our sakes became poor, that we through his poverty might become rich! I have been recommending him this morning, and purpose doing so again this evening. In *Gloucestershire* the word hath been gladly received, and here we have had pleasant gales. O my dear Sir, follow me with your prayers. The LORD be with your spirit. I commend you to his never-failing mercy, and am, my very dear friend,

Yours most affectionately,

G. W.

LETTER DCCCLXXXVII.

To Mr. B———.

Bristol, March 22, 1751.

Reverend and very dear Sir,

I Lately received your last kind letter, and am glad to find that you are enabled to joy in tribulation, and to say, "Father, not my will, but thine be done." May the LORD increase your faith, and if you should be called to give up your *Isaac*, your dear yoke-fellow, may you, *Aaron* like, hold your peace, and by an undissembled resignation to the divine will, glorify your GOD! My wife has been in pitiable circumstances for some time. The LORD only knows what will be the issue of them. This is my comfort, "all things work together for good to those that love GOD." He is the father of mercies, and the GOD of all consolation. He can bring light out of darkness, and cause the barren wilderness to smile. This I trust will be verified in *Georgia*. Thanks be to GOD, that the time for favouring that Colony seems to be come. I think now is the season for us to exert our utmost for the good of the poor *Ethiopians*. We are told, that even they are soon to stretch out their hands unto GOD. And who knows but their being settled in *Georgia*, may be over-ruled for this great end? As for the lawfulness of keeping slaves, I have no doubt, since I hear of some that were bought with *Abraham*'s money, and some that were born in his house. — And I cannot help thinking, that some of those servants mentioned by the Apostles in their epistles, were or had been slaves. It is plain, that the *Gibeonites* were doomed to perpetual slavery, and though liberty is a sweet thing to such as are born free, yet to those who never new the sweets of it, slavery perhaps may not be so irksome. However this be, it is plain to a demonstration, that hot countries cannot be cultivated without negroes. What a flourishing country might *Georgia* have been, had the use of them been permitted years ago? How many white people have been destroyed for want of them, and how many thousands of pounds spent to no purpose at all? Had Mr. *Henry* been in *America*, I believe he would have seen the lawfulness and necessity of having negroes there. And though it is true, that they are brought in a wrong way from their

their own country, and it is a trade not to be approved of, yet as it will be carried on whether we will or not; I should think myself highly favoured if I could purchase a good number of them, in order to make their lives comfortable, and lay a foundation for breeding up their posterity in the nurture and admonition of the LORD. You know, dear Sir, that I had no hand in bringing them into *Georgia*; though my judgment was for it, and so much money was yearly spent to no purpose, and I was strongly importuned thereto, yet I would not have a negro upon my plantation, till the use of them was publicly allowed in the colony. Now this is done, dear Sir, let us reason no more about it, but diligently improve the present opportunity for their instruction. The trustees favour it, and we may never have a like prospect. It rejoiced my soul, to hear that one of my poor negroes in *Carolina* was made a brother in CHRIST. How know we but we may have many such instances in *Georgia* ere it be long? By mixing with your people, I trust many of them will be brought to JESUS, and this consideration, as to us, swallows up all temporal inconveniencies whatsoever. Thus, my dear Sir, I have opened my mind to you on this head; if it satisfies you, I shall be glad; though I suppose what holy Mr. Z———*n* has already written, has been sufficient. His heart seems touched with a sympathy for these poor creatures, and in the fall, GOD willing, I intend seeing what can be done towards laying a foundation. LORD prosper this work of our hands upon us, prosper thou, O GOD, our handy work! I am now entering upon my spring campaign, and long for the time to embark for *Georgia*. This I believe will shortly come. Blessed be GOD, the work on this side increases daily. You will help me with your prayers, and you will remember me in the kindest manner to your collegue, your wife and dear congregation, and believe me to be, reverend Sir,

 Your most unworthy, but affectionate brother and
  fellow-labourer in the kingdom of our LORD,
          G. W.

LETTER DCCCLXXXVIII.

To Mr. H———ly.

Plymouth, March 30, 1751.

My very dear Friend,

I Am perfuaded you was furprized to find our elect Lady gone from *Afhby*, and I was as much furprized to fee her Ladyfhip at *Briftol*. I hope her journey was of GOD. The waters agree with her wonderfully already, and I truft fhe will be reftored to perfect health. As dear Mr. H—— cannot be prevailed upon to come down, if it would any way fuit you to be with her Ladyfhip a month, it would much refrefh her, and I believe be very agreeable to you. Some pulpits would be open for you, and who knows but you might catch fome great fifh in the gofpel net? But I need not enforce this, fince her Ladyfhip hath written to you herfelf. May the bleffed Redeemer direct your going in his way! Put up the fame requeft for me. I have thoughts of going to *Wales*, *Ireland* and *Scotland*. We have had good feafons in *Gloucefterfhire*, and at *Briftol*, and the LORD enabled me to fow fome gofpel feed at *Taunton* and *Wellington* in my way hither. O that ever fuch a wretch as I fhould be thus honoured!

> *If thou excufe,* LORD, *work thy will*
> *By fo unfit an inftrument ;*
> *It will at once thy goodnefs fhew,*
> *And prove thy power omnipotent.*

For the prefent adieu. It is a grief to me that I cannot write oftener and longer. I fuppofe the death of our prince has affected you. It has given me a fhock. "The LORD reigneth." That is our comfort. That he may reign more and more every day, and every hour, in our fouls, is the hearty prayer of, my very dear friend,

Yours moft affectionately,

G. W.

LETTER DCCCLXXXIX.

To Mr. M―――.

Dear Sir, Plymouth, March 30, 1751.

YOUR letter came safe to hand in due season, but I have been straitened how to answer it. I would write as I preach; I mean I would speak the truth as it is in JESUS, without endeavouring to blacken any denomination whatsoever. I think *Gamaliel*'s advice is good at all times, and in all ages, and our LORD's promise will be fulfilled, " That every plant that our heavenly Father hath not planted, shall be rooted up." This makes me to bear and forbear with many who widely differ from me both in principles and practice. This, as you observe, dear Sir, you may know by my poor discourses, and I find as yet no reason to alter my sentiments. I doubt not but there are many holy souls among the *M―――s*; but their not preaching the law, either as a *Schoolmaster* to shew us the need of CHRIST, or as a *rule of life* after we have closed with him, is what I can in no wise concur with. These seem to be two grand mistakes, and which with their various unscriptural expressions in their hymns, and several superstitious fopperies lately intruded among them, make me to think, they are sadly departed from the simplicity of the gospel. But to their own master they stand or fall. *Exitus acta probat.* My prayer for myself and all GOD's children is, " LORD JESUS, rectify all that is wrong, and bless and prosper all that is right!" I bless GOD, dear Sir, that you are appearing valiant for the truth. You will find more and more by happy experience, that to him that hath shall be given, and he shall have abundance. CHRIST never sends a person on a warfare at his own charges. Do not despair of Mr. G―――. As the love of GOD comes in, the fear of man goes out. By and by I trust he will set his face on a flint. It is high time for some to appear for JESUS. What pain did he endure? What shame did he suffer for us? Strange! that we should be so unwilling to go without the camp, to share with Him in his sacred reproach. Alas, what cowards are we! Dear Sir, let us pray for each other, that we may be strong in the grace which is in the CHRIST JESUS, and never fear what men and devils can say, or do unto us.

CHRIST is worth all, or he is worth nothing. I thank you for your invitation in his great name. If providence should bring me into the North, I hope to wait upon you. At present, I am bound for *Wales*. I have good news from abroad, and I believe the work is upon the advance at home. That you may be abundantly blessed, is the earnest prayer of, dear Sir,

Your affectionate though unworthy brother in CHRIST,

G. W.

LETTER DCCCXC.

To Mr. H——.

Exeter, April 11, 1751.

My very dear Mr. H——,

I Was pleased last night to find by my wife's letters, that your sister was delivered, and more so, because my wife wrote as though you was again under my roof. This I count a great honour, and such a privilege, that I wish to have the favour conferred on me as long as I live. These my hands (could they work, and was there occasion for it,) should readily minister to your necessities. If my wife should come down to *Bristol*, pray let not my dear Mr. H—— move. If *Molly* stays in *London*, she will take care of you; if not, *Polly* and Mr. D——n will gladly wait upon you. As I have been under some trying exercises for this month past, I have often wished to see you. But my blessed master hath given me access to himself, and he will make me more than conqueror through his love. I find *Luther*'s words truly applicable to myself, "He was never employed about any fresh work, but he was either visited with a fit of sickness or some violent temptations." Some good I trust is to be done this Spring to many souls. This Western circuit I believe hath been blessed already. I have preached about forty times since I left *London*, and have been enabled several times to ride forty miles in a day. I find that this sensibly refreshes me. I wish you could say so too;—your *Biddeford* friends would then see you.—They hold on their way, and long to have a line from you. Old Mr. W—— is dead. I providentially met Mr. T—— at his son's house. At *Plymouth* we had sweet seasons, and on *Tuesday* last I met with a young clergyman

man who was awakened under my preaching seven years ago. He hath been at *Cambridge*, and was ordained last Lent by the bishop of *Exeter*. He is followed much, and I suppose will soon be reproached for his master's sake. What cannot JESUS do? I hope you find that he gives you strength to proceed in your book. It is enquired much after. The LORD be with you, and bless your pen, and your heart. I send my hearty love to your brother and whole houshold, and am, very dear Mr. *H*——,

Yours most affectionately in our common LORD,

G. W.

LETTER DCCCXCI.

To Lady H———.

Dublin, May 30, 1751.

Ever-honoured Madam,

I Was uneasy that I had no opportunity of writing to your Ladyship a longer letter than my last, at leaving *Wales*; but it could not be avoided, and Mr. *P*—— (to whom I delivered your Ladyship's message) promises to supply my deficiency. I am now at *Dublin*, where I arrived the 24th instant. Mr. *L*—— gladly received me into his house, and I have been enabled to preach twice every day this week. Some seasons have been very powerful indeed, and the congregations increase daily. Last *Sunday* I believe ten thousand heard with great attention. After staying one LORD's day more, I shall set out for a month's circuit, and then purpose going to *Scotland*. I find that providence has wonderfully prepared my way, and over-ruled every thing for my greater acceptance. O that I could be more humble and thankful! Surely here are many converted souls, amongst whom are two or three students, and several soldiers. May the LORD JESUS add to their number daily such as shall be saved! I know not where this will find your Ladyship, but where-ever you are, my heart's desire and prayer to GOD is, that you may have a thriving soul in a healthy body, and be rewarded ten thousand fold for all favours conferred on, ever-honoured Madam,

Your Ladyship's most dutiful, obliged and
ready servant for CHRIST's sake,

G. W.

LETTER DCCCXCII.

To Mr. D———.

Dublin, June 1, 1751.

My very dear Friend,

I Fully proposed to have written to you from *Wales*, but was prevented by travelling and preaching. In about three weeks, I rode perhaps above five hundred miles, and preached generally twice a day. Congregations were as large as usual, and I trust an unusual power accompanied the word. After being about five days on the water, I arrived here the 24th ult. At first the greatness and hurry of the place surprized me; but thanks be to the LORD of the harvest, here as well as elsewhere the fields are white ready unto harvest. I have now preached about fourteen times, and find great freedom in dealing out the bread of life. Congregations are large, and hear as for eternity. Perhaps last LORD's day upwards of ten thousand attended. It much resembled a *Moor-fields* auditory. Next *Monday*, GOD willing, I leave *Dublin*, and set out on a circuit to *Limerick, Cork, Athlone, Waterford*, &c. I now lodge at a banker's, who purposes to come to *London* shortly. He is a follower of CHRIST, and will be glad of your acquaintance. I purpose giving him a letter. Have you heard nothing of Captain *Grant?* I long to hear of his arrival, because I would fain go over with him to *America*. Pray give me the first intelligence concerning him. A long journey is before me, but I would be at home every where, and yet never at home, till I come to heaven. There, the wicked will cease from troubling; there, the weary will be at rest. There, before men and angels will I declare how kind, yea exceeding kind, you and yours have been to, my very dear friend,

Yours most affectionately in our common LORD,

G. W.

LETTER DCCCXCIII.

To Lady H————n.

Athlone, June 10, 1751.

THIS morning I had the wished-for favour and honour of your Ladyship's lettter. O that it had acquainted me of your Ladyship's better health! But our LORD knows what

what is best. May patience have its perfect work, and your Ladyship come out of the furnace like gold tried seven times in the fire! Every day I can sympathise with your Ladyship. As the weather grows warmer, my body grows weaker, and my vomitings follow me continually. But all is little enough to keep me down, and prepare me for the service in which I am engaged. My last from *Dublin*, acquainted your Ladyship of my being owned of GOD there. By a letter from Mr. L――, I am informed, that *Dublin* is in a ferment, and that my hearers will be much more numerous at my return. Oh the blessedness of leaving all for JESUS! For this week past, I have been preaching twice almost every day in some country towns, and yesterday I sounded the gospel trumpet here. Every where, there seems to be a stirring among the dry bones, and the trembling lamps of GOD's people have been supplied with fresh oil. I find, through the many offences that have lately been given, matters were brought to a low ebb. But the cry now is, " Methodism is revived again."—Thanks be to GOD, that I have an opportunity of shewing my disinterestedness, and that I preach not for a party of my own, but for the common interest of my blessed master. May he keep me thus minded, and then I am sure all will go well at last. Your Ladyship would smile, to see how the wise have been catched in their own craftiness. O that this good news from a far country may prove a cordial to your Ladyship's soul! I pity your solitary state. I pity the deadness of all around you; but your Ladyship knows, whose brethren did not believe on him; it was even that GOD-man, who spoke a parable for this end, that men ought always to pray and not to faint. Happy trials, that drive us to our knees. Ever-honoured Madam, I could enlarge, but must not. Your Ladyship shall hear, GOD willing, how the glorious *Emmanuel* deals with me in *Ireland*. In the mean while, with the warmest sense of your Ladyship's unmerited favours, I subscribe myself, ever-honoured Madam,

Your Ladyship's most dutiful, obliged and
ready servant for CHRIST's sake,
G. W.

LETTER DCCCXCIV.

To Mr. Z———.

Honoured Sir, *Limerick, June* 14, 1751.

MY last was written on board the *Crawford*, and sent immediately upon my arrival at *Dublin*. Blessed be GOD, the word ran and was glorified there. I preached above fourteen times, and every day great multitudes attended. A friend, since my departure, writes me, that the city was in a ferment. For about a week I have been preaching twice a day in several country towns and villages. At *Athlone* I preached four times, and last night was gladly received here at *Limerick*. Every where our LORD hath vouchsafed us his blessed presence. That supports me under the heat of the weather, the weakness of my body, and the various trials which exercise my mind. I am now earnestly asking counsel from above. A wide door is open in *Dublin*; but after I have visited *Cork*, I believe I must cut short my circuit, lest I should have a winter's voyage. I should have been heartily glad to have heard from or seen you, but I trust, honoured Sir, you will have a heart given you to pray for me, and then, one way or another, my way will be made plain before me. Hitherto (thanks be to his free grace) my master supports and comforts me. He administers seed to the sower, and as far as I can hear, blesses it when sown. O that his mercies humbled me! O that I may never provoke him to leave me, or lay me aside! Some dreadful offences have been given in *Ireland*, but I trust all will work for good. My coming was very opportune and providential. May I learn to follow the Lamb blindfold, whithersoever he shall be pleased to lead me! Be pleased to remember me at his throne, and as he enables, you shall hear, from time to time, how he vouchsafes to deal with, honoured Sir,

Your most obliged, affectionate younger
brother, and unworthy fellow-labourer
in our LORD's vineyard,

G. W.

LETTER DCCCXCV.

To Lady H———.

Ever-honoured Madam, Cork, *June* 19, 1751.

STILL does the father of mercies, and the GOD of all consolation and comfort, follow me with his blessing. Since my last from *Athlone*, I have been at *Limerick*, where I preached seven times to large and affected auditories. Much freedom of spirit did I enjoy there indeed.—Yesterday I came hither (the seat of the late persecution) and thanks be to GOD, have preached twice to a great body of people, with all quietness. Both the Mayor and Sheriff have absolutely forbidden all mobbing. Now have the people of GOD rest. O that they may improve it, by walking in the comforts of the Holy Ghost! Next week, GOD willing, I shall return to *Dublin*, and from thence purpose going through the north of *Ireland* to *Scotland*. So long a circuit in this kingdom will be inconvenient for my voyage to *America*; but as divine providence seems to point out the way,

> *Lord at thy bidding I will go,*
> *And gladly to poor sinners tell,*
> *That they a blessed* CHRIST *may know,*
> *That they his peace and joy may feel.*

I hope your Ladyship enjoys a large share of this, under all your trials. They are great, but greater is he who hath promised to make his strength perfect in our weakness. I commit your Ladyship to his never-failing mercy, and beg the continuance of your fervent prayers in behalf of, ever-honoured Madam,

Your Ladyship's most dutiful, obliged,
chearful servant for CHRIST's sake,

G. W.

LETTER DCCCXCVI.

To Lady H———.

Ever-honoured Madam, Dublin, *June* 28, 1751.

MY last from *Cork*, informed your Ladyship of my having preached twice there to large and attentive auditories. From thence I went to *Bandon* and *Kinsale*, where a like

blessing attended the word. At my return to *Cork*, I preached five or six times more, and every time, both the power of the word and numbers of hearers increased. I believe on *Sunday* evening there might be more than three thousand people. Hundreds prayed for me, when I took my leave, and many of the papists said, " if I would stay, they would leave their priests." After preaching twice in the way, I came here on *Wednesday* evening, where I have again published the everlasting gospel. Next *Monday*, GOD willing, I set out for *Belfast*, and hope in about ten days to be in *Scotland*. From thence, by GOD's leave, your Ladyship shall hear from me again : but what return shall I make for your Ladyship's two kind letters? I can only repeat my old tribute, my poor but I trust unfeigned thanks. O for sincerity! O for a simple, disinterested heart. I think that low politics are below the children of GOD, and if we will be quiet, our LORD will speak for us. One to whom I had been represented in black colours, writes thus from *Dublin* to a preacher in *Cork*,—" What blessed seasons have we had since Mr. *Whitefield* came,—his coming hath been unspeakably blest to many. Thousands constantly attended the word. His word is attended with power. I never heard a man preach holiness of heart in a clearer manner.—He powerfully preaches CHRIST for us and in us. I confess I had strange ideas about him, but blessed be GOD, I have not now. GOD be praised that ever I saw his face, &c.———" Thus it hath been elsewhere. O that I was humble! O that I was thankful! Not unto me, O LORD, not unto me, but to thy free unmerited grace be all the glory?—May I learn more and more to leave all to GOD, even a GOD in CHRIST! If his cause be promoted, my end is answered. Let souls go where they please to hear, and welcome. Thanks be to JESUS for giving your Ladyship a disinterested catholic spirit. However afflicted, and in pain on earth, you shall shine ere long in the kingdom of heaven. CHRIST hath prepared a place for you, and is daily and hourly preparing your Ladyship for the place. I am glad you are like to have some company. I beg that my most hearty respects and acknowledgments may find acceptance with them and good Lady *H*———. I hope the waters will agree with the young Ladies. Above all, I pray that they, and the whole circle of your Ladyship's relations and friends, may drink
plentifully

plentifully of that water, whose streams refresh the city of GOD. I can now add no more, but to subscribe myself, ever-honoured Madam,

   Your Ladyship's most dutiful, obliged and
      ready servant for CHRIST's sake,
             G. W.

LETTER DCCCXCVII.

To Mr. T——.

Dear Mr. T——,   *Belfast, July* 4, 1751.

VERY providentially, your kind letter reached me this morning. As I am detained by the importunity of the people, I must snatch a few moments to answer it. Thanks be to the LORD of all Lords, if my poor administrations have been any ways blessed, either to you or others. "Not unto me, not unto me, but unto thy free and unmerited grace, O LORD, be all the glory!" Preaching CHRIST, I find to be the best means of winning sinners, and of building up saints. This done with a single eye and disinterested heart, will make its way through all opposition, and stand fast, when all other schemes built on a legal bottom, and supported by low politics, will fall to the ground. I wish you may have grace given you to act aright in your present circumstances. Let all bitterness and wrath and clamour be put away from you. Go on simply preaching the everlasting gospel; and if rejected for that, and freely discharged from your present connection, I shall do all in my power to promote your usefulness. I suppose, you will hear from other hands what hath been doing in *Dublin*. I hope the LORD of all Lords hath been with us. Thousands flock in this place also, to hear the word preached. I thought to have left *Belfast* to-day, but have complied with the people's earnest requests, to continue in these parts till *Monday*. O for a pilgrim heart with my pilgrim life! At present, I have no thoughts of nestling. Fain would I be kept from flagging in the latter stages of my road. I beg the continuance of your prayers. My prayer to GOD for you and yours is, "that you may live together as heirs of the grace of life, and walk in all the ordinances and commandments of the LORD blameless." You are entered upon a new scene, and will require more grace to act your parts well, than at present you may be aware of: But there is an all-sufficiency in CHRIST, who hath promised, that as our day is, so our strength shall be. I commend you and yours, and all the followers of CHRIST, to his never-failing mercy, and subscribe myself, for his great name's sake, dear Sir,

Your affectionate friend and servant,

G. W.

LETTER DCCCXCVIII.

To Lady H————n.

Ever-honoured Madam, *Belfast, July 7, 1751.*

LAST *Monday* about noon I left *Dublin*, but with what concern in respect to many poor weeping souls, cannot well be exprest. On *Wednesday* evening I came hither, and intended to embark immediately for *Scotland*, but the people by their importunity prevailed on me to stay. In about an hour's time, thousands were gathered to hear the word. I preached morning and evening, and since that have preached at *Lisburn*, *Lurgan*, the *Maize*, and *Lambag*, towns and places adjacent. So many attend, and the prospect of doing good is so promising, that I am grieved I came to the north no sooner. The country round about is like *Yorkshire* in *England*, and quite different from the most southern parts of *Ireland*. I am now waiting for a passage to *Scotland*, which I hope to get either to-morrow or on *Tuesday*. From thence your Ladyship shall hear from me again; in the mean while, having preached to many thousands again this morning, I must content myself with praying, that the best of blessings may descend on your Ladyship, and subscribe myself, ever-honoured Madam,

Your Ladyship's most dutiful,

obliged, and ready servant, &c.

G. W.

LETTER DCCCXCIX.

To the Reverend Mr. Z——.

Glasgow, July 12, 1751.

Reverend and very dear Sir,

AT length, a good and gracious GOD hath brought me out of *Ireland*, where to the very last, the people heard the gospel gladly. In the northern parts, multitudes attended, and was I not bound for *America*, I would have stayed there much longer. People flock here as usual, and I am enabled to preach twice every day. In about ten days I purpose moving towards *London* in order to embark. How my wife is, I cannot tell, having not heard from her for some time; but I hope she will be resigned. This, this is the cry of my soul,—

> *Bind, Father, hand and foot thy son,*
> *Nor leave thy work till all be done;*
> *O never let me,* LORD, *go free,*
> *Till all my heart's resign'd to thee.*
> *Then quickly to the altar lead,*
> *And suffer me no more to plead;*
> *No longer with the old* Adam *bear,*
> *Lead on, dear* LORD, *consume him there.*

Surely I shall be taken at my word. May JESUS support me in a trying hour! I still beg a continued interest in your prayers,—and hoping this will find you with a thriving soul in a healthy body, I subscribe myself, honoured Sir,

Your most obliged, affectionate, though unworthy
younger brother, in the glorious Gospel,

G. W.

LETTER DCCCC.

To Lady H——.

Ever-honoured Madam, Glasgow, July 12, 1751.

I Think it long ere I send your Ladyship another letter.— My last was from *Belfast*, where I preached twice on yesterday sevennight, and immediately after took shipping and arrived the next evening at *Erwin*. On *Wednesday* morning, at the desire of the magistrates, I preached to a great congregation, and ever since have been preaching twice every day in this city. Thousands attend every morning and evening. They seem never to be weary, and I am more followed than ever. Though I preached near eighty times in *Ireland*, and God was pleased to bless his word, yet *Scotland* seems to be a new world to me. To see the people bring so many bibles, turn to every passage, when I am expounding, and hang as it were upon me to hear every word, is very encouraging. I feel uncommon freedom of heart here, and talking with the winter, as well as summer saints, feeds and delights my heart. My body is kept pretty healthy, and my voice greatly strengthened, so that I think God is preparing me for more work, or that some trial is at hand. This I suppose will find your Ladyship yet in the furnace, but CHRIST is in the midst of the bush, and in the fiery furnace too; he will quench the violence of the flames, or cause the fire of his love to burn higher. I could enlarge, but am straitened. Some ministers wait for me. Your Ladyship would be delighted with our morning and evening auditories. This day in the church we have had a blessed feast. To-morrow I take my leave, and then for *Edinburgh*. There I expect to stay near a fortnight. Glad shall I be to hear of your Ladyship's welfare. You have always my poor prayers, and my poor, but hearty thanks; being, ever-honoured Madam,

Your Ladyship's most dutiful, obliged,
and ready servant, for CHRIST's sake,

G. W.

LETTER DCCCCI.

To Mr. M——.

Edinburgh, July 29, 1751.

THROUGH the tender mercies of a never-failing Redeemer, I came here safe yesterday noon. In the evening, and this morning, I preached the everlasting gospel to thronged auditories, and met with a very kind reception from my friends. LORD make me humble, LORD JESUS make me truly thankful! As his interest seems to be concerned, and the King's business requires haste, I take this first opportunity of writing about the *Virginia* affair. In that province, there has been for some years past, a great awakening, especially in *Hanover* county, and the countries adjacent. As the ministers of the establishment did not favour the work, and the first awakened persons put themselves under the care of the *New-York* synod, the poor people were from time to time fined, and very much harrassed for not attending on the church service:—And as the awakening was supposed to be begun by the reading of my books, at the instigation of the council a proclamation was issued out to prohibit itinerant preaching. However, before I left *Virginia*, one Mr. D—— (an excellent young man) was licensed, and settled over a congregation. Since that, the awakening has increased, so that Mr. D—— writes, " that one congregation is multiplied to seven." He desires liberty to license more houses, and to preach occasionally to all, as there is no minister but himself. This, though allowed of in *England*, is denied in *Virginia*, which grieves the people very much. The commissary is one of the council, and with the rest of his brethren, I believe no friend to the Dissenters. The late Lieutenant-Governor was like-minded.—I therefore think that Mr. D—— is raised up to succeed him, in order to befriend the church of GOD, and the interest of CHRIST's people. They desire no other privileges than what dissenting protestants enjoy in our native country. This I am persuaded your brother-in-law will be glad to secure to them. I shall write to Mr. D—— to wait upon his Honour immediately after his arrival. I pray the GOD of the sea, and the GOD of the dry land, to send him a safe and speedy passage, and make him a long and great blessing to the inhabitants of *Virginia*. You may improve these hints as you please. I beg the prayers both of yourself and dear yoke-fellow, and assure you, that neither you nor yours are forgotten by, reverend and dear Sir,

  Yours most affectionately in our common LORD,
            G. W.

LETTER DCCCCII.

To the Reverend Mr. Z——.

Honoured Sir,   *Edinburgh, July* 29, 1751.

SINCE I wrote to you from *Glasgow*, a never-failing JESUS hath vouchsafed to help me every day in preaching the everlasting gospel. The congregations morning and evening amount to many thousands. People flock more than ever, and are desirous of my longer stay, but I purpose moving next week. I thank you, honoured Sir, for paying my wife a visit. The inclosed letter I believe helped to make her sick; I have sent it with this: be pleased to keep it to yourself, and let me have the letter at my return. I little thought I was so much behind hand; but GOD will keep me dependent. " Having nothing, yet possessing all things," must be my motto still. Honoured Sir, I hear that a ship is going to *Georgia* with more *Saltzburghers*. Are you concerned? Could I go myself in her? Or could I send two or three little passengers? Mr. D—— shall call for an answer to these last questions. I trust, honoured Sir, you are enabled to pray for me. I dread coming to *London*, and think it would be best to part at a distance.—But, Father, not my will, but thine be done! In heaven these trials will be over. LORD, hasten thy coming! Come, LORD JESUS, come quickly! With difficulty I get time to write this. But whether I write or not, you and your collegue are never forgotten by, honoured Sir,

Yours, &c.
G. W.

LETTER DCCCCIII.

To Lady H————.

Edinburgh, July. 30, 1751.

Ever-honoured Madam,

I Think it a long time, since I last wrote to your Ladyship. Continual preaching twice a day, and paying and receiving visits, quite prevented my putting pen to paper, as I would have done. However, thanks be to GOD, matters go on in *Scotland* better and better. The parting at *Glasgow* was very sorrowful indeed. Numbers set out from the country, to hear the word, by three or four in the morning. Congregations increase greatly. I now preach twice daily to many thousands. Many of the best rank attend. My body is almost worn out, but in the LORD have I righteousness and strength. I purposed to move as to-morrow, but through the importunity of friends, have been prevailed upon to stay till next *Monday*. O that it may be for a further blessing! I have been to *Musselburgh* to see Captain G—— and his Lady.—They hold on.— Mr. W—— has been there, and intends setting up societies,

which

which I think imprudent. I was glad to hear that your Ladyship was strong in body, and rejoicing in your soul. The joy of the LORD shall be your strength. Letters from *Georgia* inform me, that my family is well. My eyes wait upon JESUS, from whom alone comes all my salvation. He gives me hints, that he will provide. I sometimes wish your Ladyship here. Such composed, thronged, continued, attentive, judicious auditories perhaps were seldom seen. Your Ladyship is often remembered by *Scotch* friends, and never forgotten by, ever-honoured Madam,

Your Ladyship's most dutiful, obliged,
and ready servant, for CHRIST's sake,
G. W.

LETTER DCCCCIV.

To Lady H———n.

Ever-honoured Madam, *Kendal, Aug.* 10, 1751.

AS a good and gracious GOD hath vouchsafed to bring me thus far on my way, I cannot help dropping your Ladyship a few lines. Preaching, bodily weakness, and a variety of business, prevented my writing again before I left *Edinburgh*. O *Edinburgh! Edinburgh!* Surely thou must never be forgotten by me! The longer I stayed, the more eagerly both rich and poor attended on the word preached. Perhaps for near twenty-eight days together in *Glasgow* and *Edinburgh*, I preached to near ten thousand souls every day. It would have melted your Ladyship's heart to have seen us part. Ninety-four pounds were collected for the *Edinburgh* orphans, and I hear of seven or eight students awakened about ten years ago, that are likely to turn out excellent preachers. Praise the LORD, O my soul.—Two of them came with me on the road, and parted with broken hearts. Lord and Lady L——behaved very respectfully. To the LORD of all Lords be all the glory! I am now on my way to *London*, in order to embark for *America.* Thanks be to GOD, the seed sown in *Kendal* last year hath sprung up, and borne fruit. One woman hath been with me, that seems to have received GOD's pardoning love. I leave it on *Monday*, and hope to be in town on *Saturday*. Glad should I be, to hear of your Ladyship's welfare. I threw up much blood in *Edinburgh*, but riding recruits me.

O that I may begin to work for Him, who bled and died for me! To his most tender mercies do I humbly recommend your Ladyship, and beg leave, from the very bottom of my heart, to subscribe myself, ever-honoured Madam,

Your Ladyship's most dutiful, obliged and
chearful servant, for CHRIST's sake,

G. W.

LETTER DCCCCV.

To the Reverend Mr. T———.

My very dear Friend, London, *Aug.* 29, 1751.

AT length the struggle is over;—I have been dying daily for some time, in taking leave of friends; and this afternoon I expect to go on board the *Antelope*, Captain *Maclelan*, bound for *Georgia*, with *Germans*.—I take several children with me.—Surely you will see the *American* land.—Mr. *E———*, with your other friends, seem to concur in thinking that a little travelling would do you service.—May the LORD direct and bless you! Will you not write to me by *Cowan*? If my dear friend Mr. *P———* could speak to that brewer that is so well disposed, and he or any other would send in *Cowan* a little good beer, it would be acceptable in yonder wilderness.—Pray what says Mr. *W———*? If he should agree to go over, Mr. *W——— R———* may be applied to for cash.—I have several sweet little ones to put under his care;—GOD's will be done in this also! He reigneth, that is my unspeakable consolation.—By next ship I believe will come a parcel directed to Mr. *T———*, with a folio book, and an hundred pictures of *Aaron* the *Indian* preacher, from good Lady *H———*, who is yet but poorly.—Sixty may be disposed of among *Edinburgh* friends, and forty sent to Mr. *M———*. The book you are to peruse, and then it must go with the pictures to *Glasgow*.—Be pleased to apprize Mr. *T———* of it, and desire him to send me a line by *Cowan*.—If possible, I will answer Mr. *B———* before we leave the *Downs*. My tender love and thanks await your dear father, family, and all friends. The LORD be with you all, Amen and Amen! My horses sold for fourteen pounds. GOD reward my benefactors! Perhaps Mr. *T———* and Dr. *Doddridge* may go off about the same time. *I præsequar.* Mr. *H———* is better. And now, my dear Sir, farewel! Be strong in the grace which is in CHRIST JESUS. I commend you to his never-failing mercy, and, for his great name's fake, fubfcribe myfelf,

Yours moft affectionately,
G. W.

LETTER DCCCCVI.

To the Reverend Mr. G——.
On board the Antelope, Sept. 2, 1751.

Reverend and very dear Sir,

THOUGH I could not, through hurry of bufinefs, write to you on fhore, yet I would fain fend you a few lines from on board. We are now near the *Downs*, and, I truft, fhall fail comfortably on.—The Captain is civil; and the cabin paffengers feem to be very agreeable company. Parting feafons of late have been to me dying feafons.—Surely they have broken my very heart: but it is for JESUS, and therefore all is well. Remember, my dear, dear Sir, a floating pilgrim.—If poffible, fend me a line.—Young Mr. T——r knows how to direct. I fhall rejoice to hear of your profperity. Before my embarkation, I ordered forty of *Aaron*'s pictures, and the folio book concerning the *Moravians*, to be fent to Mr. M———. They will be committed to the care of Mr. T——, in *Edinburgh*. And now, my dear Mr. G——, farewel, farewel! The LORD be with you and Mr. M———, Mr. N——, Mr. S——, and all my dear, very dear *Glafgow* friends. I falute you all much in the LORD, and beg the continuance of your moft earneft prayers in behalf of, very dear Sir,

Yours moft affectionately in our bleffed JESUS,
G. W.

LETTER DCCCCVII.

Dear Sir,   *On board the Antelope, Oct. 6, 1751.*

I Have been juft writing to one, to whom I know you will gladly convey the inclofed. I muft now fend you a few lines: may the Redeemer attend them with his bleffing! At the great day, you fhall know how often you have been remembered by me at the throne of grace, this voyage. Blessed be GOD, hitherto it has been a short and easy one! We are now within a few hundred miles of shore; and He that hath hitherto helped, I trust will help us even to the end. O that the blessings bestowed upon us, may, through the thanksgiving of many, redound to thy glory, O GOD! O that I could do something to promote this! As yet alas! alas! how little have I done! Stir up then, my sluggish soul, and begin to exert thyself for Him, who hath shed his dear and precious heart's blood for thee! O my dear Sir, is it not strange that we should forget this love? Strange, that a little silver dust, should blind our eyes, and divert us from beholding Him, who indeed is altogether lovely! A word to the wife is enough. Our LORD hath dealt wonderously kind with each of us, with us, and with ours. What shall we render unto him? My obligations are much increased by the mercies of this voyage. Your kind present was very useful. I pray the LORD of all lords to reward you ten thousand-fold. You will remember me to your dear partner, and all enquiring friends. That grace, mercy, and peace may be multiplied on you all, is the earnest prayer of, dear Sir,

Yours most affectionately in our common LORD,

G. W.

LETTER DCCCCVIII.

To Mr. J—— T——.

Bethesda, in Georgia, Nov. 20, 1751.

My dear Mr. T——,

ERE this can reach you, I suppose you will have heard of our safe arrival in *Georgia*; for which, I trust, you and my other dear friends will be thankful in our behalf. Blessed be GOD, I found the Orphan-house in as good a situation as could be expected. The children have much improved in their learning; and I hope a foundation is now laid for a future useful seminary. I want to know what answer Mr. *W*——'s hath given. I expect letters by *C*——, when I go to *Charles-town* next month. I was there about ten days ago, and had some close talk with Mr. *L*——, and several of Mr. *S*——'s congregation concerning you. All seemed to be unanimous,

nimous, in giving you a call. I need only obferve, that if GOD fhould direct your courfe to them, you will find a generous, loving people, who will ftudy to make your labours profitable and delightful to you. I doubt not but in the congregation there are many dear children of GOD. And as there will be fuch an harmony between you and Mr. L———, I hope you will be an happy inftrument of promoting peace between all parties, and adding fuch to the church as fhall be finally faved. Very near you, are feveral pious minifters of other denominations, who will be glad to keep up a chriftian correfpondence with you, and ftrengthen your hands in the work of the LORD. As far as I can judge of your difpofition, and all other concurring circumftances, your fituation will be very agreeable to others, and to yourfelf. However, a trial can do no hurt to either fide. A voyage to fea, and the feeing and converfing with many of GOD's people and minifters on this fide the water, will make it worth your while to leave your native country. Travelling improved, will enlarge your ideas, and promote your future ufefulnefs. May the glorious *Emmanuel* direct your goings in his way! If it fhould appear to be the divine will that you fhould come over to *Charles-Town*, I am perfuaded, the good old man your father will chearfully let his *Benjamin* go; and he will find his bleffed Mafter to be better to him than feven fons. Pray falute him and all dear friends in the kindeft manner. I would write to many, but as yet have not time. Brethren, pray for us. My very dear friend,

Yours moft affectionately in our common LORD,

G. W.

LETTER DCCCCIX.

To Mr. K———.

Charles-Town, Dec. 26, 1751.

My dear Mr. K———,

MAY this find you getting out of your eclipfe, and determining, through the ftrength of CHRIST, that the earth fhall never get in between your foul and the Son of Righteoufnefs any more! What mercies, fignal mercies hath the LORD JESUS conferred on you and me! What fhall we render unto the LORD? Shall we not give him our whole hearts?

hearts? O let us not follow afar off. Let his love constrain us to an holy, universal, chearful obedience to all his commands. You have a wife that will provoke you to love, and to good works. Make much of her; and present her, and your mother, and all her children, with my most cordial salutations. I do not forget them, or you, or dear Mr. R——. For CHRIST's sake forget not unworthy me. I am now returning to the Orphan-house, which I trust will be like the burning bush indeed. My poor labours are accepted here; and in the Spring I purpose going to the *Bermudas*. JESUS is very good to me. Help me to praise him; and believe me to be, my dear Sir,

Your affectionate friend for CHRIST's sake,

G. W.

LETTER DCCCCX.

To Mr. William L——.

Very dear Sir, *Bethesda, Jan* 25, 1752.

MAN appoints, but GOD disappoints. Though we missed seeing each other on earth, yet if JESUS CHRIST be our life, we shall meet never to part again in the kingdom of Heaven. Your kind letter found me employed for the fatherless, in this wilderness, and am almost ready to enter upon my Spring campaign. The news from *Ireland*, does not at all surprize me. Weak minds soon grow giddy with power; and then they become pests, instead of helps to the church of GOD. You have done well, dear Sir, not to desist from doing good, on account of some rubs you meet with in the way. *Benefacere et male pati, vere christianum est.* Go on, therefore, to lay up treasures in heaven; and let the world see, that you have been with JESUS, by imitating him in going about doing good. I intend, by his assistance, now to begin; for as yet alas! I have done nothing. Continue to pray for me; and be pleased to assure our *Irish* friends, that they are not forgotten by me. Who knows but I may see them once more on this side eternity? As soon as possible, some of them shall hear from me. Thanks be to GOD, the Orphan-house flourishes. That the work of CHRIST may flourish amongst all persons of all denominations, and that you and yours may be always abounding

ing in the work of the LORD, is the earnest prayer of, very dear Sir,

Yours most affectionately in our common LORD,

G. W.

LETTER DCCCCXI.

To the Rev. Mr. H———.

My very dear Friend,   *Charles-Town, Feb.* 1, 1752.

I Long to write to, and inform you, that I love you in the bowels of JESUS CHRIST, and earnestly pray, that you may go on from strength to strength, and increase with all the increase of GOD. This leaves unworthy me, endeavouring to do something for Him on this side the water. Glory be to his great name, he causes his work to prosper in my worthless hands. The Orphan-house is in a flourishing way, and I hope will yet become a useful seminary. My poor labours in this place meet with acceptance; and after one more trip to *Georgia*, I purpose setting out upon my Spring campaign. Follow me with your prayers; and who knows but we may meet once more on this side heaven. Our dear Mr. *H———* I find is to be detained longer from thence. I think he will live to bury many stronger men. I wish *Lisbon* may be blessed to Dr. *D———*; and O how do I wish that dear Dr. *S———* was fully employed in preaching the everlasting gospel! Pray salute him tenderly in my name, and beg him to renounce the world for CHRIST. I hope you both write to, and see our good Lady *H———n* frequently. I was rejoiced to hear, from my dear yoke-fellow, that her Ladyship was bravely: this was joy indeed. May she long live to be a blessing! That is all in all. O that I may begin to be in earnest! It is a new year; GOD quicken my tardy pace, and help me to do much work in a little time! This is my highest ambition. The LORD JESUS fill me with this ambition more and more! For the present, adieu. Accept this as a token of your not being forgotten by, reverend and very dear Sir,

Yours most affectionately in our dear LORD JESUS,

G. W.

LETTER DCCCCXII.

To Mr. S—— C——.

Charles-Town, Feb. 5, 1752.

AS I love you most tenderly in the bowels of JESUS CHRIST, you may easily guess, what great pleasure both your kind letters gave me. They came attended with a great blessing, and knit my heart, if possible, nearer to you than ever. Part of the first, indeed, I mean that which respected the Tabernacle-house, gave me uneasiness; but your last removed it, and made me thankful to our common Redeemer, who in spite of all opposition, I find will cause his word to run and be glorified. Poor Mr. *W*—— is striving against the stream; strong assertions will not go for proofs, with those who are acquainted with the divine life, and are sealed by the Holy Spirit even to the day of redemption. They know, that their stock is now put into safe hands; that the covenant of grace is not built upon the faithfulness of a poor fallible, changeable creature, but upon the never-failing faithfulness of an unchangeable GOD. This is the foundation whereon I build. " LORD JESUS, I believe, help my unbelief! Having once loved me, thou wilt love me to the end; thou wilt keep that safe, which I have committed unto thee: establish thy people more and more in this glorious truth; and grant that it may have this blessed effect upon us all, that we may love thee more, and serve thee better!" All truths, unless productive of holiness and love, are of no avail. They may float upon the surface of the understanding; but this is to no purpose, unless they transform the heart. This, I trust, the dear Tabernacle preachers and people will always have deeply impressed upon their minds. Let us not dispute, but love. Truth is great, and will prevail. I am quite willing that all our hearers shall hear for themselves. The Spirit of CHRIST is a Spirit of liberty. You remember what I have often told you about *Calvin*. He was turned out of *Geneva* for several years; but in less than twelve years time they wished for their *Calvin* again. But what is *Calvin*, or what is *Luther?* Let us look above names and parties; let JESUS, the ever-loving, the ever-lovely JESUS, be our all in all.—So that he be preached, and his divine image stamped more and more upon people's souls, I care not who is uppermost. I know my place, (LORD JESUS enable me to keep it!) even to be the servant of all. I want not to have a people called after my name, and therefore I act as I do. The cause is CHRIST's, and he will take care of it. I rejoice that you go on so well at the Tabernacle. May the shout of a king be always in the midst of you, and the glory of GOD be your reward. I am apt to believe you will pray me over. But future things belong to him, whose I am, and whom I endeavour to serve. After one more trip to the Orphan-house, I purpose going to the *Northward*, where I expect more letters by Captain *Grant*. Thanks be to GOD, all is well at *Bethesda*. A most excellent tract of land is granted to me very near the house, which in a few years I hope will make a sufficient provision for it. Pray give my tenderest and most hearty love to all your dear family, and all the Tabernacle people, and all enquiring friends. Entreat them, I pray you, to be mindful of a poor pilgrim, who night and day is never unmindful of you or them. Doctor *Doddridge* I find is gone; LORD JESUS prepare me to follow after!—With real and great affection, I subscribe myself, very dear *Jemmy*,

Yours, &c.
G. W.

LETTER DCCCCXIII.

To Mr. J—— H——.

My very dear Friend,   London, *May* 26, 1752.

HEARING that Mr. N—— is to go shortly from *Leith*, I cannot help sending you a few lines. They leave me at *London*, where, through the divine goodness, I am safely arrived, after a passage of near five weeks on board the *Henry*. People have received me with great affection; and I never saw the work of GOD go on in a more promising way. Thousands and thousands hear the gospel gladly. LORD, what am I? Not unto me, not unto me, but unto thy free grace and unmerited mercy be all the glory! I wish I could send you good news about your minister. But alas! I now almost despair of procuring one. I waited upon Dr. G—— immediately after

after my arrival;—he gave me no hopes. The person that was fixed upon, declined it. Several of the large congregations in *London*, besides many more in the country, are without pastors: they are obliged to make use of our preachers. O that the LORD of the harvest may thrust out more labourers into his harvest! Who can tell but some ministers may be raised up at *Bethesda?* At *Midsummer* the King takes *Georgia* into his own hands: blessed be GOD for sending me over at such a juncture. He hath given me already good success concerning Mr. B———'s scheme. I am come to a determination, if I can dispose of *Providence* plantation, to carry all my strength to the Orphan-house. May the LORD JESUS prosper more and more this work of our hands upon us! Prosper thou, O GOD, this handy work! I trust he will. I could enlarge, but have not time. You may expect to hear from me again by Dr. B———, whom I expect to see next week. Your *Rapin* is bought, and shall be sent with the other; I thank you for the loan of it, and for all other favours. The GOD whom I serve, will richly reward both you, and all my other dear *Charles-Town* friends. My very dear Sir, cease not to pray for

Your most affectionate, obliged friend,
and ready servant for CHRIST's sake,
G. W.

LETTER DCCCCXIV.

To Mr. T———.

My dear Mr. T———,   *London, June* 4, 1752.

I Doubt not of your being directed in your late choice. If we acknowledge GOD in all our ways, he hath promised to direct our paths. I pity poor *Carolina*. But what shall we say? JESUS may do what he will with his own. I must look out for a tutor for my orphans. When our LORD's time is come, some one or other will be stirred up to care for these sheep in yonder wilderness. Blessed be GOD, it begins to smile. You will see by the inclosed, what a prospect I have of providing for *Bethesda's* future support. The letter was sent me by Mr. *J——— B———*, a worthy christian planter, who is lately come from *Carolina* to settle in *Georgia*. He was

awakened

awakened at the Orphan-house about ten years ago. At *Midsummer*, *Georgia* is to be taken into the Government's hands. It will then be put on the same footing with the other provinces; and in all probability will be a flourishing province. I am come in the very best time. O what a blessed thing is it to follow JESUS blindfold! He hath enabled me once more to take the field. The fields seem as white as ever; and I never saw the Tabernacle so well attended. If GOD should so direct me, would the middle of *August* not be too late to come to *Edinburgh*? I cannot well come before. Does Mr. R—— go directly for *Charles-Town*? How will he be paid for the Offnaburghs he was so kind as to send over? I would fain send a few letters by him. My hearty love to him and his. Ten thousand thanks to you, for caring so friendly for my dear wife in my absence.—The LORD JESUS will care for you and my other kind friends. She is pretty well, and joins in sending cordial respects and thanks.—My young man returns his. Letters from those you mention, will be very acceptable. I hope to write to several shortly. I must now away; but not before I have wished Mr. *Gillespie* joy. The Pope I find has turned Presbyterian. O this power, when got into wrong hands, what mischief does it occasion! "The LORD reigns:"—that is enough for us. Adieu. My love to your honoured father, and all dear friends. Accept the same in the tenderest manner from, my dear *Timothy*,

Yours most affectionately in our common LORD,

G. W.

LETTER DCCCCXV.

To Mr. H——.

My very dear Friend, London, *June* 9, 1752.

I Have received and read your manuscripts; but for me to play the critic on them, would be like holding up a candle to the sun. However, before I leave town, I will just mark a few places as you desire, and then send the manuscripts to your brother. I foretell their fate: nothing but your scenery can screen you. Self will never bear to die, though slain in so genteel a manner, without shewing some resentment against its artful murderer. I am glad you have written to *South-*

Audley-

Audley-street. You are resolved not to die in my debt. I think to call your intended purchase WESTON, and shall take care to remind him by whose means he was brought under the everlasting gospel. O that Doctor S—— may be brought out to preach it! If you do not take the other living yourself, I think your giving it to the Doctor is a glorious scheme. I lay at your brother's house last week: your sister seemed to love to talk of JESUS CHRIST and her own heart. She got up early, and came after me and my wife to Madam T——'s. You know how to improve this hint at a proper season. Your brother hath been so kind as to let me have the little mare again. My Master walked, I ride to preach the glorious gospel. Whether riding or walking, LORD JESUS, let my whole heart be taken up with thee! Adieu, my dearest Sir, adieu. Cease not to pray for,

Ever yours whilst
G. W.

LETTER DCCCCXVI.

To Dr. S——.

My dear Doctor, *London, June 9, 1752.*

GLAD shall I be to hear that you are a poor despised preacher of the everlasting gospel. I long to direct *to the Reverend Mr. S——*. I believe if you once was gone so far that you could not retreat, you would do very well. If Mr. H—— does not take the two livings, I think your scheme is glorious. May the LORD thrust you out some way or another! I am sure the harvest is great: people seem more eager than ever to hear the word. May I die preaching! Next *Thursday* se'nnight I leave *London*, and purpose to take a long circuit. I should be glad to see you in the mean while. O that the love of CHRIST may burn all the love of the world out of your heart! Adieu. Never fear the Bishop: let your eye be only on the great Shepherd and Bishop of souls! He will make your way plain. I must away. Business obliges me to hasten to subscribe myself, dear Sir,

Yours, &c.
G. W.

LETTER DCCCCXVII.

To Lady H——.

Ever-honoured Madam, London, *June* 12, 1752.

THIS day about noon I received your Ladyship's wished-for letter, which brought me the welcome news of your Ladyship's safe arrival at *Bath.* May the waters be abundantly blessed to the restoring of your bodily health, and may the comforts of the ever-loving, ever-lovely JESUS, fill and refresh your soul! Your Ladyship judges right of dear Mr. Z——: he is a blessed man, a father in CHRIST indeed? I hope to see both him and your Ladyship, about the twenty-fourth of this month. Next week, GOD willing, I shall go to *Portsmouth,* from thence to *Bath,* then to the West, then to *Wales*; and from thence, may be, to *Scotland* and *Ireland.* O that I could fly from pole to pole publishing the everlasting gospel! Every day we hear of fresh conquests gained. Grace! Grace! Yesterday I had several pleasing particulars told me about *Georgia.* The having my work so divided, is a great trial to me; but what is undertaken for GOD, ought to be carried on for him. He can and will do wonders for those who put their trust in him. O for faith, precious faith! It is all in all. Old times seem to be coming about here. My body is much enfeebled, but the joy of the LORD is my strength. Hoping shortly to see your Ladyship prospering both in soul and body, and begging a continual interest in your Ladyship's prayers, I subscribe myself, ever-honoured Madam,

Your Ladyship's most dutiful, obliged,
and ready servant for CHRIST's sake,
G. W.

LETTER DCCCCXVIII.

To Mr. I——.

Dear Mr. I——, London, *June* 16, 1752.

YOUR last letter brought strange things to my ears, and put me upon considering how to act. You know, my dear friend, that I hate to head a party, and that it is absolutely inconsistent with my other business, to take upon me the care of societies in various parts. I therefore cannot promise to come to *Ireland* for that purpose, neither do I ever intend to engage in building any houses. My intention is to come your way, but whether it will be this summer or not I cannot tell. Mr. *A——* was very desirous of seeing you and his sister, and goes through *Wales* to *Ireland*. As you seem to have taken *Skinner's Alley*, I suppose he may preach there, and if a larger place could be procured, I doubt not of its being filled. The LORD direct you how to act, so as most to promote his glory, and the good of souls.—I hope you will all, if possible, avoid the very appearance of a party spirit, and evidence to the world, that the principles we hold are indeed of GOD, by their moulding us more and more into the divine image. This is indeed all in all. I hope the people here are in a growing way. Glory be to GOD, we have happy days. What shall we render unto the LORD? All he requires, is our poor hearts. May he have them without reserve! My hearty love to your wife, Mr. *C——* and his wife, and all that love CHRIST JESUS in sincerity. If I am prayed over, come I must. The LORD be with you. I am so wearied by preaching, &c. that I can scarce subscribe myself, my dear friend,

Yours most affectionately in our common LORD,

G. W.

LETTER DCCCCXIX.

To Mr. L——.

Dear Sir, *Portsmouth, June* 19, 1752.

YOUR kind letter I received immediately after my last return to *Scotland*, but I was so exceedingly busied in preparing for my voyage to *America*, that I had not time to answer it. Being once more unexpectedly brought back to my native country, I send my sincere, though late acknowledgments, and hope this will find you and yours, fighting the good fight of Faith, and resolved never to desist, till you have laid hold on eternal life. Let not what has happened, draw off your mind from the Captain of your salvation. He is altogether lovely, and worthy of your highest regard. But alas! All his servants, even the best of them, are but weak fallible men at the best. Happy they, who by seeing the imperfections of the creature, are led to adhere more closely to

the

the all-sufficient and most adorable Creator. If you and yours are taught this lesson by past occurrences, you will have no reason to complain, but on the contrary will be excited to praise him, who causes, that out of the eater there shall come forth meat, and out of the strong shall come forth sweetness. Be pleased to accept this in love. I send my most cordial respects to your whole self and family, and beg their and your prayers in behalf of, dear Sir,

Your affectionate friend and ready
servant, for CHRIST's sake,
G. W.

LETTER DCCCCXX.

To Mr. T——.

My dear Friend, *Portsmouth, June* 19, 1752.

I Thank you for your very kind letter, and thank the LORD of all Lords for honouring dear Mr. G——. Now he will do more good in a week, than before in a year. Where the carcase is, there the eagles will be gathered together. Last *Monday* we sung for him the following lines;

> *Give him thy strength, O God of power,*
> *Then let winds blow, or thunders roar;*
> *Thy faithful witness shall he be,*
> *'Tis fixed—he can do all through Thee.*

How blind is Satan! What does he get by casting out CHRIST's servants? I expect that some great good will come out of these confusions. We wait for thy salvation, O LORD! I hope your soul prospers. I long to see you, and my other *Scotch* friends, but question whether I can come this summer. The LORD direct me to act as shall be most conducive to his glory and the good of souls! We have had blessed seasons in *London*; there I must be again in about a fortnight. On next *Tuesday* the Trustees give up *Georgia* to the King; the King of Kings has appeared for *Bethesda*. I cannot think of seeing it again, till next year. In the mean while you must pray that I may be busy for CHRIST. And in so doing you will strengthen the hands of, my dear, dear friend,

Yours, &c.
G. W.

Very dear Sir, Bristol, *July* 13, 1752.

I Am quite sorry to hear that you are so much indisposed. But what shall we say? The LORD JESUS orders all things well. He knows of what we are made; he remembers that we are but dust. As our day is, so shall our strength be. I see more and more, that, like our great Exemplar, we must be made perfect through sufferings. Ere long, the time of reigning will come, and one sight of the ever-loving, ever-lovely JESUS, will make amends for all. O glorious prospect! Well might the apostle say, " that the sufferings of this present time, are not worthy to be compared with the glory that shall be revealed in us." *O gloriam quantam et qualem!* Courage then, my dear Sir; he that cometh will come, and will not tarry. I dare not give vent; business obliges me to be short. Here, as well as at *London*, the fields are white, ready unto harvest. This week I pass over to *Wales*. I am a poor, but happy pilgrim. Thanks be to free grace for it. My dutiful respects await good Lady *Jane*, and the young Ladies. Be pleased to accept the same from, very dear Sir,

Yours most affectionately in our common LORD,

G. W.

LETTER DCCCXXII.

To Mr. S——.

My very dear Friend, Cardiff, *July* 17, 1752.

WHEREVER I am, you and yours, you and your kindnesses, are always upon my heart. I think of them at my down-sitting and mine up-rising, and to refresh myself, must express my gratitude. Indeed I thank you both ten thousand times, and as a poor tribute, I send you word that the LORD of all Lords is pleased to smile upon, and bless my feeble labours. I was at *Bristol* four days, and preached nine times. To my great surprize, thousands (very near as many as attended at *Moorfields*) came out every evening to hear the word. A blessed influence attended it; and I have

reason

reason to believe much good was done. Old times seemed to be revived again. Praise the LORD, O my soul! The last evening it rained a little, but few moved. I was wet, and contracted a cold and hoarseness; but I trust, that preaching will cure me again. This is my grand Catholicon. O that I may drop and die in my blessed master's work!

> *For this let men revile my name,*
> *I'll shun no cross, I'll fear no shame;*
> *All hail reproach, and welcome pain;*
> *Only thy terrors, LORD, restrain.*

I am now entering upon *Wales*. What success my Master gives me, you may hear some time hence. I beg your prayers, that I may be kept from robbing GOD of his glory, or of any more of my precious time. What said my dear Mr. S—— when I saw him last? What!—" You the biggest robber? No, no,—I am the man." But thanks be to GOD, as you observed, " our judge is our advocate." I thank you for the hint. The LORD give me to improve it! Farewell! I must soon away, to preach about eight miles off. We have had a comfortable meeting this morning. My tender love to dear Mrs. S—— and your little daughter; accept the same in the most endearing manner from me, who in the strongest terms that words can express, am, my very dear friend,

Yours most affectionately in our common LORD,

G. W.

LETTER DCCCCXXIII.

To Lady H———.

Haverford-west, July 25, 1752.

Ever-honoured Madam,

AS this is the first day of rest from journeying, since my coming into *Wales*, and also the extent of my *Welsh* circuit, I must not omit sending your Ladyship a few lines. They inform your Ladyship of the continued goodness of my blessed master, to the most unworthy servant he ever sent forth. As my day, so hath my strength been. Abundance of souls, especially in *Pembrokeshire*, have attended; and I hope that seed hath been sown, which will spring up to eternal life. On *Monday* next, I shall begin to return back, and some time this day sevennight hope to wait upon your Ladyship at *Clifton*. On the following day, I propose to preach at *Bristol*, and the next day shall set out for *Gloucestershire*, to keep an association there. The LORD help me to hold on and hold out unto the end! I dread the thoughts of flagging in the latter stages of my road. JESUS is able to keep me from being either weary or faint in my mind. In him, and in him alone is all my strength found. I hope your Ladyship finds both your bodily and spiritual strength repaired day by day. That you may mount on wings like an eagle, walk and not be weary, hold on and not be faint, is the continual prayer of, ever-honoured Madam,

Your Ladyship's most dutiful,
obliged, and ever ready servant,
G. W.

LETTER DCCCCXXIV.

To Mr. R—— W——.

Dear Sir, *Haverford-west, July* 25, 1752.

I Love and honour you too much, to have let yours lie so long unanswered, had not travelling and preaching prevented me. This is the only quiet day that I have had for a long season. At *London*, the work seemed to be as it were but just beginning. At *Bristol* we had blessed seasons indeed, and in *Wales* the fields are white, ready unto harvest. Had I not been pre-engaged in these parts, I should certainly have come, and mounted my despised throne. I love state too well, especially in *Scotland*, not to take it upon me as often as possible. I think sometimes, that it is almost a pity one cannot have more bodies and more souls. They should all run about, and be employed for JESUS. What an honour to be employed in doing or suffering for him? Happy Mr. G——; I fancy he must preach quite well now. I dare say, you had no hand in casting him out; GOD forgive those that had. In heaven there will be none of this stuff. Thanks be to GOD, the church is militant only here below. The LORD help us to fight the good fight of Faith, till we lay hold on life eternal! Dear Mr. H—— hath taken up his weapons again; he is now Rector of a parish, and preaches twice every Lord's day. I thank you and yours, for your kind invitation of us to your

pleasant

pleasant villa; had I wings I could fly thither to talk of JESUS, and sing an hymn, but the cloud seems to move westward, and I fear my visit to beloved *Scotland* must be deferred till next spring. May the LORD enable me to fill up every hour, every moment with duty! I believe dear Mr. R—— had a narrow escape the other day: if with you, pray remember me to him and his, in the kindest manner. I most heartily salute all enquiring friends, beseeching you all, for JESUS CHRIST's sake, never to cease praying for, reverend and very dear Sir,

Yours most affectionately in our common LORD,

G. W.

LETTER DCCCCXXV.

To Mr. S——.

My very dear Friend,   *Bristol, August* 1, 1752.

SINCE I wrote my last, I have been off my horse but one day. The glorious *Emmanuel* hath carried me through the *Welch* circuit in peace and comfort. In the fortnight past, from my leaving this place, I preached twenty times, and have travelled above three hundred miles. Congregations were very large. Last Lord's day was a high day indeed; the number of hearers at seven in the morning, as well as in the evening, at *Haverford-west*, was almost incredible. The LORD was in the midst of them. My body was weak in speaking to them, but JESUS hath strengthened me again. O that I was humble and thankful! In my way hither, we held an association; there were present about nine clergy, and near forty other labourers. I trust all are born of GOD, and desirous to promote his glory, and his people's good. All was harmony and love. Yesterday I came here. It is fair time, and to-morrow, GOD willing, I purpose to expose the gospel wine and milk to sale. This I have been doing this morning. O that the hearers may be made to come down to the price, and willing to be saved by grace:—GOD knows I have nothing else to depend upon.

> *Grace!—it's a sweet, a charming theme,*
> *My soul exults at* JESU's *name;*
> *Of him, who did salvation bring,*
> *I could for ever speak and sing.*

But

But how poorly do I speak of and for him? GOD be merciful to me a sinner? He does show he will have mercy, and therefore it is that I am not consumed.

If all the world his goodness knew,
They must adore and love him too.

Blessed be GOD for manifesting himself to us, as he doth not unto the world! You will join in crying Grace! Grace! Grace! Love bids me to enlarge, though business obliges me to be brief. In about ten days I hope to be in *London*. In the mean while, pray accept these poor lines as a token of love unfeigned, and of grateful respect, from, my very dear friend,

Yours most affectionately in our common LORD,

G. W.

LETTER DCCCCXXVI.

To Mr. F——.

Dear Mr. F——, *London, Aug.* 17, 1752.

INCLOSED you have a letter for Mr. R——. I hope that promotion will do him no hurt. May GOD help him to make a stand against vice and prophaneness, and to exert his utmost efforts in promoting true religion and virtue! This is the whole of man. I find that you grow more and more famous in the learned world. As you have made a pretty considerable progress in the mysteries of electricity, I would now humbly recommend to your diligent unprejudiced pursuit and study the mystery of the new-birth. It is a most important, interesting study, and when mastered, will richly answer and repay you for all your pains. One at whose bar we are shortly to appear, hath solemnly declared, that without it, "we cannot enter the kingdom of heaven." You will excuse this freedom. I must have *aliquid Christi* in all my letters. I am yet a willing pilgrim for his great name sake, and I trust a blessing attends my poor feeble labours. To the giver of every good gift be all the glory. My respects await your whole self, and all enquiring friends, and hoping to see you yet once more in this land of the dying, I subscribe myself, dear Sir,

Your very affectionate friend, and obliged servant,

G. W.

LETTER

LETTER DCCCCXXVII.

To Mr. S——.

Chester in the street, near Newcastle, Aug. 28, 1752.

My very dear Mr. S——,

THUS far hath a good and gracious GOD brought a poor and worthless pilgrim on his way towards *Edinburgh*. Last Lord's day I preached twice at *Lutterworth*, the famous *John Wicliffe*'s parish, and have since received a letter giving me an account of the Redeemer's blessing my poor labours. On the *Monday*, I began in the name of the almighty husbandman, to plow up some fallow ground at *Leicester*; several thousands attended, and some endeavoured to disturb us, but the opposition was nothing like what I expected. In the evening all was hushed, and I trust our LORD left a blessing behind us. In my way to *Lutterworth*, my heart was encouraged by the coming of a young man, who had been awakened under my preaching about four years ago at *Oulney*. He was before that time a bitter scoffer, but hath now been a student for a year and a half under Doctor *Doddridge*, and I believe will be admitted into the *London* academy. You may know more of him hereafter. Is not this as much as to say, " Go forwards.—In the morning sow thy seed, and in the evening with-hold not thy hand, since thou knowest not which may prosper, this or that." Yes, my blessed JESUS, through thy grace strengthening me, I will continue to go out into the highways and hedges; only vouchsafe to uphold me with thy right hand, and keep me from flagging in the latter stages of my road. I know you will say, *Amen* and *Amen*. This will increase my obligations, which are already more than I can express. GOD will reward both you and yours for them, a thousand fold. Accept repeated thanks for repeated favours, and depend on hearing as often as possible, how the ever-lovely, ever-loving JESUS is pleased to deal with, my very dear Sir,

Yours most affectionately in our common LORD,

G. W.

LETTER DCCCCXXVIII.

To Mr. B——.

Newcastle, Aug. 30, 1752.

My dear Mr. B——.

YOUR laſt kind letter came to hand, only a few days before I left *London*. Buſineſs prevented my anſwering it then: accept a few lines from hence. They leave me on my way to *Scotland.* Thither the cloud ſeemed to move, and I purpoſe to call on you, GOD willing, in my return to *London.* Could you meet me at *Leeds?* I have thoughts of coming that way back. I have written to Mr. *S——,* and as I expect to ſee him, you need ſay nothing about the books. I wrote alſo to Mr. *G——.* A ſhort interview will ſettle every thing. Do not let my friend be ſo ſolicitouſly anxious about perſons or things. "The LORD reigneth," was the anſwer that *Luther* ſent to over-careful *Melancthon.* Never fear.—Our LORD knows how to over-rule all for good. So that his work goes on, let you and I be content to be forgotten, nay to be trodden under foot, and ſlighted by our own ſpiritual children and friends. This is bitter, but wholſome phyſic. The all-wiſe phyſician I truſt will make us drink it, till every evil, fretful, and uneaſy temper be purged out of us. Let us then, my dear man, chearfully take the cup out of his bleſſed hands, and leave all to Him. A word to the wiſe is enough. I muſt not enlarge. How goes on brother *W——b?* I hope he does not preach in a controverſial way; I ſuppoſe I ſhall ſee him in the North. My ſtay in *Scotland* will be about a month. You may direct for me at *Edinburgh.* I hope that a door is opened at *Leiceſter* and *Lutterworth* for field-preaching. We have had glorious ſeaſons in *Glouceſterſhire* and *London.* O for a good gate in the North! It is harveſt time.—All hands to work. My love to Mrs. *B——* and all that love CHRIST, whether they think in all things as I do or not. I ſend Mr. ——*ly* my cordial reſpects, and beg you to accept the ſame from, my dear Mr. *B——,*

Yours, &c.

G. W.

LETTER DCCCCXXIX.

To Lady H——.

Edinburgh, Sept. 22, 1752.

Ever-honoured Madam,

THE day after I wrote to your Ladyship, I left *London*, and in my way to *Scotland* I preached twice at *Lutterworth*.—The auditories were very numerous, and very quiet; but at *Leicester* some turnips were thrown at me during the first sermon; at the second all was hushed, and I hear since that good was done. Some of *Ashby* society came thither to hear me. At *Aberford* I called on Lady *Margaret*, who behaved very friendly, and enquired much after your Ladyship's welfare. At *Newcastle* I was, as it were, arrested to stay. I preached four times, and indeed a whole shower of divine blessings descended from heaven on the great congregations. I came hither last *Wednesday* was sevennight, and have preached twice a day in the open air, to very large and polite auditories. Abundance of the better sort constantly attend. Next *Tuesday* I thought to move, but they have prevailed upon me to stay a little longer. I hope the great GOD will give me a useful journey back again to *London*. I design keeping from thence as long as I can, before I go into my Winter quarters. Alas, how little is to be done even in the Summer season! One had need work whilst it is day; the night comes on apace, when no man can work. I need not tell your Ladyship of this, who are always employed for your GOD. O that the rich and great would learn to copy after your example! Surely all your Ladyship's efforts will not be lost upon them! My heart's desire and continual prayer to the LORD of all Lords is, that your Ladyship may be long continued, and find your rod budding and blossoming more and more every day. Hoping to send your Ladyship more good news in my next, and commending my poor unworthy self to your Ladyship's prayers, I beg leave to subscribe myself, ever-honoured Madam,

Your Ladyship's most dutiful, obliged and very ready servant for CHRIST's *sake,*

G. W.

Glasgow, Sept. 29, 1752.

My very dear friend,

AS you are no day out of my thoughts, so you must needs think it hath seemed a long time since I wrote to you last. But what has hindered me? Not want of love, but opportunity. For this fortnight last past, I have been preaching twice every day at *Edinburgh*, where a great multitude, as well of polite as common sort of people, attended continually. I wondered they were not wearied, but the more they heard, the more they seemed desirous of hearing. Many young ministers and students were close attendants, and I trust through grace good has been done. I expected to have left *Scotland* as last *Tuesday*, but through the importunity of friends have been prevailed on to come to *Glasgow*, and shall not return for *England* till *Tuesday* sevennight. Then I hope to begin to preach my way up to *London*. In this blessed delightful work, I hope to live and die; I think it is worth dying for. The LORD make me sensible of the honour put upon me, and lay me lower at his feet every day, every hour, and every moment! I have here a flaming minister that is my friend, and I hear sweet work is going on in the highlands. Praise the LORD, O our souls! Inclosed you have a letter from the young student mentioned in my last. I think it is a pity that such a youth, when pious students are so much wanting, should go back to business for want of a little help. I doubt not but the LORD will provide for him some way or other. He generally brings those low, whom he intends to exalt, and make use of. I have glad tidings from *Newcastle* and *Leicester*. Methinks every thing concurs to bid me go out into the highways and hedges.

> LORD, *at thy command I'll go,*
> *And unto sinners gladly tell,*
> *That they a risen* CHRIST *may know,*
> *That they the love of* CHRIST *may feel.*

This is a heaven upon earth. Of this, I pray the GOD of love to give you and yours a double portion. I know you pray for me. I send you and your dear yoke-fellow ten thousand thanks, and am, my very dear Sir,

Yours most affectionately in our common LORD,

G. W.

LETTER DCCCCXXXI.

To Madam C———.

Dear Madam,   *Glasgow, Sept.* 29, 1752.

IT is no small pleasure to me, that providence hath once more opened a way for a further correspondence with one, who for many years hath been my friend, and strengthened my hands in the work of our common LORD and master JESUS CHRIST. He will richly reward you for it in the great day of accounts; though I am persuaded you think the work itself, its own reward. Indeed it is. Blessed be GOD, I find CHRIST's service to be perfect freedom. He hath vouchsafed to encourage and comfort me in *Scotland.* At *Edinburgh* great multitudes, among whom were abundance of the better sort, attended twice every day. After a short continuance here, I am to return to *Edinburgh,* and next *Tuesday* sevennight purpose to set out for *England.* Many young ministers and students have given close attendance, and I hear of several persons that have been brought under deep convictions. As soon as they are put into my hands, I intend to send you copies of two letters from a High-land schoolmaster, who is honoured of GOD to do much good among the poor Highland children. —By this post I have also sent a letter to Mr. *D*———, which I received from a young student; he wants some little assistance, to help him to go on in his studies, but I did not send his letter to you, because he informs me that you had taken one of Mr. *G*———'s spiritual children under your care. Blessed be GOD, that makes you, Madam, a mother in *Israel.* Every student's name is Legion. Helping one of those, is helping thousands. I think this young man's case, as laid down in the letter, is very remarkable, and matter of praise. LORD JESUS add to the blessed number, for thy great name's sake! I have brave news sent me from *Leicester* and *Newcastle,* and have strong invitations to *Yorkshire* and *Lancashire.* What a pity is it, that the year goes round so soon? O my GOD, my GOD in CHRIST, how little can I do for thee! Dear Madam, be pleased to increase my obligations by praying for me. I never forget you or your houshould, and as a proof of it, promise that you shall hear at all opportunities, from, dear Madam,

Your most affectionate, obliged friend,
and ready servant for CHRIST's sake,
G. W.

LETTER DCCCCXXXII.

To Mr. A———.

Dear Mr. A———,   *Glasgow, Sept.* 29, 1752.

I Received your kind letter, but till now have not had time to answer it. However, I have not, and, GOD willing, shall not be unmindful of you. I think you have nothing to do, but by prayer and supplication with thanksgiving, to make your wants known unto GOD. He careth for you, and will some way or other provide both for soul and body. I have always found him a present help in every time of need. As means ought to be used, I have just written to some *London* friends, who under GOD may serve you. When we meet, you shall hear what success.—The hearts of all are in CHRIST's hands. Wait on him, and your eyes shall behold his great salvation. If he calls you to the ministry, as I hope he does, he will make your way plain. The cloud of his providence shall go before you, and you shall hear a voice behind you, saying, "This is the way, walk in it." Though your father should die, and your mother forsake you, the LORD JESUS CHRIST will take you up. Keep close to your GOD, and your book. Prayer, reading, meditation, and temptation make a minister. The LORD be with you. Pray for me, and assure yourself of my being, for CHRIST's sake,

Your affectionate friend and ready servant,
G. W.

LETTER DCCCCXXXIII.

To G—— P——, Esq;

Dear Sir,   *Glasgow, Sept.* 30, 1752.

MR. S——, in a letter, insists upon my sending you a few lines: I care not to refuse him, and yet I know not well how to use so much freedom. If it be too great, you
will

will excuse it; it proceeds from love, love to your better part, for I have nothing to write about, but the invisible realities of another world. These I trust, dear Sir, you and yours will be experimentally acquainted with more and more every day. Herein lies all our present peace, and the only solid preparation for future comfort in the coming world. The love of JESUS shed abroad in the heart by the Holy Ghost, is indeed all in all; this is glory begun; this is the opening of the kingdom of heaven in the soul; this is a never-failing well of water, which will at last spring up to life eternal. And yet all this is the gift, the free gift of GOD in CHRIST JESUS. It cost him dearly, even his own heart's blood, but flows down to us in a free channel; yea and that too even to the very chief of sinners. Therefore I have hope, and, blessed be GOD, good hope through grace. Is not the same grace, dear Sir, sufficient for you and yours? Let us then come boldly to CHRIST's throne. He sits encircled with a rainbow; his name and his nature is Love. He came into the world, to seek and save those that feel themselves lost; this I trust you do. Salvation then is just coming to your soul, even a present and great salvation. Only believe, and yours is the kingdom of heaven. But whither am I running? I forget myself when writing of redeeming love. O, my dear Sir, do not rest, do not let GOD have any rest, till your heart is filled with it. It is worth asking, seeking, knocking, and striving for. But I must have done. My cordial respects await your Lady. That you may both go on hand in hand to heaven, is the hearty prayer of, dear Sir,

Your affectionate friend and ready
servant for CHRIST's sake,
G. W.

LETTER DCCCCXXXIV.

To Lady H———n.

Newcastle, Oct. 15, 1752.

Ever-honoured Madam,

THUS far hath a never-failing Redeemer brought me in my way towards *London.* With all humility and thankfulness of heart I desire to set up my *Ebenezer:* for surely hitherto hath the LORD helped me. Since my writing last to your Ladyship, I went and preached for about a week at *Glasgow*, where the word of the LORD ran and was glorified. I preached twice a day, and rather more attended than at *Edinburgh*. We had a sorrowful parting at both places. For about twenty-eight days, I suppose I did not preach to less than ten thousand every day. This hath weakened my body, but the Redeemer knows how to renew my strength. At present, I am as well as a pilgrim can expect to be. About seventy pounds were collected for the *Edinburgh* orphans, and I hear that near a dozen young men that were awakened about ten years ago, have since entered upon the ministry, and are likely to prove very useful. Praise the LORD, O my soul!—In my way hither, I preached at *Berwick*, *Alnwick* and *Morpeth*; and next *Monday*, after preaching at *Sunderland*, as is intended, I am to go into *Yorkshire*. I know your Ladyship wishes me much prosperity. That your Ladyship may prosper more and more, and be in health both in soul and body, is the continual prayer of, ever-honoured Madam,

Your Ladyship's most dutiful, obliged,
and ready servant for CHRIST's sake,
G. W.

LETTER DCCCCXXXV.

To Mr. S——.

Sheffield, Nov. 1, 1752.

My very dear Friend,

SINCE I left *Newcastle*, I have scarce known sometimes whether I have been in heaven or on earth. At *Leeds*, *Burstall*, *Howarth*, *Hallifax*, &c. thousands and thousands have flocked twice and thrice a day to hear the word of life. A gale of divine influence hath every where attended it. I am now come from *Bolton*, *Manchester*, *Stockport* and *Chinly*. —Yesterday I preached in a church, where I believe execution was done. Four ordained ministers, friends to the work of GOD, have been with me. The word hath run so swiftly at *Leeds*, that friends are come to fetch me back, and I am now going to *Rotheram*, *Wakefield*, *Leeds*, *York*, and *Epworth*, and purpose returning to this place next Lord's day. GOD favours us with weather, and I would fain make hay whilst the sun shines. My dear Sir, pray follow me with your prayers.

Fain would I spend and be spent for the good of souls. This is my meat and drink. The LORD bless you and yours! I can no more, but only subscribe myself, my very dear friend,

Yours most affectionately in our common LORD,

G. W.

LETTER DCCCCXXXVI.

To the Reverend Mr. Z———.

Wakefield, Nov. 3, 1752.

Reverend and very dear Sir,

I Have been upwards of three weeks out of *Scotland*, but scarce ever had more encouragement in preaching the everlasting gospel, since the LORD of the harvest was pleased to send me forth into the harvest. At *Newcastle, Sunderland,* and several places in *Yorkshire, Lancashire,* and *Cheshire,* thousands and thousands have daily attended on the word preached. The glorious *Emmanuel* caused life and power to follow it, and I hear that the arrows have stuck fast in many hearts. The stir hath been so great at *Leeds,* that at the desire of friends, I am returning thither again. From thence I shall go to *York,* and several places in *Lincolnshire,* and am to preach at *Sheffield* next Lord's day. My return to *London* must be determined by the weather. It hath been uncommonly favourable, and methinks it is pity to go into Winter quarters, so long as work can be done in the fields.—O that I had as many tongues, as there are hairs upon my head! The ever-loving, ever-lovely JESUS should have them all. Be so good, honoured Sir, to pray that he may not turn me out of his service, but employ me as a poor pilgrim till I die. Fain would I die preaching.—I hear that Mr. *H——* is gone. The LORD JESUS quicken my tardy pace, and prepare me to follow! I know you say *Amen* in my behalf, and thereby add to the obligations you have already laid upon, honoured and dear Sir,

Your most affectionate, though unworthy son
and servant in the glorious gospel,

G. W.

LETTER DCCCCXXXVII.

To Mr. S——.

My dear Friend, London, *Nov.* 11, 1752.

THROUGH the good providence of an ever-lovely, ever-loving Redeemer, I came safe hither last night. My *Sunday's* work, sickness, the change of weather, and affecting parting from friends, so enfeebled this tottering tabernacle, that I was in hopes on the road the imprisoned soul would have been set at liberty, and fled to those blissful regions,

Where pain, and sin, and sorrow cease,
And all is calm and joy and peace.

At *Northampton* I took coach, and am now, blessed be GOD, arrived at my Winter quarters. My poor wife I found an invalid. Our LORD can restore her, for he came to heal our sicknesses, and bear our infirmities. I hope this will meet my dear friend and his wife leaning on this all-sufficient, never-failing *Emmanuel.* I have remembered you ever since my departure, and now, with groanings that cannot be uttered, pray that your souls, and the souls of all the dear people around you, may prosper and increase with all the increase of GOD. O, my dear friend, what manner of love is this, that we should be called the sons of GOD! Excuse me. I must pause a while.—My eyes gush out with water. At present they are almost fountains of tears. But thanks be to GOD, they are tears of love. O what shall I do for Him who hath loved and given himself for ill and hell-deserving, ungrateful, unfruitful me! Add to my obligations by praying for me! My unfeigned love to Mr. *L——.* If I can, he shall soon hear from me. With the box for Mr. *G——,* I shall send a few pictures, which you may present to Mr. and Mrs. *N——,* as you think best. O that the blessed and divine image of the adorable JESUS may be stamped in most lively colours on all our hearts! It will, it will. JESUS is the author, and he is also the finisher of our faith. Let us not be faithless but believing. Let us not trust in ourselves, but in him who hath promised never to leave nor forsake us. I can no more.

The LORD be with you and yours.—My hearty love to all that love CHRIST JESUS in sincerity; accept the same in the most tender manner from, my very dear friend.

Yours most affectionately in our common LORD,

G. W.

LETTER DCCCCXXXVIII.

To Mr. J——.

My dear Friend, London, *Nov.* 11, 1752.

LAST night the glorious *Emmanuel* brought me hither, after having given me and his dear people many blessed seasons in *Scotland*, and the North of *England*. O that with all his other mercies, he may vouchsafe to give me a thankful and humble heart! This morning I have been talking with dear Mr. J——, and cannot help thinking, but that you have run before the LORD, in forming yourselves into a public society, as you have done. I was afraid poor Mr. C—— would not do. Mr. A——'s visit was designed to be transient, and I cannot promise you any settled help from hence. I am sincere, when I profess, that I do not choose to set myself at the head of any party. When I came last to *Ireland*, my intention was to preach the gospel to all.—And if it should ever please the LORD of all Lords to send me thither again, I purpose to pursue the same plan. For I am a debtor to all of all denominations, and have no design, if I know any thing of this desperately wicked and deceitful heart, but to promote the common salvation of mankind. The love of CHRIST constrains me to this. Accept it as wrote from that principle. That He, who is the wonderful counsellor, may in all things direct and rule your hearts, is the earnest prayer of, my dear friend,

Yours most affectionately,

G. W.

LETTER DCCCCXXXIX.

To the Reverend Mr. H——.

My very dear Friend, London, *Nov.* 14, 1752.

I Am quite sorry that I missed seeing you, but glad and thankful that you condescended to write to me. I find you are resolved to outdo me in love; this I would prevent if possible. May the glorious JESUS shed abroad his love abundantly in your dear heart, by the Holy Ghost, and give you to increase with all the increase of GOD. He will bless you for vindicating the honour of his sacred volumes in your last pamphlet, for which, as well as for all other unmerited favours, I most heartily thank you. I have just now read it, and doubt not of its being greatly blessed and owned, and going through many editions. I cannot discern any errata or inaccuracies in the composition. Surely GOD hath raised my dear friend up, to let the polite world see how amiable are the doctrines of the gospel. Why will you weary the world, and your friends, by delaying to publish your other long wished-for performance? Glad shall I be to peruse any of the dialogues. The favour of the last is not of my mind. Pray let them see the light this Winter. They will delight and warm many a heart. O that we may have a warm season at the Tabernacle! My country circuit was exceedingly delightful. When the weather altered, my health was much affected; but a little rest hath already in some degree repaired it. You and I perhaps are not to see heaven as yet: I have waited for it long, but alas! my appointed time is not yet come. Thanks be to GOD, there is such a thing as having a heaven upon earth; CHRIST in us is the heaven of heavens. My dear, very dear friend, good night. I am called away. My love to the Doctor. O that he was wise! How glad should I have been to have seen dear Mr. *H——!* My kind respects await your mother and sister. My wife, who is quite an invalid, joins heartily with me, who am, my very dear Sir,

Yours most affectionately in our common LORD,

G. W.

LETTER DCCCCXL.

My dear Nat,   London, *Nov.* 21, 1752.

YOUR letters have all been brought safe to hand, and have given me no small satisfaction. I doubt not but the LORD, whom you seek, will in his own time come and visit the temple of your heart. Fear not, neither be dismayed. Be found in the way of duty; go on feeding his lambs, and you shall find, that the great Shepherd and Bishop of souls will bless and comfort you. I know not of a more profitable situation, that you could be in than at present. Next year, GOD willing, you will have a fellow-student. I have agreed with him, as I wrote you from *Edinburgh*, for three years at least. I am of your mind in respect to boarders. As affairs stand, I think the less the family is at present, the better. Nothing seems to be wanted but a good overseer, to instruct the negroes in sawing and planting. Let me know how Mr. *M*——behaves, and whether the Lumber trade is begun. I have consented to Mr. *E*——'s going to Mr. *Z*——, and to *Margaret*'s leaving *Bethesda*. You will see what I have wrote to Mrs. *W*——. Pray make *George* and the children to write often. He should not have written to me, *Honoured Master*, but—*Sir*. I am glad to hear that some of the children promise well. Surely some good will in the end come out of that institution. I am only afraid of its growing too great one day or another, in a worldly way. O that I may be directed to such managers, that will act with a single eye to GOD's glory, and his people's good! I have great confidence in you. I am glad you live in peace. May the Prince of peace cause his grace and mercy to be multiplied upon you! I shall be glad to live to see you a preacher. It is a delightful employment, when done out of love to JESUS: that sweetens all. In about ten weeks I have travelled above a thousand miles, and was enabled to preach sometimes twice and thrice a day to many thousands. I trust a great blessing was left behind with the word preached. O that *Georgia*'s wilderness may blossom like 'a rose! It will, when GOD's set time is come. Never mind a few evil reports. No one need be ashamed of *Bethesda* children. Blessed be GOD, they are taken care of, and the LORD will reward you. Ah my dear *Nat*, you are highly honoured. I hope you often bow down before the blessed Redeemer, and out of the fulness of your heart say, "Why me, LORD? why me?" Pray, pray, I beseech you continually, that you may be cloathed with humility. How many young men have I known ruined for the want of it! "GOD resisteth the proud, but giveth grace unto the humble." Pray that I may have an humble and thankful heart. I would vie with a seraph, if I could, in humility and thankfulness. Adieu. The LORD be with you! My wife sends her love; accept the same from, my dear *Nat*,

Your most assured friend for CHRIST's sake,

G. W.

LETTER DCCCCXLI.

To Mr. V—— B——.

London, Nov. 22, 1752.

My dear Mr. V—— B——,

I Hope this will find you and your yoke-fellow parents of a living and well formed child. May the Redeemer sanctify it from the womb, and cause it to live to his glory, and your comfort! I see you are taught to live more and more by faith. This may be tried, but never disappointed. The LORD JESUS never did, and never will forsake those who put their trust in him. I believe Mrs. H—— will not suffer you or yours to want any thing that *Bethesda* affords. I thank you for your kind offer, but suppose ere now you have been enabled to purchase some negroes, and go upon your own land. If not, I have written to Mr. B—— to make what agreement you shall mutually judge to be most proper: I cannot say more at this distance. It is hard to determine any thing four thousand miles off. GOD willing, I hope to see you next year; though it is difficult to leave thousands and ten thousands, who gladly receive the gospel, to come to a wilderness, where it has been, alas! too, too often most wretchedly despised, and slighted by many. But I trust we shall yet see better times. Happy they who have learned to live on JESUS; and by keeping up a daily and hourly fellowship with him, can maintain a comfortable frame, when all is cold and dead around them. This is the happiness I wish my dear Mr. B———. May it increase day by day, moment after moment! Then, if we never should see each other again on earth, we shall meet, never to part again, in the kingdom of heaven. I am endeavouring to call as many thither as I can. Power seems to attend it, and many seem to have their faces set *Zion-ward.* May they and we be kept from looking back! JESUS is able to keep us. To his almighty never-failing mercy do I commend you, as being, my dear Sir, for CHRIST's sake,

Your most affectionate friend, brother, and servant,

G. W.

LETTER DCCCCXLII.

To Mr. L———.

My dear Friend,   London, *Nov.* 28, 1752.

YOUR letter came safe to hand yesterday. The contents of it humbled and gladdened me, and led me directly to my knees, to intercede for you and yours, and all the dear people at *Leeds,* who are either seeking after, or have actually found redemption in the blood of JESUS. Many here, blessed be GOD, are in like circumstances. Our LORD seems to ride triumphantly on in the chariot of his everlasting gospel; and the shout of a king is indeed amongst us. Blessed are the eyes that see the things which we see. What shall we render unto the LORD? Our two mites, a vile body, and a sinful soul, are all that he requires: and shall he not have these? Yes, I trust the language of both our hearts is this:

> *Be gone, vain world, my heart resign,*
> *For I must be no longer thine;*
> *A nobler, a diviner guest,*
> *Now claims possession of my breast.*

As this is your case, I wonder not at your being so solicitous for your dear children's welfare. The LORD give you faith and patience, and help you in every respect so to behave, that you may win them over to the choice of true and undefiled religion! Courage, my dear brother, courage.—Who knows, but they may be made willing in a day of the Redeemer's power? He that hath given your dear yoke-fellow a heart to seek after the pearl of great price, can make your children like-minded. But faith must be tried, patience must be exercised, and our stubborn will brought into a chearful resignation to the holy sovereign will and good pleasure of GOD.

> *What though thou rulest not,*
> *Yet heaven, and earth and hell*
> *Proclaim GOD sitteth on the throne,*
> *And ordereth all things well.*

A variety of business prevents my enlarging. I should not have troubled you with such a speedy answer, had you not seemed to desire it, as a token of my love. I think it is cordial and unfeigned. None of you are forgotten by me before the throne. There, my dear friend, let us meet often. Remember it is a throne of grace; we may, therefore, come with boldness. JESUS is our advocate, even JESUS CHRIST the righteous. I thank you ten thousand times for all respect shewn me for his great name's sake, and command you (since love will make you wait for orders) to believe me to be, my dear Sir,

Your very affectionate friend, brother, and ready servant in our common but dearest LORD,

G. W.

LETTER DCCCCXLIII.

To Mr. ———.

My dear Friend, London, *Dec.* 5, 1752.

HOW does love meet love! Your long expected letter came last night, and as the box of books hath been gone some days, I answer you before day this morning. My dear friend, good-morrow! Blessed be GOD, that the day dawns, and that the day-star hath risen in your heart. May the Redeemer give you a *Benjamin*'s mess every hour! He is our great *Joseph,* and loves to say to his guilty brethren, "Come near me." Out of his fulness we may all receive even grace for grace. O how does he continually watch over us for good! I thought the obstructions that lay in my way to *York,* were
not

not for nothing. Our times are in our LORD's hands. We are immortal till our work is done. This, this shall be the cry of my soul:

> LORD, *at thy command I'll go,*
> *And to the world will gladly tell,*
> *That they a risen* CHRIST *may know,*
> *That they the love of* CHRIST *may feel.*

Assured of such a bidding, we may say with *Luther,* "If there was as many devils lying in wait, as there are tiles on the houses, we need not fear." Who knows but in Spring we may have a fair field fight? We can do all things through CHRIST strengthening us. Methinks I long to range in your parts, and come to *Leeds* again. The persons mentioned need not bid me to remember them. I cannot forget either them or you night or day. O that we may make some large advances in the divine life, before we see each other. When will that be? Perhaps in Spring; perhaps not till we meet in heaven.

> *There we shall see* CHRIST's *face,*
> *And never, never sin;*
> *There, from the riches of his grace,*
> *Drink endless pleasures in.*

Hasten, LORD, that blessed time! Till then, grant us, we beseech thee, an heaven upon earth! Such we have at the Tabernacle indeed. Last Lord's-day we had, if possible, a more blessed sacrament than the former.

> *How sweet, how awful was the place,*
> *With* CHRIST *within the doors,*
> *When everlasting Love display'd,*
> *The choicest of his stores!*

I must break off this delightful subject. Farewel. Pray for us. Remember me in the kindest manner to all. My wife heartily joins with

Yours, &c.
G. W.

LETTER

My dear Brother, London, Dec. 9, 1752.

IF your heart was full, so was mine when we parted. Such seasons make me long for that happy time when we shall neither part from each other, nor depart from the blessed Jesus any more. Our wanderings and tossings, fightings without, and fears within, will then all be over. Here the church is, and will be militant; in heaven it shall be altogether triumphant. Let us go on, my dear brother, fighting the good fight of faith. Ere long we shall be called to lay hold on life eternal. CHRIST is our captain; we are therefore assured of conquest.

A feeble saint shall win the day,
Though death and hell obstruct the way.

Endeavour to obstruct they will, and young converts little know how resolutely, how unweariedly. The way to heaven is a round-about way: we must go through a wilderness. GOD suffers this, to prove and try us, and to shew us what is in our hearts. Humility must be taught us, as *Gideon* taught the men of *Succoth*, with briars and thorns: these will frequently fetch blood from the old man. O that we may be made willing to have him bleed to death! " Away with him, away with him; crucify him, crucify him." May this be the language of your heart and mine! To have this prayer answered, what trials must we necessarily meet with from the devil, the world, the flesh, and even from GOD's own children? All little enough to lead us into that mortified, pacific, resigned, and disinterested mind, which was in CHRIST JESUS. The more we suffer, and the less we are esteemed for doing, or attempting to do good for his great name's sake, the more we are conformed to his blessed example. In heaven, justice will be done to all. Strange! that we cannot wait more patiently till the great day of retribution. LORD, help us to walk more by faith, and less by sense! " Help, O help us to leave ourselves and all with thee." I know you will say, *Amen!*" But I forget myself. How willingly does the pen write, when

when love, love for CHRIST's sake dictates and indites! I thank you for enquiring after my welfare: thanks be to GOD, I am as well as a poor, but happy pilgrim can expect to be. The shout of a king is amongst us. The glory of the LORD fills the Tabernacle; and we hear every day of persons brought under fresh awakenings, as well as of GOD's people being comforted. We have had two most awful sacramental occasions. Help me to cry, Grace! grace! I shall be glad to hear that the gospel runs and is glorified at *Wakefield*. Who knows but the last may be yet first? Is any thing too hard for the LORD? Continue to remember us at the throne of grace; and accept this speedy answer as a token of respect and love unfeigned, from, my dear brother,

Yours, &c.

G. W.

LETTER DCCCCXLV.

To Lady H————n.

Ever-honoured Madam, London, *Dec.* 15, 1752.

I Think it a long time since I heard from, or wrote to your Ladyship. My hands are full of work; and I trust I can say, the LORD of all lords causes his work to prosper in my unworthy hands. More blessed seasons we never enjoyed. Our sacramental occasions have been exceedingly awful and refreshing. I cannot help crying out night and day, Grace! grace! Last week we had another repast in *South Audley-street*. Lady F—— grows surprizingly. She increases much in the knowledge of herself, and of JESUS CHRIST. May she and all that profess to love him, increase with all the increase of GOD! I have glorious news from *Yorkshire*. Inclosed your Ladyship hath a letter, which I hope will please you. Ships will be going to *Philadelphia* soon after *Christmas*. Has your Ladyship read the awful account of the hurricane in *South-Carolina?* I do not find that it hath reached *Georgia*. Happy they who have laid up treasure in heaven, and have fled to CHRIST for refuge; such are safe from every storm. This is your Ladyship's happiness; and blessed be GOD, this is the happiness of unworthy, ill, and hell-deserving me. LORD, why am I a guest?

Through

Through all eternity to Thee,
A grateful song I'll raise;
But O eternity's too short,
To utter all thy praise.

Business prevents my enlarging.—I commend your Ladyship, and all your concerns, to the tender mercies of a never-failing Redeemer; and beg leave to subscribe myself, with all possible gratitude and respect, ever-honoured Madam,

Your Ladyship's most dutiful, obliged, and ready servant for CHRIST's sake,

G. W.

LETTER DCCCCXLVI.

To Mrs. K——.

Dear Mrs. K——, London, Dec. 16, 1752.

YOUR kind letter lies by me unanswered, because I had written to your dear husband just before it came to hand. Ere now I hope he hath received it with the books, and is with you, and the other true followers of our most adorable Redeemer, pressing forwards towards the mark of the prize of our high calling in CHRIST JESUS. O that nothing may hinder us in this heavenly race! O that we may remember *Lot's* wife, and never look back! Alas! what is there in this world worth looking back upon? It is nothing, less than nothing. Thanks be to that precious CHRIST, who hath redeemed us out of it. To Him that hath thus loved us, be ascribed all honour and glory now and for ever! My obligations to bless and magnify our LORD increase daily. It would delight you to see, how his glory is manifested among his poor despised ones. To-morrow we are again to celebrate the memorials of his dying love. O that we may be prepared according to the preparation of the sanctuary! Blessed be GOD for a compleat and an everlasting righteousness to appear in; this is the wedding garment; this every poor sinner is cloathed with, that truly puts on the LORD JESUS. Well may such despise outward ornaments, and trample upon the pride of life. Such things are food only for those that know not GOD. Go on then, dear Mrs. K——; go on, all ye my female fellow-soldiers, who are listed under the Redeemer's banner.

banner. As your day is, so shall your strength be. Look up continually to JESUS; and be so good as always to remember, when before his throne,

Your assured friend and ready servant,
G. W.

LETTER DCCCCXLVII.

To Governor B————.

Honoured Sir,   *London, Dec.* 20, 1752.

WITH great pleasure and satisfaction, I received and read your kind letter, and took the first opportunity of transmitting the inclosed to good Lady H————n, who is now near *Bristol*. If the ship which brings this, doth not sail soon, I believe your Excellency will have an answer by the same conveyance. She is an elect lady indeed; one who hath fairly renounced the world, and scorns to divide her affections between it and her GOD. Her Ladyship corresponds with the Dutchess of ————, but I fear that the latter doth not glory in the cross of CHRIST, so much as might be wish'd. You know, honoured Sir, that we must have true self-denial, and a disinterested spirit, before we can be sincerely willing to be accounted fools for CHRIST's sake. And yet there is no going to heaven without it. Blessed be GOD, your fight, honoured Sir, is almost over; the days are now coming wherein you must necessarily say, "I have no pleasure in them." The 71st psalm, translated by Dr. *Watts*, seems to be sweetly adapted to your circumstances. Part of it was lately sung for your Excellency, by many true followers of the Lamb.

I.

Still hath his life new wonders seen,
   Repeated every year;
Behold his days which yet remain,
   We trust them to thy care.

II.

Cast him not off, should health decline,
   Or hoary hairs arise;
And round him let thy glories shine,
   Whene'er thy servant dies.

I doubt

I doubt not but the LORD JESUS will say, *Amen*. Whether I shall have the pleasure of seeing you on this side eternity, is uncertain. It was no small self-denial for me to leave *America* without going to the *Northward*; but the cloud moved towards *England*. Here (O amazing condescension!) the glorious *Emmanuel* vouchsafes still to own and bless my feeble labours. In *Scotland*, *Wales*, and the parts in and near *Yorkshire*, we have seen blessed days of the Son of Man. I am now in my Winter quarters, longing for Spring, to take the field again. Had I a thousand tongues and lives, JESUS should have them all. I am sorry, quite sorry that not one of his ministers could venture over the *Atlantick* for *New-Jersey* College. Two general collections have lately been made upon other occasions in *Scotland*. What a pity, when all circumstances concurred, that such a favourable opportunity should have been lost? I can only lament that, which I did all I could to prevent. And now, honoured Sir, I must bid you farewel. Ere long I hope to see you in a better world: perhaps we may meet again in this. Dear *America* is much upon my heart. Thanks be to GOD, *Bethesda* is now put on a good and flourishing foundation, and I hear hath escaped the late hurricane in *South-Carolina*. Great are thy judgments, O GOD;—and great are thy mercies also! both past finding out. To the infinitely great and gracious I AM, do I most earnestly commend both you and yours, and with ten thousands thanks for all your unmerited favours, I beg leave to subscribe myself, honoured Sir,

Your Excellency's most obliged, dutiful, and ready servant for CHRIST's sake,

G. W.

LETTER DCCCCXLVIII.

To Captain G——.

My dear Captain, *London, Dec.* 20, 1752.

ONE would imagine, that you and I were never to meet any more on this side eternity. I often, often think of you, and long to see and converse with you; but GOD only knows when. We are now about to erect a *new Tabernacle* eighty foot square, which I fear will detain me in *England* the ensuing

enſuing Summer. Pen cannot well deſcribe, how white the fields have been, and how ready to harveſt, in *Wales*, *Scotland*, and the *North* of *England*. I could ſometimes ſcarce tell, whether I was in or out of the body. Grace! grace! I am now in Winter quarters, where our LORD gives us freſh conqueſts, gained by his word every day. We do not diſpute, but love. I find more and more that truth is great; and however ſeemingly cruſh'd for a while, will in the end prevail. But there muſt be a kind of death upon every promiſe, and upon every thing that is done for GOD. Thus hath it been with *Georgia* and *Bethesda*. O that we may learn to wait! Then ſhall we certainly ſee the ſalvation of GOD. I pity our dear friends in *Charles-Town*. O GOD, how great are thy judgments, as well as thy mercies! May they hear the rod, and who hath appointed it! My ſoul is diſtreſſed for them. May this ſevere correction make them truly great! When you ſend any thing to *Savannah*, I ſhould be obliged to you, if you would ſend a few things to *Bethesda*. Our LORD will bleſs you for it. I hope there are now above twenty negroes at work upon the new plantation. May the LORD JESUS convert them, and every other member of my family! And O that I may be converted myſelf more and more every day and hour! I am aſhamed of my being ſuch a dwarf in religion, and of my having ſo little of the mind of CHRIST. I hope you, my dear old friend, do find his grace ſufficient for you, to keep your heart above the world, and continually alive to GOD. My prayer for you is, that you may have power to get wealth, and grace to improve it for the Redeemer's glory, and his people's good: then you will be rich for both worlds, and GOD, even your own GOD, will give you and yours his bleſſing. Why do you not write to dear Mr. S——? He is a heavenly-minded man indeed, and my boſom friend. I ſuppoſe Mr. D—— will acquaint you of my having been at his houſe; we are kind friends ſtill: he and his very much regard you. What cannot GOD do? How faithful is he to thoſe, who " ſeek firſt his kingdom, and the righteouſneſs thereof." Let theſe words be written over your ſtore-houſe door; or rather let them be written on the table of your heart. I can add no more. A variety of buſineſs demands my attention. My dear man, farewel. Had I wings, I would fly

and

and see you, and my other never to be forgotten *Philadelphia* friends. Continue to pray, and perhaps I may yet come sooner than expectation. My wife joins in sending love to you and your houshold. Accept the same in the most endearing manner, from one that loves you more than a brother; even

Yours, &c.
G. W.

LETTER DCCCCXLIX.

To Mr. C—— W——.

My dear Friend, London, *Dec.* 22, 1752.

I Have read and pondered upon your kind letter with some degree of solemnity of spirit. In the same frame I would now sit down to answer it. And what shall I say? Really I can scarce tell. The connection between you and your brother, hath been so close and continued, and your attachment to him so necessary to keep up his interest, that I would not willingly for the world do or say any thing that may separate such friends. I cannot help thinking, but he is still jealous of me and my proceedings; but, I thank GOD, I am quite easy about it. Having the testimony of a good conscience, that I have a disinterested view to promote the common salvation only, I can leave all to him, who I am assured will in the end speak for me, and make my righteousness as clear as the light, and my just dealing as the noon-day. I more and more find, that he who believeth doth not make haste; and that if we will have patience, we shall find that every plant, which our heavenly Father hath not planted, however it may seem to have taken very deep root, shall be plucked up. As I wrote to good Lady H———n, so I write to you, dear Sir.—I bless GOD for my stripping seasons. I have seen an end of all perfection, and expect it only in him, where I am sure to find it, even in the ever-loving, ever-lovely JESUS. He knows how I love and honour you, and your brother, and how often I have preferred your interest to my own. This, by the grace of GOD, I shall still continue to do. My reward is with the LORD. If he approves, it is enough. More might be said, were we face to face. When this will be, I cannot tell. Several things,

things, especially our design of building a new tabernacle; which I hope will succeed, detain me in town this Winter. GOD only knows what course I am to steer in the Spring. I would be a blank;—let my heavenly Father fill it up as seemeth him good. I am glad you are with our elect Lady; she will shine indeed in heaven as a common friend. O how amiable is a truly catholic spirit! LORD, make us all partakers of it more and more! I beg the continuance of your prayers: I need them much. GOD willing, you shall have mine in return. That you and yours may increase with all the increase of GOD, is the earnest request of, my dear friend,

Yours, &c.

G. W.

LETTER DCCCCL.

To Lady H———n.

Ever-honoured Madam, London, Dec. 22, 1752.

WITH great pleasure I received your Ladyship's letter, which hath drawn me to the Father of Spirits, that the meek, lowly, loving, zealous, and heavenly-minded temper which was in CHRIST JESUS, may be stamped more and more upon your Ladyship's heart. A growth in these blessed graces and fruits of the divine Spirit, I am persuaded is what your Ladyship desires above all things under heaven, and I doubt not but all the trials and afflictions you meet with, both from friends and foes, will be sanctified to the promoting this glorious end. Many of these I meet with; but if I come purified out of the furnace, and am at length any way conformed to my dear and blessed Exemplar, I rejoice, yea and will rejoice. Experience, if attended with this effect, cannot be bought too dear. But alas, how unwilling is the old man to be crucified and slain! How hard is even the mind that is renewed in part, how hard to be brought off low and selfish and party views. With how much reluctance doth it give up the uppermost place, and submit to be accounted in the church, as well as in the world, less than the least of all. Yet this is a lesson the witnesses of JESUS must learn. O that I had learnt only my A B C in it! I beg the continuance of your Ladyship's prayers, for which I thank your Ladyship a thousand times.

May the LORD of all lords return them seven-fold into your bosom, and give your Ladyship success in your endeavours to serve the persons mentioned in your last! It is but for your Ladyship to try. I shall observe your Ladyship's hints about Mr. ———. I believe our visits will not be very frequent.— But I am easy, having no scheme, no design of supplanting or resenting, but I trust a single eye to promote the common salvation, without so much as attempting to set up a party for myself. This is what my soul abhors. Being thus minded, I have peace; peace which the world knows nothing of, and which all must necessarily be strangers to, who are fond either of power or numbers. GOD be praised for the many strippings I have met with: it is good for me that I have been supplanted, despised, censured, maligned, judged by, and separated from my nearest, dearest friends. By this I have found the faithfulness of him, who is the friend of friends; by this I have been taught to wrap myself in the glorious *Emmanuel*'s everlasting righteousness, and to be content that He, to whom all hearts are open, and all desires are known, now sees, and will let all see hereafter, the uprightness of my intentions towards all mankind. But whither am I going? I run too fast. Your Ladyship's kind letter hath extorted this from me. I will weary your Ladyship no longer, but hasten to subscribe myself, what I really am, ever-honoured Madam,

Your Ladyship's most dutiful, obliged,
and very chearful servant for CHRIST's sake,

G. W.

LETTER DCCCCLI.

To Mr. R———.

My very dear Friend, London, *Dec.* 22, 1752.

WITH great pleasure I received your kind and wished-for letter; and heartily bless GOD that your whole self is in such comfortable circumstances, and that honest D——— is so blest in his work. I read his two letters about ten days ago, and many joined in singing for him the following verses:

The

> *The isles in the North,*
> *Remember, O* GOD,
> *And feed thy sheep there,*
> *With pure gospel food.*
> LORD, *revive thy blest work*
> *In every place,*
> *Till thousands and thousands*
> *Do triumph through grace.*

Do you not think the blessed JESUS will say, *Amen?* Yes, assuredly he will. And if he will work, who shall hinder?

> *Thoughts are vain against the* LORD,
> *All subserve his mighty word;*
> *Wheels encircling wheels shall run,*
> *Each in course to bring it on.*

Fear not, my dear Sir; if CHRIST hath work for you to do, he will put you into a proper station. But would you be a *Nehemiah*, and have no *Sanballat* to oppose you? Building the walls of the *New-Jerusalem*, is what the profane and formalists do not approve of. We must expect the serpent will hiss, whenever the gospel seed of the woman is coming into a place to bruise his head. Courage, my dear Sir, courage. GOD is on your side.

> *The world, with sin and Satan,*
> *In vain our march opposes;*
>   *Through* CHRIST *we shall*
>   *Break through them all,*
> *And sing the song of* Moses.

You see, my dear Sir, how freely I write. The love of CHRIST constraineth me. I am much indebted to you, and hope to see you in *London* soon. My wife longs to have you under our roof: she hath been ill, but blessed be GOD is now better. We both send cordial and grateful respects to your whole self and all enquiring friends. We have had most solemn sacramental occasions. I sympathize with both our suffering friends: from what unexpected quarters do troubles come! Who would sing a requiem to himself, whilst here below?

Lord God, prepare us for whatever thou hast prepared for us! I must bid you farewel. A variety of business obliges me to hasten to subscribe myself,

Yours, &c.

G. W.

LETTER DCCCCLII.

To Lady H———m.

Honoured Madam, *London, Jan.* 1, 1753.

YOUR Ladyship's kind letter hath added to the obligations already laid on me. I can only say, the Lord knows that you and yours, are remembered by me before his throne. This is the reward, which the Redeemer promises to those who do good to a disciple, in the name of a disciple. O happy they who are rich in faith and good works! These are the true riches; they are durable; they follow us beyond the grave, and we shall be reaping the fruit of them through the endless ages of eternity. Eternity! eternity! The very writing or hearing this word, is enough to make one dead to the world, and alive unto God. The Lord quicken my tardy pace! I am now thirty-eight years of age, and entering upon another new year; Alas! alas! How little have I done for that Jesus, who hath done and suffered so much for me! I want to begin to begin to act and preach for God. Blessed be his name, that his spirit is moving on precious souls at *Bristol.* For ever adored be his rich, free, and unmerited grace, the same may be said of *London.* We have had blessed holidays, and I have had good news from the Orphan-house.

A life that all things casts behind,
Springs forth obedient at his call.

Had I a thousand lives, the Lord Jesus should have them. I wish your Ladyship, and honoured daughters, much of his divine love shed abroad in your hearts. That is the best new year's compliment, and the best new year's gift. I hope, the young ladies through grace are kept unspotted from the world. I would come and wait upon our elect Lady at *Clifton,* but am engaged in forwarding the building of a new tabernacle; I hope it will be accomplished, and that God's presence fence will fill it when erected. I could enlarge, but am called away, and therefore subscribe myself,

Your Ladyship's most dutiful, obliged, and
ready servant for CHRIST's sake,

G. W.

LETTER DCCCCLIII.

To Mr. L——.

London, Jan. 3, 1753.

My very dear Friend and Brother,

THOUGH I am very much straitened for time, yet I must sit down, (since you so earnestly desire it) and answer your kind letter. My love does not shift with my scene of action; I would have it in some degree, like my LORD's to me and his people, " Permanent and unchangeable." Blessed be GOD for such a JESUS, who is the same yesterday, to-day, and for ever. What can we want then? Or of whom should we be afraid? All his attributes are engaged to keep us on earth, and to set us upon thrones in his glorious kingdom in heaven. Last night I buried one, who I believe is seated there.—Ah lovely appearance of death! Surely my turn will come soon. I am now thirty-eight years of age; little did I think of staying in the land of the dying so long. Well, if it be to call more souls to the ever-loving, ever-lovely JESUS, Father, thy will be done!

> *If thou excuse, then work thy will,*
> *By so unfit an instrument;*
> *It will at once thy goodness show,*
> *And prove thy power omnipotent.*

I hope you have had a happy *Christmas* at *Leeds.* We have kept holidays here indeed. Sinners have been pricked to the heart, and saints refreshed in their spirits. To the Father of spirits be all the glory. I forgot none of you in my poor prayers: fear not; let us continue to pray, and we shall always find, that our extremity will be GOD's opportunity to help and appear for us. But there must be a seeming death upon every promise.

Where reason fails with all it's powers,
There faith prevails and love adores.

LORD, increase our faith.—LORD, quicken my sluggish heart! I commend you and yours to GOD, and to the word of his grace. I am sorry dear Mr. S—— is disabled from writing. When his hand is well, I hope to hear from him. In the mean while, tell him, and his, and all dear friends, that I am, for CHRIST's sake, my dear Sir,

Theirs and yours, &c. &c.

G. W.

LETTER DCCCCLIV.

To Mr. C——.

My dear Mr. C——, London, *Jan.* 7, 1753.

I Received your kind letter, for which I send you most hearty thanks. I see that you strive, and I fear you will succeed, to outdo me in love and kindness. However, I will endeavour to copy after you, and, if possible, not die in your debt. But who can ever pay his debt of love, either to GOD, or the brethren? Alas! Alas! I run in arrears every day. GOD's favours are continually multiplied upon me, and he seems to let us know that we shall see greater things than ever. We have had a blessed *Christmas* season. I trust our LORD hath imparted many a new year's gift. You know what that is, even a *new heart.* "A new heart also will I give thee." Thus run the words of our LORD's last will and testament. O for faith to prove this will! O for a willingness to receive so invaluable a legacy! LORD, I believe, help my unbelief!

Thou wilt give strength, thou wilt give power,
Thou wilt in time set free;
This great deliverance let us hope,
Not for ourselves but thee.

Come, my dear brother, let us take courage: "He is faithful, who hath promised, who also will do it."

O unbelief, injurious bar,
Source of tormenting, fruitless care.

Sure'y it is the womb of misery, and grave of comfort. Had we faith but as a grain of mustard seed, how should we trample

ple the world, the flesh, the devil, death, and hell under foot? LORD, increase our faith! I know you say *Amen.* " Even so LORD JESUS, Amen and Amen!" But whither am I going? Love makes me forget myself. Adieu—my dear Sir, adieu. Pray tell Mr. G—— that I intend answering his kind letter shortly. I send cordial love to him, and all the followers of the Lamb.

> *O may we find the ancient way,*
> *Our wand'ring foes to move;*
> *And force the heathen world to say,*
> *See how these christians love!*

I can now no more, but subscribe myself, dear Sir,
Yours most affectionately in our common LORD,
G. W.

LETTER DCCCCLV.

To Mr. H—— B——.

My very dear Friend, London, *Jan.* 7, 1753.

BY this conveyance I send you a power of attorney to dispose of *Providence Plantation,* and leave it to your discretion to sell at what price you please. I would only observe, that I had rather it should be sold for somewhat less than its real value, than to keep it any longer in my hands. I do not choose to keep two families longer than needs must. Be pleased to pay what you receive for it, into the hands of Mr. *Charles* H——n of *Charles-Town.* Blessed be GOD for remembering mercy in the midst of judgments. O that with his rod he may also send his spirit! For without it, as dear Mr. V—— B—— observes, " We shall be chastened, but not changed." The world after the deluge, was as bad as before. Nothing but the blood of JESUS CHRIST, applied by faith, can cleanse the soul from sin.—

> *To this blest fountain of thy blood,*
> *Incarnate* GOD *I fly;*
> *Here let me wash my spotted soul,*
> *From sins of deepest dye.*

My dear Sir, add to my obligations, by praying, that the foot of pride may never come against me. This is what turned fair angels into foul devils; and yet alas, how prone are we to it! Surely it is the first enemy we fight with, and the last that is totally conquered. O that I was humble! then would the LORD delight to own and honour me more and more. I am amazed he doth not throw me aside. But (O unchangeable love!) still he causeth my rod to bud and blossom. The Winter season hath been very blessed, and we hear daily of fresh inroads made into Satan's kingdom. GOD seems determined to throw down *Jericho's* walls by rams-horns, yea by very crooked rams-horns. Even so, Father, for so it seemeth good in thy sight! My dear Sir, once more I intreat you to pray for me. Neither you nor yours are forgotten by me. The money you receive for *Providence*, will be immediately wanted to buy more land, and to pay for opening *Bethesda's* new plantation.—I have desired your brother to agree with Mrs. P—— for hers, if she can give a good title. I am sorry to hear she is declining.—But why so? Is not death an entrance into life everlasting?

There sin and pain and sorrow cease,
And all is calm and joy and peace.

Hearty love and prayers attend her and all enquiring friends. That this new year may be filled with millions of new blessings, both to your souls and bodies, is and shall be the constant prayer of, very dear Sir,

Yours most affectionately in our common LORD,

G. W.

LETTER DCCCCLVI.

To Mr. S——.

My dear Mr. S——,   *London, Jan.* 9, 1753.

I Received your kind letter yesterday, and suppose, ere this can reach you, my last will be come to hand. What say you? If I should be detained in *England* this year, are you willing to put your life in the Redeemer's hands and go immediately? A ship is bound for *Savannah* about ten miles from the Orphan-house, the beginning of next month. Methinks I hear you say to the glorious *Emmanuel,*

A life that all things casts behind,
Springs forth obedient at thy call.

Such

Such a spirit is fit for *Bethesda*; such a spirit becomes one who desires to be a teacher of youth, and a faithful minister of the ever-loving ever-lovely JESUS. Let me know your mind. If you come immediately, may the LORD come and go with you! That is company enough.—But there are others going in the same ship. The LORD direct and bless you! He will vouchsafe to countenance my feeble labours. I have yet more good news from the North. Last night was an awful night, we carried three saints together to the grave; thousands attended, and both within and without doors, the word I trust came with power. O that the dead may be made to hear the voice of the Son of GOD, and to come forth! I rejoice if any of his dear people have been quickened at *Glasgow*. Perhaps next Summer, I may see them in my way to, or return from *Ireland*. The LORD help all to pray for me. " Less than the least of all," shall be still my motto. To me nothing belongs, but shame and confusion of face. I must away. The LORD direct and bless you. I commend you to his never-failing mercy, and am

Your assured friend for CHRIST's sake,
G. W.

LETTER DCCCCLVII.

To Mr. Z———.

London, *Jan.* 10, 1753.

Honoured and very dear Sir,

THIS morning, before I received your kind packet, I was finishing my answer to the good Professor, and then intended to send it to you with the inclosed extracts. LORD, what am I, that any of thy faithful servants should write to, or concern themselves about me or my affairs! With all thy other favours, give me, O GOD, an humble and grateful heart; so shall thy mercies not prove my ruin! I hope to answer good Mr. *U———* and dear Mr. *B———s* speedily. A ship goes to *Savannah* the begining of next month. Mrs. *V———B———* is safely delivered of a daughter; the forts being destroyed by the late dreadful hurricane, the Governor and Council of *South-Carolina*, have sent for her husband to *Charles-Town*. Blessed be GOD, *Bethesda* hath received but little damage. Several of the orphans have sent me pretty letters,

letters, and I trust it will yet prove an useful sominary for both white and black persons. I wait to see this great salvation, O LORD! To-morrow, GOD willing, I shall dine with Mr. L———, and on *Friday* morning if possible will endeavour to wait upon you. My hands are full of work, and I hear every day of fresh persons awakened; but I can do so little, and what I do is done so bad'y, that I fear sometimes my LORD will throw me aside like a broken vessel.—Very dear and honoured Sir, for CHRIST's sake do you and your worthy collegue continue to pray for me; surely it is an act of the greatest charity. Less than the least of all, shall be my motto still. My heart is full; GOD forgive me. I am now beginning to enter upon my thirty-ninth year. LORD JESUS quicken my tardy pace! I can no more. But hoping to see you on *Friday*, and to be furthered in my work and way by your fatherly counsel and instruction, I subscribe myself, very dear and honoured Sir,

Your most affectionate, obliged son, and
ready servant in our glorious Head,
G. W.

LETTER DCCCCLVIII.

To Lady H———n.

London, Jan. 13, 1753.

Ever-honoured Madam,

YOUR Ladyship's very kind and christian letter, I have read over and over again. It drew my heart towards the Redeemer, and caused me to pray, that your present retirement, may be a glorious preparative for further, and yet more public usefulness in his mystical body. To have one's hands or tongue tied from acting or speaking for GOD, is, to a new and heaven-born soul, one of the greatest pieces of self-denial in the world. But this hath been the lot of many of the most choice and holy souls under heaven. It is a mercy, that where there is a willing mind, it is accepted according to that which a man hath, and not according to that which he hath not. I beg that your Ladyship would not have the least thought about my concerns, otherwise than at a throne of grace. Your Ladyship wants a bridle, rather than a spur. My highest ambition is to spend and be spent for JESUS, and

to

to be not the head, but servant of all. When your Ladyship mentioned the word *ambition*, I could not help thinking of the saying of the *Eunuch*, "Speaketh the prophet this of himself, or of some other man?" But we know not what is in our hearts. LORD, keep me from being led into, and falling by temptation. I wish your Ladyship much success with B——, but worldly wise men, serpent-like, so turn and wind, that they have many ways to slip through and creep out at, which simple-hearted single-eyed souls know nothing of, and if they did, could not follow after them. Honesty is the best policy, and will in the end (whether we seek it or not) get the better of all. Your Ladyship's intended letter to Governor B——, will be very acceptable. I hope the inclosed will give your Ladyship pleasure. O that I may be enabled to give the LORD JESUS all the glory! To me nought belongs, but confusion of face. Surely I am the chief of sinners, less than the least of all saints, but for CHRIST'S sake, ever-honoured Madam,

Your Ladyship's most dutiful, obliged
and very ready servant,
G. W.

LETTER DCCCCLIX.

To Mr. C——.

My dear Mr. C——,   *London, Jan.* 15, 1753.

I Owe you a letter and much love. The one I will now pay you, the other debt our common common LORD must discharge. I despair of doing it, because I run upon fresh arrears to him and his dear people every day and every hour. I willingly therefore own myself a debtor to high and low, rich and poor, to all, of all denominations whatsoever.—What have we to do with a party or sectarian zeal? Why should not our heaven begin on earth?

All that we know they do above,
Is, that they sing, and that they love.

O for some fresh anointings of the blessed spirit! Then will the scales fall more and more from our eyes, and the veil of ignorance be taken more and more from our hearts. Then shall

shall we be more and more content to think, and let think, and be studious to be of one heart, where we cannot be of one judgment or mind. The sweetness of such a spirit, is unspeakable; it brings with it its own reward; it frees the soul from a thousand needless jealousies, and selfish passions, and enables it to put the reins of government into his hands, who alone orders all things well. LORD, increase in us this spirit, and give us more and more to love all that bear thy image, though they may not in all things agree with us!

> *O may we find the ancient way,*
> *Our wond'ring foes to move;*
> *And force the heathen world to say,*
> *See how these christians love!*

My dear brother, your kind letter constrains me to write thus. —Blessed be GOD for what has been done at any time, by any instrument, at *Newcastle*. I still pray that the town may be full of new creatures. In *London* we have reason to rejoice. Yesterday was a great day of the Son of man; both at the sacrament, and under the word preached, our LORD gave us to drink of the wine of the kingdom. On *Monday* last we followed three believers to the grave, and triumphed over death on his own ground. O what a CHRIST have we! GOD help us to love him more, and serve him better! I salute all most heartily with whom you are in fellowship.—Grace, mercy and peace be multiplied upon you. I beg a continued interest in all your prayers, and subscribe myself, dear Sir,

Your affectionate friend,
and ready servant for CHRIST's sake,
G. W.

LETTER DCCCCLX.

To C——— W———.

My dear Friend,   *Chatham, Jan.* 19, 1753.

A Multiplicity of business prevented my answering your kind letter, before my coming out of *London*. Lest I should be prevented by the same means at my return thither, I write you a few lines in the way. I have been among some new-awakened souls, who seem to be taking the kingdom of
GOD

God by a holy violence. At *London*, God hath lately caused his people's cups to run over with strong consolation, and many sturdy sinners have been made to cry out, "What shall we do to be saved?" I thank you for the caution about the new building; a burnt child dreads the fire. I shall not begin, till we have a thousand pounds in hand, and then shall contract for a certain sum for the whole. This affair will detain me till the days are long enough to travel, and set out upon a fresh pursuit after poor sinners, who have wandered from their God.—The Lord be with you and yours. May the gospel plough be prospered, whatever hand is employed to lay hold of it. This, as far as I know my treacherous heart, is the sincere language of, dear Sir,

Yours most affectionately in our common Lord,

G. W.

LETTER DCCCCLXI.

To Mr. O——.

London, Jan. 23, 1753.

My dear Mr. O——,

I Received your kind letter, and have since shewn it to the secretary for *Georgia*, who approved of it very much. I am glad we are to have you in that infant province, and could heartily wish you was nearer *Bethesda*. I doubt not of its becoming a seat of learning in time, but it is good for every thing to rise gradually. I have engaged a dear youth, who I trust will suit the Orphan-house infant state very well. It hath scarce learnt as yet to stand upon its own legs; as it grows I expect it will give me more trouble. To have young men educated there, and then turned out into the church graceless and unconverted would break my heart. Father, if it be thy will, let this cup pass from me! I suppose we shall now soon know, who is to be Governor; every thing is to be ordered as I informed you in my last. My eyes are waiting upon Him, from whom alone cometh all our salvation. We see wonders every day on this side the water. Glorious days of the Son of man indeed! Notwithstanding, I long to take another trip to yonder new world. Time will determine, wherefore this attraction. He that believeth doth not make haste. God forbid that "Chastened,'

but

but not changed," should always be *Charles-Town* motto. LORD, let them hear thy rod, and who hath appointed it! What a dreadful thing is it to come cankered out of the furnace? It befpeaks further trials yet behind;—but I need not tell you this.—Excufe this freedom: be pleafed to give my hearty love to all, and I befeech you continue to pray for, my dear friend and brother,

Yours moft affectionately in our common LORD,

G. W.

LETTER DCCCCLXII.

To Mr. V—— B——.

My very dear Sir, London, *Jan.* 19, 1753.

A Few days ago I was with good Mr. Z——, who affured me that Mr. V—— had written him, that two hundred pounds fterling were ordered you to be difpofed of as you fhould judge proper. I hope you will find this to be true, if you have not found it fo already. Is there no way of making the breach up between you and Mr. B——? Mr. U——r, from whom I heard very lately, and alfo all your *German* friends, defire it extremely. I promifed Mr. Z—— that I would ufe my intereft for your own fake, but above all for the fake of JESUS CHRIST our common LORD. My very dear Sir, do forgive and forget, and if you are confcious you have been too hafty in any refpect, pray fend to Mr. B—— a few lines of love. We never lofe any thing by ftooping.—GOD will always exalt the humble foul. O that the prince of peace would honour me to be a peace-maker!— Do, my dear friend, comply with my requeft, and thereby give further proofs that you are indeed converted, and become a little child. May this bleffing defcend on your new-born babe! Our joint refpects await Mrs. V—— and yourfelf. You may well wifh yourfelf at the tabernacle. All is alive there.—Thoufands flock to hear, and thoufands feel the power of the living GOD.—Dear *Charles-Town,* I pity thee! O that thou knoweft the day of thy vifitation! If this meets you there employed as an engineer, may the LORD own, blefs and direct you, and keep you unfpotted from the world! If elfewhere, I hope you are where GOD would have you be,

and

and that is enough,—I commend you to his never-failing mercy, and defiring a continued intereft in your prayers, beg leave to fubfcribe myfelf, very dear Sir,

Yours, &c.

G. W.

LETTER DCCCCLXIII.

To the Reverend Mr. H―――.

My very dear Friend, London, *Jan.* 27, 1753.

I Thank you a thoufand times for the trouble you have been at, in revifing my poor compofitions, which I am afraid you have not treated with a becoming feverity. How many pardons fhall I afk for mangling, and I fear murdering your dear *Theron* and *Afpafia?* You will fee by *Monday*'s coach; which will bring a parcel directed for you, to the care of Doctor S―――. It contains one of your dialogues, and two more of my fermons, which I do not like very well myfelf, and therefore fhall not wonder if you diflike them. If you think they will do for the public, pray return them immediately, becaufe the other two go to the prefs next *Monday.* I have nothing to comfort me but this, " that the LORD choofes the weak things of this world to confound the ftrong, and things that are not, to bring to nought the things that are." I think to fell all four fermons for fix-pence. I write for the poor, you for the polite and the noble; GOD will affuredly own and blefs what you write.—As yet I have only had time to perufe one of your fweet dialogues; as faft as poffible I fhall read the reft. I am more than paid for my trouble by reading them. The LORD be with your dear heart! Continue to pray for me. The LORD be with us. Grace! Grace! I am, deareft Sir, in very great hafte, but greater love,

Yours, &c.

G. W.

LETTER DCCCCLXIV.

To the Reverend Mr. B―――.

Reverend and very dear Sir, London, *Jan.* 31, 1753.

YOUR kind letter came fafe to hand, and according to your defire, I fend you a little bell, as a fmall token of my unfeigned love to your dear congregation. I have written

ftrongly

strongly to Professor *Frank* for some Negroes for you, and heartily pray the LORD of all Lords to put it into our power to serve that black generation. Their souls are equally precious in the eyes of an all gracious Redeemer, as ours. O that we may yet see some good come out of *Georgia*. I would take another trip over this spring, but am hindered by our building a new place of worship, and by the continual calls that are given me to preach the everlasting gospel.—Indeed we see most glorious days of the Son of man. The cup of GOD's people is made to run over, and every day we hear of somebody or another brought under new awakenings, and pricked to the heart; notwithstanding this, I find a continual attraction to *America*. The event will prove wherefore all this happens to me. LORD help me to walk by faith and not by sight! My dear Sir, you and yours will not forget to pray for me. I am the chief of sinners, and less than the least of all saints —What shall I render unto the LORD? Write every opportunity. Dear Mr. Z—— will take care of your child. Cannot matters be made up between you and Mr. V——? Is it not a pity that any of us should fall out in our way to heaven? When we meet next, remember that a floor and blanket is all the lodging, and a chick or fowl, boiled or roasted, is all the food I desire at *Ebenezer*. What is a pilgrim life without a pilgrim heart? O that I was like my LORD! Then should I endure hardness, like a good soldier of JESUS CHRIST.—The encouragement for raising silk will be continued. O that *Georgia* may prove a fruitful soil for raising children unto *Abraham*! We wait for thy salvation, O LORD. For the present, reverend Sir, adieu. My wife joins in sending cordial salutations to your whole self, to Mr. L—— and his wife, and all the dear people at *Ebenezer*. That you all may at all times have reason to say, "hitherto hath our LORD helped us," is the earnest prayer of, reverend and very dear Sir,

  Your most affectionate, though unworthy younger
   brother, and fellow-labourer in our common LORD,
                G. W.

The END *of the* SECOND VOLUME.

www.ingramcontent.com/pod-product-compliance
Lightning Source LLC
Chambersburg PA
CBHW031153020526
44117CB00042B/357